NINA IKRAM
BA ACCOUNTS AND F.

Paper 2.6

AUDIT AND
INTERNAL REVIEW

For exams in December 2006 and June 2007

Study Text

In this June 2006 new edition

- A new **user-friendly format** for easy navigation

- **Exam-centred topic coverage**, directly linked to ACCA's syllabus and study guide

- **Exam focus points** showing you what the examiner will want you to do

- Regular **fast forward** summaries emphasising the key points

- **Questions** and **quick quizzes** to test your understanding

- **Exam question bank** containing exam standard questions with answers

- A full index

BPP's **i-Learn** and **i-Pass** products also support this paper.

FOR EXAMS IN DECEMBER 2006 AND JUNE 2007

PROFESSIONAL EDUCATION

First edition 2001
Sixth edition July 2006

ISBN 0 7517 2669 9 (Previous edition 0 7517 2320 7)

British Library Cataloguing-in-Publication Data
A catalogue record for this book
is available from the British Library

Published by

BPP Professional Education
Aldine House, Aldine Place
London W12 8AW

www.bpp.com

Printed in Great Britain by W M Print Ltd,
Frederick Street, Walsall,
West Midlands,
WS2 9NE.

We are grateful to the Association of Chartered
Certified Accountants for permission to reproduce past
examination questions. The suggested solutions in the
exam answer bank have been prepared by BPP
Professional Education.

Contents

Introduction

The introduction pages contain lots of valuable advice and information. They include tips on studying for and passing the exam, also the content of the syllabus and what has been examined.

The BPP Effective Study Package – How the BPP Study Text can help you pass – Help yourself study for your ACCA exams – Syllabus and Study Guide – Examinable documents – The exam paper – Oxford Brookes BSc (Hons) in Applied Accounting – ACCA professional development requirements – Syllabus mindmap

Computer-based learning products from BPP

If you want to reinforce your studies by **interactive** learning, try BPP's **i-Learn** product, covering major syllabus areas in an interactive format. For **self-testing**, try **i-Pass,** which offers a large number of **objective test questions**, particularly useful where objective test questions form part of the exam.

Learn Online

Learn Online uses BPP's wealth of teaching experience to produce a fully **interactive** e-learning resource **delivered via the Internet**. The site offers comprehensive **tutor support** and features areas such as **study, practice, email service, revision** and **useful resources**.

Visit our website www.bpp.com/acca/learnonline to sample aspects of Learn Online free of charge.

Learning to Learn Accountancy

BPP's ground-breaking **Learning to Learn Accountancy** book is designed to be used both at the outset of your ACCA studies and throughout the process of learning accountancy. It challenges you to consider how you study and gives you helpful hints about how to approach the various types of paper which you will encounter. It can help you **focus your studies on the subject and exam**, enabling you to **acquire knowledge, practise and revise efficiently and effectively**.

The BPP Effective Study Package

Recommended period of use	The BPP Effective Study Package
From the outset and throughout	**Learning to Learn Accountancy** Read this invaluable book as you begin your studies and refer to it throughout your studies.
Three to twelve months before the exam	**Study Text and i-Learn** Use the Study Text to acquire knowledge, understanding, skills and the ability to apply techniques. Use BPP's **i-Learn** product to reinforce your learning.
Throughout	**Learn Online** Study, practise, revise and use other helpful resources with BPP's fully interactive e-learning site, including full tutor support.
Throughout	**i-Pass** **i-Pass**, our computer-based testing package, provides objective test questions in a variety of formats and is ideal for self-assessment.
One to six months before the exam	**Practice & Revision Kit** Try the numerous examination-format questions in our Kit and compare your answers with the suggested solutions. Examiners emphasise that tackling exam-standard questions is essential preparation for your exams. Then attempt the two mock exams.
From three months before the exam until the last minute	**Passcards** Work through these short, memorable notes which are focused on the topics most likely to come up in your exam and which you can take anywhere.
One to six months before the exam	**Success CDs** The CDs cover the vital elements of your syllabus in less than 90 minutes per subject. They also contain exam hints to help you fine tune your strategy.

You can purchase these products by visiting www.bpp.com/mybpp

How the BPP Study Text can help you pass

It provides you with the knowledge and understanding, skills and application techniques that you need to be successful in your exams

This Study Text has been targeted at the **Audit and Internal Review** syllabus.

- It is **comprehensive**. It covers the syllabus content. No more, no less.

- It is written at the **right level**. Each chapter is written with ACCA's syllabus and study guide in mind.

- It is aimed at the **exam**. We have taken account of recent exams, guidance the examiner has given and the assessment methodology.

It allows you to study in the way that best suits your learning style and the time you have available, by following your personal Study Plan (see page (viii))

You may be studying at home on your own or you may be attending a full-time course. You may like to read every word, or you may prefer to skim-read and practise questions the rest of the time. However you study, you will find the BPP Study Text meets your needs in designing and following your personal Study Plan.

It ties in with the other components of the BPP Effective Study Package to ensure you have the best possible chance of passing the exam (see page (v))

Help yourself study for your ACCA exams

Exams for professional bodies such as ACCA are very different from those you have taken at college or university. You will be under **greater time pressure before** the exam − as you may be combining your study with work. Here are some hints and tips.

The right approach

1   **Develop the right attitude**

Believe in yourself	Yes, there is a lot to learn. But thousands have succeeded before and you can too.
Remember why you're doing it	You are studying for a good reason: to advance your career.

2   **Focus on the exam**

Read through the Syllabus and Study Guide	These tell you what you are expected to know and are supplemented by **Exam focus points** in the text.
Study the Exam paper section	Past papers are likely to be good guides to what you should expect in the exam.

3   **The right method**

See the whole picture	Keeping in mind how all the detail you need to know fits into the whole picture will help you understand it better. • The **Introduction** of each chapter puts the material in context. • The **Syllabus content, Study guide** and **Exam focus points** show you what you need to **grasp**.
Use your own words	To absorb the information (and to practise your written communication skills), you need to **put it into your own words**. • **Take notes.** • Answer the **questions** in each chapter. • Draw **mindmaps**. We have an example for the whole syllabus. • Try **'teaching' a subject** to a colleague or friend.
Give yourself cues to jog your memory	The BPP Study Text uses **bold** to **highlight key points**. • Try **colour coding** with a highlighter pen. • Write **key points** on cards.

4   **The right recap**

Review, review, review	Regularly reviewing a topic in summary form can **fix it in your memory**. The BPP Study Text helps you review in many ways. • **Chapter roundups** summarise the 'Fast forward' key points in each chapter. Use them to recap each study session. • The **Quick quiz** actively tests your grasp of the essentials. • Go through the **Examples** in each chapter a second or third time.

Developing your personal Study Plan

BPP's **Learning to Learn Accountancy** book emphasises the need to use a study plan. Planning and sticking to the plan are key elements of learning successfully.
There are five steps you should work through.

Step 1   **How do you learn?**

First you need to be aware of your style of learning. BPP's **Learning to Learn Accountancy** book commits a chapter to this **self-discovery**. What types of intelligence do you display when learning? You might be advised to brush up on certain study skills before launching into this Study Text.

BPP's **Learning to Learn Accountancy** book helps you to identify what intelligences you show more strongly and then details how you can tailor your study process to your preferences. It also includes handy hints on how to develop intelligences you exhibit less strongly, but which might be needed as you study accountancy.

Step 2   **What do you prefer to do first?**

If you prefer to get to grips with a theory before seeing how it is applied, we suggest you concentrate first on the explanations we give in each chapter before looking at the examples and case studies. If you prefer to see first how things work in practice, skim through the detail in each chapter, and concentrate on the examples and case studies, before supplementing your understanding by reading the detail.

Step 3   **How much time do you have?**

Work out the time you have available per week, given the following.

- The standard you have set yourself
- The time you need to set aside later for work on the Practice & Revision Kit and Passcards
- The other exam(s) you are sitting
- Practical matters such as work, travel, exercise, sleep and social life

		Hours
Note your time available in box A.	A	

Step 4   **Allocate your time**

- Take the time you have available per week for this Study Text shown in box A, multiply it by the number of weeks available and insert the result in box B.   B ☐

- Divide the figure in box B by the number of chapters in this text and insert the result in box C.   C ☐

Remember that this is only a rough guide. Some of the chapters in this book are longer and more complicated than others, and you will find some subjects easier to understand than others.

Step 5   Implement

Set about studying each chapter in the time shown in box C, following the key study steps in the order suggested by your particular learning style.

This is your personal **Study Plan**. You should try to combine it with the study sequence outlined below. You may want to modify the sequence to adapt it to your **personal style**.

> BPP's **Learning to Learn Accountancy** gives further guidance on developing a study plan, and deciding where and when to study.

Tackling your studies

The best way to approach this Study Text is to tackle the chapters in order. Taking into account your individual learning style, you could follow this sequence for each chapter.

Key study steps	Activity
Step 1 **Topic list**	This topic list helps you navigate each chapter; each numbered topic is a numbered section in the chapter.
Step 2 **Introduction**	This sets your objectives for study by giving you the big picture in terms of the context of the chapter. The content is referenced to the Study Guide, and Exam guidance shows how the topic is likely to be examined. The Introduction tells you **why** the topics covered in the chapter need to be studied.
Step 3 **Knowledge brought forward boxes**	These highlight information and techniques that it is assumed you have 'brought forward' with you from your earlier studies. Remember that you may be tested on these areas in the exam. If you are unsure of these areas, you should consider revising your more detailed study material from earlier papers.
Step 4 **Fast forward**	Fast forward boxes give you a quick summary of the content of each of the main chapter sections. They are listed together in the roundup at the end of each chapter to help you review each chapter quickly.
Step 5 **Explanations**	Proceed methodically through each chapter, particularly focussing on areas highlighted as significant in the chapter introduction, or areas that are frequently examined.
Step 6 **Key terms and Exam focus points**	• Key terms can often earn you **easy marks** if you state them clearly and correctly in an exam answer. They are highlighted in the index at the back of this text. • Exam focus points state how the topic has been or may be examined, difficulties that can occur in questions about the topic, and examiner feedback on common weaknesses in answers.
Step 7 **Note taking**	Take brief notes, if you wish. Don't copy out too much. Remember that being able to record something yourself is a sign of being able to understand it. Your notes can be in whatever format you find most helpful; lists, diagrams, mindmaps.
Step 8 **Examples**	Work through the examples very carefully as they illustrate key knowledge and techniques.
Step 9 **Case studies**	Study each one, and try to add flesh to them from your own experience. They are designed to show how the topics you are studying come alive in the real world.
Step 10 **Questions**	Attempt each one, as they will illustrate how well you've understood what you've read.

Key study steps	Activity
Step 11 **Answers**	Check yours against ours, and make sure you understand any discrepancies.
Step 12 **Chapter roundup**	Review it carefully, to make sure you have grasped the significance of all the important points in the chapter.
Step 13 **Quick quiz**	Use the Quick quiz to check how much you have remembered of the topics covered and to practise questions in a variety of formats.
Step 14 **Question practice**	Attempt the Question(s) suggested at the very end of the chapter. You can find these in the Exam Question Bank at the end of the Study Text, along with the answers so you can see how you did. If you have bought i-Pass, use this too.

Short of time: Skim study technique?

You may find you simply do not have the time available to follow all the key study steps for each chapter, however you adapt them for your particular learning style. If this is the case, follow the **skim study** technique below.

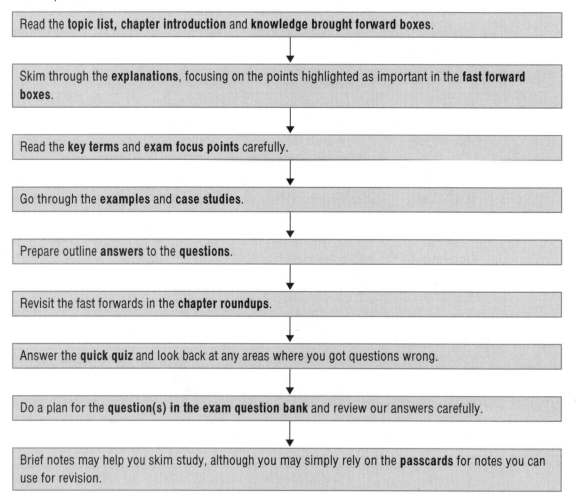

Read the **topic list, chapter introduction** and **knowledge brought forward boxes**.

Skim through the **explanations**, focusing on the points highlighted as important in the **fast forward boxes**.

Read the **key terms** and **exam focus points** carefully.

Go through the **examples** and **case studies**.

Prepare outline **answers** to the **questions**.

Revisit the fast forwards in the **chapter roundups**.

Answer the **quick quiz** and look back at any areas where you got questions wrong.

Do a plan for the **question(s) in the exam question bank** and review our answers carefully.

Brief notes may help you skim study, although you may simply rely on the **passcards** for notes you can use for revision.

Moving on...

When you are ready to start revising, you should still refer back to this Study Text.

- As a source of **reference** (you should find the index particularly helpful for this)

- As a way to **review** (the Fast forwards, Exam focus points, Chapter roundups and Quick quizzes help you here)

Remember to keep careful hold of this Study Text – you will find it invaluable in your work.

> More advice on Study Skills can be found in BPP's **Learning to Learn Accountancy** book.

Syllabus

Aim

To develop knowledge and understanding of the audit process and its application in the context of the external regulatory framework and for business control and development.

Objectives

On completion of this paper, candidates should be able to:

- understand the nature, purpose and scope of auditing and internal review, including the role of external audit and its regulatory framework, and the role of internal audit in providing assurance on risk management and on the control framework of an organisation

- identify risks, describe the procedures undertaken in the planning process, plan work to meet the objectives of the audit or review assignment and draft the content of plans

- describe and evaluate accounting and internal control systems and identify and communicate control risks, potential consequences and recommendations

- explain and evaluate sources of evidence, describe the nature, timing and extent of tests on transactions and account balances (including sampling and analytical procedures) and design programs for audit and review assignments

- evaluate findings, investigate inconsistencies, modify the work program as necessary, review subsequent events, and justify and prepare appropriate reports for users within and external to the organisation, including recommendations to enhance business performance

- discuss and apply the requirements of relevant International Standards on Auditing

- demonstrate the skills expected in Part 2.

Position of the paper in the overall syllabus

Paper 2.6 builds on the knowledge and understanding by Paper 1.1 Preparing Financial Statements and to a lesser extent Paper 1.2 Financial Information for Management.

Candidates will be expected to be familiar with Paper 2.5 Financial Reporting, including the requirements of the accounting standards examined within it. They will also be expected to be familiar with Paper 2.1 Information Systems.

Paper 2.6 provides the knowledge and understanding of the audit process which is then developed in Paper 3.1 Audit and Assurance Services.

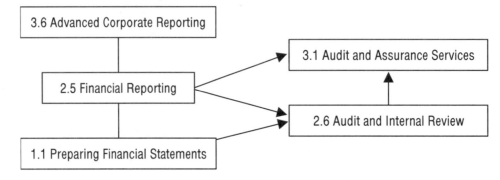

1   **Audit framework**

   (a)   The development and changing nature of audit, the social role of audit.

   (b)   Statutory audits, accountability, stewardship and agency.

   (c)   Professional ethics and codes of conduct, their application to external audit and internal audit, responsibility for fraud and error.

2   **Internal audit and internal review**

   (a)   The role of internal audit and internal review and their relationship with:

      (i)   Corporate governance
      (ii)   Risk management
      (iii) Organisational control
      (iv) Corporate objectives

   (b)   Scope and functions of internal audit, the nature and extent of internal audit assignments.

   (c)   Outsourced internal audit functions.

   (d)   The nature and extent of internal review assignments including operational, systems, value for money and financial reviews.

3   **Regulation**

   (a)   Statements of Auditing Standards:

      (i)   Their development and role
      (ii)   Their relationship with International Standards of Auditing.

   (b)   Auditors:

      (i)   Regulation and supervision
      (ii)   Their relationship with Government
      (iii) The role of the Auditing Practices Board and other UK standard-setting bodies.

4   **Planning and risk**

   (a)   Objectives of audit and review assignments, the relevance of stakeholder dialogue.
   (b)   Communicating the objectives of audit and review assignments.
   (c)   Analytical procedures.
   (d)   Risk assessment.
   (e)   Materiality, tolerable error, and sample sizes.
   (f)   Design and documentation of the plan and work program.
   (g)   Co-ordination of the work of others.
   (h)   Information Technology in planning and risk assessment.

5   **Internal control**

   (a)   Objectives of internal control systems.

   (b)   Inherent weaknesses in internal control systems.

   (c)   The use of internal control systems by auditors.

   (d)   Transaction cycles (revenue, purchases, payroll, inventory, capital expenditure).

   (e)   The evaluation of internal control systems by auditors including internal control checklists and tests of control.

   (f)   Communication with management.

6   **Other audit and internal review of evidence**

   (a)   Financial statement assertions: assets, liabilities, income and expenditure, including accounting estimates.

   (b)   Assertions reported on and opinions provided in review assignments.

   (c)   Analytical procedures as substantive evidence.

   (d)   Balance and transaction testing.

   (e)   Computer-assisted audit techniques, their uses and limitations.

   (f)   Management representations.

   (g)   Audit sampling and other selective testing procedures.

   (h)   Subsequent events review.

   (i)   Going concern reviews.

   (j)   The overall review of evidence obtained.

   (k)   Modifications to the plan and work program in the light of findings.

7   **Reporting**

   (a)   Format and content of unqualified and qualified external audit reports on financial statements.

   (b)   Format and content of review reports and other reports on assignment objectives.

   (c)   Recommendations for the enhancement of business performance.

Excluded topics

Audit of groups is not examinable at this level. Candidates should be aware of the content, wording and meaning of audit reports and they may be asked to prepare the explanatory paragraphs for inclusion in a qualified audit report. However, candidates are not expected to draft full audit reports.

Exposure drafts (EDs) are not examinable for Paper 2.6.

Key areas of the syllabus

The key topic areas are as follows:

- Professional ethics as they apply to accountants working in public practice and in business
- Risk assessment and the response to assessed risks for external auditors
- The role of internal audit in risk management and corporate governance
- Internal controls
- Substantive audit evidence

Paper 2.6

Audit and Internal Review
(United Kingdom)

Study Guide

1 THE NATURE, PURPOSE AND SCOPE OF AUDIT AND REVIEW

Explain the:

- Nature and development of audit and review
- Concepts of accountability, stewardship and agency
- Concepts of materiality, true and fair presentation and reasonable assurance
- Reporting as a means of communication to different stakeholders
- Need for auditors to communicate with those charged with governance
- High level of assurance provided by audit assignments and risk-based approaches; the moderate level of assurance provided by review assignments and procedural approaches; assignments in which no assurance is provided

NB: Students are expected to be aware of the nature and purpose of non-financial audit and review services as described in Session 6. Internal review questions will focus on financial and systems reviews in the context of companies and small not-for-profit organisations.

2 STATUTORY AUDITS

Describe the:

- UK regulatory framework in which statutory audits take place
- Development and status of the Auditing Practices Board Statements of Auditing Standards and their relationship with International Standards on Auditing
- Reasons for, and mechanisms for, the regulation of auditors by Government and other regulatory agencies including other UK standard-setters
- Types of opinion provided in statutory audit assignments
- Limitations of statutory audits

3 INTERNAL AUDIT AND INTERNAL REVIEW I

Explain the:

- Development and role of internal audit in achieving corporate objectives and as part of good corporate governance practice
- Relative merits of out-sourcing internal audit and internal review services to external auditors and others, and the associated problems

- Difference between the role of external audit and internal audit

4 REGULATORY ENVIRONMENT

Corporate governance

- Explain the objective, relevance and importance of corporate governance
- Discuss the relative merits and disadvantages of voluntary codes and legislation

Code of best practice

- Outline the provisions of the Code of Best Practice (based on the Cadbury Report) that are most relevant to auditors
- Outline the requirements of the Combined Code (of the Committee on Corporate Governance) relating to directors' responsibilities (eg for risk management and internal control) and the reporting responsibilities of auditors

Audit committees

- Explain the structure and roles of audit committees and discuss their benefits and drawbacks
- Discuss the relative merits and disadvantages of regulation by a voluntary code of practice rather than law

Internal financial control effectiveness

- Outline the importance of internal control and risk management

- Compare the responsibilities of management and auditors (internal and external) for the design and operation of systems and controls, and the reliability of management information (financial and non-financial)

- Describe the factors to be taken into account when assessing the need for an internal audit function

5 INTERNAL AUDIT AND REVIEW III

Describe the:

- Elements of best practice in the structure and operations of an internal audit function

- Scope of internal audit work and the limitations of the internal audit function

- Types of report provided in internal audit and internal review assignment

6 INTERNAL AUDIT AND INTERNAL REVIEW II

Describe and illustrate the:

- Nature and purpose of internal review assignments including:

  - value for money
  - best value
  - IT
  - financial

- Nature and purpose of operational internal audit and review assignments including:

  - procurement
  - marketing
  - treasury
  - HR

7 PROFESSIONAL ETHICS AND PROFESSIONAL CODES OF CONDUCT I

- Describe the sources of, and enforcement mechanisms associated with, professional ethics and professional codes of conduct

- Define the fundamental concepts of professional ethics

- Define the detailed requirements of, and illustrate and analyse the application of, professional ethics in the context of independence objectivity and integrity

- Distinguish between the elements of professional ethics applicable to internal auditors and those applicable to external authors

- Describe the responsibilities of internal and external auditors for the prevention and detection of fraud and error

8 PROFESSIONAL ETHICS AND PROFESSIONAL CODES OF CONDUCT II

- Describe the requirements of professional ethics and other requirements in relation to the acceptance of audit and review assignments, including situations in which there is an imposed limitation in audit scope

- Define the detailed requirements of, and illustrate and analyse the application of, professional ethics in the context of confidentiality and conflicts of interest

- Describe the importance of engagement letters and describe their contents

9 PRELIMINARY PLANNING PROCEDURES

- Distinguish between risk-based, procedural and other approaches to audit and review work

- Describe the sources and nature of information gathered in planning audit and review assignments

- Describe the knowledge of the business required by auditors

- Describe the purpose of analytical procedures in planning and illustrate the application of such procedures

- Describe the components of risk and use of information technology in risk analysis

- Illustrate and explain the importance of the application of risk analysis

- Define and illustrate the concepts of materiality and tolerable error

- Evaluate misstatements

10 THE WORK PLAN, THE WORK PROGRAM AND DOCUMENTATION

- Describe and illustrate the contents of work plans, work programs and working papers

- Describe the nature of documentation required for different types of assignment
- Explain the importance of documentation
- Illustrate the use of information technology in the audit

11 THE WORK OF OTHERS

Describe the:

- Extent to which external auditors are able to rely on the work of:
  - internal audit
  - experts
  - service organisations and recognise where reliance is needed
- Extent to which internal auditors are able to rely on the work of:
  - experts
  - service organisations
- Conditions that must be met before reliance can be placed on the work of others and the planning considerations in co-ordinating the work of others
- Division of responsibilities between auditors and others
- Extent to which reference to the work of others can be made in the audit and review reports

12 INTERNAL CONTROL I

- Describe the objectives of internal control systems and the responsibility for internal control systems in the context of organisational objectives

- Describe the importance of internal control to auditors
- Describe and illustrate the limitations of internal control systems in the context of fraud and error
- Explain the need to modify the audit plan in the light of the results of tests of control
- Distinguish between tests of control and substantive tests

13 INTERNAL CONTROL II – SALES, PURCHASES AND STOCK

- Describe, illustrate and analyse how internal control systems over sales, purchases and stock cycles operate in both large and small entities
- Describe and illustrate the use by auditors of internal control checklists for sales, purchases and stock cycles
- Describe and tabulate tests of control of sales, purchases and stock for inclusion in a work program
- Explain and illustrate how structural and operational weaknesses in sales, purchases and stock systems should be reported to management and how recommendations should be made

14 INTERNAL CONTROL III – REVENUE EXPENDITURE AND CAPITAL EXPENDITURE

- Describe, illustrate and analyse how internal control systems over revenue and capital

expenditure transaction cycles operate in both large and small entities

- Describe and illustrate the use by auditors of internal control checklists for revenue and capital expenditure transaction cycles
- Describe and tabulate tests of control of revenue and capital expenditure for inclusion in a work program
- Explain and illustrate how structural and operational weaknesses in revenue and capital expenditure systems should be reported to management and how recommendations should be made

15 INTERNAL CONTROL IV – PAYROLL

- Describe, illustrate and analyse how internal control systems over the payroll transaction cycle operate in both large and small entities
- Describe and illustrate the use by auditors of internal control checklists for the payroll transaction cycle
- Describe and tabulate tests of control of payroll for inclusion in a work program
- Explain and illustrate how structural and operational weaknesses in payroll systems should be reported to management and how recommendations should be made

16 INTERNAL CONTROL V – BANK AND CASH

- Describe, illustrate and analyse how internal control systems over the bank and cash transaction cycle operate in both large and small entities

- Describe and illustrate the use by auditors of internal control checklists for the bank and cash transaction cycle

- Describe and tabulate tests of control of bank and cash for inclusion in a work program

- Explain and illustrate how structural and operational weaknesses in bank and cash systems should be reported to management and how recommendations should be made

17 OTHER AUDIT AND REVIEW EVIDENCE I

- Describe the sources and relative merits of the different types of evidence available

- Describe the financial statement assertions commonly reported on and the principles and objectives of balance and transaction testing

- Distinguish between the interim and the final audit

- Describe and illustrate how analytical procedures are used as substantive procedures

- Explain the problems associated with the audit and review of accounting

estimates

- Describe the types of evidence available in smaller entities

- Evaluate the quality of evidence collected

18 OTHER AUDIT AND REVIEW EVIDENCE II – DEBTORS AND PREPAYMENTS

- Describe and tabulate for inclusion in a work program the substantive procedures, including debtors circularisations, used in obtaining evidence in relation to debtors and prepayments, and the related income statement entries

- Explain the purpose of substantive procedures in relation to financial statement assertions concerning debtors and prepayments

19 OTHER AUDIT AND REVIEW EVIDENCE III – STOCK

- Explain the importance of stock

- Describe stock counting procedures

- Explain cut off

- Describe and tabulate for inclusion in a work program the substantive procedures used in obtaining evidence in relation to stock, including the auditors' attendance at stocktaking

- Explain the purpose of substantive procedures including direct confirmation of stock held by third parties in relation to financial statement assertions concerning stock

20 OTHER AUDIT AND REVIEW EVIDENCE IV – CURRENT LIABILITIES AND ACCRUALS

- Describe and tabulate for inclusion in a work program the substantive procedures including supplies statement reconciliations and creditor circularisations used in obtaining evidence in relation to current liabilities and accruals, and the related income statement entries

- Explain the purpose of substantive procedures in relation to financial statement assertions concerning current liabilities and accruals

21 OTHER AUDIT AND REVIEW EVIDENCE V – BANK AND CASH

- Describe and tabulate for inclusion in a work program the substantive procedures including bank confirmation reports used in obtaining evidence in relation to bank and cash, and the related income statement entries

- Explain the purpose of substantive procedures in relation to financial statement assertions concerning bank

22 OTHER AUDIT AND REVIEW EVIDENCE VI –FIXED ASSETS AND LONG-TERM LIABILITIES

Syllabus reference 6a

- Describe and tabulate for inclusion in a work program the substantive procedures used in obtaining evidence in relation to fixed assets and long-term liabilities and the related income statement entries

- Explain the purpose of substantive procedures in relation to financial statement assertions concerning fixed assets and long-term liabilities

23 OTHER AUDIT AND REVIEW EVIDENCE VII

- Explain the need for sampling
- Distinguish between statistical and non-statistical sampling
- Describe and illustrate the application of the basic principles of statistical sampling and other selective testing procedures
- Describe and illustrate the use of computer assisted techniques in obtaining evidence

(Note: candidates will not be required to perform detailed sampling calculations)

24 GOING CONCERN REVIEWS

- Explain the importance of going concern reviews
- Describe the procedures to be applied in performing going concern reviews
- Describe the disclosure requirements relating to going concern issues
- Describe the reporting implications of the findings of going concern reviews

25 AUDIT FINALISATION AND THE FINAL REVIEW

Describe the:

- Quality of management representations as audit evidence
- Circumstances in which obtaining management representations is necessary and the matters on which representations are commonly obtained
- Purpose of the subsequent events review
- Procedures to be undertaken in performing a subsequent events review
- Importance of the overall review of evidence obtained
- Problems associated with the application of accounting treatments
- Significance of unadjusted differences

26 REPORTING I

Syllabus reference 7a

- Describe, illustrate and analyse the format and content of unqualified and qualified statutory audit reports

27 REPORTING II

Describe, illustrate and analyse the format and content of:

- Internal review reports and other reports dealing with recommendations for the enhancement of business performance

28 NOT-FOR-PROFIT ORGANISATIONS

- Apply audit and review techniques to small not-for-profit organisations
- Explain how the audit and review for small not-for-profit organisations differs from the audit and review of for-profit organisations

Examinable documents

Accounting standards

The accounting knowledge that is assumed for Paper 2.6 is the same as that examined in Paper 2.5. Therefore, candidates studying for Paper 2.6 should refer to the International Accounting Standards listed under Paper 2.5. However, Paper 2.6 only assumes a detailed knowledge of accounting standards that are examined in Paper 1.1.

International Standards on Auditing (ISAs)(UK and Ireland)

No	Title
	Glossary of terms – revised Oct 2004
	International Framework for assurance assignments
	Preface to International Standards on quality control, auditing, assurance and related services
200	Objective and general principles governing an audit of financial statements
210	Terms of audit engagements
230	Audit documentation (revised)
240	The auditor's responsibility to consider fraud in an audit of financial statements
250	Consideration of laws and regulations in an audit of financial statements
260	Communications of audit matters with those charged with governance
300	Planning an audit of financial statements
315	Understanding the entity and its environment and assessing the risks of material misstatement
320	Audit materiality
330	The auditor's procedures in response to assessed risks
402	Audit considerations relating to entities using service organisations
500	Audit evidence
501	Audit evidence – additional considerations for specific items
505	External confirmations
510	Initial engagements – opening balances
520	Analytical procedures
530	Audit sampling and other means of testing
540	Audit of accounting estimates
560	Subsequent events
570	Going concern
580	Management representations
610	Considering the work of internal auditing
620	Using the work of an expert
700	The independent auditor's report on a complete set of general purpose financial statements
701	Modifications to the independent auditor's report
710	Comparatives
720	Other information in documents containing audited financial statements

Ethical Standards (ESs)

No	Title	Issue date
ES1	Integrity, objectivity and independence	Dec 2004
ES2	Financial, business, employment and personal relationships	Dec 2004
ES3	Long association with the audit engagement	Dec 2004
ES4	Fees, remuneration and evaluation policies, litigation, gifts and hospitality	Dec 2004
ES5	Non audit services provided to audit clients	Dec 2004
	Glossary	
ES	Provisions available for small entitites	April 2005

Other documents

No	Title	Issue date
	The Combined Code (of the Committee on Corporate Governance)	
	Scope and Authority of APB Pronouncements (Revised)	Dec 2004
PN13	The audit of small businesses	July 1997
PN16	Bank reports for audit purposes	Aug 1998
PN25	Attendance at stocktaking	Jan 2004
Bulletin 2001/02*	Revisions to the working of auditors' reports on financial statements and the interim review report	Jan 2001
Bulletin 2001/03	E-business: identifying financial statement risks	April 2001
Briefing paper	Providing assurance on the effectiveness of internal control	July 2001
Briefing paper	Effective communication between audit committees and external auditors	Sept 2002

* Students will not be examined on those sections of this document that deal with the review report or Stock Exchange requirements.

Note

1   Students are advised that questions will be based on the principles and good practice set out in the International Standards on Auditing.

Other guidance

ACCA's 'Rules of Professional Conduct'

Documents under 'Other guidance' are examinable only to the extent that they are relevant to topics specified in the syllabus and study guide.

Exam focus point

These are the examinable documents for June 2006. You must check the up to date examinable documents on ACCA's website or in *Student Accountant* before your exam.

The exam paper

The examination is a three hour paper constructed in two sections. The bulk of the questions will be discursive but some questions involving computational elements will be set from time to time.

Section A is compulsory. The questions will cover the key elements of the syllabus relevant to both internal and external audit assignments. Section B requires candidates to answer two out of three questions. The questions will cover all areas of the syllabus.

		Number of Marks
Section A:	3 compulsory scenario-based questions (no single question will exceed 25 marks)	60
Section B:	Choice of 2 from 3 questions (20 marks each)	40
		100

Additional information

This paper encompasses:

1   Internal review, which may be provided either by internal auditors or may be outsourced to external auditors.

2   External audit.

References to audit and auditors mean both internal and external audit and auditors, except where otherwise indicated.

Candidates need to be aware that questions involving knowledge of new examinable regulations will not be set until at least six months after the last day of the month in which the regulation was issued.

The Study Guide provides more detailed guidance on the syllabus. Examinable documents are listed in the 'Exam Notes' section of *Student Accountant*.

Analysis of past papers

The analysis below shows the topics which have been examined in all sittings of the current syllabus so far and in the Pilot Paper.

December 2005

Section A

1   Audit procedures on stock counts and valuations
2   Internal audit and outsourcing
3   Planning and audit strategy

Section B

4   Subsequent events
5   Audit procedures on sales tax and depreciation, removal of auditors
6   CAATs, test data and audit software

June 2005

Section A

1   Audit risk, going concern
2   Letters of representation
3   Sales and fixed assets

Section B

4   Internal audit, corporate governance, audit committees
5   Responsibilities of directors/auditors, reports
6   Evidence and procedures

December 2004

Section A

1   Responsibilities for fraud and error; scenario on fraud and error
2   Planning and risk assessment; audit working papers
3   Review of internal controls and suggestions for improvement

Section B

4   Financial statement assertions; payroll audit
5   Audit of smaller entities
6   Audit of larger entities

June 2004

Section A

1   Debtors, risk and internal control
2   Acceptance of appointment, engagement letters
3   Audit procedures on stock

Section B

4   Creditors, audit evidence
5   Internal audit, controls over outsourced activities
6   Methods of obtaining evidence

December 2003

Section A

1   Internal audit risk assessment, controls and control procedures
2   Payroll, controls and tests
3   Group concern

Section B

4   Overall review and subsequent events
5   Risks in NFP, tests on income and expenditure
6   Confidentiality

June 2003

Section A

1   Audit risk assessment
2   Stock count procedures
3   Conflict of interest, audit evidence (FRS 12), impact on audit report

Oxford Brookes BSc (Hons) in Applied Accounting

The standard required of candidates completing Part 2 is that required in the final year of a UK degree. Students completing Parts 1 and 2 will have satisfied the examination requirement for an honours degree in Applied Accounting, awarded by Oxford Brookes University.

To achieve the degree, you must also submit two pieces of work based on a **Research and Analysis Project.**

- A 5,000 word **Report** on your chosen topic, which demonstrates that you have acquired the necessary research, analytical and IT skills.

- A 1,500 word **Key Skills Statement**, indicating how you have developed your interpersonal and communication skills.

BPP was selected by the ACCA and Oxford Brookes University to produce the official text *Success in your Research and Analysis Project* to support students in this task. The book pays particular attention to key skills not covered in the professional examinations.

BPP also offers courses and mentoring services.

For further information, please see BPP's website: www.bpp.com/bsc

ACCA professional development requirements

Soon, you will possess a professional qualification. You know its value by the effort you have put in. To uphold the prestige of the qualification, ACCA, with the other professional bodies that form the International Federation of Accountants (IFAC), requires its members to undertake continuous professional development (CPD). This requirement applies to all members, not just those with a practising certificate. Happily, BPP Professional Education is here to support you in your professional development with materials, courses and qualifications.

> For further information, please see ACCA's website: www.accaglobal.com

Professional development with BPP

You do not have to do exams for professional development (PD) – but you need relevant technical updating and you may also benefit from other work-related training. BPP can provide you with both. Visit our professional development website, www.bpp.com/pd for details of our PD courses in accounting, law, general business skills and other important areas. Offering defined hours of structured CPD, and delivered by top professionals throughout the year and in many locations, our courses are designed to fit around your busy work schedule. Our unique PD passport will give you access to these PD services at an attractive discount.

> For further information, please see BPP's website: www.bpp.com/pd

Master of Business Administration (MBA)

ACCA and Oxford Brookes University, a leading UK university, have worked together on an MBA programme. The MBA, accredited by AMBA (the Association of MBAs), lasts 21 months for ACCA members, and is taught by distance learning with online seminars delivered to a global student base over the Internet. BPP provides the user-friendly materials. As an ACCA member, you will receive credits towards this MBA and you can begin your studies when you have completed your ACCA professional exams. Flexibility, global reach and value for money underpin a high quality learning experience.

The qualification features an introductory module (*Foundations of Management*). Other modules include *Global Business Strategy, Managing Self Development*, and *Organisational Change and Transformation*.

Research Methods are also taught, as they underpin the **research dissertation**.

> For further information, please visit: www.accaglobal.com, www. brookes.ac.uk or www.bpp.com/mba

Diploma in International Financial Reporting

The ACCA's Diploma in International Financial Reporting is designed for those whose country-specific accounting knowledge needs to be supplemented by knowledge of international accounting standards. BPP offers books and courses in this useful qualification – it also earns you valuable CPD points.

> For further information, please see ACCA's website: www.accaglobal.com and BPP's website: www.bpp.com/dipifr

Tax and financial services

If you are interested in tax, BPP offers courses for the ATT (tax technician) and CTA (Chartered Tax Adviser, formerly ATII) qualifications. You can also buy our user-friendly CTA texts to keep up-to-date with tax practice.

> For further information, please see BPP's website: www.bpp.com/att and www.bpp.com/cta

If your role involves selling financial services products, such as pensions, or offering investment advice, BPP provides learning materials and training for relevant qualifications. BPP also offers training for specialist financial markets qualifications (eg CFA®) and insolvency.

> For further information, please see BPP's website: www.bpp.com/financialadvisers

Other business qualifications

BPP supports many business disciplines, such as market research, marketing, human resources management and law. We are the official provider of distance learning programmes for the Market Research Society. We train for the Chartered Institute of Personnel and Development qualification, with a number of other supporting qualifications in training and personnel management. BPP's law school is an industry leader.

> Visit www.bpp.com for further details of all that we can offer you. BPP's personalised online information service, My BPP, will help you keep track of the details you submit to BPP.

Syllabus mindmap

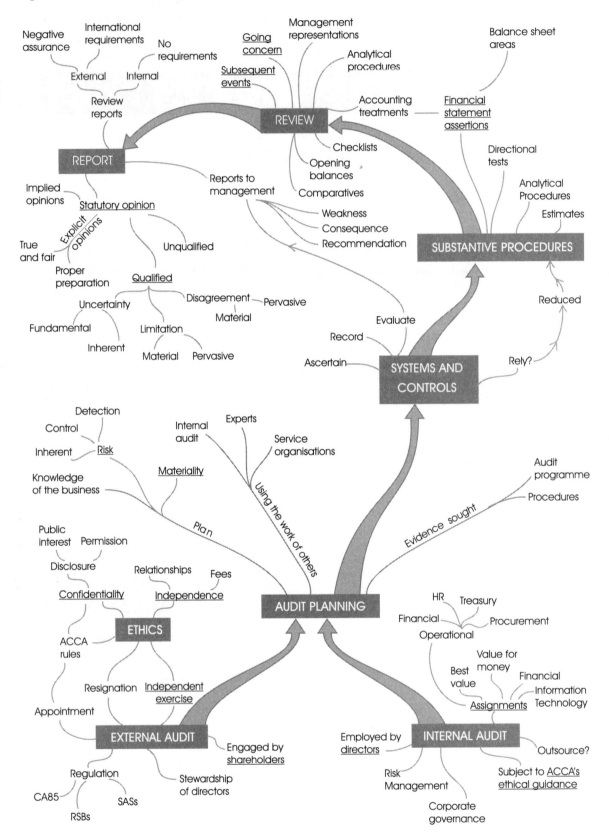

BPP
PROFESSIONAL EDUCATION

Part A
Framework

BPP
PROFESSIONAL EDUCATION

The nature and
purpose of assurance

Topic list	Syllabus reference
1 The purpose of assurance	1
2 The nature of assurance services	1
3 Assurance and reports	1

Introduction

First we need to consider **why there is a need for assurance in relation to financial and non-financial information**. You learnt about the nature of a company in Paper 2.2. The main reason an assurance service is required is the fact that the ownership and management of a company are not necessarily the same thing. In Section 1 we will introduce concepts of **agency, accountability** and **stewardship.**

Second, it is important to understand **what assurance services exist**. The key assurance services which your syllabus concentrates on are the audit (statutory and non-statutory), reviews, and internal reviews. Although it is strictly defined, many people do not understand what an audit is and what it is designed to achieve. This is discussed in Section 2.

The effect of audits and reviews is that people interested in the accounts of an entity are given a level of **assurance** as to the quality of the contents of the accounts. The audit report focuses on the truth and fairness of the accounts. It gives reasonable assurance, rather than an absolute assurance. The degrees of assurance given by audits and reviews are discussed in section 3.

While audits will vary according to the nature of the clients' businesses, most will follow standard stages overall. The **chronology of a typical external audit** is set out in section 4.

The rest of the Study Text builds on themes identified in this chapter.

Study guide

1 – The nature, purpose and scope of audit and review

Explain the:

- Nature and development of audit and review
- Concepts of accountability, stewardship and agency
- Concepts of materiality, true and fair presentation and reasonable assurance
- Reporting as a means of communication to different stakeholders
- Need for auditors to communicate with those charged with governance
- High level of assurance provided by audit assignments; the moderate level of assurance provided by review assignments; assignments in which no assurance is provided.

Note. Students are expected to be aware of the nature and purpose of non-financial review services as described in Session 6. Internal review questions may deal with these subjects, as well as financial and systems reviews in the context of companies and small not-for-profit organisations.

2 – Statutory audits

- Explain the objectives and principal characteristics of statutory audit and discuss its value (eg in assisting management to reduce risk and improve performance)
- Limitations of statutory audits

Exam guide

This chapter explains the basis of auditing and explains the distinction between audit and review. The mechanics of these issues are explained throughout the text. Questions in the exam could draw on matters in this chapter, **in conjunction** with the knowledge you will obtain later in the Study Text.

1 The purpose of assurance

FAST FORWARD >> An assurance engagement is essentially an **impartial**, **knowledgeable** scrutiny and review.

1.1 Accountability and stewardship

The key reason for having an audit or review can be seen by working through the following case study.

 Case Study

Laine decides to set up a business selling flowers. She gets up early in the morning, visits the market, and then sets up a stall by the side of the road. For the first year, all goes well. She sells all the flowers she is able to buy and she derives some income from the business.

However, Laine feels that she could sell more flowers if she was able to transport more to the place where she sells them, and also knows that there are several other roads nearby where she could sell flowers, if she could be in two places at once. She could achieve these two things by buying a van, and by employing other people to sell flowers on the other roads.

Laine needs more money to achieve this expansion of her business. She decides to ask her rich friend Glyn to invest in the business.

Glyn can see the potential of Laine's business and wants to invest, but he doesn't want to be involved in the management of the business. He also does not want to have ultimate liability for the debts of the business if the business fails. He therefore suggest that they set up a limited company. He will own the majority of the shares and be entitled to dividends. Laine will be managing director and be paid a salary for her work.

At the end of the first year of trading as a limited company, Glyn receives a copy of the financial statements. Profits are lower than expected, so his dividend will not be a large as he had hoped. He knows that Laine is paid a salary so does not care as much as him that profits are low.

Glyn is concerned by the level of profits and feels that he wants further assurance on the accounts. He doesn't know whether they give a true reflection on the last year's trading, particularly as the profits do not seen as high as those Laine had predicted when he agreed to invest.

The solution is that the **assurance** Glyn is seeking can be given by an independent **audit or review** of the financial statements. An auditor can provide the two things that Glyn requires:

- A **knowledgeable review** of the company's business and of the accounts
- An **impartial view**, since Laine's view might be partial.

Other people will also view the company's accounts with interest, for example:

- Creditors of the company
- Taxation authorities

The various people interested in the accounts of a company are sometimes referred to as **stakeholders**. Although they will all judge the accounts by different criteria, **they will all gain assurance** from learning that the accounts they are reading have been subject to an independent report.

The example of Glyn and Laine is a simple one. In practice companies may have thousands of shareholders and may not know the management personally. It is therefore important that directors are **accountable** to shareholders. Directors act as **stewards** of the shareholders' investments. They are **agents** of the shareholders.

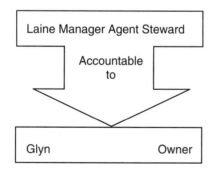
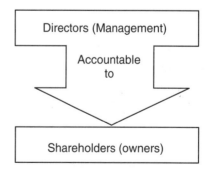

Key terms

> **Accountability** is the quality or state of being accountable, that is, being required or expected to justify actions and decisions. It suggests an obligation or willingness to accept responsibility for one's actions.
>
> **Stewardship** is the practice of being a steward, that is, someone employed to manage another person's property.
>
> **Agents** were introduced in paper 2.2 *Corporate and Business Law*. Agents are people employed or used to provide a particular service. In the case of a company, the people being used to provide the service managing the business also have the second role of being people in their own right trying to maximise their personal wealth.

You may ask, 'what are the directors accountable for?' It is important to understand the answer to this question. The directors are accountable for the **shareholders' investment**. The shareholders have bought shares in that company (they have invested). They **expect a return** from their investment. As the **directors** manage the company, they are **in a position to affect that return.**

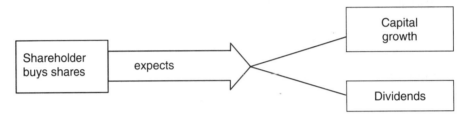

The exact nature of the return expected by the shareholder will depend on the type of company he has chosen to invest in: that is part of his investment risk analysis. Certain issues are true of any such investment, however. For example, if the directors **mismanage** the company, and it goes **bankrupt**, it will neither provide a source of future dividends, not will it create capital growth in the investment – indeed, the opposite is true, and even the original investment is likely to be lost.

Accountability therefore covers a range of issues:

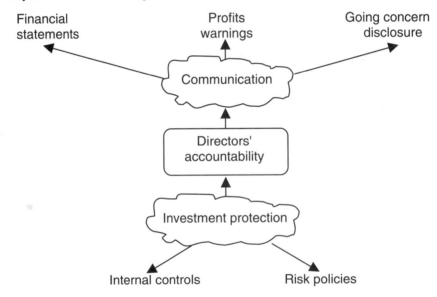

These issues are often discussed under the umbrella title '**corporate governance**', where 'governance' indicates the management (governing) role of the directors, and 'corporate' indicates that the issue relates to companies (bodies corporate). This is illustrated by our scenario, where we saw Laine taking up a corporate governance position in relation to Glyn. We shall consider corporate governance more in Chapter 2.

1.2 Assurance provision

Many of the requirements in relation to corporate governance necessitate **communication** between the directors and the shareholders.

By law, **directors** of all companies are usually **required to produce financial statements** annually which give a **true and fair view** of the affairs of the company and its profit or loss for the period. They are also **encouraged** to **communicate with shareholders** on matters relating to **directors' pay** and benefits (this is required by law in the case of public limited companies), **going concern** and **management of risks.**

But how are the shareholders to know whether the directors' communications are **accurate**, or present a **fair picture?** We are back to the problem that Glyn had in the scenario we presented at the beginning of this section. He knew that Laine's view might be **biased** in a different way to his own, and he sought **assurance** on the information he was presented with. An **assurance engagement** is one where a professional accountant evaluates or measures a subject matter that is the responsibility of another party against suitable criteria, and expresses an opinion which provides the intended user with a level of assurance about that subject matter.

Key term

An **assurance engagement** is one in which a practitioner expresses a conclusion designed to enhance the degree of confidence of the intended users other than the responsible party about the outcome of the evaluation or measurement of a subject matter against criteria.

2 The nature of assurance services

FAST FORWARD

This syllabus is particularly concerned with **audit** (both statutory and non statutory), **review** and the assurance provided to management by **internal audit**.

Exam focus point

A definition of an assurance service according to the International Framework for assurance engagements was given above. It is an engagement to express an opinion giving assurance to a set of people on information which is the responsibility of others. That definition sums up two of the major features of the audit and internal review syllabus, audits and reviews.

2.1 Statutory and non-statutory audits

Key term

'The objective of an **audit** of financial statements is to enable the auditor to express an opinion whether the financial statements are prepared, in all material respects, in accordance with an applicable financial reporting framework. The phrases used to express the auditor's opinion are 'give a true and fair view' or 'present fairly, in all material respects', which are equivalent terms. A similar objective applies to the audit of financial or other information prepared in accordance with appropriate criteria.'

The purpose of an audit is to enable auditors to **give an opinion** on the financial statements. While an audit might produce by-products such as advice to the directors on how to run the business, the point of an audit is **solely to report to shareholders.**

In most countries, audits are required under national statute in the case of a large number of undertakings, including limited liability companies. Other organisations and entities requiring a statutory audit may include charities, investment businesses, trade unions and so on.

Audits are required under statute in the case of a large number of undertakings. In the UK, registered companies legislation (currently Companies Act 1985), most companies are required to have an audit. There are also requirements for:

- Building Societies (Building Societies Act 1965)
- Trade Unions/employer associations (Trade Union and Labour Relations Act 1974)
- House Associations (various pieces of related legislation)
- Certain charities (various pieces of legislation, depending on status)

This legislation is not examinable, it is for illustration only.

The statutory audit can bring various advantages to the company and shareholders. The key benefit to shareholders is the impartial view provided by the auditors. However, the company benefits from professional accountants reviewing the accounts and system as part of the audit. Benefits might include recommendations being made in relation to accounting and control systems and the possibility that auditors might detect fraud and error.

Points to note

> Statutory audits will be discussed in more detail in Chapter 3. A chronology of a typical audit showing the auditors' work on accounts and systems is given in Section 4 of this Chapter. The techniques auditors use will be discussed in Parts B-E of this Study Text.

Non-statutory audits are performed by independent auditors because the owners, proprietors, members, trustees, professional and governing bodies or other interested parties want them, rather than because the law requires them. In consequence, **auditing may extend** to every type of undertaking which produces accounts, including:

- Clubs
- Charities (some of these will require statutory audits as well)
- Sole traders
- Partnerships

Point to note

> Some of these organisations do not operate for profit, and this has a specific impact on the nature of their audit. The audit of not for profit organisations will be considered in more detail in Chapter 21.

Auditors may also give an **opinion** on **statements other than annual accounts**, including:

- Summaries of sales in support of a statement of royalties
- Statements of expenditure in support of applications for regional development grants
- The circulation figures of a newspaper or magazine

In all such audits the auditors must take into account any **regulations** contained in the internal rules or constitution of the undertaking. Examples of the regulations which the auditors would need to refer to in such assignments would include:

- The rules of clubs, societies and charities
- Partnership agreements

2.1.1 Advantages of the non-statutory audit

In addition to the advantages common to all forms of audit, a non-statutory audit can bring other advantages. For example, the audit of the accounts of a **partnership** may be seen to have the following advantages.

(a)   It can provide a means of **settling accounts** between the partners.

(b)   Where audited accounts are available this may make the **accounts more acceptable** to the **taxation authorities** when it comes to agreeing an individual partner's liability to tax. The partners may well wish to take advantage of the auditors' services in the additional role of tax advisers.

(c) The **sale of** the business or the **negotiation of loan** or overdraft facilities may be facilitated if the firm is able to produce audited accounts.

(d) An audit on behalf of a **'sleeping partner'** is useful since generally such a person will have little other means of checking the accounts of the business, or confirming the share of profits due to him or her.

Question	Non-statutory audit

Some of the advantages above will also apply in the audit of the accounts of a sole trader, club or charity. Which ones? And can you think of others?

2.2 Reviews

An audit can be used to give assurance to a variety of stakeholders on a variety of issues. However, an audit is an exercise designed to give a high level of assurance (as we shall see later) and involves a high degree of testing and therefore cost. In some cases, stakeholders may find that they receive **sufficient assurance** about an issue from a less detailed engagement, for example, a review. A review can provide a cost-efficient alternative to an audit where an audit is not required by law.

Key term

> The objective of a **review engagement** is to enable an auditor to state whether, on the basis of procedures which do not provide all the evidence that would be required in an audit, anything has come to the auditor's attention that causes the auditor to believe that the financial statements are not prepared, in all material respects, in accordance with an identified financial reporting framework.

The major result for recipients of a review engagement is that the **level of assurance** they gain from a review engagement is not as high as from an audit, although the procedures carried out in a review engagement are similar to an audit. This is discussed in Section 4.

Points to note

> As the techniques used in audits and reviews are similar, the methods and procedures you will encounter in Parts B-E of this Study Text are relevant to both audits and reviews. Bear in mind that for a review, less detailed procedures will be carried out and sample sizes are likely to be smaller. Analytical procedures, which are used heavily in review engagements, are discussed in Chapter 12.

2.3 Internal audit

FAST FORWARD

> **Internal auditors** are employed as part of an organisation's system of controls. Their responsibilities are determined by management and may be wide-ranging.

Key term

> **Internal auditing** is an appraisal or monitoring activity established within an entity as a service to the entity. It functions by, amongst other things, examining, evaluating and reporting to management and the directors on the adequacy and effectiveness of components of the accounting and internal control systems.

Up to now in this Chapter we have discussed assurance services where an independent outsider provides an opinion on financial information. However, the syllabus is also concerned with the assurance that can be provided to management (and by implication, to other parties) by **internal auditors**.

As we shall see in the next chapter, as part of their corporate governance duties, listed company directors are required, and all directors are advised, to review the effectiveness of the company's risk management and internal control systems. They should also consider the need for an **internal audit function to help them carry out their duties.**

Larger organisations may therefore appoint full-time staff whose **function is to monitor and report on the running of the company's operations**. Internal audit staff members are one type of control. Although some of the work carried out by internal auditors is similar to that performed by external auditors, there are **important distinctions** between the two functions in terms of their responsibilities, scope and relationship with the company.

Point to note

> Internal audit will be discussed in more detail in Chapter 4.

3 Assurance and reports

12/01

FAST FORWARD

> The auditors' report on company accounts is expressed in terms of **truth** and **fairness**. This is generally taken to mean that accounts:
>
> - Are factual
> - Are free from bias
> - Reflect the commercial substance of the business's transactions

3.1 Truth and fairness

External auditors give an opinion on the **truth and fairness** of financial statements. This is not an opinion of absolute correctness. 'True' and 'fair' are not defined in law or audit guidance, but the following definitions are generally accepted.

Key terms

> **True**. Information is factual and conforms with reality, not false. In addition the information conforms with required standards and law. The accounts have been correctly extracted from the books and records.
>
> **Fair**. Information is free from discrimination and bias and in compliance with expected standards and rules. The accounts should reflect the commercial substance of the company's underlying transactions.

The audit report refers to the fact that an auditor obtains evidence 'on a test basis', he does not check everything. He is therefore giving 'reasonable' not 'absolute' assurance.

Key term

> An audit gives the reader **reasonable assurance** on the truth and fairness of the financial statements. The audit report does not guarantee that the financial statements are correct, but that they are true and fair within a reasonable margin of error.

One of the reasons that an auditor does not give absolute assurance is the **inherent limitations** of audit.

3.2 Limitations of audit

6/02

FAST FORWARD

> Audits give **reasonable assurance** that the accounts are free from material misstatement.

The assurance auditors give is governed by the fact that auditors use **judgement** in deciding what audit procedures to use and what conclusions to draw, and also by the limitations of every audit.

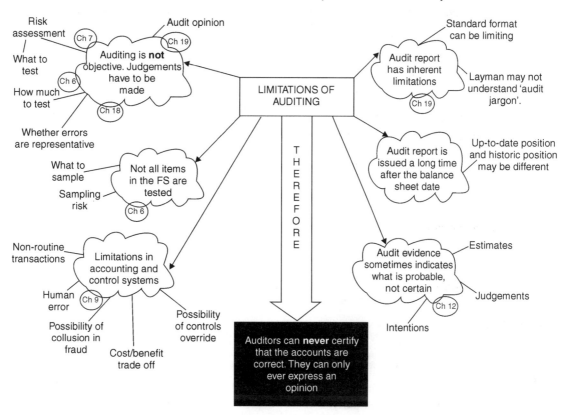

Misstatements which are significant to readers may exist in financial statements and auditors will plan their work on this basis, that is, with **professional scepticism**. The concept of 'significance to readers' is the concept of materiality.

Key term

> **Materiality** is an expression of the relative significance or importance of a particular matter in the context of financial statements as a whole.
>
> A matter is material if its omission or misstatement would reasonably influence the decisions of an addressee of the auditors' report.
>
> Materiality may also be considered in the context of any individual primary statement within the financial statements or of individual items included in them.
>
> Materiality is not capable of general mathematical definition as it has both qualitative and quantitative aspects.

Point to note

> Materiality will be discussed in Chapter 7.

The auditors' task is to decide whether accounts show a **true and fair view**. The auditors are not responsible for establishing whether the accounts are correct in every particular.

- It can take a great deal of time and trouble to check the correctness of even a very small transaction and the resulting benefit may not justify the effort.
- Financial accounting inevitably involves a degree of estimation which means that financial statements can never be completely precise.

Although the definition of materiality refers to the decision of the addressees of the audit report (the company's members), their decisions may well be influenced by other entities who use the accounts, for example, the bank.

Question   **Materiality**

Define the term 'not material' and state in which context it might be used.

Answer

Generally speaking, transactions or other events will be seen as material in the context of an enterprise's financial statements, if their omission or misstatement would reasonably influence the decisions of an addressee of the auditors' report. The report lends some credibility to those statements which will have been prepared by the management of the enterprise.

In order to form an opinion on truth and fairness, the auditors will need to exercise their professional judgement and experience in relation to the question of materiality. It will be important for the auditors to assess materiality not merely in monetary terms but also in the overall context of the company's financial statements, statutory requirements and recognised best accounting and auditing practice.

3.3 Levels of assurance

FAST FORWARD   The degree of assurance given by the impartial professional will depend on the nature of the exercise being carried out.

'Assurance' here means **the auditors' satisfaction as to the reliability of the assertion made by one party for use by another party**.

Directors prepare financial statements for the benefit of members. They **assert** that the financial statements give a true and fair view. The auditors provide **assurance** on that assertion. To provide such assurance, the auditors must:

- Assess risk
- Plan procedures
- Conduct procedures
- Assess results
- Express an opinion

The degree of satisfaction achieved and, therefore, **the level of assurance which may be provided**, is **determined by** the **nature** of **procedures performed** and their results.

An **audit** can be distinguished from other assurance engagements in the following ways.

(a)   **Audit engagement:** the auditor provides a high, but not absolute, level of assurance that the information audited is free of material misstatement. This is expressed positively in the audit report as **reasonable assurance.**

(b)   **Review engagement:** the auditor provides a moderate level of assurance that the information subject to review is free of material misstatement. This is expressed in the form of **negative assurance.**

Key term

> **Negative assurance** is when an auditor gives an assurance that nothing has come to his attention which indicates that the financial statements have not been prepared according to the framework. In other words, he gives his assurance in the absence of any evidence to the contrary.

(c)   **Agreed-upon procedures:** the auditor simply provides a report of the actual findings, so **no assurance** is expressed. Users of the report must instead judge for themselves the auditor's procedures and findings, and draw their own conclusions from the auditor's work.

(d)   **Compilation engagement:** users of the compiled information gain some benefit from the accountant's (as opposed to auditor's) involvement, but **no assurance** is expressed in the report.

Chapter Roundup

- An assurance engagement is essentially an **impartial**, **knowledgeable** scrutiny and review.

- This syllabus is particularly concerned with **audit** (both statutory and non statutory), **review** and the assurance provided to management by **internal audit**.

- **Internal auditors** are employed as part of an organisation's system of controls. Their responsibilities are determined by management and may be wide-ranging.

- The auditors' report on company accounts is expressed in terms of **truth** and **fairness**. This is generally taken to mean that accounts:

    - Are factual
    - Are free from bias
    - Reflect the commercial substance of the business's transactions

- Audits give **reasonable assurance** that the accounts are free from material misstatement.

- The degree of assurance given by the impartial professional will depend on the nature of the exercise being carried out.

Quick Quiz

1   Complete the definition of an audit:

The objective of an .... of .... is to enable the auditor to .... an .... whether the financial statements are prepared, in all .... respects, in accordance with an identified financial reporting framework. The phrases used to express the auditors' opinion are 'give' a .... and .... view' or '............. .... in all material respects', which are equivalent terms.

2   Link the correct definition to each term.

(i)   Accountable   (iv)   True
(ii)   Steward   (v)   Fair
(iii)   Agent   (vi)   Materiality

(a)   An expression of the relative significance or importance of a particular matter in the context of the financial statements as a whole.

(b)   A person employed to provide a particular service.

(c)   Factual and conforming with reality. In conformity with relevant standards and law and correctly extracted from accounting records.

(d)   A person employed to manage other people's property.

(e)   Free from discrimination and bias and in compliance with expected standards and rules. Reflecting the commercial substance of underlying transactions.

(f)   Being required or expected to justify actions and decisions.

3   For which of the following is an audit a statutory obligation? (There is more than one correct answer.)

| Limited companies | Clubs | Charities |

| Building societies | Partnerships | Trade Unions |

| Housing associations | Sole traders |

4   Tests of control cover a large number of transactions while walkthrough tests will be limited to one or two.

True ☐

False ☐

5   A partnership might benefit from having an audit even though it is not required to do so by law. Tick the correct advantages below.

(a)   Means of settling accounts between partners ☐

(b)   Ensures that partners' remuneration will be made public ☐

(c)   May make the accounts more acceptable to the HM Revenue and Customs ☐

(d)   The individual partners will not have to prepare tax returns ☐

(e)   May facilitate the negotiation of a loan ☐

(f)   May benefit a 'sleeping partner' who otherwise has little knowledge of partnership affairs ☐

Answers to Quick Quiz

1   Audit, financial statements, express, opinion, material, true, fair, present fairly.

2   (i)   (f)   (iv)   (c)
     (ii)   (d)   (v)   (e)
     (iii)   (b)   (vi)   (a)

3   Limited companies, building societies, trade unions, housing associations, **some** charities.

4   True

5   (a), (c), (e) and (f). (b) would not necessarily be a result of an audit and would not be an advantage anyway. (d) is simply untrue.

Now try the question below from the Exam Question Bank

Number	Level	Marks	Time
Q1	Introductory	n/a	15 mins

Corporate governance

Topic list	Syllabus reference
1 Introduction to corporate governance	1
2 Codes of best practice	1
3 Audit committees	1
4 Internal control effectiveness	1

Introduction

The concept of corporate governance was introduced in Chapter 1. In Section 2 of this chapter we will look at the codes of practice that have been set in place to ensure that companies are well managed.

The audit carried out by the external auditors is an extremely important part of corporate governance, as it is an independent check on what the directors are reporting to the shareholders.

Auditors of all kinds have most contact with the audit committee, a sub-committee of the board of directors. External auditors liaise with the audit committee over the audit, and internal auditors will report their findings about internal control effectiveness to the audit committee. We shall look at audit committees in Section 3 and internal control effectiveness in Section 4.

Study guide

4 – Regulatory environment

Corporate governance

- Explain the objective, relevance and importance of corporate governance
- Discuss the relative merits and disadvantages of voluntary codes and legislation

Code of best practice

- Outline the provisions of the Code of Best Practice (based on the Cadbury Report) that are most relevant to auditors
- Outline the requirements of the Combined Code (of the committee on corporate governance) relating to directors' responsibilities (eg for risk management and internal control) and the reporting responsibilities of auditors

Audit committees

- Explain the structure and roles of audit committees and discuss their benefits and drawbacks
- Discuss the relative merits and disadvantages of regulation by a voluntary code of practice rather than law

Internal financial control effectiveness

- Outline the importance of internal control and risk management
- Compare the responsibilities of management and auditors (internal and external) for the design and operation of systems and controls, and the reliability of management information (financial and non-financial)
- Describe the factors to be taken into account when assessing the need for an internal audit function

Exam guide

Corporate governance was introduced into the 2.6 syllabus in 2005. Questions on corporate governance questions could be either knowledge based or application based. You should read the examiner's article on the regulatory environment in *Student Accountant*, January 2005.

1 Introduction to corporate governance   6/05

FAST FORWARD

Good corporate governance is important because the owners of a company and the people who manage the company are not always the same people.

1.1 The importance of corporate governance

Key term

'**Corporate governance** is the system by which companies are directed and controlled.'

(Report of the Cadbury Committee)

There are various stakeholders in companies, as we discussed in Chapter 1. The Cadbury Report (a report commissioned by the UK government concerning corporate governance) identified the following:

- **Directors**: responsible for corporate governance
- **Shareholders**: (owners) linked to the directors by the financial statements
- **Other relevant parties**: such as employees, customers and suppliers.

The roles of the parties can be seen in the diagram of two companies shown below.

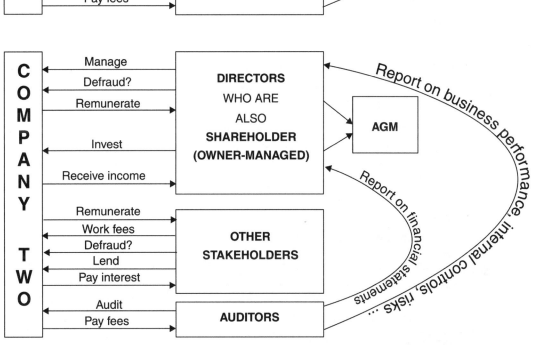

The diagram shows two companies and their relationships with the key people associated with corporate governance.

The key difference between the companies is that in **company two**, the **shareholders** are **fully informed about** the **management** of the business, being directors themselves, in **company one**, the **shareholders** only have an opportunity to find out about the management of the company at the **AGM**.

The **day-to-day running of a company is the responsibility of the directors** and other management staff to whom they delegate, and although the company's results are submitted for shareholders' approval at the annual general meeting (AGM), there is often apathy and acquiescence in director's recommendations.

AGMs are often very poorly attended. For these reasons, there is the **potential** for **conflicts of interest** between management and shareholders.

The importance of good corporate governance was summed up by another report to the UK government, 'good governance ensures that the constituencies (STAKEHOLDERS) with a relevant interest in the company's business are fully taken into account.' (Hampel Committee Report)

In other words, it is necessary for structures to be in place to ensure that every stakeholder in the company is not disadvantaged. As it is the directors that manage the company, the burden of good corporate governance falls on them. It is important that they manage the company in the best way for the shareholders, employees and other parties.

1.2 Voluntary codes?

An important question to consider is 'will the same way of managing companies be the best way for all companies?' The answer is likely to be no. Companies are different from each other, and globally, they operate in different legal systems with different institutions, frameworks and different traditions. It would not be possible to construct one single way of operating companies that could be described as good practice for all.

The key issue in corporate governance is that 'a high degree of priority [is] placed on the interests of shareholders, who place their trust in corporations to use their investment funds wisely and effectively'. Bear in mind that, as companies are different, so might these shareholders be. Shareholders in a company might be a family, they might be the general public or they might be institutional investors representing, in particular, people's future pensions. These shareholders will vary in their degree of interaction with the company and their directors. For example, a pension fund manager who has made investment in a company is far more likely to interact closely with the directors (for example at an AGM) than a member of the public with a general share portfolio.

In the context of this great variety in the basic element of these companies, the Organisation for Economic Co-operation and Development (OECD) has established a number of **principles** of Corporate Governance which are to serve as a **reference point** for countries (to develop corporate governance codes if they so wish) and companies. The UK has developed the Combined Code, which is recommended best practice for companies, particularly listed companies.

1.2.1 Advantages of voluntary codes

If such codes are kept **voluntary**, they maintain their **flexibility** to suit all the different situations companies are in. In addition, where certain elements of codes do not seem relevant to certain companies (particularly smaller or owner-managed companies), they can be left unapplied. This will also save companies unnecessary implementation costs.

1.2.2 Disadvantages of voluntary codes

However, if such codes are voluntary, there is a danger that some companies will not comply with the codes, and shareholders in those companies will be disadvantaged. It also adds to a lack of comparability in the market, if not all companies are meeting the same requirements, and makes it harder for shareholders to make investment decisions.

1.2.3 Solutions

In order to obtain the best of the advantages and avoid the worst disadvantages, countries may take a hybrid approach and make some elements of corporate governance mandatory and some voluntary. For instance, in the UK, companies are required to comply with **legislation** (the Companies Act, for example, which contains things directors are not allowed to do) and there is also a **voluntary corporate governance code**, the Combined Code, which contains some **mandatory elements** for companies which are listed on the Stock Exchange. For example, such companies must have an audit committee.

2 Codes of best practice

FAST FORWARD

The OECD principles of corporate governance set out the rights of shareholders, the importance of disclosure and transparency and the responsibilities of the board(s) of directors. The Combined Code contains detailed guidance for UK companies.

2.1 Principles

OECD Principles of Corporate Governance	
I	The corporate governance framework should protect shareholders' rights.
II	The corporate governance framework should ensure the equitable treatment of all shareholders, including minority and foreign shareholders. All shareholders should have the opportunity to obtain effective redress for violation of their rights.
III	The corporate governance framework should recognise the rights of stakeholders as established by law and encourage active co-operation between corporations and stakeholders in creating wealth, jobs and the sustainability of financially sound enterprises.
IV	The corporate governance framework should ensure that timely and accurate disclosure is made on all material matters regarding the corporation, including the financial situation, performance, ownership and governance of the company.
V	The corporate governance framework should ensure the strategic guidance of the company, the effective monitoring of management by the board, and the board's accountability to the company and the shareholders.

Principles of the Combined Code (for listed UK companies)	
The board	Every company should be headed by an effective board, which is collectively responsible for the success of the company.
	There should be clear division of responsibilities at the head of the company between the running of the board and the executive responsibility for the running of the company's business. No one individual should have unfettered powers of decision.
	The board should include a balance executive and non-executive directors (and in particular independent non-executive directors) such that no individual or small group of individuals can dominate the board's decision taking.
	There should be formal, rigorous and transparent procedure for the appointment of new directors to the board.
	The board should be supplied in a timely manner with information in a form and of a quality appropriate to enable it to discharge its duties. All directors should receive induction on joining the board and should regularly update and refresh their skills and knowledge.
	The board should undertake a formal and rigorous annual evaluation of its own performance and that of its committees and individual directors.
	All directors should be submitted for re-election at regular intervals, subject to continued satisfactory performance. The board should ensure planned and progressive refreshing of the board.

Principles of the Combined Code (for listed UK companies)	
Remuneration	Level of remuneration should be sufficient to attract, retain and motivate directors of the quality required to run the company successfully, but a company should avoid paying more than is necessary for this purpose. A significant proportion of executive directors' remuneration should be structured so as to link rewards to corporate and individual performance.
	There should be formal and transparent procedure for developing policy on executive remuneration and for fixing the remuneration packages of individual directors. No director should be involved in deciding his or her remuneration.
Accountability and audit Depending on the size of the company, this may involve setting up an internal audit	The board should present a balanced and understandable assessment of the company's position and prospects.
	The board should maintain a sound system of internal control to safeguard shareholders' investment and the company's assets.
	The board should establish formal and transparent arrangements for considering how they should apply the financial reporting and internal control principles and for maintaining an appropriate relationship with the company's auditors.
Relations with institutional shareholders	There should be a dialogue with shareholders based on the mutual understanding of objectives. The board as a whole has responsibility for ensuring that satisfactory dialogue with shareholders takes place.
	The board should use the AGM to communicate with investors and to encourage their participation.

2.2 Auditors

FAST FORWARD

The principles state that an annual audit of financial statements by an independent auditor should be carried out.

There are three key issues in relation to auditors suggested by the principles.

2.2.1 Annual audit

The principles strongly recommend that all companies have an annual, independent audit of financial statements. As we shall see in Chapter 3, many countries have made this a legal necessity for companies, which it is in the UK.

2.2.2 High quality standards

The principles state that information should be disclosed and audited according to high quality standards. This is in order to increase **reliability** and **comparability** of reporting, allowing investors to make better investment decisions.

You have already learnt about the importance of accounting standards in other papers. In Chapter 3 of this Study Text we shall look at the standards used to ensure that high quality audits are carried out.

2.2.3 Other information

The principles also imply that shareholders will benefit if other information is subject to checks by auditors. This information includes disclosure relating to:

- Financial and operating results of the company
- Company objectives
- Major share ownership and voting rights

- Members of the board and key executives, and their remuneration
- Material foreseeable risk factors
- Material issues regarding employees and other stakeholders
- Governance structures and policies

So for example, auditors could be asked to check whether companies are applying certain aspects of corporate governance codes. Auditors in the UK are required to report on whether listed companies comply with the following aspects of the Combined Code.

- Directors' responsibility for preparing financial statements explained in report

- System of internal control reviewed and reported on

- Audit committee of at least three non-executive directors set up

- Audit committee terms of reference set out in writing

- Audit committee terms of reference available/described in report

- Audit committee arrange methods for staff to report impropriety in financial reporting

- Audit committee monitor and review effectiveness of internal control

- Audit committee has primary responsibility for appointment of external auditors

- If external audit provide non-audit services, annual report sets out how independence maintained

2.3 Directors

FAST FORWARD

> Directors should set company policy, including risk policy, and are responsible for the company's systems and controls

2.3.1 Policy

Directors are responsible ultimately for managing the company, and this includes setting strategy, budgets, managing the company's people, maintaining company assets, and ensuring corporate governance rules are kept. An important element of setting strategies is determining and managing risks. We shall outline in Chapter 4 how internal audit may have a role in this area. The Combined Code requires that there is clear division of responsibility at the head of a company between chairman and chief executive. It requires that no one individual has unfettered powers of discretion.

The board should be supplied with information in a timely manner to enable it to carry out its duties and directors should receive induction on joining the board and should regularly update and refresh their skills.

2.3.2 Systems, controls and monitoring

Directors are responsible for the systems put in place to achieve the company policies and the controls put in place to mitigate risks. These issues will be considered further in section 4. Under the Combined Code, UK boards are required to consider annually whether an internal audit department is required.

They are also responsible for **monitoring** the effectiveness of systems and controls. **Internal auditors** have an important role in this area as we shall discuss in Chapter 4, but remember that the directors are responsible for determining whether to have an internal audit department to assist them in monitoring in the first place.

In the UK, a report issued by a government committee considering companies and internal control set out the following recommendations:

Turnbull Guidelines
Have a **defined process** for the effectiveness of internal control
Review **regular reports** on internal control
Consider **key risks** and how they have been managed
Check the **adequacy** of **action taken** to remedy weaknesses and incidents
Consider the **adequacy** of **monitoring**
Conduct an **annual assessment** of risks and the effectiveness of internal control
Make a **statement** on this process in the **annual report**

2.3.3 Non-executive directors

An important recommendation of the principles is that boards contain some non-executive directors to ensure that the board exercises **objective judgement**. The Combined Code requires 'a balance' of executive and non-executive directors on the board.

Key term

> **Non-executive directors** are directors who do not have an executive function in the company.

Such non-executive directors may have a particular role in some sensitive areas such as company reporting, nomination of directors and remuneration of executive directors. Often companies will set up sub-committees of the board to deal with such issues. We are now going on to consider one such sub-committee, the audit committee, in more detail.

Exam focus point

> Auditors' and directors' reporting responsibilities were examined in June 2005.

3 Audit committees   6/05

FAST FORWARD

> An audit committee can help a company maintain objectivity with regard to financial reporting and the audit of financial statements

3.1 Role and function of audit committees

An **audit committee** is a sub-committee of the board of directors, usually containing a number of non-executive directors.

The role and function of the audit committee is described by the Cadbury report:

'If they operate effectively, audit committees can bring significant benefits. In particular, they have the potential to:

(a)   improve the quality of financial reporting, by reviewing the financial statements on behalf of the Board;

(b)   create a climate of discipline and control which will reduce the opportunity for fraud;

(c)   enable the non-executive directors to contribute an independent judgement and play a positive role;

(d)   help the finance director, by providing a forum in which he can raise issues of concern, and which he can use to get things done which might otherwise be difficult;

(e)   strengthen the position of the external auditor, by providing a channel of communication and forum for issues of concern;

(f)   provide a framework within which the external auditor can assert his independence in the event of a dispute with management;

(g)   strengthen the position of the internal audit function, by providing a greater degree of independence from management;

(h)   increase public confidence in the credibility and objectivity of financial statements.'

Combined Code provisions

The board would establish an audit committee of at least three, or in the case of smaller companies, two members.

The main role and responsibilities should be set out in **written terms of reference** and should include:

(a)   To monitor the integrity of the financial statements of the company and any formal announcements relating to the company's financial performance, reviewing significant financial reporting issues and judgements contained in them.

(b)   To review the company's internal financial controls and, unless expressly addressed by a separate board risk committee composed of independent directors or by the board itself, the company's control and risk management systems.

(c)   To monitor and review the effectiveness of the company's internal audit function.

(d)   To make recommendations to the board for it to put to the shareholders for their approval in general meeting in relation to the appointment of the external auditor and to approve the remuneration and terms of engagement of the external auditors.

(e)   To monitor and review the external auditor's independence, objectivity and effectiveness, taking into consideration relevant UK professional and regulatory requirements.

(f)   To develop and implement policy on engagement of the external auditor to supply non-audit services, taking into account relevant ethical guidance regarding the provisions of non-audit services by the external audit firm and to report to the board, identifying any matters in respect of which it considers that action or improvement is needed, and making recommendations as to the steps to be taken.

The audit committee should be provided with **sufficient resources** to undertake its duties.

3.2 Advantages and disadvantages of audit committees

The key advantage to an auditor of having an audit committee is that a committee of independent non-executive directors provides the auditor with an independent point of reference other than the executive directors of the company, in the event of disagreement arising.

Other **advantages** that are claimed to arise from the existence of an audit committee include:

(a)   It will lead to **increased confidence** in the credibility and objectivity of financial reports. This is particularly important for listed companies and companies seeking listing.

(b)   By specialising in the problems of financial reporting the internal auditors will be able to assist the directors, allowing the **executive** directors to **devote their attention to management**.

(c)   In cases where the interests of the company, the executive directors and the employees conflict, the audit committee might provide an **impartial body** for the auditors to consult. It will also provide a channel for international and external auditors to communicate through.

(d)   The internal auditors will be able to report to the audit committee, rather than the main board, enhancing their objectivity.

(e)   The audit committee can be a 'critical friend' to the board in ensuring that the company keeps up to date with corporate governance requirements.

Opponents of audit committees argue that:

(a)   The executive directors may not understand the purpose of an audit committee and may perceive that it detracts from their authority.

(b)   There may be **difficulty selecting** sufficient non-executive directors with the necessary competence in auditing matters for the committee to be really effective.

(c)   The establishment of such a **formalised reporting procedure** may **dissuade** the **auditors** from raising matters of judgement and limit them to reporting only on matters of fact.

(d)   **Costs** may be **increased**.

3.3 Voluntary or mandatory?

We have already discussed the general benefits of having a voluntary code above at paragraph 1.2. Specifically with regard to audit committees, it should be observed that it can be difficult to find suitably qualified individuals who are prepared to be non-executive directors in companies. If such individuals are tempted by large salaries, they lose some of their objectivity.

However, this difficulty should not prevent companies from having the correct corporate governance arrangements, and arguably, if audit committees were made mandatory, the corporate culture would have to change, and it might more often become the case that executive directors from the company became non-executives in other companies not in competition with their primary company.

4 Internal control effectiveness

FAST FORWARD   Directors must ensure that a company's system of controls is effective.

4.1 Importance of internal control and risk management

Internal controls are essential to management, as they contribute to

- Safeguarding the company's assets
- Helping to prevent and detect fraud
- Therefore, safeguarding the shareholders' investment

Good internal control helps the business to run efficiently. A control system reduces identified risks to the business. It also helps to ensure reliability of reporting, and compliance with laws.

4.2 Directors' responsibilities

The **ultimate responsibility** for a company's system of internal controls lies with the board of directors. It should set procedures of internal control and regularly monitor that the system operates as it should.

Part of setting up an internal control system will involve **assessing the risks** facing the business, so that the **system** can be **designed** to ensure those **risks are avoided**.

Internal control systems will always have **inherent limitations**, the most important being that a system of internal control cannot eliminate the possibility of human error, or the chance that staff will collude in fraud.

Once the directors have set up a system of internal control, they are responsible for **reviewing** it regularly, to ensure that it **still meets its objectives**.

The board may decide that in order to carry out their review function properly they have to employ an **internal audit function** to undertake this task. When deciding whether an internal audit function is required, directors will need to consider the extent of systems and controls, and the relative expense of obtaining checks from other parties, such as the external auditors. These issues will be considered in more detail in Chapter 4.

If the board does not see the need for an internal audit function, in the UK, the Combined Code requires companies to consider the need for one annually, so that the **need for internal audit is regularly reviewed**.

The Combined Code, also recommends that the board of directors **report** on their review of internal controls as part of their annual report.

The statement should be based on an annual assessment of internal control which should confirm that the board has considered **all significant aspects** of internal control. In particular the assessment should cover:

(a) The **changes** since the last **assessment** in **risks** faced, and the company's **ability** to **respond** to **changes** in its business environment

(b) The **scope** and **quality** of management's monitoring of risk and internal control, and of the work of internal audit, or consideration of the need for an internal audit function if the company does not have one

(c) The **extent** and **frequency** of reports to the board

(d) **Significant controls**, **failings** and **weaknesses** which have or might have material impacts upon the accounts

(e) The effectiveness of the public reporting processes

4.3 Auditors' responsibilities

The auditors' detailed responsibilities with regard to reporting on the requirements of the Combined Code are set out in a Bulletin, which is not examinable. However, in summary, the auditors should review the statements made concerning internal control in the annual report to ensure that they appear true and are not in conflict with the audited financial statements.

Auditors should concentrate on the review carried out by the board. The objectives of the auditors' work is to assess whether the company's summary of the process that the board has adopted in reviewing the effectiveness of the system of internal control is supported by the documentation prepared by the directors and reflects that process.

The auditors should make appropriate enquiries and review the statement made by the board in the accounts and the supporting documentation.

Auditors will have gained some understanding of controls due to their work on the accounts; however what they are required to do by auditing standards is narrower in scope than the review performed by the directors.

Auditors therefore are not expected to assess whether the directors' review covers all risks and controls, and whether the risks are satisfactorily addressed by the internal controls.

It is particularly important for auditors to communicate quickly to the directors any material weaknesses they find, because of the requirements for the directors to make a statement on internal control.

The directors are required to consider the material internal control aspects of any significant problems disclosed in the accounts. Auditors work on this is the same as on other aspects of the statement; the auditors are not required to consider whether the internal control processes will remedy the problem. The auditors may report by exception if problems arise such as:

(a)   The **board's summary** of the process of review of internal control effectiveness does **not reflect** the **auditors' understanding** of that process.

(b)   The **processes** that **deal with** material internal control aspects of **significant problems** do **not reflect** the **auditors' understanding** of those processes.

(c)   The board has **not made** an **appropriate disclosure** if it has **failed** to **conduct** an **annual review**, or the disclosure made is not consistent with the auditors' understanding.

Question   Risk management effectiveness

There is a growing call internationally for public reporting about the control effectiveness of companies not just from a narrow statutory audit perspective but more from the wider perspective of corporate governance.

Required

(a)   Explain the key enquiries that an auditor would make in order to ensure that a company is managing effectively its corporate business risk.

(b)   Explain what you understand by the term audit committee.

Answer

(a)   **Corporate business risk**

The questions the auditor should ask include:

(i)   Does the company address the issues?

The auditors should ensure that the company is aware of the issues raised by the Turnbull guidance and that they have taken steps to follow the guidance. Indicators of such steps might include having one director put in charge of complying with the Turnbull guidance, and information issued to staff about what this will involve.

(ii)   Do the directors identify significant risks?

It is possible that 'risks' are defined narrowly by the directors, in other words that they have tried to set out what issues the company might face, and that other significant risks may slip through the net.

Again, reading the documentation that has been prepared for staff may indicate whether this is the case. It might also emerge in the course of discussions with the director designated to control compliance.

(iii)   Does the board evaluate and manage significant risks?

The board must be able to do this stage effectively, or the entire process is pointless. The auditors should assess the director's action plan in the event of significant risks being identified, and perhaps review minutes of past meetings when the directors have had to respond to a risk.

(iv)   Does the board consider the probability of the risk arising?

(v)   Does the board consider the potential operational and financial impact in the event of the risk arising?

(vi)   Have the board implemented controls which would maintain the business risk between certain specified tolerance limits? (Have the directors set specified tolerance limits?)

(vii)   Does the board regularly review its processes for identifying and dealing with risks arising?

(viii)   Does the board include meaningful reports about the systems to identify and manage risks in the annual report so that shareholders can understand their actions?

(b)   An audit committee reviews financial information and liaises between the auditors and the company. It normally consists of the non-executive directors of the company, though there is no reason why other senior personnel should not be involved.

Chapter Roundup

- Good corporate governance is important because the owners of a company and the people who manage the company are not always the same people.

- The OECD principles of corporate governance set out the rights of shareholders, the importance of disclosure and transparency and the responsibilities of the board(s) of directors. The Combined Code contains detailed guidance for UK companies.

- The principles state that an annual audit of financial statements by an independent auditor should be carried out.

- Directors should set company policy, including risk policy, and are responsible for the company's systems and controls

- An audit committee can help a company maintain objectivity with regard to financial reporting and the audit of financial statements

- Directors must ensure that a company's system of controls is effective.

Quick Quiz

1   Name three different types of **shareholder** that might be found in companies.

    1....................
    2....................
    3....................

2   An advantage of voluntary codes is that they are flexible and therefore suit different kinds of companies in different situations.

    True   ☐

    False   ☐

3   The OECD principles strongly recommend:

    A   An annual audit
    B   Internal audit
    C   Directors should not receive pay
    D   Directors should be non-executive

4   Complete the blanks

    An audit.............is a sub-committee of the............. ...., usually containing a number of.........................directors.

5   When a company cannot easily find non-executive directors it should not have an audit committee.

    True   ☐

    False   ☐

6   Why are internal controls important in a company?

Answers to Quick Quiz

1   1   Family
     2   General public
     3   Institutional investors

2   True

3   A

4   An audit **committee** is a sub-committee of the **board of directors**, usually containing a number of **non-executive** directors.

5   False. It should have an audit committee if required, or if the directors feel it is in the best interests of the shareholders, even if it is difficult to find non-executive directors.

6   Internal controls contribute to:

     •   Safeguarding company assets
     •   Preventing and detecting fraud
     •   As a result, safeguarding the shareholder's investment

Now try the question below from the Exam Question Bank

Number	Level	Marks	Time
Q2	Examination	20	45 mins

Statutory audit and regulation

Topic list	Syllabus reference
1 The statutory audit requirement	1
2 Audit regulation	3
3 Auditor rights and duties	3
4 Auditing standards	3

Introduction

This chapter describes the main bodies and the major factors which govern auditing. You should particularly note how the **audit monitoring regime** works and what inspectors are looking for.

The chapter then goes on to discuss the role of the Auditing Practices Board and the scope of the guidance it issues. You should understand the authority of auditing standards. The detailed requirements of the auditing standards you are required to know (most of them) are discussed throughout the rest of this Study Text.

The regulatory framework for auditors discussed in this chapter and the ethical framework discussed in Chapter 5 are very important. They could be examined together as part of a scenario question on planning or accepting appointment.

Study guide

2 – Statutory audits

Describe the:

- UK Regulatory framework in which statutory audits take place
- Development and status of the Auditing Practices Board Statements of Auditing Standards and their relationship with International Standards on Auditing
- Reasons for, and mechanisms for, the regulation of auditors by Governments and other regulatory agencies including other UK standard setters
- Types of opinion provided in statutory audit assignments

Exam guide

The previous examiner stated that an understanding of the overall regulatory regime is essential to an understanding of external audit and could be examined in the compulsory section of the exam. The removal of auditors was examined in December 2005.

1 The statutory audit requirement

FAST FORWARD ▶▶ Most companies are required to have an audit by law, but some small companies are exempt.

The majority of companies are required by national law to have an audit. A key exception to this requirement is that given to small companies. For example, many EC countries have a small company exemption from audit. The exemption is based on the turnover of the companies. The maximum turnover of a company which qualifies as exempt under EC rules is £5.6m.

1.1 Small company audit exemption

In most countries, the majority of companies are very small, employing few staff (if any) and are often owner-managed, ie the owner of the company manages the business directly. This is very different from a large business where the owners (the shareholders) devolve the day-to-day running of the business to a group of managers or directors.

Key term

> A **small entity** is any enterprise in which:
>
> (a) There is concentration of ownership and management in a small number of individuals (often a single individual), and
>
> (b) One or more of the following are also found:
>
> (i)   Few sources of income and uncomplicated activities
>
> (ii) Unsophisticated record-keeping
>
> (iii) Limited internal controls together with potential for management override of internal controls

In the UK, the following rules apply in respect of audit exemption:

(a) A company is **totally exempt** if it qualifies as a small company under s 246 of the Companies Act 1985, its **turnover is not more than £5.6m** and its **balance sheet total is not more than £2.8m**.

(b)   These **exemptions do not apply to public companies, banks, insurers, insurance brokers, those authorised under the Financial Services Act, trade unions, employers' associations, parent companies or subsidiaries**.

(c)   Members of **groups** can claim exemption from audit.

(d)   A company is not exempt if **members holding 10%** or more of its shares **demand an audit** at least a month before the end of the financial year.

(e)   Where a company takes advantage of an exemption its directors must make a **statement on the balance sheet**. Among other things, this statement must acknowledge the directors' responsibility for ensuring that proper accounting records are kept, and for preparing accounts that give a true and fair view and comply with the Companies Act.

There has long been a **debate over the benefits of audit to small companies.** As seen above, where small companies are owned by the same people that manage them, there is significantly less value in an independent review of the stewardship of the managers than where management and ownership are divorced.

The case for retaining the small company audit rests on the value of the statutory audit to those who have an interest in audited accounts, that is, the users of accounts. From the viewpoint of each type of user, the arguments for and against abolition are as follows.

(a) Shareholders	
Against change	Shareholders not involved in management need the reassurance given by audited accounts. Furthermore, the existence of the audit deters the directors from treating the company's assets as their own to the detriment of minority shareholders.
	Audited financial statements are invaluable in arriving at a fair valuation of the shares in an unquoted company either for taxation or other purposes.
For change	Where all the shareholders are also executive directors or closely related to them, the benefit gained from an audit may not be worth its cost.

(b) Banks and other institutional creditors	
Against change	Banks rely on accounts for the purposes of making loans and reviewing the value of security.
For change	There is doubt whether banks rely on the audited accounts of companies to a greater extent than those of unincorporated associations of a similar size which have not been audited.
	A review of the way in which the bank accounts of the company have been conducted and of forecasts and management accounts are at least as important to the banks as the appraisal of the audited accounts.
	There is no reason why a bank should not make an audit a precondition of granting a loan.

(c) Trade creditors	
Against change	Creditors and potential creditors should have the opportunity to assess the strength of their customers by examining audited financial statements either themselves or through a credit company.
For change	In practice, only limited reliance is placed on the accounts available from the regulatory authority as they are usually filed so late as to be of little significance in granting short term credit.

(d) Tax authorities	
Against change	The authorities rely on accounts for computing corporation tax and checking returns.
For change	There is little evidence to suggest that the tax authorities rely on audited accounts to a significantly greater extent than those, which, whilst being unaudited have been prepared by an independent accountant.

(e) Employees	
Against change	Employees are entitled to be able to assess audited accounts when entering wage negotiations and considering the future viability of their employer.
For change	There is little evidence to suggest that, in the case of small companies, such assessments are made.

(f) Management	
Against change	The audit provides management with a useful independent check on the accuracy of the accounting systems and the auditor is frequently able to recommend improvements in those systems.
For change	If the law were changed, the management of a company could, if they so desired, still elect to have an independent audit. It is likely, however, that a systems review accompanied by a management consultancy report would represent a greater benefit for a similar cost.

1.2 The statutory audit opinion

The Companies Act requires the auditors to state **explicitly** (s 235) whether in their opinion the annual accounts have been properly prepared in accordance with the Act and in particular whether a **true and fair view** is given. The law has recently changed so that they are also required to state if the directors' report agrees with the financial statements.

EXPLICIT OPINIONS
In the balance sheet, of the **state of the company's affairs** at the end of the financial year
In the profit and loss account, of the **company's profit or loss** for the financial year
The **information** given in the **directors' report** is **consistent** with the **accounts**.

In addition certain requirements are reported on **by exception**. The auditor only has to report if they have not been met. The following are matters with which the auditors **imply** satisfaction in an unqualified report under s 237 of the Companies Act 1985.

IMPLIED OPINIONS
Proper accounting records have been kept.
Proper returns adequate for the audit have been received from branches not visited.
The **accounts** are in **agreement** with the **accounting records** and returns.
All information and **explanations** have been **received** as the auditors think necessary and they have had access at all times to the company's books, accounts and vouchers.
Details of **directors' emoluments** and other benefits have been correctly **disclosed** in the financial statements.
Particulars of loans and other **transactions** in favour of **directors** and others have been correctly **disclosed** in the financial statements.

1.3 The standard report

A report containing a number of elements is required by ISA 700 *The auditor's report on financial statements.*

Independent auditors' report to the shareholders of XYZ Limited

We have audited the financial statements of (name of entity) for the year ended ... which comprise (state the primary financial statements such as the profit and loss account, the balance sheet, the cash flow statement, the statement of total recognised gains and losses) and the related notes. These financial statements have been prepared under the historical cost convention (as modified by the revaluation of certain fixed assets) and the accounting policies set out therein.

Respective responsibilities of directors and auditors

The directors' responsibilities for preparing the annual report and the financial statements in accordance with applicable law and United Kingdom Accounting Standards (United Kingdom Generally Accepted Accounting Practice) are set out in the statement of directors' responsibilities.

Our responsibility is to audit the financial statements in accordance with relevant legal and regulatory requirements and International Standards on Auditing (UK and Ireland).

We report to you our opinion as to whether the financial statements give a true and fair view and are properly prepared in accordance with the Companies Act 1985. We report to you whether in our opinion the information given in the directors' report is consistent with the financial statements. [The information given in the directors' report includes that specific information presented in the Operating and Financial Review that is cross referred from the Business Review section of the directors' report.] We also report to you if, in our opinion, the company has not kept proper accounting records, if we have not received all the information and explanations we required for our audit, or if information specified by law regarding directors' remuneration and transactions with the company is not disclosed.

We read other information contained in the annual report and consider whether it is consistent with the audited financial statements. This other information comprises only (the Chairman's Statement, the Operating and Financial Review). We consider the implications for our report if we become aware of any apparent misstatements or material inconsistencies with the financial statements. Our responsibilities do not extend to any other information.

Basis of audit opinion

We conducted our audit in accordance with International Standards on Auditing (UK and Ireland) issued by the Auditing Practices Board. An audit includes examination, on a test basis, of evidence relevant to the amounts and disclosures in the financial statements. It also includes an assessment of the significant estimates and judgements made by the directors in the preparation of the financial statements, and of whether the accounting polices are appropriate to the company's circumstances, consistently applied and adequately disclosed.

We planned and performed our audit so as to obtain all the information and explanations which we considered necessary in order to provide us with sufficient evidence to give reasonable assurance that the financial statements are free from material misstatement, whether caused by fraud or other irregularity or error. In forming our opinion we also evaluated the overall adequacy of the presentation of information in the financial statements.

Opinion

In our opinion the financial statements:

- Give a true and fair view of the state of the company's affairs as at ... and of its profit (loss) for the year then ended and
- Have been properly prepared in accordance with the Companies Act 1985
- The information given in the directors' report is consistent with the financial statements

Registered auditors   *Address*
Date

Points to note

This report will be looked at in detail in Chapter 19. A list of the International Standards on Auditing (UK and Ireland) relevant to this syllabus is given in Section 4.

Exam focus point

You should be able to list the contents of an unqualified audit report.

2 Audit regulation

FAST FORWARD

Requirements for the **eligibility**, **registration** and **training** of auditors are extremely important as they are designed to maintain standards in the auditing profession.

In the UK there are a large number of different accountancy, or accountancy-related, institutes and associations, such as the Association of Chartered Certified Accountants (ACCA) or the Chartered Institute of Management Accountants (CIMA).

All these bodies vary from each other, depending on the nature of their aims and the specialisms their members wish to attain. They are all, however, characterised by various attributes, stringent entrance requirements (examinations and practical experience), strict codes of ethics and technical updating of members. The membership of all these bodies is scattered through practice, industry, government and public bodies.

2.1 Recognised Supervisory Bodies

The EC 8th Directive on company law requires that persons carrying out statutory audits must be approved by the authorities of EU member states. The authority to give this approval in the UK is delegated to Recognised Supervisory Bodies (RSBs). An auditor must be a member of an RSB and be eligible under its own rules. The ACCA is a RSB as are some of the institutes and associations mentioned above.

The RSBs are required to have rules to ensure that persons eligible for appointment as a company auditor are either (4(1), Sch 11, CA 1989):

- Individuals holding an appropriate qualification
- Firms controlled by qualified persons

A number of other requirements concern the procedures which RSBs must follow to **maintain** the **competence** of **members**. Professional qualifications, which will be prerequisites for membership of an RSB, will be offered by Recognised Qualifying Bodies ('RQBs') approved by the Secretary of State.

2.2 Eligibility as auditor

Membership of a Recognised Supervisory Body is the main prerequisite for eligibility as an auditor. An audit firm may be either a body corporate, a partnership or a sole practitioner. The Companies Act 1985 also requires an auditor to hold an **'appropriate qualification'**. A person holds an 'appropriate qualification' if he or she has gained one of the following.

- Acknowledgement that he or she has met **existing criteria** for appointment as an auditor under CA 1985

- A **recognised qualification** obtained in the UK

- An **approved overseas qualification**

2.3 Ineligibility as auditor

The Companies Act sets out the following reasons that a person would be **ineligible** for appointment as company auditor.

Being an **officer** or **employee** of the company
Being a **partner** or **employee** of such a person
Being a **partnership** in which such a person is a partner
Ineligible by any of the above three reasons for appointment as auditor of any parent or subsidiary undertaking or a subsidiary undertaking of any parent undertaking of the company
There exists between him or her or any associate (of his or hers) and the company (or any company) a **connection** of any description as may be specified in regulations laid down by the Secretary of State

The legislation does **not** disqualify the following from being an auditor of a limited company:

- A shareholder of the company
- A debtor or creditor of the company
- A close relative of an officer or employee of the company

However, the regulations of the accountancy bodies applying to their own members are stricter than statute in this respect.

Under the Companies Act 1985, a person may also be ineligible on the grounds of **'lack of independence'**. The definition of lack of independence is to be determined by statutory instrument following consultation with the professional bodies.

Under s 389 CA 1985, if during their term of office a company auditor becomes ineligible for appointment to the office, he must vacate office and give notice in writing to the company.

Question	Audit regulation

Outline the role of the Recognised Supervisory Bodies (RSBs).

Answer

See Paragraph 2.1

2.4 Legal requirements on appointment to a company audit

The auditors should be appointed by and therefore be **answerable** to the **shareholders**. The table below shows what the position should ideally be.

RIGHTS OF APPOINTMENT	
Members	Appoint auditors at each **general meeting** where accounts are laid by **positive resolution** (re-appointment of existing auditor not automatic)
	Auditors hold office until conclusion of next general meeting at which accounts are laid
Directors	Can appoint auditor:
	(a) Before company's **first general meeting** at which accounts are laid; auditors hold office until conclusion of that meeting
	(b) To fill **casual vacancy**
Secretary of State	Can appoint auditors if **no auditors** are **appointed** or reappointed at general meeting at which accounts are laid

2.4.1 Special notice of appointment

In certain cases relating to appointment of an auditor reasonable notice is required for the appropriate resolutions at a general meeting.

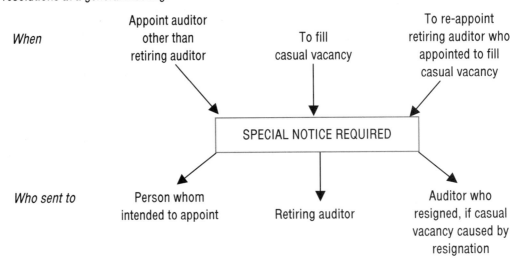

2.4.2 Remuneration

The remuneration of the auditors, which will include any sums paid by the company in respect of the auditors' expenses, will be fixed either by **whoever made** the **appointment** or in **such manner** as the **company in general meeting** may determine.

However the auditors' remuneration is fixed, in many countries it must be disclosed in the annual accounts of the company.

2.5 Legal requirements at the end of an audit relationship   12/05

You will have learnt the legal requirements for resignation and removal of auditors in your studies for paper 2.2 *Corporate and Business Law.*

However, it is relevant to revise them briefly here. It is important that auditors know the procedures because as part of their client acceptance, they have a duty to ensure the old auditors were properly removed from office.

BPP
PROFESSIONAL EDUCATION

RESIGNATION OF AUDITORS		
1	Resignation procedures	Auditors deposit **written notice** together with **statement of circumstances** relevant to members/creditors or statement that no circumstances exist
2	Notice of resignation	Sent by **company** to regulatory authority
3	Statement of circumstances	Sent by: (a) Auditors to regulatory authority (b) Company to everyone entitled to receive a copy of accounts
4	Convening of general meeting	**Auditors** can **require directors** to call extraordinary general meeting to discuss circumstances of resignation Directors must send out notice for meeting within **21 days** of having received requisition by auditors
5	Statement prior to general meeting	**Auditors** may require company to circulate (different) **statement of circumstances** to everyone entitled to notice of meeting
6	Other rights of auditors	Can **receive all notices** that relate to: (a) A general meeting at which their term of office would have expired (b) A general meeting where casual vacancy caused by their resignation to be filled Can **speak** at these meetings on **any matter** which **concerns them as auditors**

REMOVAL OF AUDITORS		
1	Notice of removal	**Either special notice** (28 days) with copy sent to auditor **Or** if elective resolution in place, **written resolution** to terminate auditors' appointment Directors must convene meeting to take place within reasonable time
2	Representations	**Auditors** can make **representations** on why they ought to stay in office, and may require company to state in notice representations have been made and send copy to members
3	If resolution passed	(a) Company must **notify** regulatory authority (b) Auditors must **deposit statement of circumstances** at company's registered office **within 14 days** of ceasing to hold office. Statement must be sent to regulatory authority
4	Auditor rights	Can **receive notice** of and **speak** at: (a) General meeting at which their term of office would have expired (b) General meeting where casual vacancy caused by their removal to be filled

2.6 Independent regulation

The professional bodies (RSBs) which carry out audit work in the UK have long been self-regulating. Currently, the role of regulator is devolved to the Financial Reporting Council (FRC), which is partly funded by the profession. The FRC is a unified, independent regulator. It has three key roles:

- To set accounting and auditing standards

- To proactively enforce and monitor them

- To oversee the self-regulatory professional bodies

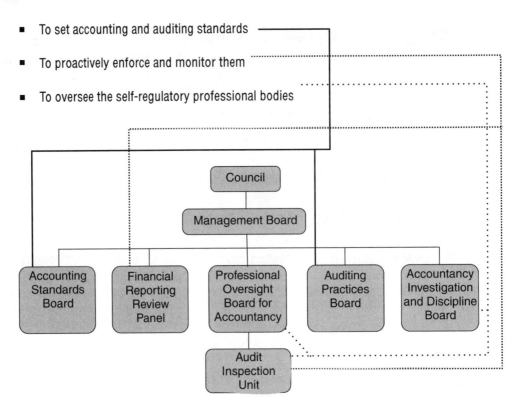

The above diagram shows the various arms of the FRC, and how it carries out its main aims. We shall look in detail at the Auditing Practices Board in section 4.

The FRC contains the **Professional Oversight Board**. This has a wide remit in overseeing the conduct of accountants generally. It will also set up a new inspection unit to monitor the audits of listed companies, major charities and pension funds. The Professional Oversight Board will also oversee the ethical agenda of accountants. A new **Investigation and Discipline Board** will be created as part of the FRC to provide an independent forum for hearing significant public interest disciplinary cases.

The regulator has not currently been given **statutory backing**. The Government believes that there is a strong case that statutory regulation will be necessary to ensure that the regulator operates effectively, but is currently considering the matter further.

The FRC is **funded** jointly by the **accountancy profession** (through the Consultative Committee of Accountancy Bodies – CCAB), the **City** (the London Stock Exchange together with the banking and investment community) and the **Government**.

2.6.1 Other supervision and monitoring

RSBs must also implement procedures for inspecting their registered auditors on a regular basis. ACCA has a **monitoring unit**.

The frequency of inspection depends on the number of partners, number of offices and number of listed company audits (these factors are also reflected in the size of annual registration fees payable).

The following features should be apparent in each practice visited by the monitoring unit.

- A **properly structured audit approach**, suitable for the range of clients served and work undertaken by the practice

- Carefully instituted **quality control procedures**, revised and updated constantly, to which the practice as a whole is committed. This will include:

    - Staff recruitment
    - Staff training
    - Continuing professional development

-     –   Frequent quality control review
- **Commitment to ethical guidelines**, with an emphasis on independence issues
- An emphasis on **technical excellence**
- Adherence to the **'fit and proper'** criteria by checking personnel records and references
- Use of internal and, if necessary, external **peer reviews** or consultations
- **Appropriate fee** charging per audit assignment

3 Auditor rights and duties

> The law gives auditors both rights and duties.

The audit is primarily a statutory concept, and eligibility to conduct an audit is often set down in statute. Similarly, the rights and duties of auditors can be set down in law, to ensure that the auditors have sufficient power to carry out an effective audit.

3.1 Duties

The auditors should be required to report on every balance sheet and income statement laid before the company in general meeting.

The auditors are required to consider the following.

Compliance with legislation	Whether the accounts have been prepared in accordance with the relevant legislation
Truth and fairness of accounts	Whether the balance sheet shows a true and fair view of the company's affairs at the end of the period and the income statement (and a cash flow statement) show a true and fair view of the results for the period
Proper records and returns	Whether proper accounting records have been kept and proper returns adequate for the audit received from branches not visited by the auditor
Agreement of accounts to records	Whether the accounts are in agreement with the accounting records
Consistency of other information	Whether the other information published with the accounts is consistent with the accounts

3.2 Rights

The auditors must have certain rights to enable them to carry out their duties effectively.

The principal rights auditors should have, excepting those dealing with resignation or removal, are set out in the table below.

Access to records	A right of access at all times to the books, accounts and vouchers of the company
Information and explanations	A right to require from the company's officers such information and explanations as they think necessary for the performance of their duties as auditors
Attendance at/notices of general meetings	A right to attend any general meetings of the company and to receive all notices of and communications relating to such meetings which any member of the company is entitled to receive
Right to speak at general meetings	A right to be heard at general meetings which they attend on any part of the business that concerns them as auditors
Rights in relation to written resolutions	A right to receive a copy of any written resolution proposed
Right to require laying of accounts	A right to give notice in writing requiring that a general meeting be held for the purpose of laying the accounts and reports before the company (if elective resolution dispensing with laying of accounts in force)

3.2.1 Rights to information

If auditors have not received all the information and explanations they consider necessary, they should state this fact in their audit report.

Laws may make it an offence for a company's officer knowingly or recklessly to make a statement in any form to an auditor which:

- Purports to convey any information or explanation required by the auditor
- Is materially misleading, false or deceptive

4 Auditing standards   12/01

FAST FORWARD You must be able to discuss the scope and authority of **International Standards on Auditing (ISAs)** (UK and Ireland).

4.1 Rules governing audits

We discussed in Chapter 1 the various stakeholders in a company, and the number of people who might read a company's accounts. Consider also that a number of these readers will not just be reading a single company's accounts, but will also be reading the accounts of a large number of companies, and making comparisons between them.

Readers **want assurance** when making comparisons **that the reliability of the accounts does not vary from company to company**. This assurance will be obtained not just from knowing each set of accounts has been audited, but knowing that each set of accounts has been audited to **common standards**.

Hence there is a need for audits to be **regulated** so that auditors follow the same standards. As we see in this chapter, auditors have to follow rules issued by a variety of bodies. As we saw above, some obligations are imposed by governments in law, or statute. Some obligations are imposed by the professional bodies to which auditors are required to belong (such as the **ACCA**).

4.2 The APB and auditing guidance

Auditing Standards are set by the Auditing Practices Board (APB) which is a part of the Financial Reporting Council. The APB:

- Can issue auditing standards in its own right without having to gain the approval of all the professional accounting bodies

- Has strong representation from outside the accounting profession

- Has a commitment to openness, with agenda papers being circulated to interested parties and an annual report being published

The APB makes three categories of pronouncement:

- Auditing Standards (Quality control, engagement and ethical)
- Practice notes
- Bulletins

We are primarily concerned with the auditing standards. The scope of these is as follows: 'APB quality control and engagement standards contain basic principles and essential procedures (identified in bold type lettering) together with related guidance in the form of explanatory and other material, including appendices. The basic principles and essential procedures are to be understood and applied in the context of the explanatory and other material that provide guidance for their application. It is therefore necessary to consider the whole text of a Standard to understand and apply the basic principles and essential procedures.'

The APB has adopted International Standards on Auditing. In many cases, the Standards have been augmented by UK requirements (shown in grey shade in the Standards) so in UK, ISAs are styled International Standards on Auditing (UK and Ireland). Complying with these is a requirement when carrying out statutory audits.

International Standards on Auditing are produced by the International Audit and Assurance Standards Board (IAASB), a technical standing committee of the International Federation of Accountants (IFAC). An explanation of the workings of the IAASB, the authority of the ISAs and so on are laid out in the *Preface to International Standards on Quality Control, Auditing, Assurance and Related Services*.

The *Preface* restates the mission of IFAC as set out in its constitution: 'The development and enhancement of an accountancy profession with harmonised standards able to provide services of consistently high quality in the public interest'.

In working toward this mission, the Council of IFAC established the International Auditing Practices Committee, precursor to IAASB, to develop and issue, on behalf of the Council, standards and statements on auditing and related services. Such standards and statements improve the degree of uniformity of auditing practices and related services throughout the world.

Within each country, local regulations govern, to a greater or lesser degree, the practices followed in the auditing of financial or other information. Such regulations may be either of a statutory nature, or in the form of statements issued by the regulatory or professional bodies in the countries concerned.

National standards on auditing and related services published in many countries differ in form and content. The IAASB takes account of such documents and differences and, in the light of such knowledge, issues ISAs which are intended for international acceptance.

4.2.1 The authority attached to ISAs

The Preface also lays out the authority attached to ISAs in general.

Authority of International Standards on Auditing

International Standards on Auditing (ISAs) are to be applied in the audit of historical financial information.

The IAASB's Standards contain basic principles and essential procedures (identified in bold type black lettering) together with related guidance in the form of explanatory and other material, including appendices. The basic principles and essential procedures are to be understood and applied in the context of the explanatory and other material that provide guidance for their application. It is therefore necessary to consider the whole text of a standard to understand and apply the basic principles and essential procedures.

In exceptional circumstances, an auditor may judge it necessary to depart from an ISA in order to more effectively achieve the objective of an audit. When such a situation arises, the auditor should be prepared to justify the departure.

Any **limitation** of the applicability of a specific ISA is made clear in the standard, for example, it might contain a passage such as the following:

Application to public sector

The Public Sector Perspective (PSP) issued by the Public Sector Committee of the International Federation of Accountants is set out at the end of an ISA. Where no PSP is added, the ISA is applicable in all material respects to the public sector.

ISAs do **not** override the local regulations referred to above governing the audit of financial or other information in a particular country.

(a) To the extent that ISAs **conform** with local regulations on a particular subject, the audit of financial or other information in that country in accordance with local regulations will automatically comply with the ISA regarding that subject.

(b) In the event that the local regulations **differ from**, or conflict with, ISAs on a particular subject, member bodies should comply with the obligations of members set forth in the IFAC Constitution as regards these ISAs (ie **encourage changes** in local regulations to comply with ISAs).

4.2.2 Working procedures of the IAASB

The working procedure of the IAASB is to select subjects for detailed study by a **subcommittee** established for that purpose. The IAASB delegates to the subcommittee the initial responsibility for the preparation and drafting of accounting standards and statements.

As a result of that study, an **exposure draft** is prepared for consideration by the IAASB. If approved, the exposure draft is widely distributed for comment by member bodies of IFAC, and to such international organisations that have an interest in auditing standards as appropriate.

The comments and suggestions received as a result of this exposure are then considered by the IAASB and the exposure draft is **revised** as appropriate. Provided that the revised draft is approved it is issued as a definitive **International Standard on Auditing** or as an **International Auditing Practice Statement** and becomes operative.

Point to note

> The examiner has written an article on ISAs and how they are made, 'ISAs and SASs' *Student Accountant* March 2006. You should read this article.

4.3 Current ISAs (UK and Ireland)

No	Title
200	Objective and general principles governing an audit of financial statements
210	Terms of audit engagements
220	Quality control for audits of historical financial information
230	Audit documentation
240	The auditor's responsibility to consider fraud in an audit of financial statements
250	Consideration of laws and regulations in an audit of financial statements
260	Communication of audit matters with those charged with governance
300	Planning an audit of financial statements
315	Obtaining an understanding of the entity and its environment and assessing the risks of material misstatement
320	Audit materiality
330	The auditor's procedures in response to assessed risks
402	Audit considerations relating to entities using service organisations
500	Audit evidence
501	Audit evidence – additional considerations for specific items
505	External confirmations
510	Initial engagements – opening balances and continuing engagements – opening balances
520	Analytical procedures
530	Audit sampling and other means of testing
540	Audit of accounting estimates
545	Auditing fair value measurements and disclosures
550	Related parties
560	Subsequent events
570	Going concern
580	Management representations
600	Using the work of another auditor
610	Considering the work of internal audit
620	Using the work of an expert
700	The auditor's report on financial statements
710	Comparatives
720	Other information in documents containing audited financial statements and the auditors' statutory reporting responsibility in relation to directors' reports

Notes

1   Students should be aware of the nature and meaning of the audit report and should be able to discuss the contents and wording of the report. Students would not be asked to reproduce the audit report in full in an exam question, but they may be requested to prepare explanatory paragraphs for inclusion in the report particularly in situations leading to a modified report.

2   Students are advised that questions will be based on the principles and good practice set out in the International Standards on Auditing.

Exam focus point

> International standards are quoted throughout this text and you must understand how they are applied in practice. Not all the standards listed above are examinable, you should review the list of examinable documents in the front pages and check the list of examinable documents for your exam in *Student Accountant* prior to your sitting.

Point to note

> Throughout the rest of this book, for convenience, ISAs (UK and Ireland) are referred to simply as ISAs. Note that if you need to refer to an ISA in the exam, you should give it its full title, eg ISA (UK and Ireland) 200 *Objective and general principles governing an audit of financial statements*. However, it is unlikely that you will need to refer to an ISA by name in the exam.

4.4 Application of ISAs to smaller entities

You should refer back to the definition of small entities given on page 32. Although ISAs apply to the audit of financial information of any entity regardless of its size, small businesses possess a combination of characteristics which make it necessary for the auditors to adapt their audit approach to the circumstances surrounding the small business engagement.

An International Auditing Practice Statement on the audit of small businesses, IAPS 1005 *The Special Considerations in the Audit of Small Entities* was issued in March 1999. The IAPS discusses how various ISAs apply to the audit of small enterprises. The UK has not adopted this IAPS at this time.

Chapter Roundup

- Most companies are required to have an audit by law, but some small companies are exempt.

- Requirements for the **eligibility**, **registration** and **training** of auditors are extremely important as they are designed to maintain standards in the auditing profession.

- The law gives auditors both rights and duties.

- You must be able to discuss the scope and authority of **International Standards on Auditing (ISAs)** (UK and Ireland).

Quick Quiz

1   People can be ineligible to be company auditors under

- The Companies Act 1985
- The requirements of their RSB

Using the reasons given, fill in the table below.

Reasons

(a)   Officer or employee of the company

(b)   Creditor of the company

(c)   Not a member of an RSB

(d)   A partner of someone in (a)

(e)   A close relative of an officer of the company

(f)   Does not hold a recognised qualification

Ineligible under law	Ineligible under RSB rules

2   (a)   A person does not have to satisfy membership criteria to become a member of a Recognised Supervisory Body

True   ☐

False   ☐

(b)   Auditing is regulated by the government in the UK.

True   ☐

False   ☐

(c)   The Auditing Practices Board issues auditing standards which auditors are required to follow.

True   ☐

False   ☐

3   Which of the following features should the Joint Monitoring Unit not expect to find when visiting audit firms?

(a)   Properly structured audit approach

(b)   Quality control procedures

(c)   Peer reviews

(d)   Charging of unsubstantiated fees

Answers to Quick Quiz

1

Ineligible under law	Ineligible under RSB rules
(a) Officer/employee	(a) Officer/employee
(c) Not a member of an RSB	(b) Creditor
(d) A partner of someone in (a)	(d) A partner of someone in (a)
(f) No appropriate qualification	(e) Close relative of officer

2   (a)   False. All RSBs have stringent membership requirements.
      (b)   False. It is regulated by RSBs and the FRC.
      (c)   True. Auditors face discipline by their RSB if they do not.

3   (d)

Now try the question below from the Exam Question Bank

Number	Level	Marks	Time
Q3	Introductory	n/a	30 mins

Internal audit and regulation

4

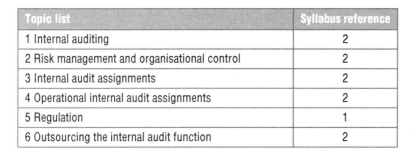

Topic list	Syllabus reference
1 Internal auditing	2
2 Risk management and organisational control	2
3 Internal audit assignments	2
4 Operational internal audit assignments	2
5 Regulation	1
6 Outsourcing the internal audit function	2

Introduction

Internal auditing is **different from external auditing**, although the techniques used are very similar to those which will be outlined in Parts B, C and D of this Study Text.

Internal audit is **established by management** to **assist in corporate governance** by assessing internal controls and helping in risk management. It can be a department of employees, or, as discussed in Section 2, can be **outsourced** to expert service providers.

The ethical requirements differ from those of external auditors due to the nature of the function. This is discussed in Chapter 5.

Various **assurance assignments** which may be undertaken by internal auditors are outlined in Sections 3 and 4, and their role with regard to **fraud** is discussed briefly in Section 5. While the techniques used may be similar to external auditors, the **focus and reasons** behind the audit may **differ**.

There are usually no statutory requirements in relation to internal audit. Reporting will be discussed in detail in Part E of this Study Text.

Study guide

3 – Internal audit and review I

Explain the:

- Development and role of internal audit in achieving corporate objectives and as part of good corporate governance practice

- Relative merits of out-sourcing internal audit and internal review services to external auditors and others, and the associated problems

- Difference between the role of external audit and internal audit

5 – Internal audit and review III

Describe the:

- Elements of best practice in the structure and operations of an internal audit function

- Scope of internal audit work and the limitations of the internal audit function

- Types of report provided in internal audit and internal review assignments

6 – Internal audit and internal review IV

Describe and illustrate the:

- Nature and purpose of internal review assignments including:

  - Value for money
  - Best value
  - IT
  - Financial

- Nature and purpose of operational internal review assignments including:

  - Procurement
  - Marketing
  - Treasury
  - HR

Exam guide

Internal review is an important part of the syllabus, which is likely to feature in every exam. In June 2005 it was examined in the context of corporate governance. In December 2005, outsourcing IA was examined.

1 Internal auditing   Pilot paper, 12/01, 6/02, 12/02, 6/05

FAST FORWARD Internal audit assists management in achieving corporate objectives, particularly in achieving good corporate governance.

1.1 Definition

The following definition was given in Chapter 1, for comparison with other forms of assurance service and providers.

Key term

> **Internal auditing** is an appraisal or monitoring activity established within an entity as a service to the entity. It functions by, amongst other things, examining, evaluating and reporting to management and the directors on the adequacy and effectiveness of components of the accounting and internal control systems.

Internal audit is generally a feature of large companies. It is a function, provided either by employees of the entity or sourced from an external organisation to assist management in **achieving corporate objectives.**

If internal audit exists to assist management in achieving corporate objectives, it is important to ask '**what are corporate objectives**?' Obviously, these will vary from company to company, and will be found, for example, in companies' mission statements and strategic plans.

However, other corporate objectives will not vary so much between companies, and are linked to a key corporate issue we have already discussed at length, the issue being **good corporate governance**.

The codes of corporate governance that we have already looked at highlight the need for businesses to maintain **good systems of internal control** to manage the risks the company faces. **Internal audit** can play a **key role in assessing and monitoring** internal control policies and procedures.

The internal audit function can assist the board in other ways as well:

- By, in effect, acting as auditors for board reports not audited by the external auditors.

- By being the experts in fields such as auditing and accounting standards in the company and assisting in implementation of new standards.

- By liasing with external auditors, particularly where external auditors can use IA work and reduce the time and therefore cost of the external audit. In addition, IA can check that external auditors are reporting back to the board everything they are required to under auditing standards.

The Combined Code highlights the importance of internal audit by stipulating that directors of companies that do not have an internal audit department should re-consider the need for one annually.

1.2 Distinction between internal and external audit

FAST FORWARD

> Although many of the techniques internal and external auditors use are similar, the basis and reasoning of their work is different.

The best way to see the difference between internal and external audit is to revise a key term.

Key term

> An **external audit** is an exercise whose objective is to enable auditors to express an opinion whether the financial statements give a true and fair view (or equivalent) of the entity's affairs at the period end and of its profit and loss for the period then ended and have been properly prepared in accordance with the applicable reporting framework.

Contrast the definition of external audit with the definition of internal audit given at the beginning of this chapter. The external audit is focused on a very small item, the financial statements, whereas the internal audit is focused on the operations of the entire business.

The following table highlights the differences between internal and external audit.

	Internal audit	External audit
Reason	Internal audit is an activity designed to add value and improve an organisation's operations.	An exercise to enable auditors to express an opinion on the financial statements.
Reporting to	Internal audit report to the Board of directors, or other people charged with governance, such as the audit committee	The external auditors report to the shareholders, or members, of a company on the truth and fairness of the accounts
Relating to	As demonstrated in the reason for their existence, internal audit's work relates to the operations of the organisation	External audit's work relates to the financial statements. They are concerned with the financial records that underlie these.
Relationship with the company	Internal auditors are very often employees of the organisation, although sometimes the internal audit function is outsourced.	External auditors are independent of the company and its management. They are appointed by the shareholders.

The table shows that although some of the procedures that internal audit undertake are very similar to those undertaken by the external auditors, the **whole basis and reasoning of their work is fundamentally different**.

2 Risk management and organisational control

FAST FORWARD

Internal audit has two key roles to play in relation to organisational risk management:

- Ensuring the company's risk management system operates effectively
- Ensuring that strategies implemented in respect of business risks operate effectively

2.1 Risk

The Turnbull guidelines refers to risk. All companies face risks arising from their activities. This risk is known as business risk.

Key term

Business risk is the risk inherent to the company in its operations. It is risks at all levels of the business.

Business risk cannot be eliminated, but it must be **managed** by the company.

Designing and operating internal control systems is a key part of a company's risk management. This will often be done by employees in their various departments, although sometimes (particularly in the case of specialised computer systems) the company will hire external expertise to design systems.

2.2 The role of internal audit

The internal audit department has a two-fold role in relation to risk management.

- Monitoring the company's overall risk management policy to ensure it operates effectively.
- Monitoring the strategies implemented to ensure that they continue to operate effectively.

Going back to the diagram in used earlier, this can be shown as:

As a significant risk management policy in companies is to implement internal controls to reduce them, internal audit have a key role in assessing systems and testing controls.

Point to note

> Internal audit's work on operational systems and controls will be looked at in more detail later in this chapter and also in Chapter 11.

Internal audit may assist in the development of systems. However, their key role will be in **monitoring the overall process** and in **providing assurance** that the **systems** which the departments have designed **meet objectives** and **operate effectively**.

It is important that the internal audit department retain their **objectivity** towards these aspects of their role, which is another reason why internal audit would generally not be involved in the assessment of risks and the design of the system.

3 Internal audit assignments

FAST FORWARD

> Internal audit can be involved in many different assignments as directed by management.

In the next two sections we will consider a number of the detailed assignments which an internal auditor could get involved in.

Exam focus point

> You should read through these two sections now to learn **what an internal auditor does** and to **reinforce the difference between an internal audit and the statutory (external) audit** introduced in Chapter 3. However, don't worry too much about the mechanics of **how** they test the following things – you are going to be introduced to the techniques of auditing in the next few part of the Text.

3.1 Value for money

3.1.1 Example

A good example of value for money is a bottle of Fairy Liquid. If we believe the advertising, Fairy is good 'value for money' because it washes half as many plates again as any other washing up liquid. Bottle for bottle it may be more expensive, but plate for plate it is cheaper. Not only this but Fairy gets plates 'squeaky' clean. To summarise, Fairy gives us VFM because it exhibits the following characteristics.

- Economy (more clean plates per dollar)
- Efficiency (more clean plates per squirt)
- Effectiveness (plates as clean as they should be)

These are the three Es of VFM.

3.1.2 The three Es

A 1990 CCAB Audit brief on VFM audit defined the three Es as follows.

(a) **Economy**: attaining the appropriate quantity and quality of physical, human and financial resources (**inputs**) at lowest cost. An activity would not be economic, if, for example, there was over-staffing or failure to purchase materials of requisite quality at the lowest available price.

(b) **Efficiency**: this is the relationship between goods or services produced (**outputs**) and the resources used to produce them. An efficient operation produces the maximum output for any given set of resource inputs; or it has minimum inputs for any given quantity and quality of product or service provided.

(c) **Effectiveness**: this is concerned with how well an activity is achieving its policy objectives or other intended effects.

The internal auditors will **evaluate these three factors** for any given business system or operation in the company. Value for money can often only be judged by **comparison.** In searching for value for money, present methods of operation and uses of resources must be **compared with alternatives.**

Economy, efficiency and effectiveness can be studied and measured with reference to the following.

Inputs	Economy
Inputs means money or resources – the labour, materials, time and so on consumed, and their cost. For example, a VFM audit into state secondary education would look at the efficiency and economy of the use of resources for education (the use of schoolteachers, school buildings, equipment, cash) and whether the resources are being used for their purpose: what is the pupil/teacher ratio and are trained teachers being fully used to teach the subjects they have been trained for?	Economy is concerned with the cost of inputs, and it is achieved by obtaining those inputs at the lowest acceptable cost. Economy does not mean straightforward cost-cutting, because resources must be acquired which are of a suitable quality to provide the service to the desired standard. Cost-cutting should not sacrifice quality to the extent that service standards fall to an unacceptable level. Economising by buying poor quality materials, labour or equipment is a 'false economy'.

Outputs	Efficiency
Outputs mean the results of an activity, measurable as the services actually produced, and the quality of the services. In the case of a VFM audit of secondary education, outputs would be measured as the number of pupils taught and the number of subjects taught per pupil; how many examination papers are taken and what is the pass rate.	Efficiency means the following. (a) Maximising output for a given input, for example maximising the number of transactions handled per employee or per £1 spent (b) Achieving the minimum input for a given output

Impacts	Effectiveness
Impacts are the effect that the outputs of an activity or programme have in terms of achieving policy objectives. Policy objectives might be to provide a minimum level of education to all children up to the age of 16, and to make education relevant for the children's future jobs and careers. This might be measured by the ratio of jobs vacant to unemployed school leavers.	Effectiveness means ensuring that the outputs of a service or programme have the desired impacts; in other words, finding out whether they succeed in achieving objectives, and if so, to what extent. In a profit-making organisation, objectives can be expressed financially in terms of target profit or return. In NFP (not-for-profit) organisations, effectiveness cannot be measured this way, because the organisation has non-financial objectives. The effectiveness of performance in NFP organisations could be measured in terms of whether targeted non-financial objectives have been achieved.

3.1.3 Selecting areas for investigation

Value for money checklists can be used. The following list identifies areas of an organisation, process or activity where there might be scope for significant value for money improvements. Each of these should be reviewed within individual organisations, with a view to assessing its economy, efficiency and effectiveness.

- Service delivery (the actual provision of a public service)
- Management process
- Environment

An alternative approach is to look at areas of spending. A value for money assessment of economy, efficiency, and effectiveness would look at whether:

- Too much money is being spent on certain items or activities, to achieve the targets or objectives of the overall operation.

- Money is being spent to no purpose, because the spending is not helping to achieve objectives.

- Changes could be made to improve performance.

An illustrative list is shown below of the sort of spending areas that might be looked at, and the aspects of spending where value for money might be improved.

- Employee expenses
- Premises expenses
- Suppliers and services
- Establishment expenses
- Capital expenditure

Problems with VFM auditing	
Measuring outputs	For example, the outputs of a fire brigade can be measured by the number of call-outs, but it is not satisfactory to compare a call-out to individuals stuck in a lift with a call-out to a small house fire or a major industrial fire or a road accident etc.
Defining objectives	In not for profit organisations the quality of the service provided will be a significant feature of their service. For example, a local authority has, amongst its various different objectives, the objective of providing a rubbish collection service. The effectiveness of this service can only be judged by establishing what standard or quality of service is required.
Sacrifice of quality	Economy and efficiency can be achieved by sacrificing quality. Neither outputs nor impacts are necessarily measured in terms of quality. For example, the cost of teaching can be reduced by increasing the pupil:teacher ratio in schools, but it is difficult to judge the consequences of such a change on teaching standards and quality.
Measuring effectiveness	For example, the effectiveness of the health service could be said to have improved if hospitals have greater success in treating various illnesses and other conditions, or if the life expectancy of the population has increased, but a consequence of these changes will be overcrowded hospitals and longer medical waiting lists.
Overemphasis in cost control	There can be an **emphasis** with VFM audits on **costs and cost control** rather than on achieving more benefits and value, so that management might be pressurised into 'short term' decisions, such as abandoning capital expenditure plans which would create future benefits in order to keep current spending levels within limits.

Problems with VFM auditing	
Measuring efficiency	In profit-making organisations, the efficiency of the organisation as a whole can be measured in terms of return on capital employed. Individual profit centres or operating units within the organisation can also have efficiency measured by relating the quantity of output produced, which has a **market value** and therefore a quantifiable financial value, to the inputs (and their cost) required to make the output.
	In NFP organisations, output does not usually have a market value, and it is therefore more difficult to measure efficiency. This difficulty is compounded by the fact that, since NFP organisations often have many different activities or operations, it is difficult to compare the efficiency of one operation with the efficiency of another. For example, with the police force, it might be difficult to compare the efficiency of a serious crimes squad with the efficiency of the traffic police.

3.2 Best value

'Best value' is a performance framework introduced into local authorities by the government. They are required to publish annual best value performance plans and review all of their functions over a five year period.

As part of 'Best value' authorities are required to strive for continuous improvement by implementing the '4 Cs':

- **Challenge**. How and why is a service provided?
- **Compare**. Make comparisons with other local authorities and the private sector.
- **Consult**. Talk to local taxpayers and services users and the wider business community in setting performance targets.
- **Compete**. Embrace fair competition as a means of securing efficient and effective services.

The **external auditors** will report on the annual best value performance plan.

3.2.1 Internal auditors and best value

One of internal audit's standard roles in a company is to provide assurance that internal control systems are adequate to promote the effective use of resources and that risks are being managed properly.

In relation to best value, this role can be extended to ensure that the authority has arrangements in place to achieve best value, that the risks and impacts of best value are incorporated into normal audit testing and that the authority keeps abreast of best value developments.

As best value depends on assessing current services and setting strategies for development, internal audit can take part in the 'position audit', as they should have a good understanding of how services are currently organised and relate to each other.

As assurance providers, the key part internal audit will play is in giving management assurance that their objectives and strategies in relation to best value are being met.

3.3 Information technology

An information technology audit is a test of control in a specific area of the business, the computer systems. Increasingly in modern business, computers are vital to the functioning of the business, and therefore the controls over them are some of the most important in the business.

It is likely to be necessary to have an IT specialist in the internal audit team to undertake an audit of the controls, as some of them will be programmed into the computer system.

The diagram below shows the various areas of IT in the business which might be subject to a test of controls by the auditors.

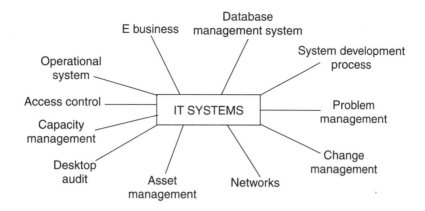

3.4 Financial

The financial audit is internal audit's traditional role. It involves reviewing all the available evidence (usually the company's records) to substantiate information in management and financial reporting.

This role in many ways echoed the role of the external auditor, and was not a role in which the internal auditors could add any particular value to the business. Increasingly, it is a minor part of the function of internal audit.

3.5 Fraud   12/01

Internal auditors may have a role in preventing and detecting fraud.

Fraud is a **key business risk**. It is the responsibility of the directors to prevent and detect fraud. As the **internal auditor has a role in risk management** he is involved in the process of managing the risk of fraud.

The internal auditor can help to **prevent** fraud by their work **assessing the adequacy and effectiveness of control systems** and **detect** fraud by **being mindful** when carrying out their work and **reporting any suspicions**.

The very **existence of an internal audit** department may act as a **deterrent** to fraud. The internal auditors might also be called upon to undertake special projects to investigate a suspected fraud.

4 Operational internal audit assignments   12/03

Internal auditors traditionally undertake operational audits.

Key term

> **Operational audits** are audits of the operational processes of the organisation. They are also known as management or efficiency audits. Their prime objective is the monitoring of management's performance, ensuring company policy is adhered to.

4.1 Approaching operational internal audit assignments

There are two aspects of an operational assignment:

- Ensure policies are adequate
- Ensure policies work effectively

4.1.1 Adequacy

The internal auditor will have to review the policies of a particular department by:

- Reading them
- Discussion with members of the department

Then the auditor will have to assess whether the policies are adequate, and possibly advise the board of improvement.

4.1.2 Effectiveness

The auditor will then have to examine the effectiveness of the controls by:

- Observing them in operation
- Testing them

This will be done on similar lines to the testing of controls discussed in Section D, even though the controls being tested may differ.

4.2 Procurement

Procurement is the process of **purchasing** for the business. A procurement audit will therefore concentrate on the **systems of the purchasing department(s).**

The internal auditor will be checking that the system achieves key objectives and that it operates according to company guidelines.

Point to note

> The control objectives and systems will be the same as will be discussed in Chapter 10, where we look at the purchases and expenses system. However, internal audit will also be concerned with considerations beyond the scope of the external auditor, which we shall consider in Chapter 11.

4.3 Marketing

Marketing is the **process of assessing and enhancing demand for the company's products**. Marketing and associated sales is very important for the business, and therefore, the internal auditor but as the **associated systems do not directly impact on the financial statements**, they do not usually concern the external auditor. The external auditor is concerned with systems directly relevant to sales.

It is important for the internal auditor to review the marketing processes to ensure:

- The process is **managed efficiently**
- **Information is freely available** to manager demand
- **Risks** are being **managed** correctly.

An audit may be especially critical for a marketing department which may be complex with several different teams, for example:

- Research
- Advertising
- Promotions
- After sales

It is vital to ensure that information is passed on properly within the department, and activities are streamlined.

4.4 Treasury

Treasury is a function within the finance department of a business. It **manages the funds of a business**. It is vital to a business that funds are managed so that cash is available when required.

There are risks associated with treasury, in terms of interest rate risk and foreign currency risk, and the auditor must ensure that the **risk is managed in accordance with company procedures.**

As with marketing audits, it is vital to ensure that **information is available** to the treasury department, so that they can **ensure funds are available when required**.

4.5 Human resources

The human resources department on one hand **procures a human resource** (employee) for the operation of the business and on the other **supports those employees in developing the organisation.**

It is important to ensure that the processes ensure that people are available to work as the business requires them and that the overall development of the business is planned and controlled.

Again, **ensuring company policies are maintained and information is freely available are key factors for internal audit to assess.**

Question   Internal control procedures

The growing recognition by management of the benefits of good internal control, and the complexities of an adequate system of internal control have led to the development of internal auditing as a form of control over all other internal controls. The emergence of the internal auditors as experts in internal control is the result of an evolutionary process similar in many ways to the evolution of independent auditing.

Required

(a)   Explain why the internal and independent auditors' review of internal control procedures differ in purpose.

(b)   Explain the reasons why internal auditors should or should not report their findings on internal control to the following selection of company officials:

     (i)   The board of directors
     (ii)   The chief accountant

(c)   Explain whether the independent auditors can place any reliance upon the internal auditors' work when the latter's main role is to be of service and assistance to management.

Answer

(a)   The internal auditors review and test the system of internal control and report to management in order to improve the information received by managers and to help in their task of running the company. The internal auditors will recommend changes to the system to make sure that the management receives objective information which is efficiently produced. The internal auditors will also have a duty to search for and discover fraud.

     The external auditors review the system of internal control in order to determine the extent of the substantive work required on the year end accounts. The external auditors report to the shareholders rather than the managers or directors.

     External auditors usually however issue a letter of weakness to the managers, laying out any areas of weakness and recommendations for improvement in the system of internal control. The external auditors report on the truth and fairness of the financial statements, not directly on the system of internal control. The auditors do not have a specific duty to detect fraud, although they should plan their audit procedures so as to detect any material misstatement in the accounts on which they give an opinion.

(b) (i) *Board of directors*

A high level of independence is achieved by the internal auditors if they report directly to the Board. There may be problems with this approach.

(1) The members of the Board may not understand all the implications of the internal audit reports when accounting or technical information is required.

(2) The Board may not have enough time to spend considering the reports in sufficient depth. Important recommendations might therefore remain unimplemented.

A way around these problems might be to delegate the review of internal audit reports to an audit committee, which would act as a kind of sub-committee to the main board. The audit committee might be made up largely of non-executive directors who have more time and more independence from the day-to-day running of the company.

(ii) *Chief accountant*

It would be inappropriate for internal audit to report to the chief accountant, who is largely in charge of running the system of internal control. It may be feasible for him or her to receive the report as well as the Board. Otherwise, the internal audit function cannot be effectively independent as the chief accountant could suppress unfavourable reports or could just not act on the recommendations of such reports.

(c) The internal audit function is itself part of the system of internal control: it is an internal control over internal controls. As such, the external auditors should be able to test it and, if it is found to be reliable, they can rely on it.

To check the reliability of the work of the internal auditors, I would consider the following matters.

(i) *The degree of independence of the internal auditors*

I would assess the organisational status and reporting responsibilities of the internal auditors and consider any restrictions placed upon them. Although internal auditors are employees of the enterprise and cannot therefore be independent of it, they should be able to plan and carry out their work as they wish and have access to senior management. They should be free of any responsibility which may create a conflict of interest, and of a situation where those staff on whom they are reporting are responsible for their or their staff's appointment, promotion or pay.

(ii) *The scope and objectives of the internal audit function*

I would examine the internal auditors' formal terms of reference and ascertain the scope and objectives of internal audit assignments.

(iii) *Quality of work*

I would consider whether the work of internal audit is properly planned, controlled, recorded and reviewed. Examples of good practice include the existence of an adequate audit manual, plans and procedures for supervision of individual assignments, and satisfactory arrangements for ensuring adequate quality control, reporting and follow-up.

(iv) *Technical competence*

Internal audit should be performed by persons having adequate training and competence as auditors. Indications of technical competence may be membership of an appropriate professional body or attendance at regular training courses.

(v) *Reports*

I would consider the quality of reports issued by internal audit and find out whether management considers and acts upon such reports.

If I find that the internal auditors' work is reliable, I will be able to place reliance on that work when appropriate. This may mean that I will need to carry out less audit work.

However, it should be emphasised that I cannot rely totally on the internal auditors' work in relation to any particular audit objective. Internal audit work provides only one form of evidence, and the internal auditors are not independent of company management. I may be able to reduce the number of items which I test, but I will not be able to leave a particular type of test (for example, a debtors' circularisation) entirely to internal audit. I remain responsible for the opinion which I form on the accounts.

5 Regulation

FAST FORWARD

Internal audit is not regulated in the same way as external audit.

Internal auditing is not regulated in the same ways as statutory auditing. There are **no legal requirements** associated with becoming an internal auditor. The **scope** and **nature** of **internal audit's work** is more likely to be set by **company policy** than by any external guidelines.

The Auditing Practices Board does not issue detailed auditing standards in relation to internal audit work. **Where** they are **applicable**, the standards set out in Auditing Standards are likely to be **good practice**, but they are not prescriptive in the same ways that they are for external auditors.

5.1 Institute of Internal Auditors

FAST FORWARD

Internal auditors may be members of bodies such as ACCA or IIA, or both.

In contrast to external auditors, **internal auditors are not required to be members of a professional body** such as ACCA. However, this does not mean they cannot be, and many are. There is also a global Institute of Internal Auditors (the IIA) which internal auditors **may** also become members of. Some people are members of both ACCA and IIA.

The IIA has over 6,000 members in the UK and Ireland and it is dedicated to representing and promoting the interests of internal auditors.

It issues 'Standards for the Professional Practice of Internal Auditing'. These are not examinable, so are not detailed in this Study Text, but you should be aware of the them as being another Code of Good Practice that internal auditors can follow, providing a framework for providing a wide range of internal audit services.

6 Outsourcing the internal audit function   12/01, 12/05

FAST FORWARD

Internal audit departments may consist of employees, or may be sourced from external service providers.

6.1 Sources of internal audit

While, as we have just discussed, the scope of the internal auditor's work is different to that of the external auditor, there are many features that can link them. The key linking factor is that the **techniques** which are used to carry out audits are the same for internal and external auditors.

It can be expensive to maintain an internal audit function consisting of employees. The Turnbull guidelines state that the directors should consider the need for them annually. However, the directors may conclude that the cost is prohibitive.

It is possible that the monitoring and review required by a certain company could be done in a small amount of time and full-time employees cannot be justified.

It is possible that a number of internal audit staff are required, but the cost of recruitment is prohibitive, or the directors are aware that the need for internal audit is only short-term.

In such circumstances, it is possible to **outsource the internal audit function**, that is, purchase the service from outside.

Therefore, many of the **larger accountancy firms offer internal audit services**. It is possible that the same firm might offer one client both internal and external audit services. In such circumstances the firm would have to be aware of the independence issues this would raise for the external audit team.

Question	Independence

The independence issues which would arise through the audit firm offering both internal and external audit services to the same client are referred to above.

(a)   What are the independence issues?

(b)   Why should the issues affect the external audit team rather than the internal audit team?

Answer

(a)   External auditors are employed to give an assurance to the members of a company about the stewardship of the directors and the management of that entity. They are independent verifiers. If the firm provides internal audit services to the entity, two issues arise:

   (i)   Internal auditors report to the director so there is a link between the firm and the directors which is a block to independence.

   (ii)   The firm provides 'other services' to an external audit client, and they must consider whether this affects their objectivity in relation to the audit and renders them no longer impartial.

   The specific guidance on auditors independence will be considered in more detail in Chapter 5.

(b)   The issues arise for the external audit team as independence is a key ethical issue for external auditors. As internal auditors provide a service to the directors, by whom they are employed, the issue of independence is a more tricky issue! It relates more to 'independence of mind'. Internal auditors are not required to be 'seen to been independent' in the same way that external auditors are. Ethical issues for internal audit are also discussed in Chapter 5.

6.2 Advantages of outsourcing

FAST FORWARD

Advantages of sourcing in internal audit include speed, cost, and a tailored answer to internal audit requirements.

The advantage of outsourcing internal audits is that outsourcing can overcome all the problems mentioned above.

   •   Staff do not need to be recruited, as the **service provider has good quality staff.**

- The service provider has different specialist skills and can assess what management require them to do. As they are external to the operation, this will not cause operational problems. The company will have access to a broad range of skills.

- Outsourcing can provide an **immediate** internal audit department.

- Associated costs, such as staff training, are eliminated.

- The service contract can be for the **appropriate time scale** (a two week project, a month, etc)

- Because the **time scale is flexible**, a **team of staff** can be provided if required.

- The service provider could also provide less than a team, but, for example, could provide one member of staff on a full-time basis for a short period, as a **secondment.**

Outsourced internal audit services are provided by many audit firms, particularly the large firms. This can range from a team of staff for a short term project, or a single staff member on a long term project. However, problems with such provision may include a high turnover in the staff used to provide IA services.

The fact that internal audit services are typically provided by **external auditors** can raise problems as well:

- The company might wish to **use the same firm** for internal and external audit services, but this may lead to **complications for the external auditors**, particularly in terms of independence.

- The **cost** of sourcing the internal audit function might be high enough to make the directors choose not to have an internal audit function at all.

A key advantage of outsourcing internal audit is that **outsourcing can be used on a short term basis**, to:

- Provide immediate services
- Lay the basis of a permanent function, by setting policies and functions
- Prepare the directors for the implications of having an internal audit function
- Assist the directors in recruiting the permanent function.

6.3 Managing an outsourced department

A company will need to establish controls over the outsourced internal audit department. Controls would include:

- Setting performance measures in terms of cost and areas of the business reviewed and obtaining explanations for variances.

- Ensuring appropriate audit methodology (working papers/reviews) is maintained

- Reviewing working papers on a sample basis to ensure they meet internal standards/guidelines.

- Agreeing internal audit work plans in advance of work being performed.

- If external auditor is used, ensuring the firm has suitable controls to keep the two functions separate.

Exam focus point

The question on outsourcing IA in December 2005 was an excellent example of a question candidates needed to answer using a blend of their own knowledge and facts applied from the scenario given. Such questions require practice. You will find this question in your Practice and Revision kit.

Chapter Roundup

- Internal audit assists management in achieving corporate objectives, particularly, in achieving good corporate governance.

- Although many of the techniques internal and external auditors use are similar, the basis and reasoning of their work is different.

- Internal audit has two key roles to play in relation to organisational risk management:
    - Ensuring the company's risk management system operates effectively
    - Ensuring that strategies implemented in respect of business risks operate effectively

- Internal audit can be involved in many different assignments as directed by management.

- Internal auditors may have a role in preventing and detecting fraud.

- Internal auditors traditionally undertake operational audits.

- Internal audit is not regulated in the same way as external audit.

- Internal auditors may be members of bodies such as ACCA or IIA, or both.

- Internal audit departments may consist of employees, or may be sourced from external service providers.

- Advantages of sourcing in internal audit include speed, cost, and a tailored answer to internal audit requirements.

Quick Quiz

1   What is an internal audit?

2   Complete the Turnbull Guidelines (given in Chapter 2)

TURNBULL GUIDELINES
Have a .... for the .... of effectiveness of ....
Review .... reports on ....
Consider .... and how they have been ....
Check the .... of .... to remedy weaknesses and incidents.
Consider the .... of ....
Conduct an .... of risks and the effectiveness of internal control.
Make a .... on this process in the ....

3   Name three key differences between internal and external audit.

  1   ....

  2   ....

  3   ....

4   It is possible to buy in an internal audit service from an external organisation.

  True   ☐

  False   ☐

5   Link the value for money 'E' with its definition.

(a)   Economy

(b)   Efficiency

(c)   Effectiveness

(i)   The relationships between the goods and services produced (outputs) and the resources used to produce them.

(ii)   The concern with how well an activity is achieving its policy objectives or other intended effects.

(iii)   Attaining the appropriate quantity and quality of physical, human and financial resources (inputs) at lowest cost.

6   Name five areas of the computer system which might benefit from an IT audit.

1   ....

2   ....

3   ....

4   ....

5   ....

7   Define the following areas of a business, which an internal auditor might review:

(a)   Procurement   (c)   Treasury
(b)   Marketing   (d)   Human resources

8   There are formal statutory rules governing the format of internal audit reports.

True   ☐

False   ☐

Answers to Quick Quiz

1   **Internal audit** is an appraisal or monitoring activity established by the entity as a service to the entity.

2   defined process, review, internal control
      regular, internal control
      key risks, managed
      adequacy, actions taken
      adequacy, monitoring
      annual assessment
      statement, annual report

3   1   External report to members, internal to directors
      2   External report on financial statements, internal on systems, controls and risks
      3   External are independent of the company, internal often employed by it

4   True

5   (a) (iii), (b) (i), (c) (ii)

6   Look back to the diagram in paragraph 3.3

7   (a)   The purchasing department
      (b)   The process which assesses and enhances demand for a product.
      (c)   Function (often within finance department) which manages funds.
      (d)   Department which procures a human resource and manages development of the organisation.

8   False

Now try the question below from the Exam Question Bank

Number	Level	Marks	Time
Q4	Examination	20	36 mins

Professional codes of ethics and behaviour

Topic list	Syllabus reference
1 Professional competence and due care	1
2 Code of ethics and conduct	1
3 Internal audit ethics	1
4 Areas of controversy	1
5 Accepting appointment	1
6 Engagement letters	1

Introduction

In Chapter 3 we looked at some of the regulation surrounding the auditor. Here we look at the (sometimes more stringent) **requirements of the RSBs, specifically the ethical guidance from ACCA**, the association you are studying to join. **Internal auditors** are subject to the requirements of any professional body to which they belong. The only professional body specifically for internal auditors is the Institute of Internal Auditors. We will look briefly at their guidance.

The ethical matters covered in this chapter are **very important**. Ethical matters could arise in almost every type of exam question. You must be able to apply the ACCA's guidance on ethical matters to any given situation, but remember that **common sense** is usually a good guide.

We firstly examine what a client has the **right to demand** from their auditors under the terms of their **contract**. The most important qualities are that the auditors carry out their work with due **professional care**.

Auditors are also subject to **ethical requirements imposed by their professional bodies**. The principle of **independence** – that auditors must not only be independent but must be seen to be independent – is very important. In a number of cases whether a particular situation is a threat to independence is not clear-cut; is auditor independence compromised by providing services other than audit to an audit client, for example.

One area where client requirements may conflict with the requirement for auditors to act ethically is whether the auditor should keep the affairs of clients secret, or disclose them to others without obtaining the client's consent. We shall see that professional guidance tries to strike a balance between stressing the importance of keeping the affairs of clients **confidential**, and stating that in certain instances auditors should consider (or have to) disclose client details to third parties.

Lastly we shall consider matters relating to accepting appointment.

Study guide

7 – Professional ethics and professional codes of conduct I

- Describe the sources of, and enforcement mechanisms associated with, professional ethics and professional codes of conduct

- Define the fundamental concepts of professional ethics

- Define the detailed requirements of, and illustrate and analyse the application of, professional ethics in the context of independence, objectivity and integrity

- Distinguish between the elements of professional ethics applicable to internal auditors and those applicable to external auditors

8 – Professional ethics and professional codes of conduct II

- Describe the requirements of professional ethics and other requirements in relation to the acceptance of audit and review assignments, including situations in which there is an imposed limitation in audit scope

- Define the detailed requirements of, and illustrate and analyse the application of, professional ethics in the context of confidentiality and conflicts of interest

- Describe the importance of engagement letters and describe their contents

Exam guide

Questions about independence often involve discussion of topical, controversial issues, for example provision of services other than audit to audit clients. You should keep an eye open for articles in *Student Accountant* and financial press in these areas. Exam questions will generally require you to consider both sides of a controversial topic. In December 2005, candidates had to outline what matters an audit firm offering internal audit services to a client would have to consider.

1 Professional competence and due care

 The auditors' **duty of care** has been defined by case law over time.

1.1 The auditors' duty of care

ACCA's *Code of Ethics and Conduct*

Members have a continuing duty to maintain professional knowledge and skill at a level required to ensure that a client or employer receives competent professional service based on current developments in practice, legislation and techniques. Members should act diligently and in accordance with applicable technical and professional standards when providing professional services.

All accountants (not just auditors) in public practice are obliged by law to provide services of appropriate quality. Unless an accountant and client have agreed otherwise in the UK, there is an implied duty of care that an accountant owes to a client under s 13 Supply of Goods and Services Act 1982. This relates to **all services** provided by an accountancy firm, external audit, internal audit, accounts, preparation work, tax work etc.

The professional guidance statement *Professional Liability* published in 1994 makes the following further points.

(a)   The degree of skill and care will depend on the work: a higher degree will be required for work:

- Of a **specialised nature**
- Where negligence is likely to **cause substantial loss**

These particularly apply where the accountant represented himself as being experienced.

(b)   The duty will not be absolute; opinions or advice will not give rise to claims just because they are proved wrong in the light of later events.

Thus auditors must employ **reasonable care** in all they do, in particular:

(a)   Auditors must use **generally accepted auditing techniques** when seeking to satisfy themselves that the matters upon which they reports accurately reflect the true financial state of his client's business.

(b)   If auditors come across any matter which puts them **upon inquiry** then they have a duty to investigate such a matter until they are able to resolve it to their own reasonable satisfaction. Auditors should not accept any explanation unless they have first carried out such investigations as will enable them properly to assess whether the explanation offered a reasonable one.

2 Code of ethics and conduct   Pilot paper

FAST FORWARD

Independence and objectivity are the most important characteristics of auditors.

There are a number of ethical issues which are of great importance in the client-auditor relationship.

2.1 Objectivity and independence

Why? Because, as we saw in Chapter 1 in the case of Glyn and Laine, it is important that the auditor is **impartial**, and independent of management, so that he can give an **objective** view.

The onus is always on the auditor not only to be ethical but also to be **seen** to be ethical. To this end, the Association publishes a Code of Ethics and Conduct previously called *Rules of Professional Conduct*. **All** members **and** students of the ACCA must adhere to these rules. Guidance is in the form of:

- Fundamental principles
- Guidance and explanatory notes

The Fundamental Principles	
Integrity	Members should be straightforward and honest in all business and professional relationships.
Objectivity	Members should not allow bias, conflicts of interest or undue influence of others to override professional or business judgements.
Professional competence and due care	Members have a continuing duty to maintain professional knowledge and skill at a level required to ensure that a client or employer receives competent professional service based on current developments in practice, legislation and techniques. Members should act diligently and in accordance with applicable technical and professional standards when providing professional services.

The Fundamental Principles	
Confidentially	Members should respect the confidentiality of information acquired as a result of professional and business relationships and should not disclose any such information to third parties without proper or specific authority or unless there is a legal or professional right or duty to disclose. Confidential information acquired as a result of professional and business relationships should not be used for the personal advantage of members or third parties.
Professional behaviour	Members should comply with relevant laws and regulations and should avoid any action that discredits the profession.

2.1.1 Why do independence and objectivity matter so much?   12/02

Independence and objectivity matter because of:

(a)   The **expectations** of those directly affected, particularly the members of the company. The audit should be able to provide **objective** assurance that the directors can never provide on the accounts.

(b)   The **public interest**. Companies are public entities, governed by rules requiring the disclosure of information.

Threats to independence and objectivity could arise for the following reasons.

The auditors' own **personal interest**. The auditors may fear, for example, the loss of fees.
When carrying out the audit, the auditors **review work** that their **own firm** has **done previously**, for example, preparing accounts or making a valuation.
If the auditors get involved in **disputes** concerning the client. They may end up **acting for or against** the **client**, which undermines the appearance of objectivity.
If the auditors are involved with the client for a long time, they may become **unduly sympathetic** towards directors and management, and thus too inclined to trust their unsupported word.
The auditors may be **intimidated** by a **dominant** or **aggressive atmosphere** at the clients.

What can the auditor do to preserve objectivity? The simple answer is to **withdraw from any engagement** where there is the **slightest threat** to objectivity. However there are disadvantages in this strict approach.

- Clients may lose an auditor who knows their business
- It denies clients the freedom to be advised by the accountant of their choice.

A better approach would be as follows

Step 1   **Consider** whether the **auditors' own objectivity** and the **general safeguards** operated in the professional environment are **sufficient** to offset the threat

Step 2   Consider whether **safeguards over and above** the general safeguards are required, for example specified partners or staff not working on an assignment.

However the ultimate option must always be withdrawing from an engagement or refusing to act.

2.2 Integrity, objectivity and independence

ACCA Statement

Members should consider when providing any professional service whether there are threats to compliance with the fundamental principle of objectivity resulting from having interests in, or relationships with, a client or directors, officers or employees.

Members who provide assurance services are required to be independent of the assurance client. Independence of mind and in appearance is necessary to enable members in public practice to express a conclusion, and be seen to express a conclusion, without bias, conflict of interest or undue influence of others.

'The spirit of the ACCA guidance applies to all audit situations'. The rules are given as 'guidance' so that they are matters of judgement for the auditors rather than being hard and fast rules.

Exam focus point

> You should note that legal independence is a set of relationships which are prohibited (see Chapter 3). Professional independence is however an attitude of mind; the detailed guidelines listed below are guidelines and audit firms may feel justified in taking stricter measures than the guidelines suggest.

2.3 Self-interest threat

The ACCA Code of Ethics and Conduct highlights a great number of areas in which a self-interest threat might arise.

2.3.1 Financial interests

Key term

> A financial interest exists where an audit firm has a financial interest in a client's affairs, for example, the audit firm owns shares in the client, or is a trustee of a trust that holds shares in the client.

A financial interest in a client constitutes a substantial self-interest threat. According to ACCA, **the parties listed below are not allowed to own a direct financial interest or an indirect material financial interest in a client**:

- The **assurance firm**
- A **member of the assurance team**
- An **immediate family member of a member of the assurance team**

The following safeguards will therefore be relevant:

- Disposing of the interest
- Removing the individual from the team if required
- Keeping the client's audit committee informed of the situation
- Using an independent partner to review work carried out if necessary

Such matters will involve judgement on the part of the partners making decisions about such matters. For example, what constitutes a material interest? A small percentage stake in a company might be material to its owner. How does the firm judge the closeness of a relationship between staff and their families, in other words, what does immediate mean in this context?

Audit firms should have quality control procedures requiring staff to disclose relevant financial interests for themselves and close family members. They should also foster a culture of voluntary disclosure on an ongoing basis so that any potential problems are identified on a timely basis.

2.3.2 Close business relationships

Examples of when an audit firm and an audit client have an inappropriately close business relationship include:

- Having a material financial interest in a joint venture with the assurance client

- Arrangements to combine one or more services or products of the firm with one or more services or products of the assurance client and to market the package with reference to both parties

- Distribution or marketing arrangements under which the firm acts as distributor or marketer of the assurance client's products or services or vice versa

Again, it will be necessary for the partners to judge the materiality of the interest and therefore its significance. However, **unless the interest is clearly insignificant, an assurance provider should not participate in such a venture with an assurance client**. Appropriate safeguards are therefore to end the assurance provision or to terminate the (other) business relationship.

If an individual member of an assurance team had such an interest, he should be removed from the assurance team.

However, if the firm or a member (and immediate family of the member) of the assurance team has an interest in an entity when the client or its officers also has an interest in that entity, the threat might not be so great.

Generally speaking, **purchasing goods and services from an assurance client on an arm's length basis does not constitute a threat to independence**. If there are a substantial number of such transactions, there may be a threat to independence and safeguards may be necessary.

2.3.3 Employment with assurance client

It is possible that staff might transfer between an assurance firm and a client, or that negotiations or interviews to facilitate such movement might take place. Both situations are a threat to independence:

- An audit staff member might be motivated by a desire to impress a future possible employer (objectivity is therefore affected)

- A former partner turned Finance Director has too much knowledge of the audit firm's systems and procedures

The extent of the threat to independence depends on various factors, such as the role the individual has taken up at the client, the extent of his influence on the audit previously, the length of time that has passed between the individual's connection with the audit and the new role at the client.

Various safeguards might be considered:

- Considering modifying the assurance plan

- Ensuring the audit is assigned to someone of sufficient experience as compared with the individual who has left

- Involving an additional professional accountant not involved with the engagement to review the work done

- Carrying out a quality control review of the engagement

In respect of **audit clients, a partner should not accept a key management position at an audit client until at least two years have elapsed since the conclusion of the audit he was involved with.**

An individual who has moved from the firm to a client should not be entitled to any benefits or payments from the firm unless these are made in accordance with pre-determined arrangements. If money is owed to the individual, it should not be so much as to compromise the independence of the assurance engagement.

A firm should have quality control procedures setting out that an individual involved in serious employment negotiations with an audit client should notify the firm and that this person would then be removed from the engagement.

2.3.4 Partner on client board

A partner or employee of an assurance firm should not serve on the board of an assurance client.

It may be acceptable for a partner or an employee of an assurance firm to perform the role of company secretary for an assurance client, if the role is essentially administrative.

2.3.5 Family and personal relationships

Family or close personal relationships between assurance firm and client staff could seriously threaten independence. Each situation has to be evaluated individually. Factors to consider are:

- The individual's responsibilities on the assurance engagement
- The closeness of the relationship
- The role of the other party at the assurance client

When an immediate family member of a member of the assurance team is a director, an officer or an employee of the assurance client in a position to exert direct and significant influence over the subject matter information of the assurance engagement, the individual should be removed from the assurance team.

The audit firm should also consider whether there is any threat to independence if an employee who is not a member of the assurance team has a close family or personal relationship with a director, an officer or an employee of an assurance client.

A firm should have quality control policies and procedures under which staff should disclose if a close family member employed by the client is promoted within the client.

If a firm inadvertently violates the rules concerning family and personal relationships they should apply additional safeguards, such as undertaking a quality control review of the audit and discussing the matter with the audit committee of the client, if there is one.

2.3.6 Gifts and hospitality

Unless the value of the gift/hospitality is clearly insignificant, a firm or a member of an assurance team should not accept.

2.3.7 Loans and guarantees

The advice on loans and guarantees falls into two categories:

- The client is a bank or other similar institution
- Other situations

If a lending institution client lends an immaterial amount to an audit firm or member of assurance team on normal commercial terms, there is no threat to independence. If the loan were material it would be necessary to apply safeguards to bring the risk to an acceptable level. A suitable safeguard is likely to be an independent review (by a partner from another office in the firm).

Loans to members of the assurance team from a bank or other lending institution client are likely to be material to the individual, but provided that they are on normal commercial terms, these do not constitute a threat to independence.

An audit firm or individual on the assurance engagement should not enter into any loan or guarantee arrangement with a client that is not a bank or similar institution.

2.3.8 Overdue fees

In a situation where there are overdue fees, the auditor runs the risk of, in effect, making a loan to a client, whereupon the guidance above becomes relevant.

Audit firms should guard against fees building up and being significant by discussing the issues with those charged with governance, and, if necessary, the possibility of resigning if overdue fees are not paid.

2.3.9 Percentage or contingent fees

Key term

> **Contingent fees** are fees calculated on a predetermined basis relating to the outcome or result of a transaction or the result of the work performed.

A firm should not enter into any fee arrangement for an assurance engagement under which the amount of the fee is contingent on the result of the assurance work or on items that are the subject matter of the assurance engagement.

It would also usually be inappropriate to accept a contingent fee for non assurance work from an assurance client. Factors to consider in whether a contingent fee is acceptable or not include:

- The range of possible fee outcomes
- The degree of variability in the fee
- The basis on which the fee is to be determined
- Whether the transaction is to be reviewed by an independent third party
- The effect on the transaction on the assurance engagement

In other circumstances it may be appropriate to accept a contingent fee for non assurance work if suitable safeguards are in place. Examples include:

- Making disclosures to the audit committee about the fees
- Review or determination of the fee by an unrelated third party
- Quality control policies and procedures

2.3.10 High percentage of fees

A firm should be alert to the situation arising where the total fees generated by an assurance client represent a large proportion of a firm's total fees. Factors such as the structure of the firm and the length of time it has been trading will be relevant in determining whether there is a threat to independence. It is also necessary to beware of situations where the fees generated by an assurance client present a large proportion of the revenue of an individual partner.

Safeguards in these situations might include:

- Discussing the issues with the audit committee
- Taking steps to reduce the dependency on the client
- Obtaining external/internal quality control reviews
- Consulting a third party such as ACCA

The public may perceive that a member's objectivity is likely to be in jeopardy where the fees for audit and recurring work paid by one client or group of connected clients exceed 15% of the firm's total fees. Where the entity is listed or public interest, this figure should be 10%.

It will be difficult for new firms establishing themselves to keep outside of these limits and firms in this situation should make use of the safeguards outlined.

2.3.11 Lowballing

When a firm quotes a significantly lower fee level for an assurance service than would have been charged by the predecessor firm, there is a significant self-interest threat. If the firm's tender is successful, the firm must apply safeguards such as:

- Maintaining records such that the firm is able to demonstrate that appropriate staff and time are spent on the engagement

- Complying with all applicable assurance standards, guidelines and quality control procedures

2.3.12 Recruitment

Recruiting senior management for an assurance client, particularly those able to affect the subject matter of an assurance engagement creates a self-interest threat for the assurance firm.

Assurance providers must not make management decisions for the client. Their involvement could be limited to reviewing a shortlist of candidates, providing that the client has drawn up the criteria by which they are to be selected.

2.4 Self-review threat

The key area in which there is likely to be a self-review threat is where an assurance firm provides services other than assurance services to an assurance client (providing multiple services). There is a great deal of guidance in the ACCA and IFAC rules about various other services accountancy firms might provide to their clients, and these are dealt with below.

2.4.1 Recent service with an assurance client

Individuals who have been a director or officer of the client, or an employee in a position to exert direct and significant influence over the subject matter information of the assurance engagement in the period under review or the previous two years should not be assigned to the assurance team.

If an individual had been closely involved with the client prior to the time limits set out above, the assurance firm should consider the threat to independence arising and apply appropriate safeguards, such as:

- Obtaining a quality control review of the individual's work on the assignment
- Discussing the issue with the audit committee

2.4.2 General other services

For assurance clients, accountants are not allowed to:

- **Authorise, execute or consummate a transaction**
- **Determine which recommendation of the company should be implemented**
- **Report in a management capacity to those charged with governance**

Having custody of an assurance client's assets, supervising client employees in the performance of their normal duties, and preparing source documents on behalf of the client also pose significant self-review threats which should be addressed by safeguards. These could be:

- Ensuring non assurance team staff are used for these roles
- Involving an independent professional accountant to advise
- Quality control policies on what staff are and are not allowed to do for clients
- Making appropriate disclosures to those charged with governance
- Resigning from the assurance engagement

2.4.3 Preparing accounting records and financial statements

There is clearly a significant risk of a self-review threat if a firm prepares accounting records and financial statements and then audits them.

On the other hand auditors routinely assist management with the preparation of financial statements and give advice about accounting treatments and journal entries.

Therefore, assurance firms must analyse the risks arising and put safeguards in place to ensure that the risk is at an acceptable level. Safeguards include:

- Using staff members other than assurance team members to carry out work
- Obtaining client approval for work undertaken

The rules are more stringent when the client is listed or public interest. **Firms should not prepare accounts or financial statements for listed or public interest clients**, unless an emergency arises.

For any client, assurance firms are also not allowed to:

- **Determine or change journal entries without client approval**
- **Authorise or approve transactions**
- **Prepare source documents**

2.4.4 Valuation services

Key term

> A **valuation** comprises the making of assumptions with regard to future developments, the application of certain methodologies and techniques, and the combination of both in order to compute a certain value, or range of values, for an asset, a liability or for a business as a whole.

If an audit firm performs a valuation for which will be included in financial statements audited by the firm, a self-review threat arises.

Audit firms should not carry out valuations on matters which will be material to the financial statements. If the valuation is for an immaterial matter, the audit firm should apply safeguards to ensure that the risk is reduced to an acceptable level. Matters to consider when applying safeguards are the extent of the audit client's knowledge of the relevant matters in making the valuation and the degree of judgement involved, how much use is made of established methodologies and the degree of uncertainty in the valuation. Safeguards include:

- Second partner review
- Confirming that the client understands the valuation and the assumptions used
- Ensuring the client acknowledges responsibility for the valuation
- Using separate personnel for the valuation and the audit

2.4.5 Taxation services

The provision of taxation services is generally not seen to impair independence.

2.4.6 Internal audit services

A firm may provide internal audit services to an audit client. However, it should ensure that the client acknowledges its responsibility for establishing, maintaining and monitoring the system of internal controls. It may be appropriate to use safeguards such as ensuring that an employee of the client is designated responsible for internal audit activities and that the client approves all the work that internal audit does.

2.4.7 Corporate finance

Certain aspects of corporate finance will create self-review threats that cannot be reduced to an acceptable level by safeguards. Therefore, **assurance firms are not allowed to promote, deal in or underwrite an assurance client's shares. They are also not allowed to commit an assurance client to the terms of a transaction or consummate a transaction on the client's behalf**.

Other corporate finance services, such as assisting a client in defining corporate strategies, assisting in identifying possible sources of capital and providing structuring advice may be acceptable, providing that safeguards, such as using different teams of staff, and ensuring no management decisions are taken on behalf of the client.

2.4.8 Other services

The audit firm might sell a variety of other services to audit clients, such as:

- IT services
- Temporary staff cover
- Litigation support
- Legal services

The assurance firm should consider whether there are any barriers to independence, such as if the firm were asked to design internal control IT systems, which it would then review as part of its audit, or if the firm were asked to provide an accountant to cover the chief accountant's maternity leave. The firm should consider whether the threat to independence could be reduced by appropriate safeguards.

2.5 Advocacy threat

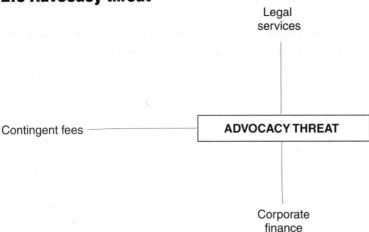

An advocacy threat arises in certain situations where the assurance firm is in a position of taking the client's part in a dispute or somehow acting as their advocate. The most obvious instances of this would be when a firm offered legal services to a client and, say, defended them in a legal case or provided evidence on their behalf as an expert witness. Advocacy threat might also arise if the firm carried out corporate finance work for the client, for example, if the audit firm was involved in advice on debt reconstruction and negotiated with the bank on the client's behalf.

As with the other threats above, the firm has to appraise the risk and apply safeguards as necessary. Relevant safeguards might be using different departments in the firm to carry out the work and making disclosures to the audit committee. Remember, the ultimate option is always to withdraw from an engagement if the risk to independence is too high.

2.6 Familiarity threat

A familiarity threat is where independence is jeopardised by the audit firm and its staff becoming over familiar with the client and its staff. There is a substantial risk of loss of professional scepticism in such circumstances.

We have already discussed some examples of when this risk arises, because very often a familiarity threat arises in conjunction with a self-interest threat.

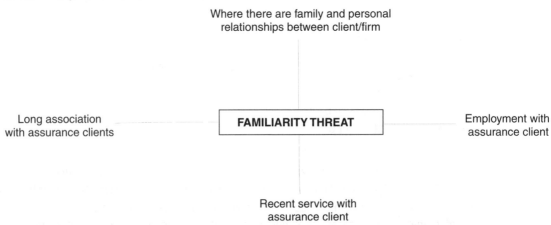

2.6.1 Long association of senior personnel with assurance clients

It can be a significant threat to independence if senior members of staff at an audit firm have a long association with a client. All firms should therefore monitor the relationship between staff and established clients and use safeguards to independence such as rotating senior staff off the assurance team, involving second partners to carry out reviews and obtaining independent (but internal) quality control reviews.

In addition, the Code of Ethics and Conduct sets out specific rules for listed and public interest entities in this situation. These state that **for the audit of listed and other public interest entities:**

- **The engagement partner should be rotated after a pre-defined period, normally no more than five years, and should not return to the engagement until a period of five years has elapsed.**

- **Other key audit partners should be rotated after a pre-defined period, normally no more than seven years, and should not return to the engagement until a period of two years (or five years if returning as engagement partner) has elapsed; and**

- **The individual responsible for the engagement quality control review should be rotated after a pre-defined period, normally no more than seven years, and should not return to the engagement until a period of two years has elapsed**

When an entity becomes a listed entity, the length of time the staff involved with the audit have been involved should be taken into consideration, but **the engagement partner, other key partners and quality control person should only continue in those position for another two years**.

These rules should be followed, but there may be circumstances in which it is necessary to be flexible, such as when the firm is so small as to make rotation impracticable and when the person involved is particularly important to the audit. However, the firm should apply safeguards in such circumstances.

2.7 Intimidation threat

An intimidation threat arises when members of the assurance team have reason to be intimidated by client staff.

These are also examples of self-interest threats, largely because intimidation may only arise significantly when the assurance firm has something to lose.

2.7.1 Actual and threatened litigation

The most obvious example of an intimidation threat is when the client threatens to sue, or indeed sues, the assurance firm for work that has been done previously. The firm is then faced with the risk of losing the client, bad publicity and the possibility that they will be found to have been negligent, which will lead to further problems. This could lead to the firm being under pressure to produce an unqualified audit report when they have been qualified in the past, for example.

Generally, assurance firms should seek to avoid such situations arising. If they do arise, factors to consider are:

- The materiality of the litigation
- The nature of the assurance engagement
- Whether the litigation relates to a prior assurance engagement

The following safeguards could be considered:

- Disclosing to the audit committee the nature and extent of the litigation
- Removing specific affected individuals from the engagement team
- Involving an additional professional accountant on the team to review work

However, if the litigation is at all serious, it may be necessary to resign from the engagement, as the threat to independence is so great.

The statement points out that, although the rules refer specifically to company audits under the Companies Acts, 'the spirit of the guidance applies equally to other audit situations'. The rules are given as 'guidance' so that they are matters of judgement for the auditors rather than being hard and fast rules.

<table>
<tr><td>**Exam focus point**</td><td>You should note that legal independence is a set of relationships which are prohibited (see Chapter 3). Professional independence is however an attitude of mind; the detailed guidelines listed below are just guidelines and audit firms may feel justified in taking stricter measures than the guidelines suggest.</td></tr>
</table>

2.8 APB's Ethical Standards

As mentioned in Chapter 2, the APB issues ethical standards also. Here is a summary of the ethical standards.

2.8.1 ES 1: Integrity, objectivity and independence

This standard outlines the general requirements with regard to these matters. It states that integrity, objectivity and confidentiality are fundamental ethical principles.

Integrity implies qualities of **confidentiality**.

Objectivity is a state of mind that excludes bias, prejudice and compromise. It requires that the auditors' judgement is not affected by conflicts of interest.

Independence is related to and underpins objectivity. However whereas objectivity is a personal behavioural characteristic concerning the auditors' state of mind, independence relates to the circumstances surrounding the audit.

In practical terms it states that firms should establish policies to ensure that the firm and everyone in a position to influence the conduct and the outcome of the audit act with integrity, objectivity and independence. An ethics partner should be designated to set and communicate these policies. For listed or public interest companies, an independent partner should review the conclusions drawn by the engagement partner as to the firm's independence.

As part of the general guidance in the standard it also outlines the types of threats to independence that the auditors face. These have been discussed at length in paragraphs 2.3-2.7.

As we have seen, these categories are not necessarily distinct. Certain circumstances may give rise to more than one type of threat. Where the audit engagement partner identifies threats to the auditors' objectivity safeguards should be applied. (ES 1 does not set out the detail of what the safeguards should include.)

2.8.2 ES 2: Financial, business, employment and personal relationships

Financial relationships

General considerations

'The audit firm, any partner in the audit firm, a person in a position to influence the conduct and outcome of the audit or an immediate family member of such a person should not hold:

(a)   any direct financial interest in an audit client or an affiliate of an audit client; or

(b)   any indirect financial interest in an audit client or an affiliate of an audit client, where the investment is material to the audit firm or the individual and to the intermediary; or

(c)   any indirect financial interest in an audit client or an affiliate of an audit client where the person holding it has both:

(i)   the ability to influence the investment decisions of the intermediary; and
(ii)   actual knowledge of the existence of the underlying investment.'

In the above cases the threats to the auditors' objectivity are such that no safeguards can eliminate them or reduce them to an acceptable level.

Where the financial interest is held by the audit firm, a partner or an immediate family member **the entire interest should be disposed of** (or a sufficient amount of an indirect interest is disposed of so that the remaining interest is no longer material) or **the firm should not accept or should withdraw from the audit**.

Where a financial interest is acquired **unintentionally**, for example through inheritance, the **disposal of the financial interest** is required immediately or as soon as possible. Where disposal does not take place immediately, the audit firm must adopt safeguards. These may include the temporary exclusion of the person in a position to influence the conduct and outcome of the audit.

Where a person in a position to influence the outcome of the audit or a partner in the audit firm becomes aware that a close family member holds a financial interest, it should be reported to the audit engagement partner. If there is any doubt as to the action to be taken the audit engagement partner should resolve the issue through **consultation with the ethics partner**.

Loans and guarantees

Audit firms, persons in a position to influence the conduct and outcome of the audit and immediate family members of such persons should not make a loan to/accept a loan from, or guarantee the borrowings of/have their borrowings guaranteed by, an audit client or its affiliates unless this represents a deposit made with a bank or similar deposit taking institution in the ordinary course of business and on normal business terms.

Business relationships

'Audit firms, persons in a position to influence the conduct and outcome of the audit and immediate family members of such persons should not enter into business relationships with an audit client or its affiliates except where they involve the purchase of goods and services from the audit firm or the audit client in the ordinary course of business and on an arm's length basis and the value involved is not material to either party.'

Where a business relationship has been entered into either the relationship is terminated or the firm does not accept (withdraws) from the engagement/or that person does not retain a position in which they exert such influence on the audit engagement.

Employment relationships

'An audit firm should not admit to the partnership or employ a person to undertake audit work if that person is also employed by the audit client or its affiliates ('dual employment').

A partner or employee of the audit firm should not accept appointment:

   (a)   to the board of directors

   (b)   to any subcommittee of that board

   (c)   to such a position in an entity which hold more than 20% of the voting rights in the audit client, or in which the audit client holds directly or indirectly more than 20% of the voting rights.'

Loan staff assignments

'An audit client should not enter into an agreement with an audit client to provide a partner or employee to work for a temporary period as if that individual were an employee unless the audit client:

   (a)   agrees that the individual concerned will not hold a management position
   (b)   acknowledges its responsibility for directing and supervising the work to be performed.'

On completion of the loan staff assignment that individual should not be given any role on the audit involving any function or activity that they performed or supervised during that assignment.

Partners and engagement team members joining an audit client

Partners, senior members of the engagement team and other members of the engagement team should notify the firm of any situation involving their potential employment with an audit client. The individual should be removed from the team and any work performed by them on the most recent audit should be reviewed.

'Where a partner leaves the firm and is appointed as a director (including as a non-executive director) or to a key management position with an audit client, having acted as audit engagement partner at any time in the **two years** prior to his appointment, the firm should resign as auditors. The firm should not accept reappointment as auditors until a two-year period, commencing when the former partner ceased to act for the client, has elapsed or the former partner ceases employment with the former client, whichever is sooner.'

Where the above situation applies to a member of the engagement team the audit firm should consider whether the composition of the audit team is appropriate.

Directors and employees joining an audit firm

Where a director or a former employee joins an audit firm that individual should not be assigned to a position in which he or she is able to influence the conduct and outcome of the audit for a period of two years.

Family members employed by an audit client

As a general governance issue ES 2 states that the audit firm should have policies and procedures that require partners and professional staff to report family relationships involving audit clients.

Where a person in a position to influence the conduct and outcome of the audit, or a partner in the firm becomes aware that an immediate family member is employed by an audit client in a position to exercise influence on the accounting records or financial statements, that individual should cease to have any further role in the audit.

In the case of a close family member the matter should be reported to the audit engagement partner to take appropriate action.

2.8.3 ES 3: Long association with the audit engagement

General provisions

Where audit engagement partners, key audit partners and staff in senior positions have a long association with the audit safeguards should be applied. **Where they cannot be applied the audit firm should either resign or not stand for reappointment**.

Safeguards include:

- **Rotating the audit partner** and other senior members of the audit team after a pre-determined number of years

- Involving an **additional partner**

- Applying **independent internal quality reviews**

Once an audit partner has held the role for a continuous period of ten years careful consideration should be given to whether objectivity would have the appearance of being impaired.

Additional provisions for listed companies

The firm should establish policies to ensure that:

(a) no one should act as audit engagement partner or independent partner for a continuous period longer than **five years**

(b) they should not hold a position of responsibility regarding this audit client again until a further period of five years has elapsed

Where senior staff have been involved on an audit for a continuous period longer than seven years the audit engagement partner should review the safeguards put in place.

In addition, key audit partners (an audit partner other than the engagement partner who is involved at a *group* level) should not act for more than seven years. If the engagement partner becomes a key partner, the total for his combined roles must not exceed seven years.

2.8.4 ES 4: Fees, remuneration and evaluation policies, litigation, gifts and hospitality

Fees

An audit should not be undertaken on a **contingent fee** basis.

The audit fee should reflect the **time spent** and the **skills and experience** of the personnel performing the audit.

Where fees are **overdue** the auditor needs to consider whether the firm can continue as auditors.

Where it is expected that the fees for both audit and non-audit services receivable from a listed audit client and its subsidiaries will regularly exceed **10% of the annual fee income of the audit firm** (15% for non-listed), the firm should **not act as the auditors** and should either resign or not stand for reappointment.

Where the above fees will regularly exceed **5% of the annual fee income** the audit engagement partner should **disclose** this to the ethics partner and those charged with governance and consider whether safeguards should be applied.

New firms should not undertake any audits of listed companies, where fees would represent 10% or more of the annual fee income of the firm. In addition, for a period not exceeding two years, independent reviews should be performed on those audits of unlisted entities that represent more than 10% of the annual fee income.

Performance criteria and remuneration of staff should not depend on the selling of non-audit services.

Threatened and actual litigation

Where litigation between the audit client and the audit firm is already in progress or is probable, the audit firm should either not continue or should not accept the engagement.

Gifts and hospitality

The audit firm, those in a position to influence the conduct and outcome of the audit and immediate family members should **not accept gifts from the audit client**, unless the value is clearly insignificant.

Hospitality should not be accepted either, unless it is **reasonable** in terms of its frequency, nature and cost.

2.8.5 ES 5: Non-audit services provided to audit clients

This standard issues general guidance regarding the approach to non-audit services but also goes on to describe how these principles should be applied to specific non-audit services.

General approach

ES 5 does not prohibit the provision of other services. However, it requires the audit engagement partner to:

- Consider whether the objectives of the proposed engagement would be perceived to be inconsistent with the objectives of the audit

- Identify and assess the significance of any related threats to the auditors' objectivity

- Identify and assess the effectiveness of the available safeguards

Where the engagement partner considers it probable that the objectives of the two assignments are inconsistent, the audit firm should either not undertake the non-audit service or not accept/withdraw from the audit engagement.

Safeguards

Where there is a threat to the auditors' objectivity the audit engagement partner should assess whether there are safeguards that could be applied which would eliminate the threat or reduce it to an acceptable level. If safeguards can be applied the non-audit service can be provided. If safeguards cannot be applied, the audit firm should either not undertake the non-audit work, or not accept, or withdraw from, the audit engagement.

2.8.6 Application of general principles to specific non-audit services

These include the following:

Internal audit services

In general term this service can be provided assuming that adequate safeguards are in place.

Safeguards include:

- Using different staff for internal and external audit purposes

- Review of the audit of the financial statements performed by a partner who is not involved with the external audit.

However the firm should not undertake the engagement where the auditor will place significant reliance on internal audit as part of the audit of the financial statements or where the audit firm would be taking on a management role.

Information technology services

The audit firm should not undertake an engagement to design, provide or implement technology systems for an audit client where:

- The system concerned would be important to any significant part of the accounting system or to the production of the financial statements and the auditor would place significant reliance upon them as part of the audit of the financial statements; or
- The audit firm would undertake part of the role of management.

Valuation services

The audit firm should not provide a valuation to a client where the valuation would:

- Involve a significant degree of subjective judgement; and
- Have a material effect on the financial statements.

Actuarial valuation services

The audit firm should not provide actuarial valuation services to an audit client unless they are satisfied the significant judgements will be made by informed management or the valuation has no material effect on the financial statements.

Tax services

In general terms tax services may be provided although the auditor must assess the possible threats to objectivity.

Safeguards would include:

- Use of different staff
- Tax services reviewed by an independent tax partner
- External independent advice on tax work
- Tax computations prepared by the audit team are reviewed by a partner or senior staff member who is not a member of the audit team

The audit firm **should not** provide tax services:

- Where the fee for tax work is calculated on a contingent fee basis and the engagement fees are material to the audit firm
- Where the engagement would involve the audit firm undertaking a management role
- Where it would involve acting as an advocate for the client.

Litigation support or legal services

The audit client should not accept such work if relevant matters might have a material impact on financial statements.

Recruitment and remuneration services

The audit firm should not provide a service which would involve the firm taking responsibility for the appointment of any director or employee of the audit client.

For a **listed company** the audit firm should not provide a recruitment service in relation to a key management position.

Corporate finance

This term covers a range of activity but the key threat is that the auditor takes on the role of management. The engagement partner needs to ensure that appropriate safeguards are applied. For example:

- The use of different staff
- Advice is reviewed by an independent corporate finance partner.

There are certain circumstances where the corporate finance work should not be undertaken. These include:

- Where the engagement would involve the audit firm taking responsibility for dealing in, underwriting or promoting shares

- Where the partner doubts the appropriateness of an accounting treatment related to the advice provided

- The corporate finance fee is calculated on a contingent basis and is material to the audit firm.

Transaction related services

Such services should not be accepted if the audit engagement partner has (or ought to) doubt about the appropriateness of accounting treatments used, or there are contingent fees and the matter is material or is dependent on significant judgements in financial statements.

Accounting services

These should not be provided to any listed client or where it would involve the auditor taking management decisions.

Glossary of terms used in the Ethical Standards

Close family	A non-dependent parent, child or sibling
Immediate family	A spouse (or equivalent) or dependent
Person in a position to influence the conduct and outcome of the audit	Any person who is directly involved in the audit including the audit partners, audit managers, audit staff, professional personnel from other disciplines involved in the audit and those who provide quality control or direct oversight of the audit. It also includes any person who forms part of the chain of command for the audit within the firm or any person within the firm who may be in a position to exert influence.

2.9 The professional duty of confidence   12/03

FAST FORWARD

> Auditors have a professional duty of **confidentiality**. However they may be compelled by law or consider it desirable in the **public interest** to disclose details of clients' affairs to third parties.

Information acquired in the course of professional work should not be disclosed except where

- **Consent has been obtained** from the client, employer or other proper source, or
- There is a **public duty** to disclose, or
- There is a **legal** or **professional right or duty** to disclose.

A member acquiring information in the course of professional work should neither use nor appear to use that information for his **personal advantage** or for the **advantage of a third party**.

In general, where there is a right (as opposed to a duty) to disclose information, a member should only make disclosure in pursuit of a public duty or professional obligation.

A member must make clear to a client that he may only act for him if the client agrees to disclose in full to the member all information relevant to the engagement.

Where a member agrees to serve a client in a professional capacity both the member and the client should be aware that it is an **implied term** of that agreement that the **member will not disclose** the client's affairs to any other person save with the client's consent or within the terms of certain recognised exceptions.

RECOGNISED EXCEPTIONS
Obligatory disclosure
If a member knows or suspects his client to have committed **money-laundering**, **treason**, **drug-trafficking** or **terrorist** offences, he is obliged to disclose all the information at his disposal to a competent authority.
Under ISA 250 *Consideration of law and regulations in an audit of financial statements* auditors should consider whether **non-compliance with laws and regulations** affects the accounts. Auditors may have to include in their audit report a statement that non-compliance has led to significant uncertainties, or non-compliance means that the auditors disagree with the way certain items have been treated in the accounts.
Voluntary disclosure
Disclosure is reasonably necessary to **protect** the **member's interests**, for example to enable him to sue for fees or defend an action for, say, negligence.
Disclosure is **compelled** by **process of law**, for example where in an action a member is required to give evidence or discovery of documents.
There is a **public duty** to disclose, say where an offence has been committed which is contrary to the public interest.
Disclosure is to **non-governmental bodies** which have statutory powers to compel disclosure.

If an ACCA member is requested to assist the police, the taxation or other authorities by providing information about a client's affairs in connection with enquiries being made, he should first enquire under what **statutory authority** the information is demanded.

Unless he is satisfied that such statutory authority exists he should decline to give any information until he has obtained his client's authority. If the client's authority is not forthcoming and the demand for information is pressed the member should not accede unless so advised by his solicitor.

If a member knows or suspects that a client has committed a wrongful act he must give careful thought to his own position. He must ensure that he has not prejudiced himself by, for example, relying on information given by the client which subsequently proves to be incorrect.

However, it would be a **criminal offence** for a **member to act positively**, without lawful authority or reasonable excuse, in such a manner as **to impede with intent the arrest** or prosecution **of a client whom he knows or believes to have committed an 'arrestable offence'**.

3 Internal audit ethics

FAST FORWARD

Internal auditors who are members of ACCA are bound by ACCA's professional guidance. **Objectivity** in each situation is a key issue for internal auditors.

It is important to remember that if the internal auditor is a member of ACCA, he is subject to the ACCA's ethical guidance, just as if he was an external auditor.

3.1 ACCA's ethical guidance

An essential feature of the ACCA's ethical guidance is that it applies to members and students of ACCA, regardless of their employment and the nature of the job they do.

Clearly, as can be seen from the analysis in Chapter 4, much of the detail of the guidance relates to external auditors. However, all members of ACCA are bound by the general ethical principles and are **expected to adhere to the spirit of the guidance**.

Therefore an internal auditor who is a member of ACCA must abide by ACCA's ethical guidelines. In particular, the issue of **objectivity** is as important for internal auditors as for external auditors. In order to ensure a professional standard, internal auditors should have care for the matter in hand and no other.

Exam focus point

Remember in exam question that an internal auditor who is a member of ACCA is bound by the guidelines of ACCA. You might also want to refer to ethical guidelines that are more directly applicable to internal audit.

3.1.1 Objectivity and independence

We have discussed various matters which affect the independence of the external auditor from the company, for example, guidance over the level of fees charged, litigation and personal relationships. It is harder to see how an internal auditor can gain 'independence' in his relationship with the company, when it employs him, pays his wages and the people he audits are his colleagues.

A key issue with regard to **objectivity** is organisational status. The internal audit department must have the support of management to enable it to function. The head of internal audit must have direct reporting access to senior management and the audit committee, if relevant.

In terms of personal objectivity, this is a matter for each internal auditor to consider personally. He must seek objectivity in mind. The following matters must be considered.

- Avoiding conflicts of interest
- Freedom from undue influences in the organisation
- No undertaking non-audit duties where possible
- Objectivity when auditing matters he has had responsibility for

3.2 Specific ethical guidance for internal auditors

The Institute of Internal Auditors was introduced in Chapter 4. There are a number of joining requirements, as there are for people seeking to join ACCA. It also issues an ethical code for members.

However, it is important to your to understand that an internal auditor is only bound by the following code of ethics if he is a member or student of the IIA. They are useful for other internal auditors as a **reference point only**.

3.2.1 Ethical guidance of the Institute of Internal Auditors

1	Members shall exercise honesty, objectivity and diligence in the performance of their duties and responsibilities.
2	Members shall exhibit loyalty in all matters pertaining to the affairs of their organisation or to whomever they may be rendering a service. However, members shall not knowingly be a party to any illegal or improper activity.
3	Members shall not knowingly engage in acts or activities which are discreditable to the profession of internal auditing or to their organisation.
4	Members shall refrain from entering any activity which may be in conflict with the interests of their organisation or which would prejudice their ability to carry out objectively their duties and responsibilities.

5	Members shall not accept anything of value from an employee, client, customer, supplier or business associate of their organisation which would impair or be presumed to impair their professional judgement.
6	Members shall undertake only those services which they can reasonably expect to complete with professional competence.
7	Members shall adopt suitable means to comply with the standards for the professional practice of internal auditing.
8	Members shall be prudent in the use of information acquired in the course of their duties. They shall not use confidential information for any personal gain nor in any manner which would be contrary to law or detrimental to the welfare of their organisation.
9	Members, when reporting on the results of their work, shall reveal all material facts known to them which, if not revealed, could either distort reports of operations under review or conceal unlawful practices.
10	Members shall continually strive for improvement in the proficiency, effectiveness and quality of their service.
11	Members, in the practice of their profession, shall be ever mindful of their obligation to maintain the high standards of competence, morality and dignity promulgated by the Institute. Members shall abide by the Articles and uphold the objectives of the Institute.

Exam focus point

> You are studying for a qualification from ACCA, not IIA. You do not have to learn this code of ethics. It is reproduced here to help you to think about the ethics of auditing form the point of view of the internal auditor.

4 Areas of controversy

FAST FORWARD

> Controversial ethical areas include when audit firms offer multiple services, opinion shopping, conflicts of interest and whistleblowing.

4.1 Multiple services

Pilot paper

ACCA Statement

> The provision of non-audit services may, however, create threats to the independence of the firm, a network firm or the member of the assurance team, particularly with respect to perceived threats to independence.

In Chapter 4 we discussed the possibility that the same firm of accountants could provide both internal and external audit services to the same client.

The issue is not restricted to offering internal audit services to external audit clients. Accountancy firms, even small ones, often offer a **wide range of business services**. An audit firm's services portfolio could also include:

- Payroll services
- Asset management/custody
- Preparing financial statements
- Preparing taxation returns
- Valuation services
- Information technology services

- Recruitment assistance
- Tax planning
- Corporate finance services
- Management consultancy

The provision of other services to audit clients is a **highly controversial** issue. As you can see from ACCA's statement above, it recognises that it can cause an auditor's **objectivity** to be **impaired** but issues no hard and fast rules about when providing other services is or is not allowed.

The following problems may be perceived:

- The perception that a company gave its auditors some lucrative consultancy work **in exchange** for a clean audit report.

- The auditors may end up making **management decisions** for the company which would harm their independence

- The auditor undertaking **self-review**, that is auditing his own work.

However the provision of other services may have **advantages** to the audit firm

- Auditors would have more confidence in work prepared by their firm.
- Carrying out accounting and tax work enhances audit staff's expertise.
- Non-audit services may smooth out seasonal audit work.

Clients may find the following benefits associated with having one firm provide all their accountancy-related services:

- They use a single adviser whom they **trust**
- The **overall** cost of all the services is likely to be lower.

The problem with small or sole practitioners auditing very small companies for whom they prepare accounts is probably insurmountable. Some small companies are not required to have an audit, and so for such companies who have dispensed with an audit this problem has been solved. Where accountants still undertake the audit, they must ensure that the **audit** work (as opposed to any accountancy or tax work) is **planned** and **executed**, and perhaps most importantly, properly **recorded**. Also if possible, they might use different staff for the accounts preparation from those carrying out the audit.

Larger audit firms have countered the problem by the use of **separate departments** for each service within the firm (consultancy, audit, taxation and so on).

Another important safeguard is the **engagement letter**, which should separately identify the non-audit services provided, make clear the extent of directors' responsibilities (responsibility for accounting records, ensuring accounts give a true and fair view, taxation matters are disclosed and so on).

Point to note	The engagement letter is discussed further in Section 6.

The response of the profession to the criticisms about the provision of other services to audit clients has been limited. The issue has been firmly placed in the spotlight again in the 21st century, in light of some major corporate failures in the US. The US Stock Exchange regulator has forbidden listed companies to purchase other services from their auditor. It is unlikely that ACCA or the APB would pursue such a measure, preferring a guidelines approach.

Exam focus point	Questions on independence often focus on provision of other services, as this has continued to be a controversial area. This was the case in December 2005, in the context of internal audit services.

PROFESSIONAL EDUCATION

4.2 Opinion shopping

If a company is unhappy with the audit opinion which it receives (or may receive) from its current auditors, then it might approach other audit firms for a second opinion. The problem will be if the current auditors are pressurised into accepting the (more favourable) second opinion.

There are two potential problems inherent in this situation.

- The other firm of auditors may form a negligent opinion because they are not necessarily in possession of all the facts.

- The original auditor may be put under pressure to accept the second opinion, which compromises his independence.

To avoid such a situation there should be constant communication between both sets of auditors. The second firm of auditors has a **professional duty to seek permission** for an approach to the current auditors from the client.

Point to note

> Professional duties on acceptance are discussed in Section 5.

4.3 Conflicts of interest   6/03

In some ways conflict of interest problems are similar to the difficulties firms have in maintaining independence. Conflicts of interest can arise in a variety of circumstances and each problem has to be dealt with on its own merits. There are no rules to deal with most of the situations, outside the Association's rules about independence and integrity, and the solution will usually be based on common sense as much as ethical behaviour.

We have already dealt with conflicts of interest in terms of auditor independence, particularly in situations where there is a financial or personal interest in a client company.

Conflicts of interest can arise when a firm has two (or more) audit clients, both of whom have reason to be unhappy that their auditors are also auditors to the other company. This situation frequently arises when the companies are in **direct competition** with each other, and particularly when the **auditors have access to** particularly **sensitive information**.

These situations are difficult for the auditors: it may involve the loss of a substantial client, even though the staff and engagement partners on each of the audits are different.

Most of these companies have this attitude because of the highly competitive nature of their industry. Others may be sensitive because of the work they do for governments in defence or other controversial areas.

4.3.1 Avoidance of conflicts of interest

In general, where conflicts of interest arise, there should be **full** and **frank explanation** to those involved by the audit firm, coupled with any action necessary to disengage from one or both positions.

Conflicts should, so far as possible, be avoided by **not accepting** any appointment or assignment in which conflict seems likely to occur.

This avoidance of clients causing a conflict of interest is more important for smaller audit firms. The larger firms can overcome a conflict by building a 'Chinese wall' within the firm. This would mean that the respective audits are undertaken by different audit 'groups', the engagement partners are different and all the other audit staff are allowed to work on one of the clients only.

Case Study

An example of very competitive companies which appeared to agree with this type of arrangement was that of **British Airways** and **British Caledonian** (before they merged). Both companies were audited by the same large accountancy firm and yet the airline business is one of the most competitive in the world and confidential information is held at a premium.

It is possible, of course, that some clients might not agree to such an arrangement. The increasing number of mergers which have taken place within the accountancy profession recently have caused conflict of interest problems.

Case Study

British Telecom was not happy when its auditors merged with the firm which audited Cable and Wireless. The new firm was forced to drop one of the audits.

Legal cases such as Prince Jefri of Brunei and KPMG, and in connection with the merger of Robson Rhodes and Parnell Kerr Forster, have also cast doubt on the ability of accountants to rely on Chinese walls.

4.3.2 Safeguards

Whenever accountants are acting for two clients who are in a **directly adversarial** situation, both should be informed and asked to **give consent** for the accountant to continue to act for both.

Other situations, for example clients in competition, might be covered by a paragraph in the **engagement letter.**

If consent has not been given in an adversarial situation, a Chinese wall may be effective providing the departments concerned are **physically separated** and there are **strict procedures** and **monitoring** in place. The Chinese wall needs to be part of the organisational culture of the organisation.

The guidance suggests firms can avoid the need for a Chinese wall in these circumstances by a paragraph in the engagement letter saying that information will be kept confidential except as required by law, regulatory or ethical guidance, and the client permits the firm to take such steps as the firm thinks fit to preserve confidentiality.

It would be better to advise the companies to obtain arbitration from an independent accountant. The auditors should not investigate one client on behalf of another, nor pass on any knowledge of either client in such a situation. This is not always easy, particularly when the auditors can see the whole picture, but the companies cannot. The auditors must be extremely tactful and firm.

Question   Other services

Southern Engineering has undergone a period of substantial growth following its establishment five years ago by two engineers. Because of a lack of accounting expertise within the company it has traditionally looked to its auditors, Smith and Jones, for accounting services in the preparation of annual financial statements as well as for the statutory audit function. Smith and Jones have also provided advice in connection with the company's accounting and internal control systems.

Smith and Jones is a two partner firm of certified accountants whose clients are mainly sole traders, partnerships and small limited companies. Although Southern Engineering was originally a typical small company client, its growth over the last five years has meant that it now accounts for approximately 20% of Smith and Jones' gross fee income and the company has indicated that it may wish to issue shares on the public exchange in the near future.

Required

(a)   Discuss the extent to which it is acceptable and desirable that Smith and Jones have in the past provided the three services of statutory audit, advice in connection with systems, and accountancy services in the preparation of annual financial statements to Southern Engineering.

(b)   Discuss the acceptability and desirability of Smith and Jones continuing to act in the future as auditors to Southern Engineering while continuing to provide the other services.

Answer

(a)   Auditors, especially of small companies, often provide other, non-audit services. The risk arises that, in such cases, the auditor's objectivity may be impaired. This is particularly possible where the auditor is involved in advising the client on systems, as it becomes difficult for the auditor to remain sufficiently detached to comment critically on any weaknesses or shortcomings which appear when systems are implemented. A clear distinction must be drawn between the auditor's advisory capacity – in systems or accountancy work – and the executive responsibility, which is still that of the company's management. Undue involvement with non-audit services must be avoided, lest it detracts from the auditor's essential independence and objectivity.

(b)   The ethical guidance of the accounting bodies recommends that fee income from a single client should not exceed 15% of a practice's total gross fees. As Southern Engineering's fees now represent 20% of fee income (and would, presumably, increase when the company makes a public issue) it seems Smith and Jones have to consider ways of reducing their dependence on this one client. This might well be done by continuing as auditors but ceasing to provide accounting services and systems advice. (In any case, the ethical guidelines suggest that the auditors of a public company should not assist with accountancy save in exceptional circumstances.)

Smith and Jones should keep the situation under review, even after they have moved to a pure audit role, to ensure that they are not again becoming unduly dependent on Southern Engineering as it expands.

Question   Other services (II)

An auditor must ensure that his independence is not being compromised by providing other services to audit clients, and by other actions.

The additional services an auditor may provide include:

(a)   Taxation, preparing the company's corporation tax computation and negotiating with the Inland Revenue; dealing with the tax affairs of the company's directors

(b)   Preparing periodic management accounts of the company, quarterly and annual accounts

(c)   Advising the directors on legal and accounting matters in relation to the company, for example, preparing submissions to the bank to obtain additional finance, advising on changes in share ownership and capital structure of the company and valuation of the company's shares

(d)   Attending meetings of the board of directors

Required

In relation to a private company, of which you are auditor, consider:

(i)   The benefits which may arise to the auditor and client in providing *each* of the above services

(ii)   The extent to which providing *each* of these services may compromise your independence, and the action you would take to minimise the risk to your independence of providing these services

Answer

In all cases, the auditor will of course enjoy income additional to the audit fee. The client will probably benefit from a saving in using the same professional for all these types of work, because information gained on one assignment can be used on others, and the client will not be paying for the learning time of a new advisor. The client's staff and management should also save time, as they should not need to explain the business repeatedly to different people. (It has to be admitted, however, that changes in audit and other staff do often result in the client's needing to explain the same point in successive years.) The following individual comments may be made.

(a)   *Taxation.* It is customary for the company's taxation liability to be at least checked, and often computed, as part of routine audit work. It is unlikely that independence would be impaired by this, or by routine correspondence with the Inland Revenue. Similarly, it is normal for an auditor to deal with directors' tax affairs. A problem would, however, arise here if there were any dispute between the company and its directors, as the auditor would suffer a conflict of interests and would probably be best advised to relinquish either the audit or the tax advisory role.

(b)   *Accounts preparation.* This clearly gives the auditor a very good opportunity to keep in touch with the company's performance during the year and to take note of any possible audit problems as soon as they arise. There is, however, a risk that the auditor will not be as detached in carrying out the audit of accounts he or she has prepared as would be the case if the client had produced the accounts.

(c)   *Advice to directors.* Clearly, the auditor will be able to draw on knowledge of the company in giving advice. There is a significant risk, however, that independence will be compromised, particularly if the advice turns out to have been mistaken. If the auditor has prepared a profit forecast for submission to the bank which subsequently proves over-optimistic, he or she may find it difficult to require the client to reflect the actual result in the year end accounts.

(d)   *Board meetings.* There is a risk here that the auditor may completely forfeit independence by becoming too closely involved in the running of the company. The Companies Act regards as a director anyone who carries out the functions of a director, and an auditor would be exposed to this presumption if he or she attended meetings regularly. It would therefore be advisable for the auditor to attend only the board meetings at which the annual accounts are approved by the board.

4.4 Whistleblowing

In the UK, the Public Interest Disclosure Act 1998 gives protection to 'workers' who make qualifying disclosures (they whistleblow).

Key term

A **qualifying disclosure** is 'any disclosure of information which, in the reasonable belief of the worker making the disclosure, tends to show one or more of the following:

(a)   That a criminal offence has been committed, is being committed or is likely to be committed

(b)   That a person has failed, is failing or is likely to fail to comply with any legal obligation to which he is subject

(c)   That a miscarriage of justice has occurred, is occurring or is likely to occur

(d)   That the health or safety of any individual has been, is being or is likely to be endangered

(e)   That the environment has been, is being or is likely to be damaged

(f)   That information tending to show any matter falling within any one of the preceding paragraphs has been, is being or is likely to be deliberately concealed.'

Whistleblowing is potentially a tricky ethical area for internal auditors for the following reasons.

- They are in a position to access knowledge they might feel necessitated a public disclosure themselves
- They may be given information by a whistleblower, or be in a position to be a point of contact for concerned employees

The internal auditor must be prepared to deal with any case individually, but should, as general policy, facilitate lines of communication within the company so as to restrict the need to whistleblow externally.

Exam focus point

Ethics is a key topic area. It is likely to be examined regularly.

5 Accepting appointment

FAST FORWARD

Auditors have guidance from ACCA on advertising and obtaining professional work.

5.1 Tendering and obtaining work

Members are entitled to advertise their services and products. The advertising medium should not reflect adversely on the member, ACCA or the accountancy profession. Adverts should not:

- Bring ACCA into disrepute or bring discredit to the member, firm or accountancy profession
- Discredit the services of others
- Be misleading
- Fall short of local regulatory or legislative requirements

5.1.1 Fee negotiation and lowballing

The audit fee is a sensitive subject for most companies. It represents a cost for something the company often does not really want and the fees may be perceived as too high just for this reason. The auditors must ensure that they can provide a quality audit for the price.

Many large companies invite **tenders** for their audit work. The directors then have the opportunity to compare directly a range of offers.

Generally, a tender will take the form of detailed written proposals and a presentation. Factors include:

- The **level** of **expertise** each firm has in the industry
- **Similar companies** audited by each firm (good for expertise, bad for confidentiality?)
- **National** and **international presence**
- The proposed fee

Audit firms which tender for such audits will usually give at least an indication of the level of fees in the next few years, including likely overall rate rises. Fee levels are very important to most companies, and are often the determining factor.

In all situations, the auditors should quote a fee based on the estimated hours worked by each member of staff required on the audit, multiplied by the hourly rate plus any travel as other expenses to be incurred during the audit. They may also charge a premium for more complex audits.

Sometimes it appears that firms are charging less than 'market rate' for an audit, especially when tendering for new clients. This practice is known as **lowballing**.

It is not considered ethically wrong to charge a low price for an audit in itself. However, the auditors must ensure that they carry out an audit of the quality demanded by auditing standards and must ensure that the 'cut-price' audit fee does not call their independence into question.

This is always going to be a topical debate, but in terms of negotiating the audit fee the following factors need to be taken into account.

(a) The audit is perceived to have a **fluctuating 'market price'** as any other commodity or service.

(b) Companies can reduce external audit costs through various **legitimate measures:**

- Extending the size and function of internal audit
- Reducing the number of different audit firms used world-wide
- Selling off subsidiary companies leaving a simplified group structure to audit
- The tender process itself simply makes auditors more competitive
- Exchange rate fluctuations in audit fees

(c) Auditing firms have **increased productivity**, partly through the use of more sophisticated information technology techniques in auditing.

In any case, an auditing firm lays itself open to accusations of loss of independence if it reduces its fees to below a certain level, particularly if it is difficult to see how such fees will cover direct labour costs. This is also true of firms which use the audit as a 'loss leader' to obtain profitable consultancy work from audit clients.

When such non-audit services are offered to a client by the auditors, there can, of course, be an apparent loss of independence. The allegation may arise that the price of an 'acceptable' audit opinion is lucrative taxation or consulting work.

5.2 Appointment ethics

FAST FORWARD The **present** and **proposed auditors** must **communicate** about the client prior to the audit being accepted.

This section covers the procedures that the **auditors must** undertake to **ensure that their appointment is valid** and that they are clear to act.

5.2.1 Before accepting nomination

FAST FORWARD The client must be asked to give permission for communication to occur. If the client **refuses** to give **permission,** the proposed auditors must **decline nomination.**

Before a new audit client is accepted, the auditors must ensure that there are no **independence** or **other ethical problems** likely to cause conflict with the ethical code. Furthermore, new auditors should ensure that they have been appointed in a proper and legal manner.

The nominee auditors must carry out the following procedures:

ACCEPTANCE PROCEDURES	
Ensure **professionally qualified** to act	Consider whether disqualified on legal or ethical grounds
Ensure **existing resources adequate**	Consider available time, staff and technical expertise
Obtain references	Make independent enquiries if directors not personally known.
Communicate with present auditors	Enquire whether there are reasons/circumstances behind the change which the new auditors ought to know, also courtesy. See flowchart over page for process

5.2.2 Example letters

This is an example of a initial communication.

> To: Retiring & Co
>   Certified Accountants
>
> Dear Sirs
>
> Re: New Client Co Ltd
>
> We have been asked to allow our name to go forward for nomination as auditors of the above company, and we should therefore be grateful if you would please let us know whether there are any professional reasons why we should not accept nomination ....
>
> Acquiring & Co
>
> Certified Accountants

Having negotiated these steps the auditors will be in a position to accept the nomination, or not, as the case may be. These procedures can be demonstrated most easily in a decision chart, as shown on the next page.

5.2.3 Procedures after accepting nomination

The following procedures should be carried out after accepting nomination.

(a)   **Ensure** that the **outgoing auditors' removal** or **resignation** has been **properly conducted** in accordance with national legislation.

The new auditors should see a valid notice of the outgoing auditors' resignation, or confirm that the outgoing auditors were properly removed.

(b)   **Ensure** that the **new auditors' appointment is valid**. The new auditors should obtain a copy of the resolution passed at the general meeting appointing them as the company's auditors.

(c)   Set up and **submit a letter of engagement** to the directors of the company.

Point to note

> Letters of engagement are discussed in Section 6 of this chapter.

5.2.4 Other matters

Where the previous auditors have fees still owing by the client, the new auditors need not decline appointment solely for this reason. They should decide how far they may go in aiding the former auditors to obtain their fees, as well as whether they should accept the appointment.

Once a new appointment has taken place, the **new auditors should obtain all books and papers which belong to the client from the old auditors**. The former accountants should ensure that all such documents are transferred, **unless** they have a lien (a legal right to hold on to them) over the books because of unpaid fees. The old auditors should also pass any useful information to the new auditors if it will be of help, without charge, unless a lot of work is involved.

Appointment decision chart

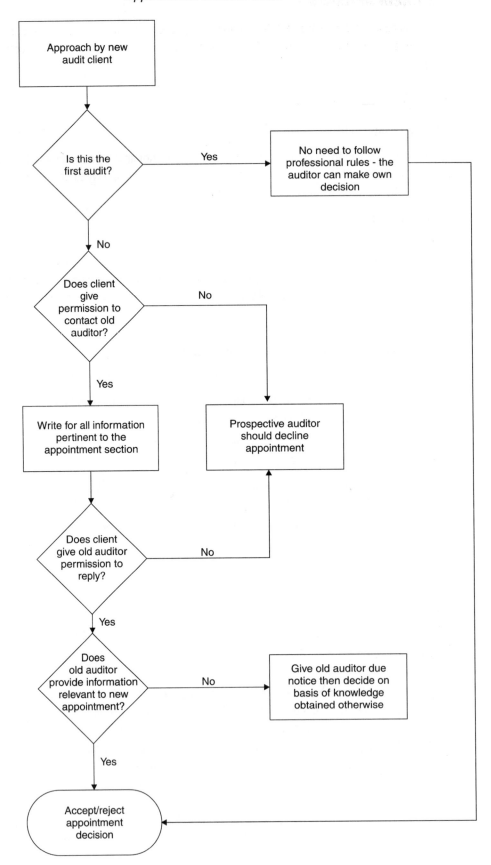

5.3 Client screening

As well as contacting previous auditors many firms, particularly larger firms, carry out **stringent checks** on potential client companies and their management. Some of the basic factors for consideration are given below.

5.3.1 Management integrity

The integrity of those managing a company will be of great importance, particularly if the company is controlled by one or a few dominant personalities.

5.3.2 Risk

The following table contrasts low and high risk clients.

LOW RISK	HIGH RISK
Good long-term prospects	Poor recent or forecast performance
Well-financed	Likely lack of finance
Strong internal controls	Significant control weaknesses
Conservative, prudent accounting policies	Evidence of questionable integrity, doubtful accounting policies
Competent, honest management	Lack of finance director
Few unusual transactions	Significant related party or unexplained transactions

Where the risk level of a company's audit is determined as anything other than low, then the specific risks should be identified and documented. It might be necessary to assign specialists in response to these risks, particularly industry specialists, as independent reviewers. Some audit firms have procedures for closely monitoring audits which have been accepted, but which are considered high risk.

5.3.3 Engagement economics

Generally, the expected fees from a new client should reflect the **level of risk** expected. They should also offer the same sort of return expected of clients of this nature and reflect the overall financial strategy of the audit firm. Occasionally, the audit firm will want the work to gain entry into the client's particular industry, or to establish better contacts within that industry. These factors will all contribute to a total expected economic return.

5.3.4 Relationship

The audit firm will generally want the relationship with a client to be **long term**. This is not only to enjoy receiving fees year after year; it is also to allow the audit work to be enhanced by better knowledge of the client and thereby offer a better service.

Conflict of interest problems are significant here; the firm should establish that no existing clients will cause difficulties as competitors of the new client. Other services to other clients may have an impact here, not just audit.

5.3.5 Ability to perform the work

The audit firm must have the **resources** to perform the work properly, as well as any **specialist knowledge or skills**. The impact on existing engagements must be estimated, in terms of staff time and the timing of the audit.

SOURCES OF INFORMATION ABOUT NEW CLIENTS	
Enquiries of other sources	Bankers, solicitors
Review of **documents**	Most recent annual accounts, listing particulars, credit rating
Previous accountants/auditors	Previous auditors should disclose fully all relevant information
Review of **rules and standards**	Consider specific laws/standards that relate to industry

5.4 Approval

Once all the relevant procedures and information gathering has taken place, the company can be put forward for approval. The engagement partner will have completed a client acceptance form and this, along with any other relevant documentation, will be submitted to the managing partner, or whichever partner is in overall charge of accepting clients.

Exam focus point

> In the exam you may be given a 'real-life' client situation and asked what factors you would consider in deciding whether to accept appointment.

6 Engagement letters

FAST FORWARD An engagement letter should be sent to all clients.

6.1 Audit engagement letters

An engagement letter should:

- Define clearly the **extent** of the **auditors' responsibilities** and so minimise the possibility of any misunderstanding between the client and the auditors

- Provide **written confirmation** of the **auditors' acceptance** of the appointment, the scope of the audit, the form of their report and the scope of any non-audit services

If an engagement letter is not sent to clients, both new and existing, there is scope for argument about the precise extent of the respective obligations of the client and its directors and the auditors. The contents of an engagement letter should be discussed and agreed with management before it is sent.

Guidance is available in the form of ISA 210 (UK and Ireland) *Terms of audit engagements*, which states 'the auditor and the client should agree on the terms of the engagement'. The agreed terms must be in writing and the usual form would be a **letter of engagement**. Any other form of appropriate contract, however, may be used.

The ISA makes this further comment about the client/auditor agreement.

- Even in countries where the audit objectives and scope and the auditor's obligations are established by law, an **audit engagement letter** may be informative for clients.

The auditors should send an engagement letter to all new clients soon after **their appointment** as auditors and, in any event, before the commencement of the first audit assignment. They should also consider sending an engagement letter to existing clients to whom no letter has previously been sent as soon as a suitable opportunity presents itself.

The engagement letter must document and confirm the auditor's acceptance of the appointment, and include a summary of the responsibilities of those charged with governance and the auditor, the scope of the audit and the form of any reports. The form and remaining content of audit engagement letters may vary for each client, but they would generally include reference to the following.

BPP
PROFESSIONAL EDUCATION

(a)   The **objective** of the **audit** of financial statements

(b)   **Management's responsibility** for the financial statements

(c)   The applicable reporting framework

(d)   The **scope** of the audit, including reference to applicable legislation, regulations, or pronouncements of professional bodies to which the auditor adheres

(e)   The fact that because of the **test nature** and other **inherent limitations** of an audit, together with the inherent limitations of any accounting and internal control system, there is an unavoidable risk that even some material misstatement may remain undiscovered

(f)   **Unrestricted access** to whatever records, documentation and other information requested in connection with the audit

(g)   The confidentiality of any reports issued, and, if relevant, the terms under which they can be shared with third parties.

The auditor may wish to include in the letter the following items.

- Arrangements regarding the **planning** of the audit

- Expectation of receiving from management **written confirmation** of **representations** made in connection with the audit

- Request for the client to **confirm the terms** of the engagement by acknowledging receipt of the engagement letter

- Description of any **other letters or reports** the auditor expects to issue to the client

- Basis on which **fees** are computed and any billing arrangements

When relevant, the following points could also be made.

- Arrangements concerning the involvement of **other auditors** and **experts** in some aspects of the audit

- Arrangements concerning the involvement of **internal auditors** and other client staff

- Arrangements to be made with the **predecessor auditor**, if any, in the case of an initial audit

- Any **restriction of the auditor's liability** when such possibility exists

- A reference to any **further agreements** between the auditor and the client

6.2 Recurring audits

Once it has been agreed by the client, an engagement letter will, if it so provides, remain effective from one audit appointment to another until it is replaced. However, the engagement letter should be **reviewed annually** to ensure that it continues to reflect the client's circumstances.

The ISA suggests that the following factors may make the agreement of a new letter appropriate.

- Any indication that the client **misunderstands** the objective and scope of the audit
- Any **revised** or **special terms** of the engagement
- A recent **change of senior management**, board of directors or ownership committee
- A **significant change** in the **nature or size** of the client's business
- **Legal requirements**

6.3 Acceptance of a change in engagement

In the case of a change in the terms of engagement prior to completion, this may result from:

(a)   A **change in circumstances** affecting the need for the service

(b)   A **misunderstanding** as to the nature of an audit or of the related service originally
        requested

(c)   A **restriction on the scope** of the engagement, whether imposed by management or caused
        by circumstances

The auditors should consider such a request for change, and the reason for it, very seriously, particularly
in terms of any restriction in the scope of the engagement.

In the case of (a) and (b) above, these would normally be acceptable reasons for requesting a change in
the engagement. A change would not be considered reasonable, however, if it seemed to relate to
information that is incorrect, incomplete or otherwise unsatisfactory.

In addition to the above, an auditor engaged to perform an audit in accordance with ISAs must consider
any legal or **contractual implications** of **the change**.

The audit report issued after such a change has been agreed (and the relevant audit work carried out)
should be appropriate to the revised terms of engagement. Such an audit report should *not* include
reference to:

•   The original engagement
•   Any procedures performed under the original engagement

The standard gives an example of where an auditor should **not** agree to a change of engagement; where
the auditor is unable to obtain sufficient appropriate audit evidence regarding receivables and the client
asks for the engagement to be changed to a review engagement to avoid a qualified audit opinion or a
disclaimer of opinion.

Question   New auditors

You are a partner in Messrs Borg Connors & Co, Certified Accountants. You are approached by Mr
Nastase, the managing director of Navratilova Enterprises Ltd, who asks your firm to become auditors of
his company. In return for giving you this appointment Mr Nastase says that he will expect your firm to
waive fifty per cent of your normal fee for the first year's audit. The existing auditors, Messrs Wade Austin
& Co have not resigned but Mr Nastase informs you that they will not be re-appointed in the future.

Required

(a)   What action should Messrs Borg Connors & Co take in response to the request from Mr Nastase to
        reduce their first year's fee by fifty per cent?

(b)   Are Messrs Wade Austin & Co within their rights in not resigning when they know Mr Nastase
        wishes to replace them? Give reasons for your answer.

Answer

(a)   The request by Mr Nastase that half of the first year's audit fee should be waived is quite improper.
        If this proposal were to be accepted it could be held that Borg Connors & Co had sought to procure
        work through the quoting of lower fees. This would be unethical and would result in disciplinary
        proceedings being taken against the firm.

        It should be pointed out to Mr Nastase that the audit fee will be determined, in accordance with
        normal practice, by reference to the work involved in completion of a satisfactory audit taking into
        consideration the nature of the audit tasks involved and the level of staff required to carry out those
        tasks in an efficient manner. Mr Nastase should further be informed that if he is not prepared to
        accept an audit fee arrived at in this way and insists on there being a reduction then regrettably the
        nomination to act as auditor will have to be declined.

(b) Wade Austin & Co have every right not to resign even though they may be aware that Mr Nastase, the managing director of the company, wishes to replace them. The auditors of a company are appointed by, and report to, the members of a company and the directors are not empowered, as directors, to remove the auditors.

If the reason for the proposed change arises out of a dispute between management and the auditors then the auditors have a right to put forward their views as seen above and to insist that any decision should be made by the members, but only once they have been made aware of all pertinent facts concerning the directors' wishes to have them removed from office as auditors.

Chapter Roundup

- The auditors' **duty of care** has been defined by case law over time.

- **Independence** and objectivity are the most important characteristics of auditors.

- Auditors have a professional duty of **confidentiality**. However they may be compelled by law or consider it desirable in the **public interest** to disclose details of clients' affairs to third parties.

- Internal auditors who are members of ACCA are bound by ACCA's professional guidance. **Objectivity** in each situation is a key issue for internal auditors.

- Controversial ethical areas include when audit firms offer multiple services, opinion shopping, conflicts of interest and whistleblowing.

- Auditors have guidance from ACCA on advertising and obtaining professional work.

- The **present** and **proposed auditors** must **communicate** about the client prior to the audit being accepted.

- The client must be asked to give permission for communication to occur. If the client **refuses** to give **permission,** the proposed auditors must **decline nomination.**

- An engagement letter should be sent to all clients.

Quick Quiz

1   Match each ethical principle.

(a) Integrity
(b) Objectivity
(c) Professional competence and due care
(d) Confidentiality
(e) Professional behaviour

(i) Not allow bias, conflicts of interest or undue influence of others to override professional or business judgements.

(ii) Have a continuing duty to maintain professional knowledge and skill at a level required to ensure that a client or employer receives competent professional service based on current developments in practice, legislation and techniques. Members should act diligently and in accordance with applicable technical and professional standards when providing professional services.

(iii) Be straightforward and honest in all business and professional relationships.

(iv) Comply with relevant laws and regulations and should avoid any action that discredits the profession.

(v)   Respect the confidentiality of information acquired as a result of professional and business relationships and should not disclose any such information to third parties without proper or specific authority or unless there is a legal or professional right or duty to disclose. Confidential information acquired as a result of professional and business relationships should not be used for the personal advantage of members or third parties.

2   ACCA Code of Ethics and Conduct applies only to statutory audits.

True   ☐

False   ☐

3   Fill in the blanks.

In general, the recurring work paid by the client or group of connected clients should not exceed ....% of the gross practice income.

In the case of .... or other .... companies, the figure should be .... % of gross practice income.

4   Using the factors given, complete the table.

(a)   Forms an independent liaison between board and auditors
(b)   Leads to increased confidence in creditability and objectivity of reporting
(c)   Formalised reporting procedure may dissuade auditors from raising matters of judgement
(d)   Impartial body for auditors to consult in the event of conflicts of interest
(e)   Difficulty in selecting sufficient non-executive directors with the necessary competence

Advantages of an audit committee	Disadvantages of an audit committee

5   (a)   Which of the following are legitimate reasons for breach of client confidentiality?

(i)   Auditor **suspects** client has committed treason
(ii)   Disclosure **needed** to protect auditor's own interests
(iii)   Information is **required** for the auditor of another client
(iv)   Auditor **knows** client has committed terrorist offence
(v)   There is a **public duty** to disclose
(vi)   Auditor **considers** there to be non-compliance with law and regulations
(vii)   Auditor **suspects** client has committed fraud

(b)   Of the above reasons, which are voluntary disclosures and which are obligatory disclosures.

6   Complete the questions that should be in the diagram which is given on the next page.

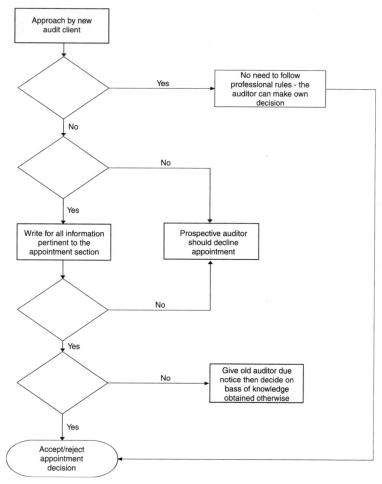

7   An engagement letter is only ever sent to a client before the first audit.

True   ☐

False   ☐

Answers to Quick Quiz

1   (a)   (iii)
     (b)   (i)
     (c)   (ii)
     (d)   (v)
     (e)   (iv)

2   False. 'The spirit of the guidance applies equally to other audit situations.'

3   15, listed, pubic interest, 10

4	Advantages of an audit committee	Disadvantages of an audit committee
	(a), (b), (d)	(c), (e)

5   (i)   O
     (ii)   V
     (iv)   O
     (v)   V
     (vi)   O

     (*NB*. In the case of (vii), the auditor should not take action outside the company until he is certain. When he is certain, he should seek legal advice.)

6   •   Is this the first audit?
     •   Does the client give permission to contact the old auditor?
     •   Does client give old auditor permission to reply?
     •   Does old auditor provide information relevant to new appointment?

7   False. It should be re-issued if there is a change in circumstances.

Now try the question below from the Exam Question Bank

Number	Level	Marks	Time
Q5	Examination	20	36 mins

Part B
Planning

Evidence, sampling and documentation

Topic list	Syllabus reference
1 Audit evidence	6
2 Audit sampling	6
3 Audit documents	4

Introduction

Before an auditor can even start putting together a strategy for the audit, he must be aware what kind of **evidence** he will be looking for. In this chapter, we introduce some fundamental auditing concepts of audit evidence and audit sampling.

We also introduce the **financial statement assertions**. These will be particularly important when we consider detailed testing, since audit tests are designed to obtain **sufficient, appropriate evidence** about the assertions for each balance or transaction in financial statements. Detailed testing may involve **substantive testing** and/or **tests of controls**. Both types of test will be introduced in this chapter, and the manner in which they are carried out will be explored.

Whatever type of test is chosen, the auditors need to decide **how they will select the items to be tested** from the whole population. The auditors will want to **select a sample** which reflects, as closely as possible, the characteristics of the population from which the sample has been selected. We will explain **practical aspects of sampling.** Sampling theory is closely associated with the definition of **audit risk** which we shall look at in detail in the next chapter.

Lastly in this chapter we shall look at **how** auditors **document** their work.

Study guide

10 – The work plan, the work program and documentation

- Describe and illustrate the contents of work plans, work programs and working papers
- Describe the nature of documentation required for different types of assignment
- Explain the importance of documentation
- Illustrate the use of information technology in the audit

12 – Internal control I

- Distinguish between tests of controls and substantive tests

17 – Other audit and review evidence I

- Describe the sources and relative merits of different types of evidence available
- Describe the financial statement assertions commonly reported on the principles and objectives of balance and transaction testing
- Distinguish between the interim and the final audit
- Describe the types of evidence available in smaller entities
- Evaluate the quality of evidence collected

23 – Other audit and review evidence VII

- Explain the need for sampling
- Distinguish between statistical and non-statistical sampling
- Describe and illustrate the application of the basic principles of statistical sampling and other selective testing procedures
- Describe and illustrate the use of computer assisted techniques in obtaining evidence (Note: candidates will not be required to perform detailed sampling calculations)

Exam guide

The issues of sampling and evidence will underpin questions about detailed testing which we shall look at in Parts C and D. In addition, you could be asked a question on the theory of evidence or sampling. Sampling was the topic of a question in June 2003.

1 Audit evidence   12/02, 6/05

FAST FORWARD

Auditors must obtain **sufficient, appropriate** audit evidence.

1.1 Sufficient appropriate audit evidence

Remember

> The objective of an audit of financial statements is to enable the auditor to express an opinion whether the financial statements are prepared, in all material respects, in accordance with an identified financial reporting framework.

In this section, we shall look at the **audit evidence** he has gathered, which **enables** the auditor to express an opinion on financial statements.

PROFESSIONAL EDUCATION

Key term

> **Audit evidence** is the information auditors obtain in arriving at the conclusions on which their report is based.

Audit evidence includes all the information contained within the accounting records underlying the financial statements, and other information gathered by the auditors, such as confirmations from third parties. Auditors are **not expected to look at all the information** that might exist. They will often select samples, as we shall see in Section 2.

FAST FORWARD ▶

Evidence can be in the form of **tests of control** or **substantive procedures.**

In order to reach a position in which they can express a professional opinion, the auditors need to gather evidence from various sources. There are two types of test which they will carry out.

Key terms

> **Tests of controls** are performed to obtain audit evidence about the effectiveness of the:
>
> - Design of the accounting and internal control systems, ie whether they are suitably designed to prevent or detect and correct material misstatements; and
>
> - Operation of the internal controls throughout the period.
>
> **Substantive procedures** are tests to obtain audit evidence to detect material misstatements in the financial statements. They are generally of two types:
>
> - Analytical procedures
>
> - Other substantive procedures such as tests of detail of transactions and balances, review of minutes of directors' meetings and enquiry.

ISA (UK and Ireland) 500 *Audit evidence* requires auditors to 'obtain **sufficient appropriate** audit evidence to be able to draw **reasonable conclusions** on which to base the audit opinion'. 'Sufficiency' and 'appropriateness' are interrelated and apply to both tests of controls and substantive procedures.

- **Sufficiency** is the measure of the **quantity** of audit evidence.
- **Appropriateness** is the measure of the **quality** or **reliability** of the audit evidence.

FAST FORWARD ▶

The **reliability** of audit evidence is influenced by its **source** and by its **nature.**

The **quantity** of audit evidence required is affected by the **level of risk** in the area being audited. We shall look at this in the next chapter. It is also affected by the **quality** of evidence obtained. If the evidence is high quality, the auditor may need less than if it were poor quality. However, obtaining a high quantity of poor quality evidence will not cancel out its poor quality. The following generalisations may help in assessing the **reliability** of audit evidence.

QUALITY OF EVIDENCE	
External	Audit evidence from **external sources** is more reliable than that obtained from the entity's records.
Auditor	Evidence obtained **directly by auditors** is more reliable than that obtained indirectly or by inference
Entity	Evidence obtained from the entity's records is more reliable when related **control system operates effectively**
Written	Evidence in the form of **documents (paper or electronic)** or **written representations** are more reliable than oral representations
Originals	Original documents are more realistic than photocopies, or facsimiles

Auditors will often use information produced by the entity when obtaining audit evidence, although this will not always be a strong form of audit evidence. When doing so, the ISA requires that the auditor 'obtain audit evidence about the **accuracy and completeness** of the information'. This may be achieved by testing controls in the related area, or by other methods, for example, computer assisted audit techniques (see below).

Exam focus point

> You may be asked to consider how strong certain evidence is from the auditor's viewpoint, for example trade debtors circularisation or third party valuation of assets.

1.2 Financial statement assertions

FAST FORWARD ⟩⟩

> Audit tests are designed to obtain evidence about the financial statement assertions.

Key terms

> **Financial statement assertions** are the representations of the directors that are embodied in the financial statements. By approving the financial statements, the directors are making representations about the information therein. These representations or assertions may be described in general terms in a number of ways.

ISA 500 states that 'the auditor should use assertions for **classes of transactions**, **account balances**, and **presentation and disclosures** in sufficient detail to form the basis for the assessment of risks of material misstatement and the design and performance of further audit procedures'. It gives examples of assertions in these areas.

Assertions used by the auditor	
Assertions about **classes of transactions** and events for the period under audit	**Occurrence**: transactions and events that have been recorded have occurred and pertain to the entity.
	Completeness: all transactions and events that should have been recorded have been recorded.
	Accuracy: amounts and other data relating to recorded transactions and events have been recorded appropriately.
	Cutoff: transactions and events have been recorded in the correct accounting period (see measurement, above).
	Classification: transactions and events have been recorded in the proper accounts.
Assertions about **account balances** at the period end	**Existence**: assets, liabilities and equity interests exist.
	Rights and obligations: the entity holds or controls the rights to assets, and liabilities are the obligations of the entity.
	Completeness: all assets, liabilities and equity interests that should have been recorded have been recorded.
	Valuation and allocation: assets, liabilities, and equity interests are included in the financial statements at appropriate amounts and any resulting valuation or allocation adjustments are appropriately recorded.
Assertions about **presentation and disclosure**	**Occurrence and rights and obligations**: disclosed events, transactions and other matters have occurred and pertain to the entity.
	Completeness: all disclosures that should have been included in the financial statements have been included.
	Classification and understandability: financial information is appropriately presented and described, and disclosures are clearly expressed.
	Accuracy and valuation: financial and other information are disclosed fairly and at appropriate amounts.

You may find the following mnemonic useful when trying to remember the financial statement assertions: ACCA COVER.

Accuracy
Completeness
Cut-off
Allocation
Classification/understandability
Occurrence
Valuation
Existence
Rights and Obligations

(Each letter of ACCA COVER is the first letter of each of the assertions listed above).

Exam focus point	When designing audit plans for specific areas, you should focus on the financial statement assertions.

1.3 Audit procedures   6/05

FAST FORWARD

Audit evidence can be obtained by inspection, observation, inquiry and confirmation, computation and analytical procedures.

Auditors obtain evidence by one or more of the following procedures.

PROCEDURES	
Inspection of assets	Inspection of assets that are recorded in the accounting records confirms existence, gives evidence of valuation, but does not confirm rights and obligations.
	Confirmation that assets seen are recorded in accounting records gives evidence of completeness.
Inspection of documentation	Confirmation to documentation of items recorded in accounting records confirms that an asset exists or a transaction occurred. Confirmation that items recorded in supporting documentation are recorded in accounting records tests completeness.
	Cut-off can be verified by inspecting reverse population ie checking transactions recorded after the balance sheet date to supporting documentation to confirm that they occurred after the balance sheet date.
	Inspection also provides evidence of valuation/measurement, rights and obligations and the nature of items (presentation and disclosure). It can also be used to compare documents (and hence test consistency of audit evidence) and confirm authorisation.
Observation	This involves watching a procedure being performed (for example, post opening).
	It is of limited use, as only confirms procedure took place when the auditor was watching.
Inquiry	This involves seeking information from client staff or external sources.
	Strength of evidence depends on the knowledge and integrity of source of information.
Confirmation	This involves seeking confirmation from another source of details in client's accounting records eg, confirmation from bank of bank balances.
Recalculation	Checking arithmetic of client's records for example, adding up ledger account.
Reperformance	Independently executing procedures or controls, either manually or through the use of CAATs (see below).
Analytical procedures	Evaluating and comparing financial and/or non-financial data for plausible relationships (see Chapter 12).

Question   Audit evidence

(a)   Discuss the quality of the following types of audit evidence, giving two examples of each form of evidence.

     (i)   Evidence originated by the auditors

     (ii)   Evidence created by third parties

     (iii)   Evidence created by the management of the client

(b)   Describe the general considerations which the auditors must bear in mind when evaluating audit evidence.

Answer

(a)   **Quality of audit evidence**

     (i)   *Evidence originated by the auditors*

         Evidence originated by the auditors is in general the most reliable type of audit evidence because there is little risk that it can be manipulated by management.

         Examples

         (1)   Analytical procedures, such as the calculation of ratios and trends in order to examine unusual variations

         (2)   Physical inspection or observation, such as attendance at physical stock counts or inspection of a fixed asset

         (3)   Re-performance of calculations making up figures in the accounts, such as the computation of total stock values

     (ii)   *Evidence created by third parties*

         Third party evidence is more reliable than client-produced evidence to the extent that it is obtained from sources independent of the client. Its reliability will be reduced if it is obtained from sources which are not independent, or if there is a risk that client personnel may be able to and have reason to suppress or manipulate it. This, for instance, is an argument against having replies to circularisations sent to the client instead of the auditors.

         Examples

         (1)   Circularisation of trade debtors or creditors and other requests from the auditors for confirming evidence, such as requests for confirmation of bank balances.

         (2)   Reports produced by experts, such as property valuations, actuarial valuations, legal opinions. In evaluating such evidence, the auditors need to take into account the qualifications of the expert, his or her independence of the client and the terms of reference under which the work was carried out.

         (3)   Documents held by the client which were issued by third parties, such as invoices, price lists and statements. These may sometimes be manipulated by the client, to the extent that items may be suppressed or altered, and to this extent they are less reliable than confirmations received direct.

     (iii)   *Evidence created by management*

         The auditors cannot place the same degree of reliance on evidence produced by client management as on that produced outside the client organisation. However, it will often be necessary to place some reliance on the client's evidence. The auditors will need to obtain audit evidence that the information supplied is complete and accurate, and apply judgement in doing so, taking into account previous experience of the client's reliability and the extent to which the client's representations appear compatible with other audit findings, as well as the materiality of the item under discussion.

Examples

(1) The company's accounting records and supporting schedules. Although these are prepared by management, the auditors have a statutory right to examine such records in full: this right enhances the quality of this information.

(2) The client's explanations of, for instance, apparently unusual fluctuations in results. Such evidence requires interpretation by the auditors and, being oral evidence, only limited reliance can be placed upon it.

(3) Information provided to the auditors about the internal control system. The auditors need to check that this information is accurate and up-to-date, and that it does not simply describe an idealised system which is not adhered to in practice.

(b) **General considerations in evaluating audit evidence**

Audit evidence will often not be wholly conclusive. The auditors must obtain evidence which is **sufficient and appropriate** to form the basis for their audit conclusions. The evidence gathered should also be **relevant** to those conclusions, and sufficiently **reliable** ultimately to form the basis for the audit opinion. The auditors must exercise skill and judgement to ensure that evidence is correctly interpreted and that only valid inferences are drawn from it.

Certain general principles can be stated. **Written evidence** is preferable to oral evidence; **independent evidence** obtained from outside the organisation is more reliable than that obtained internally; and that **evidence generated by the auditors** is more reliable than that obtained from others.

1.4 Computer assisted audit techniques

Exam focus point

> Use of computers on audits is now common practice. The examiner expects you to consider the computer aspects of auditing as a matter of course. Therefore in answering questions on obtaining evidence, remember to include reference to CAATs if they seem relevant. In December 2005, CAATs were also examined as a specific topic.

The overall objectives and scope of an audit do not change when an audit is conducted in a computerised environment. However, the application of auditing procedures may require auditors to consider techniques that use the computer as an audit tool. These uses of the computer for audit work are known as computer assisted audit techniques **(CAATs).**

(a) The absence of input documents or the lack of a visible audit trail may require the use of CAATs in the application of tests of control and substantive procedures.

(b) The effectiveness and efficiency of auditing procedures may be improved through the use of CAATs.

CAATs may be used in performing various auditing procedures, including the following.

- **Tests of details of transactions and balances**, for example the use of audit software to test all (or a sample) of the transactions in a computer file

- **Analytical review procedures**, for example the use of audit software to identify unusual fluctuations or items

- **Tests of computer information system controls**, for example the use of test data to test access procedures to the program libraries, or the functioning of a programmed procedure

The advantages of using CAATs are:

- Auditors can test programme controls as well as general internal controls associated with computers.

- Auditors can test a greater number of items more quickly and accurately than would be the case otherwise

- Auditors test transactions rather than paper records of transactions that could be incorrect

- CAATs are cost-effective in the long term if the client does not change its systems

- Results from CAATs can be compared with results from traditional testing – if the results correlate, overall confidence is increased

There are two particularly common types of CAAT, audit software and test data.

1.4.1 Audit software

Audit software consists of computer programs used by the auditors, as part of their auditing procedures, to process data of audit significance from the entity's accounting system. Regardless of the source of the programs, the auditor should substantiate their validity for audit purposes prior to use. Audit software may consist of the following.

(a) **Package programs** are generalised computer programs designed to perform data processing functions which include reading computer files, selecting information, performing calculations, creating data files and printing reports in a format specified by the auditors.

(b) **Purpose-written programs** are computer programs designed to perform audit tasks in specific circumstances. These programs may be prepared by the auditors, by the entity or by an outside programmer engaged by the auditors. In some cases, existing entity programs may be used by the auditors in their original or in a modified state because it may be more efficient than developing independent programs.

(c) **Utility programs** are used by the entity to perform common data processing functions, such as sorting, creating and printing files. These programs are generally not designed for audit purposes and, therefore, may not contain such features as automatic record counts or control totals.

Examples of uses of audit software are:

- Interrogation software, which accesses the client's data files
- Comparison programs which compare versions of a program
- Interactive software for interrogation of on-line systems
- Resident code software to review transactions as they are processed

There are a number of difficulties using audit software, such as:

- High set-up costs due to the detailed knowledge of the client's systems and files required before audit software can be used.

- Audit software may not be available for the client's specific systems, particularly if they are bespoke.

- The audit software may produce too much output if faulty and waste auditor time.

- Checking client records in a 'live' situation may cause corruption and, therefore, disruption to the client.

1.4.2 Test data

Test data techniques are used in conducting audit procedures by entering data (eg a sample of transactions) into an entity's computer system, and comparing the results obtained with predetermined results. Examples include:

(a)   Test data used to test **specific controls** in computer programs. Examples include on-line password and data access controls.

(b)   Test transactions selected from previously processed transactions or created by the auditors to test **specific processing characteristics** of an entity's computer system. Such transactions are generally processed separately from the entity's normal processing. Test data can for example be used to check the controls that prevent the processing of **invalid data** by entering data with say a non-existent customer code or worth an unreasonable amount, or a transaction which may if processed break customer credit limits.

(c)   Test transactions used in an **integrated test facility**. This is where a 'dummy' unit (eg a department or employee) is established, and to which test transactions are posted during the normal processing cycle.

A significant problem with test data is that any resulting corruption of data files has to be corrected. This is difficult with modern real-time systems, which often have built-in (and highly desirable) controls to ensure that data entered **cannot** be easily removed without leaving a mark.

Other problems with **test data** are that it only tests the operation of the system at a **single point of time**, and auditors are only testing controls in the programs being run and controls which they know about. The problems involved mean that test data is being used less as a CAAT.

Question

Invisible evidence

Try to think of examples of where visible evidence may be lacking in the accounting process.

Answer

(a)   **Input documents** may be non-existent where sales orders are entered on-line. In addition, accounting transactions, such as discounts and interest calculations, may be generated by computer programs with no visible authorisation of individual transactions.

(b)   The system may not produce a visible audit trail of **transactions processed** through the computer. Delivery notes and suppliers' invoices may be matched by a computer program. In addition, programmed control procedures, such as checking customer credit limits, may provide visible evidence only on an exception basis. In such cases, there may be no visible evidence that all transactions have been processed.

(c)   **Output reports** may not be produced by the system. In addition, a printed report may only contain summary totals while supporting details are kept in computer files.

The major steps to be undertaken by the auditors in the application of a CAAT are as follows.

- **Set the objective** of the CAAT application
- **Determine** the **content** and **accessibility** of the entity's **files**
- **Define** the **transaction types** to be tested
- **Define the procedures** to be performed on the data

- **Define** the **output requirements**

- **Identify** the audit and computer **personnel** who may participate in the design and application of the CAAT

- **Refine** the estimates of **costs** and **benefits**

- Ensure that the **use of the CAAT is properly controlled** and **documented**

- Arrange the **administrative activities**, including the necessary skills and computer facilities

- Execute the **CAAT application**

- **Evaluate the results**

Question

CAATs

(a) Outline the major types of CAATs and describe the potential benefits that might be derived from using them.

(b) Explain what is meant by a 'test pack'.

(c) Briefly explain the use that the auditors could make of such a test pack when examining a sales ledger system maintained on a computer system.

(d) Briefly outline the main practical problems encountered when using a test pack.

Answer

(a) Audit techniques that involve, directly or indirectly, the use of a client's computer are referred to as Computer Assisted Audit Techniques (CAATs), of which the following are two principal categories.

(i) *Audit software*: computer programs used for audit purposes to examine the contents of the client's computer files

(ii) *Test data*: data used by the auditors for computer processing to test the operation of the enterprise's computer programs

The benefits of using CAATs are as follows.

(i) By using computer audit programs, the auditors can scrutinise large volumes of data and concentrate skilled manual resources on the investigation of results, rather than on the extraction of information.

(ii) Once the programs have been written and tested, the costs of operation are relatively low, indeed the auditors do not necessarily have to be present during its use (though there are frequently practical advantages in the auditors attending).

(b) A 'test pack' consists of input data submitted by the auditors for processing by the enterprise's computer based accounting system. It may be processed during a normal production run ('live') or during a special run at a point in time outside the normal cycle ('dead').

The primary use of the test pack is in testing of application controls. The data used in the test pack will often contain items which should appear in exception reports produced by the system. The results of the processed test pack will be compared with the expected results.

(c) The auditors could use a test pack to test the sales ledger system by including data in the pack which would normally be processed through the system, such as:

(i) Sales
(ii) Credits allowed

(iii)   Cash receipts

(iv)   Discounts allowed

The processing of the input would involve:

(i)   Production of sales invoices (with correct discounts)

(ii)   Production of credit notes

(iii)   Posting of cash received, invoices and credit notes to individual debtor's accounts to appear on statements

(iv)   Posting all transactions to the sales ledger control account and producing balances

The result produced would be compared with those predicted in the test pack. Errors should appear on exception reports produced by the computer, for example, a customer credit limit being breached.

(d)   The practical problems involved in using a test pack are as follows.

(i)   In using 'live' processing there will be problems removing or reversing the test data, which might corrupt master file information.

(ii)   In using 'dead' processing the auditors do not test the system actually used by the client.

(iii)   The system will be checked by the test pack, but not the year end balances, which will still require sufficient audit work. Costs may therefore be high.

(iv)   Any auditors who wish to design a test pack must have sufficient skill in computing, and also a thorough knowledge of the client's system.

(v)   Any changes in the client's system will mean that the test pack will have to be rewritten which will be costly and time-consuming.

1.5 Auditing smaller entities

The quality of audit evidence available at smaller entities is likely to be affected by the size of that entity. Auditors may have particular trouble obtaining sufficient audit evidence of **completeness**, due to the fact that the owner-manager is likely to be dominant and may be able to ensure that some transactions are not recorded. In addition, the internal control procedures of a small entity may not provide documentary evidence that all transactions are recorded.

A small entity may not have a strong system of internal control, particularly because it is unlikely to be able to sustain sufficient segregation of duties. We shall look at that in more detail in Chapter 9. You should, however, note that this is likely to result in the auditor carrying out all substantive procedures rather than some tests of controls.

The following points should be given special consideration when using CAATs in a small business computer environment.

(a)   As noted above, the level of general computer information system controls may be such that the auditors will place less reliance on the system of internal control. This will result in:

(i)   **Greater emphasis** on **tests of details** of transactions and balances and analytical review procedures, which may increase the effectiveness of certain CAATs, particularly audit software

(ii)   The **application of audit procedures** to ensure the proper functioning of the CAAT and validity of the entity's data

(b)   In cases where smaller volumes of data are processed, **manual methods** may be more **cost effective**.

(c)   Adequate **technical assistance** may not be available to the auditors from the entity, thus making the use of CAATs impracticable.

(d)   Certain audit package programs **may not operate** on small computers, thus restricting the auditors' choice of CAATs. However, the entity's data files may be copied and processed on another suitable computer.

(e)   Detailed knowledge of computer **operations programs** and **files** may be confined to a few people or even a single person. This may increase the opportunity to commit an undiscovered fraud by changing **programs** or **data.**

2 Audit sampling   6/03

> Auditors usually seek evidence from less than 100% of items of the balance or transaction being tested.

2.1 Introduction to audit sampling

Auditors do not normally examine all the information available to them; it would be impractical to do so and using audit sampling will produce valid conclusions. ISA (UK and Ireland) 530 *Audit sampling and other means of testing* states that 'when designing audit procedures, the auditor should determine appropriate means for selecting items for testing so as to gather sufficient appropriate audit evidence to meet the objectives of audit procedures'.

Key terms

> **Audit sampling** involves the application of audit procedures to less than 100% of the items within an account balance or class of transactions such that all sampling units have a chance of selection. This will enable the auditor to obtain and evaluate audit evidence about some characteristic of the items selected in order to form or assist in forming a conclusion concerning the population.
>
> **Population** is the entire set of data from which a sample is selected and about which an auditor wishes to draw conclusions.

Some testing procedures do **not** involve sampling, such as:

- **Testing 100%** of items in a population (this should be obvious)
- Testing all items with a **certain characteristic** as selection is not representative

Auditors are unlikely to test 100% of items when carrying out tests of control, but 100% testing may be appropriate for certain substantive procedures. For example if the population is made up of a small number of high value items, there is a high risk of material misstatement and other means do not provide sufficient appropriate audit evidence, 100% examination may be appropriate.

The ISA requires auditors to 'determine appropriate means of selecting the items for testing'. It distinguishes between **statistically-based sampling** and **non-statistical methods**.

Key terms

> **Statistical sampling** is any approach to sampling that involves random selection of a sample, and use of probability theory to evaluate sample results, including measurement of sampling risk.
>
> **Non statistical sampling** is the approach to sampling where the auditor does not use statistical methods and draws a judgemental opinion about the population.

The auditor may alternatively select certain items from a population because of specific characteristics they possess. The results of items selected in this way cannot be projected onto the whole population but may be used in conjunction with other audit evidence concerning the rest of the population.

- **High value or key items.** The auditor may select high value items or items that are suspicious, unusual or prone to error.

- **All items over a certain amount.** Selecting items this way may mean a large proportion of the population can be verified by testing a few items.

- **Items to obtain information** about the client's business, the nature of transactions, or the client's accounting and control systems.

- **Items to test procedures,** to see whether particular procedures are being performed.

2.2 Design of the sample

When designing the sample, the ISA requires the auditor to 'consider the **objectives** of the audit procedure and the **attributes of the population** from which the sample will be drawn', and to consider 'the sampling and selection methods'.

Auditors must consider the specific audit objectives to be achieved and the audit procedures which are most likely to achieve them. The auditors also need to consider the nature and characteristics of the audit evidence sought, possible error conditions and the **rate of expected error**. This will help them to define **what constitutes an error** and **what population to use** for sampling.

Key terms

> **Error** means either control deviations, when performing tests of control, or misstatements, when performing substantive procedures.
>
> **Expected error** is the error that the auditor expects to be present in the population.

The population from which the sample is drawn must be **appropriate and complete** for the specific audit objectives. The ISA distinguishes between situations where overstatement or understatement is being tested.

The population may be divided into sampling units in a variety of ways, eg an individual accounts receivable balance or, in monetary unit sampling, £1 of the total accounts receivable balance. Auditors must **define** the **sampling unit** in order to obtain an efficient and effective sample to achieve the particular audit objectives.

Key term

> **Sampling units** are the individual items constituting a population.

The ISA requires that the auditor 'should select items for the sample with the expectation that all sampling units in the population have a chance of selection'. This requires that **all items** in the population have an opportunity be selected.

There are a number of selection methods available.

(a) **Random selection** ensures that all items in the population have an equal chance of selection, eg by use of random number tables or computerised generator.

(b) **Systematic selection** involves selecting items using a constant interval between selections, the first interval having a random start. When using systematic selection auditors must ensure that the population is not structured in such a manner that the sampling interval corresponds with a particular pattern in the population.

(c) **Haphazard selection** may be an alternative to random selection provided auditors are satisfied that the sample is representative of the entire population. This method requires care to guard against making a selection which is biased, for example towards items which are easily located, as they may not be representative. It should not be used if auditors are carrying out statistical sampling.

(d) **Sequence or block selection**. Sequence sampling may be used to check whether certain items have particular characteristics. For example an auditor may use a sample of 50 consecutive cheques to check whether cheques are signed by authorised signatories rather than picking 50 single cheques throughout the year. Sequence sampling may however produce samples that are not representative of the population as a whole, particularly if errors only occurred during a certain part of the period, and hence the errors found cannot be projected onto the rest of the population.

(e) **Monetary Unit Sampling (MUS)**. This is a selection method which ensures that every £1 in a population has an equal chance of being selected for testing. How MUS works is shown in the example below. The advantages of this selection method are that it is easy when computers are used, and that every material item will automatically be sampled. Disadvantages include the fact that if computers are not used, it can be time consuming to pick the sample and that MUS does not cope well with errors of understatement of negative balances.

2.2.1 Example: MUS

You are auditing trade creditors. Total trade creditors is £500,000 and materiality is £50,000. You will select the balances containing the 50,000th £1 from the ledger below.

CREDITOR	BALANCE	CUMULATIVE TOTAL	SELECTED
A	30,000	30,000	
B	35,000	65,000	Yes
C	45,000	110,000	Yes
D	**52,000**	162,000	Yes
E	13,000	175,000	
F	**50,000**	225,000	Yes
G	23,000	248,000	
H	500	248,500	
I	42,000	290,000	Yes
J	47,000	337,000	Yes
K	**54,000**	391,000	Yes
L	17,000	408,000	Yes
M	**80,000**	488,000	Yes
N	12,000	500,000	Yes
	500,000		

Material items are shown in bold and have all been selected. The cumulative column shows you when the next 50,000th £1 has been reached.

Stratification may be appropriate. Stratification is the process of dividing a population into subpopulations, each of which is a group of sampling units, which have similar characteristics (often in monetary value). Each sampling unit can only belong to one, specifically designed stratum, thus reducing the variability within each stratum. This enables the auditors to direct audit effort towards items which, for example, contain the greatest potential monetary error. Ways of dividing items into strata include by age or by amount.

2.3 Sample size

As we shall see in the next chapter, in obtaining evidence, the auditor should use professional judgement to assess audit risk and design audit procedures to ensure this risk is reduced to an acceptably low level. In determining the sample size, the auditor should consider whether sampling risk is reduced to an acceptably low level.

Key terms

> **Sampling risk** arises from the possibility that the auditor's conclusion, based on a sample of a certain size, may be different from the conclusion that would be reached if the entire population were subjected to the same audit procedure.
>
> **Non-sampling risk** arises from factors that cause the auditor to reach an erroneous conclusion for any reason not related to the size of the sample. For example, most audit evidence is persuasive rather than conclusive, the auditor might use inappropriate procedures, or the auditor might misinterpret evidence and fail to recognise an error.

The auditors are faced with sampling risk in both tests of control and substantive procedures, as follows.

(a) **Tests of control**

   (i) **Risk of under-reliance**. The risk that, although the sample result does not support the auditor's assessment of control risk, the actual compliance rate would support such an assessment

   (ii) **Risk of over-reliance**. The risk that, although the sample result supports the auditor's assessment of control risk, the actual compliance rate would not support such an assessment

(b) **Substantive procedures**

   (i) **Risk of incorrect rejection**. The risk that, although the sample result supports the conclusion that a recorded account balance or class of transactions is materially misstated, in fact it is not materially misstated

   (ii) **Risk of incorrect acceptance**. The risk that, although the sample result supports the conclusion that a recorded account balance or class of transactions is not materially misstated, in fact it is materially misstated

The **greater** their reliance on the results of the procedure in question, the **lower** the sampling risk auditors will be willing to accept and the **larger** the sample size will be.

Key term

> **Tolerable error** is the maximum error in the population that the auditor would be willing to accept.

Tolerable error is considered during the planning stage and, for substantive procedures, is related to the auditor's judgement about materiality. We shall look at these matters in the next chapter. The smaller the tolerable error, the greater the sample size will need to be.

(a) In tests of control, the **tolerable error** is the **maximum rate of deviation** from a **prescribed control procedure** that auditors are willing to accept in the population and still conclude that the preliminary assessment of control risk is valid.

(b) In substantive procedures, the **tolerable error** is the **maximum monetary error** in an account balance or class of transactions that auditors are willing to accept so that, when the results of all audit procedures are considered, they are able to conclude, with reasonable assurance, that the financial statements are not materially misstated.

Larger samples will be required when errors are expected than would be required if none were expected, in order to conclude that the actual error is less than the tolerable error. The size and frequency of errors is important when assessing the sample size; for the same overall error, larger fewer errors will mean a bigger sample size than for smaller more frequent errors. If the expected error rate is high then sampling may not be appropriate. When considering expected error, the auditors should consider:

- **Errors identified in previous audits**
- **Changes in the entity's procedures**
- **Evidence available from other procedures**

Most auditing firms use computer programmes to set sample sizes, based on risk assessments and materiality.

2.4 Evaluation of sample results

2.4.1 Analysis of errors in the sample

To begin with, the auditors must consider whether the items in question are **true errors**, as they defined them before the test, eg a misposting between customer accounts will not affect the total debtors.

When the expected audit evidence regarding a specific sample item cannot be found, the auditors may be able to obtain sufficient appropriate audit evidence by performing **alternative procedures**. In such cases, the item is not treated as an error.

The **qualitative** aspects of errors should also be considered, including the **nature and cause** of the error. Auditors should also consider any possible effects the error might have on **other parts of the audit** including the general effect on the financial statements and on the auditors' assessment of the accounting and internal control systems.

Where common features are discovered in errors, the auditors may decide to identify all items in the population which possess the common feature (eg location), thereby producing a sub-population. Audit procedures could then be extended in this area.

On some occasions the auditor may decide that the errors are **anomalous errors**. To be considered anomalous, the auditors have to be certain that the errors are not representative of the population. Extra work will be required to prove that an error is anomalous.

Key term

> **Anomalous error** means an error that arises from an isolated event that has not recurred other than on specifically identifiable occasions and is therefore not representative of errors in the population.

2.4.2 Projection of errors

The auditors should project the error results from the sample on to the relevant population. The auditors will **estimate the probable error** in the population by extrapolating the errors found in the sample.

For substantive tests, auditors will then **estimate any further error** that might not have been detected because of the imprecision of the technique (in addition to consideration of the qualitative aspects of the errors).

Auditors should also consider the effect of the projected error on other areas of the audit. The auditors should compare the projected population error (net of adjustments made by the entity in the case of substantive procedures) to the tolerable error, taking account of other relevant audit procedures.

2.4.3 Reassessing sampling risk

If the projected population error **exceeds** or is close to tolerable error, then the auditors should re-assess sampling risk. If it is unacceptable, they should consider extending auditing procedures or performing alternative procedures. However if after alternative procedures the auditors still believe the actual error rate is higher than the tolerable error rate, they should re-assess control risk if the test is a test of controls; if the test is a substantive test, they should consider whether the accounts need to be adjusted.

2.5 Summary

Key stages in the sampling process are as follows.

- Determining **objectives and population**
- Determining **sample size**

- Choosing method of **sample selection**
- Analysing the **results** and **projecting errors**

 Question   Statistical sampling

Present the arguments for and against the use of statistical sampling in auditing and reach a conclusion.

Answer

An inevitable characteristic of audit testing is that a sample only of transactions or items can be examined. The auditors examine a sample of items and thereby seek to obtain assurance that the whole group is acceptable.

Provided that conditions are appropriate for its use, a statistical approach to sampling is likely to have many advantages over the alternative of judgement sampling.

Conditions favouring the use of statistical sampling are:

(a) Existence of large and homogeneous groups of items
(b) Low expected error rate and clear definition of error
(c) Reasonable ease of identifying and obtaining access to items selected

If these conditions are present, statistical sampling is likely to have the following advantages.

(a) At the conclusion of a test the auditors are able to state a definite level of confidence they may have that the whole population conforms to the sample result, within a stated precision limit.

(b) Sample size is objectively determined, having regard to the degree of risk the auditors are prepared to accept for each application.

(c) It may be possible to use smaller sample sizes, thus saving time and money.

(d) The process of fixing required precision and confidence levels compels the auditors to consider and clarify their audit objectives.

(e) The results of tests can be expressed in precise mathematical terms.

(f) Bias is eliminated.

Statistical sampling is not without disadvantages.

(a) The technique may be applied blindly without prior consideration of the suitability of the statistical sampling for the audit task to be performed. This disadvantage may be overcome by establishing soundly-based procedures for use in the firm, incorporating standards on sampling in the firm's audit manual, instituting training programmes for audit staff and proper supervision.

(b) Unsuspected patterns or bias in sample selection may invalidate the conclusions. The probability of these factors arising must be carefully judged by the auditor before they decide to adopt statistical sampling.

(c) It frequently needs back-up by further tests within the population reviewed: large items, non-routine items, sensitive items like directors' transactions.

(d) At the conclusion of a statistical sampling-based test the auditors may fail to appreciate the further action necessary based on the results obtained. This potential disadvantage may be overcome by adequate training and supervision, and by requiring careful evaluation of all statistical sampling tests.

(e) Statistical sampling may be applied carelessly, without due confirmation that the sample selected is acceptably random.

(f)   The selection exercise can be time consuming.

(g)   The degree of tolerance of acceptable error must be predetermined.

The disadvantages listed above can all be overcome if the technique is applied sensibly and competently.

Provided that the conditions favouring its use are present, statistical sampling is a useful technique for several auditing tasks.

(a)   Tests of controls
(b)   Substantive procedures
(c)   Direct confirmation of debtors and creditors
(d)   Fraud investigation using discovery sampling

Statistical techniques should be used when they are convenient and of positive use to the auditors in achieving a level of reliability in their results. If they are used selectively, in cases where their advantages are conspicuous and their disadvantages can be reduced to a minimum, they can make a significant contribution towards greater quality control on an audit. But it is hard to resist the argument that properly devised and controlled 'judgmental methods' can achieve the same high standards with fewer administrative or technical problems.

Exam focus point

In the exam, you may be asked to describe sampling in general terms or how it will be used in a specific situation.

3 Audit documents   12/03

FAST FORWARD

It is important to document audit work performed in working papers to:

- Enable reporting partner to ensure all planned work has been completed adequately
- Provide details of work done for future reference
- Assist in planning and control of future audits
- Encourage a methodical approach and therefore quality

3.1 Working papers

All audit work must be documented: the working papers are the tangible evidence of the work done in support of the audit opinion. ISA 230 *Audit documentation* states that 'auditors should prepare, on a timely basis, audit documentation that provides:

(a)   A sufficient and appropriate record of the basis for the auditor's report, and

(b)   Evidence that the audit was performed in accordance with ISAs and applicable legal and regulatory requirements.'

Key term

Working papers are the record of audit procedures performed, relevant audit evidence obtained and conclusions reached.

In addition auditors record their work to:

- Assist the audit team to plan and perform the audit

- Assist relevant members of the team to direct and supervise work

- Enable the audit team to be accountable for its work (and to prove adherence to ISAs in a litigious situation)

- Retain a record of matters of continuing significance to future audits

- Enable an experienced auditor to carry out quality control reviews

- Enable an experienced auditor to conduct external inspections in accordance with applicable legal, regulatory or other requirements

3.2 Form and content of working papers

Working papers should be headed in a certain way and contain certain information. They may be automated.

The ISA requires working papers to be sufficiently complete and detailed to provide an overall understanding of the audit. Auditors cannot record everything they consider. Therefore judgement must be used as to the extent of working papers, based on the following general rule:

> What would be necessary to provide an experienced auditor, with no previous connection with the audit, with an understanding of the work performed, the results of audit procedures, audit evidence obtained, significant matters arising during the audit and conclusions reached

The form and content of working papers are affected by matters such as:

- The **nature** of the audit procedures to be performed

- The **identified risks** of material misstatements

- The **extent of judgement** required in performing the work and evaluating the results

- The **significance** of the audit evidence obtained

- The **nature** and **extent** of **exceptions** identified

- The **need to document a conclusion** or the **basis for a conclusion not readily determinable** from the documentation of the work performed or audit evidence obtained

- The **audit methodology** and **tools** used

3.2.1 Examples of working papers

- Information obtained in understanding the entity and its environment, including its internal control, such as the following:

  - Information concerning the legal documents, agreements and minutes

  - Extracts or copies of important legal documents, agreements and minutes

  - Information concerning the industry, economic environment and legislative environment within which the entity operates.

  - Extracts from the entity's internal control manual

- Evidence of the planning process including audit programs and any changes thereto

- Evidence of the auditor's consideration of the work of internal auditing and conclusions reached

- Analyses of transactions and balances

- Analyses of significant ratios and trends

- The identified and assessed risks of material misstatements at the financial statement and the assertion level

- A record of the nature, timing, extent and results of auditing procedures

- Evidence that the work performed by assistants was supervised and reviewed

- An indication as to who performed the audit procedures and when they were performed
- Details of audit procedures applied regarding components whose financial statements are audited by another auditor
- Copies of communications with other auditors, experts and other third parties
- Copies of letters or notes concerning audit matters communicated to or discussed with management or those charged with governance, including the terms of the engagement and material weaknesses in internal control
- Letters of representation received from the entity
- Conclusions reached by the auditor concerning significant aspects of the audit, including how exceptions and unusual matters, if any, disclosed by the auditor's procedures were resolved or treated.
- Copies of the financial statements and auditors' reports
- Notes of discussions about significant matters with management and others
- In exceptional circumstances, the reasons for departing from a basic principle or essential procedure of an ISA and how the alternative procedure performed achieve the audit objective

Working papers should show:

- The **name of** the **client**
- The **balance sheet date**
- The **file reference** of the working paper
- The **name of** the **person** preparing the working paper
- The **date the working paper** was **prepared**
- The **subject** of the working paper
- The **name of** the **person reviewing** the working paper
- The **date** of the **review**
- The **objective** of the work done
- The **source of information**
- How any **sample was selected** and the sample size determined
- The **work done**
- A **key** to any audit ticks or symbols
- Appropriate **cross-referencing**
- The **results obtained**
- **Analysis of errors** or other significant observations
- The **conclusions drawn**
- The **key points highlighted**

The auditor should record the identifying characteristics of specific items or matters being tested. Firms should have standard **referencing** and **filing** procedures for working papers, to facilitate their review.

3.2.2 Audit files

For recurring audits, working papers may be split between:

Permanent audit files (containing information of **continuing importance** to the audit). These contain:

- Engagement letters
- New client questionnaire
- The memorandum and articles
- Other legal documents such as prospectuses, leases, sales agreement
- Details of the history of the client's business
- Board minutes of continuing relevance

- Previous years' signed accounts, analytical review and management letters
- Accounting systems notes, previous years' control questionnaires

Current audit files (containing information of relevance to the current year's audit). These should be compiled on a timely basis after the completion of the audit and should contain:

- Financial statements
- Accounts checklists
- Management accounts details
- Reconciliations of management and financial account
- A summary of unadjusted errors
- Report to partner including details of significant events and errors
- Review notes
- Audit planning memorandum
- Time budgets and summaries
- Letter of representation
- Management letter
- Notes of board minutes
- Communications with third parties such as experts or other auditors

They also contain working papers covering each audit area. These should include the following:

- A lead schedule including details of the figures to be included in the accounts
- Problems encountered and conclusions drawn
- Audit programmes
- Risk assessments
- Sampling plans
- Analytical review
- Details of substantive tests and tests of control

If it is necessary to modify/add new audit documentation to a file after it has been assembled, the auditor should document:

- Who made the changes, and when, and by whom they were reviewed
- The reasons for making changes
- The effect of changes on the auditors' conclusions

If, in exceptional circumstances, changes are made to an audit file after the audit report has been signed, the auditor should document:

- The circumstances
- The audit procedures performed, evidence obtained, conclusions drawn
- When and by whom changes to audit documents were made and reviewed

3.3 Standardised and automated working papers

The use of **standardised** working papers, for example, checklists, specimen letters, may improve the efficiency of audit work but they can be dangerous because they may lead to auditors mechanically following an approach without using audit judgement.

Automated working paper packages have been developed which can make the documenting of audit work much easier. Such programs aid preparation of working papers, lead schedules, trial balance and the financial statements themselves. These are automatically cross referenced, adjusted and balanced by the computer.

The **advantages** of automated working papers are as follows.

- The risk of errors is reduced.
- The working papers will be neater and easier to review.

- The time saved will be substantial as adjustments can be made easily to all working papers, including working papers summarising the key analytical information.

- Standard forms do not have to be carried to audit locations.

- Audit working papers can be transmitted for review via a modem, or fax facilities (if both the sending and receiving computers have fax boards and fax software).

Question

Working papers

'Auditors base their judgement as to the extent of working papers upon what would be necessary to provide an experienced auditor, with no previous connection with the audit, with an understanding of the work performed, the results of audit procedures, audit evidence obtained, significant matters arising during the audit and conclusions reached.'

Describe four benefits that auditors will obtain from working papers that meet the above requirement.

Answer

- The reporting partner can be satisfied that work delegated by him has been completed adequately.

- Working papers are a record of work performed and conclusions drawn which might be necessary in the future, for example, in litigation.

- Good working papers and the planning and control of future audits.

- Preparing working papers encourages auditors to adopt a methodical approach. This is likely to improve quality.

3.4 Retention of working papers

Judgement may have to be used in deciding the length of holding working papers, and further consideration should be given to the matter before their destruction. The ACCA recommends seven years as a minimum period.

Working papers are the property of the auditors. They are not a substitute for, nor part of, the entity's accounting records.

Auditors must follow ethical guidance on the confidentiality of audit working papers. They may, at their discretion, release parts of or whole working papers to the entity, as long as disclosure does not undermine 'the independence or validity of the audit process'. Information should not be made available to third parties without the permission of the entity.

Chapter Roundup

- Auditors must obtain **sufficient, appropriate** audit evidence.

- Evidence can be in the form of **tests of control** or **substantive procedures.**

- The **reliability** of audit evidence is influenced by its **source** and by its **nature.**

- Audit tests are designed to obtain evidence about the financial statement assertions.

- Audit evidence can be obtained by inspection, observation, inquiry and confirmation, computation and analytical procedures.

- Auditors usually seek evidence from less than 100% of items of the balance or transaction being tested.

- It is important to document audit work performed in working papers to:

    - Enable reporting partner to ensure all planned work has been completed adequately
    - Provide details of work done for future reference
    - Assist in planning and control of future audits
    - Encourage a methodical approach and therefore quality

- Working papers should be headed in a certain way and contain certain information. They may be automated.

Quick Quiz

1   Define sufficiency and appropriateness of evidence in one line each.

2   Name seven financial statement assertions.

3   Fill in the **blanks**

Audit evidence from external sources is ………………………. ……………………. than that obtained from the entity's records.

Evidence obtained directly ………………………………….. ……………………… is more ……………………. than that obtained by or from the entity.

4   Match the definitions to the terms

   (a)   Sampling risk
   (b)   Non-sampling risk

   (i)   The risk that the auditors' conclusion, based on a sample, may be different from the conclusions that would be reached if the entire population was subject to the same audit procedure.

   (ii) The risk that the auditors might use inappropriate procedures or might misinterpret evidence and thus fail to recognise an error.

5   Name three methods of sample selection

   1   …………………………………………………..
   2   …………………………………………………..
   3   …………………………………………………..

6   Name two types of audit software

   1   …………………………………………………..
   2   …………………………………………………..

7   What is the general rule for documenting the audit process?

8   Give two advantages and one disadvantage of standardised working papers.

   1   ……………………………………………   1   …………………………………………………
   2   …………………………………………

9   Complete the table, using the working papers given below.

Current audit file	Permanent audit file

engagement letters	new client questionnaire
financial statements	management letter
accounts checklists	audit planning memo
board minutes of continuing relevance	accounting systems notes

Answers to Quick Quiz

1 Sufficiency is the measure of the quantity of audit evidence.

Appropriateness is the measure of the quality/reliability of audit evidence.

2 Existence, right and obligations, occurrence, completeness, valuation, accuracy, classification, cut off, allocation.

3 More reliable
By auditors, reliable

4 (a) (i)
(b) (ii)

5 Random
Haphazard
Systematic

6 • Package programs
• Purpose-written programs
• Utility programs

7 What would be necessary to provide an experienced auditor, with no previous connection with the audit, with an understanding of the work performed, the results of audit procedures, audit evidence obtained, significant matters arising during the audit and conclusions reached.

8 | **Advantages** | **Disadvantages** |
|---|---|
| 1 Facilitate the delegation of work | 1 Detracts from proper exercise of profession |
| 2 Means to control quality | judgement |

9

Current audit file	Permanent audit file
financial statements	engagement letters
management letter	new client questionnaire
accounts checklists	board minutes of continuing relevance
audit planning memo	accounting systems notes

Now try the question below from the Exam Question Bank

Number	Level	Marks	Time
Q6	Examination	20	36 mins

Planning and risk

Introduction

This chapter covers the aspects of the audit which will be considered at the earliest stages, during planning. It is unlikely that you will have direct experience of planning an audit, but you should acquaint yourself with all the planning documentation on any audit you attend.

Key points this chapter covers which you must understand are:

- The **purposes of planning**

- The importance of **understanding the entity and its environment**

- Using that understanding to **assess the risks** of material misstatement and **plan further procedures**

The auditor also needs to consider the risks of fraud and non compliance with law and regulations in the audit.

Lastly, the issue of planning is looked at from the point of view of the internal auditor and for a review.

Study guide

7 – Professional ethics and professional codes of conduct I

- Describe the responsibilities of internal and external auditors for the prevention and detection of fraud and error and in relation to laws and regulations

9 – Preliminary planning procedures

- Distinguish between risk-based, procedural and other approaches to audit and review work
- Describe the sources and nature of information gathered in planning audit and review assignments
- Describe the understanding of the entity required by auditors
- Describe the purpose of analytical procedures in planning and illustrate the application of such procedures
- Describe the components of risk and the use of information technology in risk analysis
- Illustrate and explain the importance of the application of risk analysis
- Define and illustrate the concepts of materiality and tolerable error
- Evaluate misstatements

Exam guide

Audit planning is extremely important. In December 2005, candidates were asked to explain why audits had to be planned and outline an overall audit strategy. Within planning, risk is a key topic area, and questions such as question 2 on the pilot paper are likely to be asked frequently. The December 2001 paper included a compulsory question on risks.

You may be asked in the exam to explain various terms such as risk and materiality. This involves not merely learning the definitions but also being able to show how in practice the auditor uses the techniques in planning an audit.

1 Planning   12/05

 FAST FORWARD

> The auditors formulate an overall audit strategy which is translated into a detailed audit plan for audit staff to follow.

1.1 The overall audit strategy

An effective and efficient audit relies on proper planning procedures. The planning process is covered in general terms by ISA (UK and Ireland) 300 *Planning*. Other more detailed areas are covered in the other ISAs covered in this chapter. ISA 300 states 'The auditor should plan the audit so that the engagement will be performed in an effective manner'.

Key term

> An overall **audit strategy** is the formulation of the general strategy for the audit, which sets the direction for the audit, describes the expected scope and conduct of the audit and provides guidance for the development of the audit plan.

Key term

> An **audit plan** is more detailed than the strategy and includes a set of instructions to the audit team that sets out the audit procedures (risk assessment procedures and further procedures) the auditors intend to adopt and may include references to other matters such as the audit objectives, timing, sample size and basis of selection for each area. It also serves as a means to control and record the proper execution of the work.

An **audit plan** sets out the nature, timing and extent of planned audit procedures required to implement the overall audit strategy. The audit plan serves as a set of instructions to assistants involved in the audit and as a means to control the proper execution of the work.

Audits are planned to:

- Develop a strategy and detailed approach for specific audit work so that the audit is carried out in a timely and efficient manner

- Ensure important areas of the audit are given proper attention and problem areas are identified and dealt with

- Determine the amount of work required, so that staff can be allocated properly

- Provide a reference for initial conversations with the client's audit committee about audit approach

- Be the basis for the production of the detailed audit plan.

Audit procedures should be discussed with the client's management, staff and/or audit committee in order to co-ordinate audit work, including that of internal audit. However, all audit procedures remain the responsibility of the external auditors.

A structured approach to planning will include:

Step 1   Ensuring that ethical requirements are met.

Step 2   Ensuring the terms of the engagement are understood

Step 3   Establishing the overall audit strategy

- Determining the relevant characteristics of the engagement, such as the reporting framework used as this will set the scope for the engagement

- Discovering key dates for reporting and other communications

- Determining materiality, preliminary risk assessment, whether internal controls are to be tested

- Consideration of resources available and how they are to be used (subject to risk procedures)

Step 4   Developing an audit plan including planned risk assessment procedures, further procedures and any other procedures necessary to comply with ISAs

'The auditor should develop an audit plan in order to reduce audit risk to an acceptably low level.' The audit plan and any significant changes to it during the audit must be documented

KEY CONTENTS OF AN OVERALL AUDIT STRATEGY	
Understanding the entity's environment	General economic factors and industry conditions
	Important characteristics of the client, (a) business, (b) principal business strategies, (c) financial performance, (d) reporting requirements, including changes since the previous audit
	The general level of competence of management.

KEY CONTENTS OF AN OVERALL AUDIT STRATEGY	
Understanding the accounting and internal control systems	The accounting policies adopted by the entity and changes in those policies
	The effect of new accounting or auditing pronouncements
	The auditors' cumulative knowledge of the accounting and internal control systems, and the relative emphasis expected to be placed on tests of control and substantive procedures
Risk and materiality	The expected assessments of risks of fraud or error and identification of significant audit areas
	The setting of materiality for audit planning purposes
	The possibility of material misstatements, including the experience of past periods, or fraud
	The identification of complex accounting areas including those involving estimates
Consequent nature, timing and extent of procedures	Possible change of emphasis on specific audit areas
	The effect of information technology on the audit
	The work of internal auditing and its expected effect on external audit procedures
Co-ordination, direction, supervision and review	The involvement of other auditors
	The involvement of experts
	The number of locations
	Staffing requirements
Other matters	The possibility that the going concern basis may be subject to question
	Conditions requiring special attention such as the existence of related parties
	The terms of the engagement and any statutory responsibilities
	The nature and timing of reports or other communication with the entity that are expected under the engagement

Exam focus point

The December 2005 exam asked candidates to produce an overall audit strategy document for a given client. You should practice this question, which you will find in your Practice and Revision Kit, to ensure you are completely aware of the contents of an audit strategy.

2 Introduction to risk   Pilot paper, 12/01, 6/03, 6/05

2.1 Overall audit risk

FAST FORWARD

The auditor usually adopts a **risk-based approach** to auditing and focuses his testing on the riskiest balances and classes of transactions.

Auditors follow a **risk-based approach** to auditing. In the risk-based approach, auditors analyse the risks associated with the client's business, transactions and systems which could lead to misstatements in the financial statements, and direct their testing to risky areas. They are therefore not concerned with individual routine transactions, although they will still be concerned with material, non-routine transactions.

Key term

Audit risk is the risk that the auditors give an inappropriate opinion on the financial statements.

Audit risk has two elements, the **risk that the financial statements contain a material misstatement** and the **risk that the auditors will fail to detect any material misstatements**.

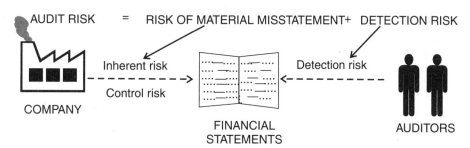

As you can see from the above diagram, audit risk has two major components. One is dependent on the entity, and is the risk of material misstatement arising in the financial statements. The other is dependent on the auditor, and is the risk that the auditor will not detect material misstatements in the financial statements.

Point to note

> We shall look in detail at the concept of materiality in the next section of this chapter.

2.2 Risk of material misstatement in the financial statements

Risk of material misstatement in the financial statement has two elements, **inherent** and **control** risk.

2.2.1 Inherent risk

Key term

> **Inherent risk** is the susceptibility of an account balance or class of transactions to misstatement that could be material individually or when aggregated with misstatements in other balances or classes, assuming there were no related internal controls.

Inherent risk is the risk that items will be misstated due to characteristics of those items, such as the fact they are estimates or that they are important items in the accounts. The auditors must use their professional judgement and all available knowledge to assess inherent risk. If no such information or knowledge is available then the inherent risk is **high**.

Inherent risk is affected by the nature of the entity; for example, the industry it is in and the regulations it falls under, and also the nature of the strategies it adopts. We shall look at more examples of inherent risks in section 4.

2.2.2 Control risk

Key term

> **Control risk** is the risk that a material misstatement would not be prevented, detected or corrected by the accounting and internal control systems.

We shall look at control risk in more detail in Chapter 9.

2.3 Risk that the auditor will not detect a material misstatement in the financial statements

The risk that the auditor will fail to detect material misstatements is known as **detection** risk.

Key term

> **Detection risk** is the risk that the auditors' substantive procedures will not detect a misstatement that exists in an account balance or class of transactions that could be material, either individually or when aggregated with misstatements in other balances or classes.

This is the component of audit risk that the auditors have a degree of control over, because, if risk is too high to be tolerated, the auditors can carry out more work to reduce this aspect of audit risk, and therefore audit risk as a whole. We have already introduced sampling and non-sampling risk in Chapter 6. These are the components of detection risk.

ISA 200 states that 'the auditor should plan and perform the audit to reduce audit risk to an acceptably low level that is consistent with the objective of the audit', that is, giving reasonable assurance on the truth and fairness of the financial statements.

Point to note

> We shall look in more detail at risk assessment procedures later in this chapter.

2.4 Management of audit risk

Auditors will want their overall audit risk to be at an acceptable level, or it will not be worth them carrying out the audit. In other words, if the chance of them giving an inappropriate opinion and being sued is high, it might better not to do the audit at all.

The auditors will obviously consider how risky a new audit client is during the acceptance process, and may decide not to go ahead with the relationship. However, they will also consider audit risk for each individual audit, and will seek to manage the risk.

As we have seen above, it is not in the auditors' power to affect inherent or control risk. As they are risks integral to the client, the auditor cannot change the level of these risks.

The auditor therefore manages overall audit risk by manipulating detection risk, the only element of audit risk the auditor has control over. This is because, the more audit work the auditors carry out, the lower detection risk becomes, although it can never be entirely eliminated due to the inherent limitations of audit.

This audit risk management can be shown crudely in a mathematical equation. The auditor will decide what level of overall risk is acceptable, and then determine a level of audit work so that detection risk makes the equation work.

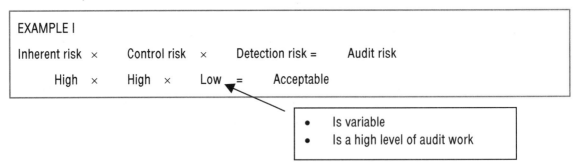

EXAMPLE I

Inherent risk	×	Control risk	×	Detection risk =	Audit risk
High	×	High	×	Low =	Acceptable

- Is variable
- Is a high level of audit work

In Example I, inherent and control risk were both high. This has the following effects on the audit.

- The auditors are unlikely to rely on tests of controls, but will carry out extended substantive tests.

- Detection risk must be rendered low, which will mean carrying out a substantial amount of substantive testing.

Audits are not all the same, however. A different company could product the following audit risk calculation.

BPP
PROFESSIONAL EDUCATION

EXAMPLE II

Inherent risk	×	Control risk	×	Detection risk	=	Audit risk
Medium	×	Low	×	Medium	=	Acceptable

In Example II, as control risk is low, the auditors are likely to carry out tests of controls and seek to rely on the client's system. Remember, this does not mean substantive tests can be eliminated entirely. Detection risk in this instance would be affected by the amount of controls and substantive testing carried out.

Lastly, it is important to understand that there is not a standard level of audit risk which is considered generally by auditors to be acceptable. This is a matter of audit judgement, and so will vary from firm to firm and audit to audit. Audit firms are likely to charge higher fees for higher risk clients. Regardless of the risk level of the audit, however, it is vital that audit firms always carry out an audit of **sufficient quality**.

Question

Audit risk

Hippo Ltd is a long established client of your firm. It manufactures bathroom fittings and fixtures, which it sells to a range of wholesalers, on credit.

You are the audit senior and have recently been sent the following extract from the draft balance sheet by the finance director.

	Budget £'000s	£'000s	Actual £'000s	£'000s
Fixed assets		453		367
Current assets				
Trade debtors	1,134		976	
Bank	–		54	
Current liabilities				
Trade creditors	967		944	
Bank overdraft	9		–	

During the course of conversation with the finance director, you establish that a major new customer the company had included in its budget went bankrupt during the year.

Required

Identify any potential risks for the audit of Hippo and explain why you believe they are risks.

Answer

Potential risks relevant to the audit of Hippo

(1)   **Credit sales**. Hippo makes sales on credit. This increases the risk that Hippo's sales will not be converted into cash. Trade accounts receivable is likely to be a risky area and the auditors will have to consider what the best evidence that customers are going to pay is likely to be.

(2)   **Related industry**. Hippo manufactures bathroom fixtures and fittings. These are sold to wholesalers, but it is possible that Hippo's ultimate market is the building industry. This is a notoriously volatile industry, and Hippo may find that their results fluctuate too, as demand rises and falls. This suspicion is added to by the bankruptcy of the wholesaler in the year. The auditors must be sure that accounts which present Hippo as a viable company are in fact correct.

(3)   **Controls**. The fact that a major new customer went bankrupt suggests that Hippo did not undertake a very thorough credit check on that customer before agreeing to supply them. This implies that the controls at Hippo may not be very strong.

(4)   **Variance**. The actual results are different from budget. This may be explained by the fact that the major customer went bankrupt, or it may reveal that there are other errors and problems in the reported results, or in the original budget.

(5)   **Receivables**. There is a risk that the result reported contains balance due from the bankrupt wholesaler, which is likely to be irrecoverable.

2.5 Business risk

The other major category of risk which the auditor must be aware of is that of **business risk**. As you shall see in more detail in Chapter 9, the auditor is required to consider the company's process of business risk management.

We briefly introduced the concept of business risk in Chapter 4 in the context of internal audit's role in risk management and organisational control.

Exam focus point

> It is vital that you do not confuse the concepts of audit and business risks. Remember – audit risk is focused on the financial statements of a company, business risk is related to the company as a whole.

3 Materiality   6/02

FAST FORWARD

> **Materiality** should be calculated at the planning stages of all audits. The calculation or estimation of materiality should be based on experience and judgement.

3.1 Applying materiality

We discussed materiality briefly in Chapter 1. Remember it relates to the level of error that affects the decisions of users of the accounts. ISA (UK and Ireland) 320 *Audit materiality* states that 'materiality should be considered by the auditor when:

(a)   Determining the nature, timing and extent of audit procedures; and
(b)   Evaluating the effect of misstatements'.

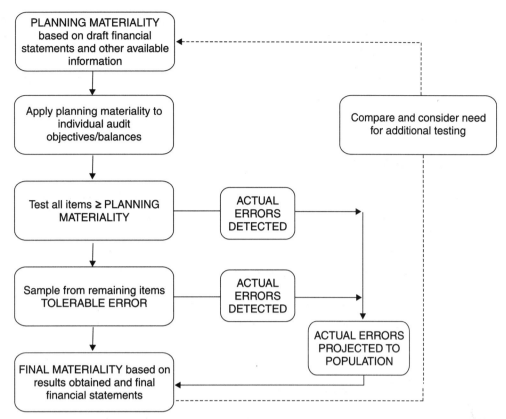

Materiality considerations during **audit planning** are extremely important. The assessment of materiality at this stage should be based on the most recent and reliable financial information and will help to determine an effective and efficient audit approach. Materiality assessment will help the auditors to decide:

- **How many** and **what items** to examine
- Whether to use **sampling techniques**
- What **level of error** is likely to lead to a modified audit opinion

The resulting combination of audit procedures should help to reduce audit risk to an appropriately low level. This is how risk and materiality are closely connected. The value of discovered errors should be aggregated at the end of the audit to ensure the total is still below tolerable error.

To set the materiality level the auditors need to decide the level of error which would distort the view given by the accounts. Because many users of accounts are primarily interested in the profitability of the company, the level is often expressed as a proportion of its profits.

Materiality can be thought of in terms of the size of the business. Hence, if the company remains a fairly constant size, the materiality level should not change; similarly if the business is growing, the level of materiality will increase from year to year.

The size of a company can be measured in terms of turnover and total assets before deducting any liabilities both of which tend not to be subject to the fluctuations which may affect profit.

Note that the auditors will often calculate a range of values, such as those shown below, and then take an average or weighted average of all the figures produced as the materiality level.

Value	%
Profit before tax	5
Gross profit	½ – 1
Turnover	½ – 1
Total assets	1 – 2
Net assets	2 – 5
Profit after tax	5 – 10

Point to note

> However, bear in mind that materiality has qualitative, as well as quantitative, aspects. You must not simply think of materiality as being a percentage of items in the financial statements.

Tolerable error may be set at planning materiality, but it is usually reduced to, say 75% or even 50% of planning materiality so as to take account of sampling risk. As we discussed in Chapter 6, the tolerable error is used to determine sample size.

3.2 Review of materiality

FAST FORWARD

> Materiality should be reviewed during the audit.

The level of materiality must be reviewed constantly as the audit progresses and **changes** may be required because:

- **Draft accounts** are **altered** (due to material error and so on) and therefore overall materiality changes.

- **External factors cause changes** in the control or inherent risk estimates.

- Such changes are caused by **errors** found during testing.

4 Understanding the entity and its environment

FAST FORWARD

> The auditor is required to **obtain an understanding of the entity and its environment** in order to be able to assess the risks of material misstatements.

4.1 Obtaining an understanding

ISA 315 *Understanding the entity and its environment and assessing the risks of material misstatement* states that 'the auditor should **obtain an understanding** of the entity and its environment, including its internal control, sufficient to **identify and assess the risks of material misstatement** of the financial statements whether due to fraud or error, and sufficient to design and perform further audit procedures'.

Summary: Obtaining an understanding of the entity and its environment	
Why?	To identify and assess the risks of material misstatement in the financial statements
	To enable the auditor to design and perform further audit procedures
	To provide a frame of reference for exercising audit judgement, for example, when setting audit materiality
What?	Industry, regulatory and other external factors, including the reporting framework
	Nature of the entity, including selection and application of accounting policies
	Objectives and strategies and relating business risks that might cause material misstatement in the financial statements
	Measurement and review of the entity's financial performance
	Internal control (which we shall look at in detail in Chapter 9)
How?	Inquiries of management and others within the entity
	Analytical procedures
	Observation and inspection
	Prior period knowledge
	Discussion of the susceptibility of the financial statements to material misstatement among the engagement team

As can be seen in the table above, the reasons the auditor is to obtain the understanding of the entity and its environment are very much bound up with assessing risks and exercising audit judgement. We shall look at these aspects more in the next two sections of this chapter.

4.2 What?

The ISA sets out a number of requirements about what the auditors must consider in relation to obtaining an understanding of the business. The general areas are shown in the following diagram.

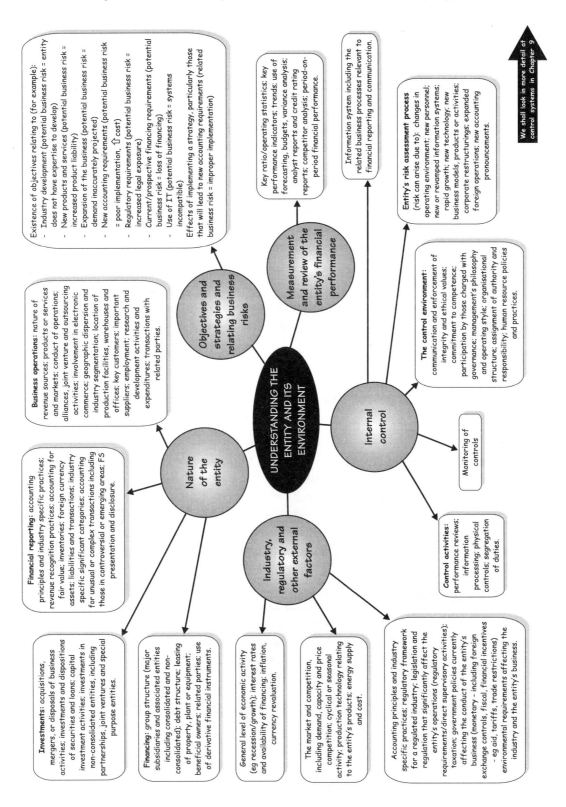

4.3 How?

ISA 315 sets out the methods that the auditor **must** use to obtain the understanding. The auditor does not have to use all of these for each area, but a combination of these procedures should be used. These are:

- Inquiries of management and others within the entity
- Analytical procedures
- Observation and inspection

The **audit team** is also required by ISA 315 to **discuss the susceptibility of the financial statements to material misstatement**. Judgement must be exercised in determining which members of the team should be involved in which parts of the discussion, but all team members should be involved in the discussion relevant to the parts of the audit they will be involved in.

Lastly, if it is a recurring audit, the auditors may have obtained a great deal of knowledge about the entity and the environment in the course of prior year audits. The auditor is entitled to use this information in the current year audit, but he must make sure that he has determined whether any **changes** in the year have affected the relevance of information obtained in previous years.

4.3.1 Inquiries of management and others within the entity

The auditors will usually obtain most of the information they require from staff in the accounts department, but may also need to make enquiries of other personnel, for example, internal audit, production staff or those charged with governance.

4.3.2 Examples

Those charged with governance may give insight into the environment in which the financial statements are prepared. In-house legal counsel may help with understanding matters such as outstanding litigation, or compliance with laws and regulations. Sales and marketing personnel may give information about marketing strategies and sales trends.

4.3.3 Analytical procedures

Analytical procedures are a useful tool in risk assessment.

Key term

> **Analytical procedures** consist of the analysis of significant ratios and trends including the resulting investigations of fluctuations and relationships that are inconsistent with other relevant information or which deviate from predictable amounts.

Point to note

> We shall look at the mechanics of analytical procedures in Chapter 12.

4.3.4 Observation and inspection

These techniques are likely to confirm the answers made to inquiries made of management. They will include observing the normal operations of a company, reading documents or manuals relating to the client's operations or visiting premises and meeting staff.

5 Assessing the risks of material misstatement   6/05

When the auditor has obtained an understanding of the entity, he must assess the risks of material misstatement in the financial statements, also identifying significant risks.

5.1 Identifying and assessing the risks

The ISA says that 'the auditor should **identify** and **assess the risks of material misstatement** at the **financial statement level**, and at the **assertion level** for classes of transactions, account balances and disclosures'. It requires the auditor to take the following steps:

Step 1   Identify risks throughout the process of obtaining an understanding of the entity

Step 2   Relate the risks to what can go wrong at the assertion level

Step 3   Consider whether the risks are of a magnitude that could result in a material misstatement

Step 4   Consider the likelihood of the risks causing a material misstatement

5.2 Example

The audit team at Ockey Ltd has been carrying out procedures to obtain an understanding of the entity. In the course of making inquiries about the stock system, they have discovered that Ockey Ltd designs and produces tableware to order for a number of high street stores. It also makes a number of standard lines of tableware, which it sells to a number of wholesalers. By the terms of its contracts with the high street stores, it is not entitled to sell uncalled stocks designed for them to wholesalers. Ockey Ltd regularly produces 10% more than the high street stores have ordered, in order to ensure that they meet requirements when the stores do their quality control check. Certain stores have more stringent control requirements than others and regularly reject some of the stock.

The knowledge above suggests two risks, one that the company may have obsolescent stock, and the other that if their production quality standards are insufficiently high, they could run the risk of losing custom.

We shall look at each of these risks in turn and relate them to the assertion level.

Stock

If certain of the stock are obsolescent due to the fact that it has been produced in excess of the customer's requirement and there is no other available market for the stock, then there is a risk that stock as a whole in the financial statements will not be carried at the **appropriate value**. Given that stock is likely to be a material balance in the balance sheet of a manufacturing company, and the misstatement could be up to 10% of the total value, this has the capacity to be a material misstatement.

The factors that will contribute to the likelihood of these risks causing a misstatement are matters such as:

- Whether management regularly review stock levels and scrap items that are obsolescent
- Whether such items are identified and scrapped at the stock count
- Whether such items can be put back into production and changed so that they are saleable

Losing custom

The long term risk of losing custom is a risk that in the future the company will not be able to operate (a going concern risk, which we shall look at in more detail in Chapter 18). It could have an impact on the financial statements, if disputed sales were attributed to customers, sales and trade debtors could be overstated, that is, not carried at the correct **value**. However, it appears less likely that this would be a material problem in either area, as the problem is likely to be restricted to a few number of customers, and only a few number of sales to those customers.

Again, review of the company's controls over the recording of sales and the debt collection procedures of the company would indicate how likely these risks to the financial statements are to materialise.

Question   Assessing the risks of material misstatement

You are involved with the audit of Tantpro Ltd, a small company. You have been carrying out procedures to gain an understanding of the entity. The following matters have come to your attention:

The company offers standard credit terms to its customers of 60 days from the date of invoice. Statements are sent to customers on a monthly basis. However, Tantpro Ltd does not employ a credit controller, and other than sending the statements on a monthly basis, it does not otherwise communicate with its customers on a systematic basis. On occasion, the sales ledger clerk may telephone a customer if the company has not received a payment for some time. Some customers pay regularly according to the credit terms offered to them, but others pay on a very haphazard basis and do not provide a remittance advice. Sales ledger receipts are entered onto the sales ledger but not matched to invoices remitted. The company does not produce an aged list of balances.

Required

From the above information, assess the risks of material misstatement arising at in the financial statements. Outline the potential materiality of the risks and discuss factors in the likelihood of the risks arising.

Answer

The key risk arising from the above information is that trade debtors will not be carried at the appropriate **value** in the financial statements, as some may be irrecoverable. Where receipts are not matched against invoices in the ledger, the balance on the ledger may include old invoices that the customer has no intention of paying.

It is difficult to assess at this stage whether this is likely to be material. Trade debtors is likely to be a material balance in the financial statements, but the number of irrecoverable balances may not be material. Analytical procedures, for example, to see if the level of accounts receivable has risen year on year, in a manner that is not explained by price rises or levels of production, might help to assess this.

A key factor that affects the likelihood of the material misstatement arising is the poor controls over the sales ledger. The fact that invoices are not matched against receipts increases the chance of old invoices not having been paid and not noticed by Tantpro Co. It appears reasonably likely that the trade debtors balance is overstated in this instance.

Exam focus point

The risk question in December 2005 required candidates to 'identify and describe the matters that give rise to audit risks associated with Parker' in a similar way as you have just done for Tantpro Co.

5.3 Significant risks

FAST FORWARD

Significant risks are complex or unusual transactions, those that may indicate fraud or other special risks.

Some risks identified may be significant risks, in which case they present **special audit considerations** for the auditors. The following factors indicate that a risk might be a significant risk:

- Risk of fraud (see Section 7)
- Its relationship with recent developments
- The degree of subjectivity in the financial information
- It is an unusual transaction
- It is a significant transaction with a related party
- The complexity of the transaction

Routine, non-complex transactions are less likely to give rise to significant risk than unusual transactions or matters of director judgement. This is because unusual transactions are likely to have more:

- Management intervention
- Complex accounting principles or calculations

- Manual intervention
- Opportunity for control procedures not to be followed

When the auditor identifies a significant risk, if he hasn't done so already, he must evaluate the design and implementation of the entity's controls in that area.

6 Responding to the risk assessment

The auditor must **formulate an approach** to assessed risks of material misstatement.

The main requirement of ISA (UK and Ireland) 330 *The auditor's procedures in response to assessed risks* is 'in order to reduce audit risk to an acceptably low level, the auditor should determine overall responses to assessed risks at the financial statement level, and should design and perform further audit procedures to respond to assessed risks at the assertion level'.

In other words, having assessed the risks of material misstatements in the financial statements, the auditor has to **plan the work** that will be carried out **to ensure** that **he can give an opinion** that the financial statements give a true and fair view, that is, that any material misstatements have been identified and amended if necessary.

6.1 Overall responses

Overall responses include issues such as emphasising to the team the importance of professional scepticism, allocating more staff, using experts or providing more supervision.

Overall responses to risks of material misstatement will be changes to the general audit strategy or re-affirmations to staff of the general audit strategy. For example:

- Emphasising to audit staff the need to maintain professional scepticism
- Assigning additional or more experienced staff to the audit team
- Using experts
- Providing more supervision on the audit
- Incorporating more unpredictability into the audit procedures

The evaluation of the control environment that will have taken place as part of the assessment of the client's internal control systems will help the auditor determine whether they are going to take a substantive approach (focusing mainly on substantive procedures) or a combined approach (tests of control and substantive procedures).

6.2 Responses to the risks of material misstatement at the assertion level

The auditor must also determine **further audit procedures** to address the risks of material misstatement.

The ISA says that 'the auditor should design and perform further audit procedures whose **nature**, **timing** and **extent** are responsive to the assessed risks of material misstatement at the assertion level'. Nature refers to the purpose and the type of test that is carried out. We have already considered the extent of audit tests in Chapter 6 when we considered sampling.

6.2.1 Tests of control

The ISA states that 'when the auditor's assessment of risks of material misstatement includes an expectation that controls are operating effectively, the auditor should perform tests of controls to obtain sufficient appropriate audit evidence that the controls were operating effectively at relevant times during the period under audit'. So, for example, if controls over sales and debtors were expected to operate effectively, auditors should test controls in that area.

It may also be necessary to undertake tests of control when it will not be possible to obtain sufficient appropriate audit evidence simply from substantive procedures. This might be the case if the entity conducts its business using IT systems which do not produce documentation of transactions.

In carrying out tests of control, auditors must use **inquiry**, but must not only use inquiry. Other procedures must also be used. In testing controls, **reperformance** by the auditor will often be a helpful procedure, as will **inspection**.

When considering timing in relation to tests of controls, the purpose of the test will be important. For example, if the company carries out a year end stock count, controls over the stock count can only be tested at the year end. Other controls will operate all year, and the auditor may need to test that controls have been effective all year.

Some controls may have been tested in prior audits and the auditor may choose to rely on that evidence of their effectiveness. If this is the case, the auditor must obtain evidence about any changes since the controls were last tested and must test the controls if they have changed. In any case, controls should be tested for effectiveness at least once in every three audits.

If the related risk has been designated a significant risk, the auditor should not rely on testing carried out in prior years, but should carry out testing in the current year.

6.2.2 Substantive procedures

FAST FORWARD

Substantive procedures must be carried out on **material** items. There are also a number of substantive procedures that must be carried out on the preparation of the financial statements.

The auditor must always carry out substantive procedures on material items. The ISA says 'irrespective of the assessed risk of material misstatement, the auditor should design and perform substantive procedures for each material class of transactions, account balance and disclosure'.

In addition, the auditor **must** carry out the following substantive procedures:

- Agreeing the financial statements to the underlying accounting records
- Examining material journal entries
- Examining other adjustments made in preparing the financial statements

As you know, substantive procedures fall into two categories: analytical procedures and other procedures. The auditor must determine when it is appropriate to use which type of substantive procedure.

Analytical procedures tend to be appropriate for large volumes of predictable transactions (for example, wages and salaries). **Other procedures (tests of detail)** may be appropriate to gain information about account balances (for example, stock or trade debtors), particularly verifying the assertions of existence and valuation.

Tests of detail rather than analytical procedures are likely to be more appropriate with regard to matters which have been identified as **significant risks**, but the auditor must determine procedures that are specifically responsive to that risk, which may include analytical procedures. Significant risks are likely to be the most difficult to obtain sufficient appropriate evidence about.

6.2.3 Timing of substantive procedures and tests of controls

Auditors may carry out their audit work for one year in two or more sittings. When they do so, they call these sittings the **interim audit**(s) and the **final audit**.

Key terms

The **final audit** is the main period of audit testing, when work is focused on the final financial statements.

Interim audits are audits undertaken prior to the final audit, often during the period under review. The auditor is likely to carry out tests of control at interim audits.

We have already highlighted the need for the auditors to obtain evidence that controls have operated effectively throughout the period. The ISA says 'when the auditor obtains evidence about the operating effectiveness of controls during an interim period, the auditor should determine what additional audit evidence should be obtained for the remaining period'.

The ISA makes a similar observation with regard to substantive procedures: 'when substantive procedures are performed at an interim date, the auditor should perform further substantive procedures or substantive procedures combined with tests of controls to cover the remaining period that provide a reasonable basis for extending the audit conclusions from the interim date to the period end'.

In addition, with regard to substantive procedures, 'the use of audit evidence from the performance of substantive procedures in a prior audit is not sufficient to address a risk of material misstatement in the current period'. In other words, because the existence of fixed assets was tested last year does not mean it does not have to be tested this year.

This is slightly different to testing the operation of controls, as the controls may be the same year on year, and operated in the same manner. Therefore, the auditor may decide that tests of controls carried out in a prior audit may be relevant to a current year audit, subject to the matters of judgement already discussed.

Point to note

We shall look at the individual tests of control and substantive procedures that auditors carry out in Parts C (Tests of controls) and D (Substantive procedures) of this Study Text.

6.3 Documentation

The need for auditors to document their audit work was discussed in the previous chapter. In this chapter we have referred to two key audit documents: the audit strategy and the audit plan. ISAs 315 and 330 contain a number of requirements about documentation, and we shall briefly run through those here.

The following matters should be documented:

- The discussion among the audit team concerning the susceptibility of the financial statements to material misstatements, including any significant decisions reached

- Key elements of the understanding gained of the entity including the elements of the entity and its control specified in the ISA as mandatory, the sources of the information gained and the risk assessment procedures carried out

- The identified and assessed risks of material misstatement

- Significant risks identified and related controls evaluated

- The overall responses to address the risks of material misstatement

- Nature, extent and timing of further audit procedures linked to the assessed risks at the assertion level

- If the auditors have relied on evidence about the effectiveness of controls from previous audits, conclusions about how this is appropriate

7 Fraud, laws and regulations

FAST FORWARD

When carrying out risk assessment procedures, the auditors should also consider the risk of fraud or non-compliance with law and regulations causing a misstatement in financial statements.

7.1 What is fraud?

Key term

> **Fraud** is an intentional act by one or more individuals among management, those charged with governance (management fraud), employees (employee fraud) or third parties involving the use of deception to obtain an unjust or illegal advantage. Fraud may be perpetrated by an individual, or colluded in, with people internal or external to the business.

Fraud is a wide legal concept, but the auditor's main concern is with fraud that causes a material misstatement in financial statements. It is distinguished from error, which is when a material misstatement is caused by mistake, for example, in the misapplication of an accounting policy.

Specifically, there are two types of fraud causing material misstatement in financial statements:

- Fraudulent financial reporting
- Misappropriation of assets

7.1.1 Fraudulent financial reporting

This may include:

- Manipulation, falsification or alteration of accounting records/supporting documents
- Misrepresentation (or omission) of events or transactions in the financial statements
- Intentional misapplication of accounting principles

Such fraud may be carried out by overriding controls that would otherwise appear to be operating effectively, for example, by recording fictitious journal entries or improperly adjusting assumptions or estimates used in financial reporting.

7.1.2 Misappropriation of assets

This is the theft of the entity's assets (for example, cash, inventory). Employees may be involved in such fraud in small and immaterial amounts, however, it can also be carried out by management for larger items who may then conceal the misappropriation, for example by:

- Embezzling receipts (for example, diverting them to private bank accounts)
- Stealing physical assets or intellectual property (inventory, selling data)
- Causing an entity to pay for goods not received (payments to fictitious vendors)
- Using assets for personal use

7.2 Responsibilities with regard to fraud

Management and those charged with governance in an entity are primarily responsible for preventing and detecting fraud. It is up to them to put a strong emphasis within the company on fraud prevention.

Auditors are responsible for carrying out an audit in accordance with international auditing standards, one of which is ISA (UK and Ireland) 240 *The auditor's responsibility to consider fraud in an audit of financial statements*, the details of which we shall look at now.

The auditors' approach to the possibility of fraud is similar to the approach to the possibility of error, which we have already considered at length in this chapter. The key requirement for an auditor is set out early in the ISA: 'In planning and performing the audit to reduce audit risk to an acceptably low level, the auditor should consider the risks of material misstatements in the financial statements due to fraud.'

An overriding requirement of the ISA is that auditors are aware of the possibility of there being misstatements due to fraud. The team must have professional scepticism and must discuss the possibility of material misstatements due to fraud (how fraud could be perpetrated and by whom, how unpredictability could be added into the audit and such like).

7.2.1 Risk assessment procedures

The auditor would undertake risk assessment procedures as set out in ISA 315 (discussed in section 5) which would include assessing the risk of fraud. These procedures will include:

- Inquiries of management and those charged with governance
- Consideration of when fraud risk factors are present
- Consideration of results of analytical procedures
- Consideration of any other relevant information

In identifying the risks of fraud, the auditor is required by the ISA to make specific enquiries of management regarding fraud (for example, what they think the risk is, what their process for identifying and responding to fraud is, management communications on the topic).

Auditors are also required to enquire of management, internal audit or others whether any alleged, actual or suspected fraud has taken place.

For example, management may have an incentive to report fraudulently if profitability is threatened by market conditions or as a result of new accounting standards, alternatively there may be pressure to meet certain targets to impress shareholders or keep funding.

Alternatively, fraudulent financial reporting could take place because the nature of the entity makes fraud more straightforward for example, if there are significant related parties or the entity is badly managed and there are few controls.

Fraud by misappropriation might be caused by unhappy employees, or opportunities arising out of poor internal controls or because the culture of the organisation is wrong and 'everybody does it'.

The auditors should be alert for evidence of incentives or opportunities for management or employees to carry out frauds.

Similarly to ISA 315, ISA 240 says, 'when identifying and assessing the risks of material misstatement at the financial statement level, and at the assertion level for classes of transactions, account balances and disclosures, the auditor should identify and assess the risks of material misstatement due to fraud. Those assessed risks that could result in a material misstatement due to fraud are significant risks and accordingly, to the extent not already done so, the auditor should evaluate the design of the entity's related controls, including relevant control activities, and determine whether they have been implemented'.

In other words, the auditor:

- Identifies fraud risks
- Relates this to what could go wrong at a financial statement level
- Considers the likely magnitude of potential misstatement
- Comes up with responses to the assessed risks.

The auditor must come up with overall responses and specific procedures to answer the risks of fraud in the audit.

7.3 Reporting

The ISA states 'if the auditor has identified a fraud or has obtained information that indicates a fraud may exist, the auditor should communicate these matters as soon as practicable to the appropriate level of **management**'.

In addition, 'if the auditor has identified fraud involving:

(a)   Management

(b)   Employees who have significant roles in internal control, or

(c)   Others, where the fraud results in a material misstatement in the financial statements the auditor should communicate these matters to **those charged with governance** as soon as practicable'.

The auditor should also make relevant parties within the entity aware of material weaknesses in the design or implementation of controls to prevent and detect fraud which have come to the auditor's attention, and consider whether there are any other relevant matters to bring to the attention of those charged with governance with regard to fraud.

The auditor may have a **statutory duty** to report fraudulent behaviour to **regulators** outside the entity. If no such legal duty arises, the auditor must consider whether to do so would breach his **professional duty of confidence**. In either event, the auditor should take **legal advice**.

7.4 Law and regulations

The auditor is also required to consider the issue of law and regulations in the audit. For example, he must consider:

- Areas of non-compliance where the matter could materially affect the financial statements
- Areas where the auditors could unwittingly become liable for failing to report matters, such as in the area of money laundering

Auditors are given guidance in ISA 250 *Consideration of law and regulations in an audit of financial statements*, which says 'when designing and performing audit procedures and in evaluating and reporting the results thereof, the auditor should recognise that non-compliance by the entity with laws and regulations may materially affect the financial statements'.

In other words, whether the entity has complied with relevant law and regulation is another factor for the auditor to consider when carrying out his procedures to gain an understanding of the entity and assessing risks of material misstatement in the financial statements.

7.4.1 When non-compliance is indicated

The auditors should gain an understanding of the situation and discuss it with management, unless they are required by law to report their findings directly to a third party. They should consider whether their discovery casts doubt on anything management has said to them during the audit.

If the auditor suspects that a particular level of management is involved in the non-compliance, he should discuss it with a higher level of management or those charged with governance.

As we shall discuss in Chapter 19, if any non-compliance has a material impact on the financial statements, the auditor may need to modify his audit opinion.

8 Reviews and internal audit

- Planning an external review is a matter of professional judgement, but should include obtaining a knowledge of the business.

- Internal audit departments need to plan also, both at an **annual department level** and at an **individual assignment level**.

8.1 Reviews

A review is an exercise similar to audit. The guidance given in ISRE 2400 relating to a review is not specifically examinable, but it is useful to consider briefly and to compare to guidance on audit planning.

ISRE 2400 states that the auditor 'should plan the work so that an effective engagement will be performed'. The standard therefore leaves this as a matter of judgement for the auditor to consider.

However, the standard also states that 'the auditor should obtain or update the knowledge of the business'. This should include consideration of the following factors:

- The entity's organisation
- The accounting systems
- The operating characteristics of the entity
- The nature of its assets, liabilities, revenues and expenses

The standard requires that the auditor have sufficient understanding of the business to be able to make appropriate enquiries as part of the review exercise.

8.2 Internal audit

Purposes of internal audit planning

- Determine priorities
- Establish the most cost-effective way of doing the work
- Assist in the direction and control of work
- Ensure that attention is devoted to critical aspects of work
- Ensure that work is completed in accordance with pre-determined targets

Key terms

The **strategic plan** is a long term plan covering a period of between 2 and 5 years. During this time, all major systems should be audited. The plan should set out the audit objectives, areas, types of activity, frequency of audit and resources to be applied.

The **periodic plan** is typically set out for a financial year and it translates the strategic plan for that year into a schedule of assignments to be carried out, allocating staff and resources. It is likely to be approved by management.

Operational work plans are those plans produced for each audit assignment. They should cover the objectives and scope of the audit, include time budgets and outline procedures and methods.

All of the types of plan outlined above should be flexible, so that the plans can be adapted to the changing needs of the business.

When the audit plans (above) are formulated, the following stages should be followed:

Stage 1 Identify the objectives of the organisation

Stage 2 Define internal audit objectives

Stage 3 Take account of relevant legal and regulatory changes

Stage 4 Obtain a comprehensive understanding of the systems, structure and operations

Stage 5 Identify, evaluate and rank risks to which the company is exposed

The issue of risk management has already been discussed in Chapter 4. The internal auditors will incorporate their knowledge and understanding of risk into all the strategic audit plans they prepare.

Stage 6 Take account of changes in structure or systems during the period, known strengths and weaknesses in the system, management concerns and expectations

Stage 7 Identify audit areas by service, function and major systems

For example, the team might audit divisions of the business separately, or focus on the Human Resources department, or the sales systems.

Stage 8 Determine the type of audit, for example, systems, verification, value for money

A systems audit might be conducted on the sales or purchase system, for example. If the internal auditors were investigating a fraud, they might use a verification or substantive approach, trying to substantiate financial results to third party evidence. Value for money audits were discussed in Chapter 4.

Stage 9 Take account of any external audit or review plans

The company will not want internal audit to carry out work that the external audit team plan to carry out as part of their audit as this is not cost-effective. On the other hand, the external audit team might make use of work performed by internal audit (see Chapter 8) which might be cheaper for the company.

Stage 10 Assess staff resources and match to requirements

We will discuss staffing in Chapter 8.

Chapter Roundup

- The auditors formulate an overall audit strategy which is translated into a detailed audit plan for audit staff to follow.

- The auditor usually adopts a **risk-based approach** to auditing and focuses his testing on the riskiest balances and classes of transactions.

- Audit risk has two elements, the **risk that the financial statements contain a material misstatement** and the **risk that the auditors will fail to detect any material misstatements**.

- Risk of material misstatements in the financial statement has two elements, **inherent** and **control** risk.

- The risk that the auditor will fail to detect material misstatements is known as **detection** risk.

- **Materiality** should be calculated at the planning stages of all audits. The calculation or estimation of materiality should be based on experience and judgement.

- Materiality should be reviewed during the audit.

- The auditor is required to **obtain an understanding of the entity and its environment** in order to be able to assess the risks of material misstatements.

- When the auditor has obtained an understanding of the entity, he must assess the risks of material misstatement in the financial statements, also identifying significant risks.

- **Significant risks** are complex or unusual transactions, those that may indicate fraud or other special risks.

- The auditor must **formulate an approach** to assessed risks of material misstatement.

- **Overall responses** include issues such as emphasising to the team the importance of professional scepticism, allocating more staff, using experts or providing more supervision.

- The auditor must also determine **further audit procedures** to address the risks of material misstatement.

- Substantive procedures must be carried out on **material** items. There are also a number of substantive procedures that must be carried out on the preparation of the financial statements.

- When carrying out risk assessment procedures, the auditors should also consider the risk of fraud or non-compliance with law and regulations causing a misstatement in financial statements.

- Planning an external review is a matter of professional judgement, but should include obtaining a knowledge of the business.

- Internal audit departments need to plan also, both at an **annual department level** and at an **individual assignment level**.

Quick Quiz

1   Complete the definitions:

An .... is the formulation of a general strategy for the audit.

An .... is a set of instructions to the audit team that sets out the further audit procedures to be carried out.

2   Complete the definitions.

.... risk is the risk that .... may give an ....opinion on the financial statements.

.... risk is the .... of an account balance or .... to material ....

3   If control and inherent risk are assessed as sufficiently low, substantive procedures can be abandoned completely.

True   ☐

False   ☐

4   Match the percentages to the values for a correct calculation of materiality

	%
Profit before tax	5
Gross profit	5–10
Turnover	1–2
Total assets	$\frac{1}{2}$–1
Net assets	2–5
Profit after tax	$\frac{1}{2}$–1

5   Which of the following procedures might an auditor use in gaining an understanding of the entity?

(a)   Inquiry
(b)   Recalculation
(c)   Analytical procedures
(d)   CAATs
(e)   Observation and inspection

6   The audit team is required to discuss the susceptibility of the financial statements to material misstatements.

True   ☐

False   ☐

7   Name four factors which might indicate a significant risk.

(1)   ....

(2)   ....

(3)   ....

(4)   ....

8   Name any three potential overall responses to assessed risks.

(1)   ....

(2)   ....

(3)   ....

9   Auditors have a duty to detect fraud.

   True   ☐
   False   ☐

10   Auditors should always report non-compliance with laws and regulations to the statutory authority.

   True   ☐
   False   ☐

Answers to Quick Quiz

1   Overall audit strategy, audit plan.

2   Audit, auditors, inappropriate

     Inherent, susceptibility, class of transactions, misstatement

3   False.

4
	%
Profit before tax	5
Gross profit	$1/2$–1
Turnover	$1/2$–1
Total assets	1–2
Net assets	2–5
Profit after tax	5–10

5   (a), (c), (e)

6   True

7   Any of:

   • Risk of fraud
   • Relationship with recent developments
   • Degree of subjectivity in the financial information
   • The fact that it is an unusual transaction
   • Transaction with a related party
   • Complexity of the transaction

8   Any of:

   • Emphasising the need for professional scepticism
   • Assigning additional/more experienced staff
   • Using experts
   • Providing more supervision
   • Incorporating more unpredictability

9   False

10   False

Now try the question below from the Exam Question Bank

Number	Level	Marks	Time
Q7	Examination	20	36 mins

Using the work of others

Topic list	Syllabus reference
1 Using the work of internal audit	4
2 Using the work of an expert	4
3 Service organisations	4
4 Reporting	4
5 Staff issues	4

Introduction

In this chapter we explore the various groups of people that can have an impact on the statutory audit and what the auditor's attitude to them should be.

Internal auditors can, and often do, carry out similar audit tests to external auditors. The external auditors will sometimes seek to use the work of internal audit. Section 1 of this chapter looks at the extent to which external auditors can use and rely on the work of internal auditors. It outlines the guidance in this matter, which is found in ISA 610.

While auditors are highly trained individuals, it is possible that when conducting an audit they encounter issues which are outside the scope of their expertise, for example, valuation of buildings. In such circumstances an auditor will have to consult an expert. ISA 620, *Using the work of an expert*, outlines the factors an auditor should bear in mind, as we seen in section 2.

It is increasingly common for companies to outsource specific functions to service organisations who have more expertise in that function, for example IT or payroll, then the business. If functions relevant to the audit have been outsourced, the auditor must consider how to obtain the audit evidence he requires to come to his opinion. In section 3, we look at the guidance in ISA 402, *Audit Considerations Relative to Entities using Service Organisations*.

Finally, we consider staffing issues in relation to both internal and external audits.

Study guide

11 – The work of others

Describe the:

- Extent to which external auditors are able to rely on the work of:

    - internal audit
    - experts
    - service organisations

    and recognise when reliance is needed

- Extent to which internal auditors are able to rely on the work of:

    - experts
    - service organisations

- Conditions that must be met before reliance can be placed on the work of others and the planning considerations in co-ordinating the work of others

- Division of responsibilities between auditors and others

- Extent to which reference to the work of others can be made in audit and review reports

Exam guide

The relationship between internal and external auditors could be examined as they are both important syllabus areas. Using the work of experts or auditing areas which have been outsourced could be examined in conjunction with a balance sheet area, for example, stock, as was the case in December 2005.

1 Using the work of internal audit   12/02, 6/03

FAST FORWARD

> External auditors may make use of work internal audit have done when carrying out external audit procedures.

ISA (UK and Ireland) 610 *Considering the work of internal audit* states that as part of their planning procedures, auditors must 'consider the activities of internal auditing and their effect, if any, on the external audit procedures'. While the external auditor has sole responsibility for the opinion expressed, some internal auditor work may be helpful to him in forming a decision.

1.1 Scope and objectives of internal auditing

As we discussed in Chapter 4, the scope and objectives of internal auditing vary widely. Normally however, internal audit operates in one or more of the following broad areas.

- Review of the accounting and internal control systems
- Examination of financial and operating information
- Review of economy, efficiency and effectiveness
- Review of compliance with laws and regulations
- Special investigations

PROFESSIONAL EDUCATION

1.2 Understanding and preliminary assessment of the role and scope of internal audit

An effective IA function may reduce, modify or alter the timing of external audit procedures, but it can **never** eliminate them entirely. Even where the IA function is deemed ineffective, it may still be useful to be aware of the IA conclusions. The effectiveness of IA will have a great impact on how the external auditors assess the whole control system and the assessment of audit risk.

The ISA goes on to say that 'the external auditor should obtain a sufficient understanding of internal audit activities to identify and assess the risks of material misstatement of the financial statements and to design and perform further audit procedures. The external auditor should perform an assessment of the internal audit function when internal auditing is relevant to the external auditor's risk assessment'. The following important criteria will be considered by the external auditors.

ASSESSMENT OF INTERNAL AUDIT	
Organisational status	Consider **to whom** internal audit **reports** (should be the board), whether internal audit has any **operating responsibilities** and constraints or restrictions on it
Scope of function	Consider **extent** and **nature** of **assignments** performed and the action taken by management as a result of internal audit reports
Technical competence	Consider whether internal auditors have adequate **technical training** and proficiency
Due professional care	Consider whether internal audit is **properly planned**, **supervised**, **reviewed** and **documented**

When reporting, internal auditors should report to the whole board or the audit committee and should be free to discuss their concerns with external auditors. They should not report to management upon whose work or responsibilities they are likely to comment; this may mean for example that they should not report to the finance director.

1.3 Using the work of internal audit

The **objectives** of internal audit will differ from those of the external auditors. However, some of the **means** of achieving their respective objectives are often **similar**, and so some of the internal auditors' work may be used by the external auditors. External auditors may use internal auditors' work on the following areas.

1.3.1 Recording an accounting system

The external auditor should carry out walkthrough tests on the records.

1.3.2 Evaluating and testing internal control

If the external auditors are to rely on the work done, say the completion of an internal control evaluation questionnaire, they should check that the method of evaluation is appropriate. They should confirm that internal audit has satisfactorily tested controls in detail by re-performing a sample of internal audit's tests; if internal audit's work is satisfactory, external auditors can make a reduced assessment of control risk as a consequence.

In particular external audit may be able to rely on internal audit's assessment of computer systems, since internal audit may have carried out extensive testing on aspects of the system including controls over development and operation of the system and general controls such as access controls.

1.3.3 Substantive procedures

As external auditors are primarily interested in internal audit's role as a control, the importance of internal audit as a source of substantive evidence will be less. However internal audit procedures may be a source of substantive evidence in particular areas, for example comparing supplier statements with the purchase ledger. If the client has several sites, internal audit may have visited sites that external auditors will not have the chance to visit, and external audit may be able to place some reliance on the work done by internal audit on those sites.

1.4 Timing of liaison and co-ordination

All timing of IA work should be agreed as early as possible, and in particular how it co-ordinates with the external auditors' work. Liaison with the internal auditors should take place at regular intervals throughout the audit. Information on tests and conclusions should be passed both to and from IA.

1.5 Evaluating specific internal auditing work

The ISA states 'when the external auditor intends to use specific work of internal audit, the external auditor should evaluate and perform audit procedures that work to confirm its adequacy for the external auditor's purpose'.

The evaluation here will consider the scope of work and related audit programmes *and* whether the assessment of the IA function remains appropriate.

Evaluation	
Training and proficiency	Have the internal auditors had sufficient and adequate technological training to carry out the work? Are the internal auditors proficient?
Supervision	Is the work of assistants properly supervised, reviewed and documented?
Evidence	Has sufficient, appropriate audit evidence been obtained to afford a reasonable basis for the conclusions reached?
Conclusions	Are the conclusions reached appropriate, given the circumstances?
Reports	Are any reports produced by internal audit consistent with the result of the work performed?
Unusual matters	Have any unusual matters or exceptions arising and disclosed by internal audit been resolved properly?
Plan	Are any amendments to the external audit plan required as a result of the matters identified by internal audit?
Testing	Has the work of internal audit been sufficiently tested by the external auditor to confirm its adequacy?

The nature, timing and extent of the testing of the specific work of internal auditing will depend upon the external auditor's judgement of the risk and materiality of the area concerned, the preliminary assessment of internal auditing and the evaluation of specific work by internal auditing. Such tests may include examination of items already examined by internal auditing, examination of other similar items and observation of internal auditing procedures.

If the external auditors decide that the IA work is not adequate, they should extend their procedures in order to obtain appropriate evidence.

1.6 Using the work of others as part of a review

When the auditor uses work carried out by another party (expert or internal auditor) as part of a review, he must be satisfied that the work is satisfactory for the purposes of the report he is issuing. This will be a matter of judgement.

1.7 Internal audit using the work of others

The situation where internal auditors use the work of experts or service organisations is different to when external auditors use them. The experts etc are **contracted** to provide the service to the organisation (of which the IA function is part).

This gives the company contractual rights when they rely on the work. If the directors permit the internal auditors to use the services of an expert, the internal auditors may seek to rely on their work and may be able to sue for negligence if the work is not of a satisfactory quality.

2 Using the work of an expert   12/05

FAST FORWARD

External auditors may make use of the work of an expert when carrying out audit procedures.

2.1 Experts

Key term

> An **expert** is a person or firm possessing special skill, knowledge and experience in a particular field other than accounting and auditing.

Professional audit staff are highly trained and educated, but their experience and training is limited to accountancy and audit matters. In certain situations it will therefore be necessary to employ someone else with different expert knowledge.

Auditors have **sole responsibility** for their opinion, but may use the work of an expert. An expert may be engaged by:

- A client to provide **specialist advice** on a particular matter which affects the financial statements
- The auditors in order to obtain **sufficient audit evidence** regarding certain financial statement assertions

The auditor will generally consider whether there is an expert in the client entity with relevant skill, or if not, whether those charged with governance will contract an expert. If they are unwilling, the auditor will consider hiring an expert.

The following list of examples is given by ISA 620 *Using the work of an expert* of the audit evidence which might be obtained from the opinion, valuation etc of an expert.

- **Valuations of certain types of assets**, eg land and buildings, plant and machinery
- **Determination of quantities or physical condition of assets**
- **Determination of amounts** using specialised methods, eg pensions accounting
- **The measurement of work completed** and **work in progress** on contracts
- **Legal opinions**

The ISA gives the following requirements in relation to using the work of an expert:

- 'When using the work performed by an expert, auditors should obtain sufficient appropriate audit evidence that such work is adequate for the purposes of an audit'

- 'When planning to use the work of an expert the auditors should assess the professional competence of the expert and the professional qualifications, experience and resources of the expert … the auditor should [also] evaluate the objectivity of the expert'

- 'The auditors should obtain sufficient appropriate audit evidence that the scope of the expert's work is adequate for the purposes of the audit'

- 'The auditors should assess the appropriateness of the expert's work as audit evidence regarding the assertion being considered'

- 'If the results of the expert's work do not provide sufficient appropriate audit evidence, or if the results are not consistent with other audit evidence, the auditor should resolve the matter'

2.2 Determining the need to use the work of an expert

When considering whether to use the work of an expert, the auditors should review:

- The **materiality** of the financial statement item being considered
- The **risk of misstatement** based on the nature and complexity of the matter
- The **quantity** and **quality** of other available **relevant audit evidence**

Once it is decided that an expert is required, the approach should be discussed with the management of the entity. Where the management is unwilling or unable to engage an expert, the auditors should consider engaging an expert themselves unless sufficient alternative audit evidence can be obtained.

2.3 Competence and objectivity of the expert

The auditors must consider:

- The expert's **professional certification**, or licensing by, or membership of, an appropriate professional body

- The expert's **experience and reputation** in the field in which the auditors are seeking audit evidence

The risk that an expert's objectivity is impaired increases when the expert is:

- **Employed** by the entity

- **Related** in some other manner to the entity, for example, by being financially dependent upon, or having an investment in, the entity

If the auditors have **reservations** about the competence or objectivity of the expert they may need to carry out other procedures or obtain evidence from another expert.

2.4 The expert's scope of work

Written instructions usually cover the expert's terms of reference and such instructions may cover such matters as follows.

- The **objectives** and **scope** of the expert's work
- A **general outline** as to the specific matters the expert's report is to cover
- The **intended use** of the expert's work
- The **extent** of the **expert's access** to appropriate records and files
- Clarification of the **expert's relationship** with the entity, if any
- **Confidentiality** of the entity's information
- Information regarding the **assumptions and methods intended** to be used

2.5 Assessing the work of the expert

Auditors should assess whether the substance of the expert's findings is properly reflected in the financial statements or supports the financial statement assertions. It will also require consideration of:

- The **source data used**
- The **assumptions and methods used**
- **When** the expert carried out the work
- The reasons for any **changes in assumptions and methods**
- The **results** of the expert's work in the light of the auditors' knowledge of the business, the results of other audit procedures, as other similar work (for example, valuation done previously by the same expert or a comparison of the expert's work against other available information).

Example

An expert valuation of a commercial building could be compared to the value of other, similar commercial building in estate agent's windows or on the web.

The auditors do **not** have the expertise to judge the assumptions and methods used; these are the responsibility of the expert. However, the auditors should seek to obtain an understanding of these assumptions etc, to consider their reasonableness based on other audit evidence, knowledge of the business and so on.

This may involve discussion with both the client and the expert. Additional procedures (including use of another expert) may be necessary.

Exam focus point

Expert opinions are generally obtained in 'difficult' audit areas, for example valuation of assets, and hence the topic is popular with auditing examiners. In December 2005, candidates were asked to explain factors to consider when relying on the work of a specialist diamond valuer for 5 marks. All the issues discussed above were relevant to the answer.

3 Service organisations

FAST FORWARD

There may be special circumstances for an auditor when the client makes use of a service organisation.

Key term

A **service organisation** is an organisation that provides services to another organisation.

ISA (UK and Ireland) 402 *Audit considerations relative to entities using service organisations* provides guidance to auditors whose client uses a 'service organisation' of this type. It describes the auditor reports from the service organisation which the client's auditors may obtain. It states that 'the auditor should consider how an entity's use of a service organisation affects the entity's internal control so as to assess the risk of material misstatement and to design and perform further audit procedures.'

A client may use a service organisation such as one that executes transactions and maintains related accountability or records transactions and processes related data (eg a computer systems service organisation).

3.1 Considerations of the client auditor

A service organisation may establish and execute policies and procedures that affect a client organisation's accounting and internal control systems. These policies and procedures are physically and operationally separate from the client organisation.

(a)   When the services provided by the service organisation are **limited to recording** and **processing client transactions** and the client retains authorisation and maintenance of accountability, the client may be able to implement effective policies and procedures within its organisation.

(b)   When the service organisation **executes** the client's **transactions** and **maintains accountability**, the client may deem it necessary to rely on policies and procedures at the service organisation.

The ISA states, 'the auditor should determine the significance of service organisation activities to the client and the **relevance** to the audit'.

The ISA lists the following activities as relevant activities. (This is not an exclusive list.)

- Maintenance of accounting records
- Other finance functions
- Management of assets
- Undertaking or making arrangements for transactions as agent of the user entity.

The ISA requires the auditor to understand the terms of the agreement between the service organisation and the user entity. '**User entity and auditors should obtain and document an understanding of:**

(a)   **The contractual terms which apply to relevant activities undertaken by service organisations and**

(b)   **The way that the user entity monitors those activities so as to ensure that it meets its fiduciary and other legal responsibilities.'**

The ISA requires the auditor to consider:

- Whether the terms contain an adequate specification of the information to be provided to the user entity and responsibilities for initiating transactions relating to the activity undertaken by the service organisation.

- The way that accounting records relating to relevant activities are maintained.

- Whether the user entity has right to access to accounting records prepared by the service organisation concerning the activities undertaken, and relevant underlying information held by it, and the conditions in which such access may be sought.

- Whether the terms take proper account of any applicable requirements of regulatory bodies concerning the form of records to be maintained, or access to them.

- The nature of relevant performance standards.

- The way in which the use entity monitors performance of relevant activities and the extent to which its monitoring process relies on controls operated by the service organisation.

- Whether the service organisation has agreed to indemnify the user entity in the event of a performance failure.

- Whether the contractual terms permit the user entity auditors access to source of audit evidence including accounting records of the user entity and the information necessary for the conduct of the audit.

In obtaining an understanding of the entity, the auditor will also consider:

- The **nature of the services** provided by the service organisation

- The **terms of contract** and **relationship** between the client and the service organisation

- The extent to which the client's **accounting and internal control systems interact** with the systems at the service organisation

- The entity's **internal controls** relevant to the service organisation activities.

- The **service organisation's capability** and **financial strength**, including the possible effect of the failure of the service organisation on the client

- Information about the **service organisation** such as that reflected in user and technical manuals

- Information available on **general controls** and **computer systems** controls relevant to the client's applications

If this leads the auditor to decide that the control risk assessment will not be affected by controls at the service organisation, further consideration of this ISA is unnecessary. However, if he concludes that risk is affected, further audit procedures should be carried out.

The client auditor should also consider the existence of **third-party reports** from service organisation auditors, internal auditors, or regulatory agencies as a means of providing information about the accounting and internal control systems of the service organisation and about its operation and effectiveness.

The ISA states that 'if the client auditor concludes that the activities of the service organisation are significant to the entity and relevant to the audit, the auditor should obtain a sufficient understanding of the entity and its environment, including its internal control, to identify and assess the risks of material misstatement and design further audit procedures in response to the assessed risk.'

If information is insufficient, the client auditor should consider asking the service organisation to have its auditor perform such procedures as to supply the necessary information, or the need to visit the service organisation to obtain the information. A client auditor wishing to visit a service organisation may advise the client to request the service organisation to give the client auditor access to the necessary information.

3.1.1 Obtaining audit evidence

The ISA states that **'based on their understanding of the aspects of the user entity's accounting system and control environment relating to relevant activities, user entity auditors should:**

(a) **Assess whether sufficient appropriate audit evidenced concerning the relevant financial statement assessment is available from records held at the user entity; and if not**

(b) **Determine effective procedures to obtain evidence necessary for the audit, either by direct access to records kept by service organisations or through information obtained from the service organisations or their auditors'.**

It also outlines a series of audit procedures

- Inspecting records and documents held by the user entity

- Establishing the effectiveness of controls

- Obtaining representations to confirm balance and transactions from the service organisation

- Performing analytical review on
  - The records maintained by the user entity, or
  - The returns received from the service organisation

- Inspecting records and documents held by the service organisation

- Requesting specified procedures re performed by

    - The service organisation
    - The user entity's internal audit department

- Reviewing information from the service organisation or its auditors concerning the design and operation of its control systems.

3.2 Service organisation auditor's reports

The ISA says 'when using a service organisation auditor's report, the client auditor should consider the nature of and content of that report. If the client auditor uses the report of a service organisation auditor, the auditor should consider making inquiries concerning that auditor's professional competence in the context of the specific assignment undertaken by the service organisation auditor'.

The report of the service organisation auditor will ordinarily be one of two types.

(a)   **Report on suitability of design**. This is the basic report.

(b)   **Report on suitability of design and operating effectiveness**. This will contain the same as a report on design, **plus** an opinion by the service organisation auditor that the accounting and internal control systems are operating effectively based on the results from the tests of control.

While reports on design may be useful to a client auditor in gaining the required understanding of the accounting and internal control systems, an auditor would not use such reports as a basis for reducing the assessment of control risk.

By contrast a report on operating effectiveness may provide such a basis since tests of control have been performed. If this type of report is maybe to be used as evidence to support a lower control risk assessment, a client auditor would have to consider whether the controls tested by the service organisation auditor are relevant to the client's transactions (significant assertions in the client's financial statements) and whether the service organisation auditor's tests of control and the results are adequate.

The auditor of a service organisation may be engaged to perform **substantive procedures** that are of use to a client auditor. Such engagements may involve the performance of procedure of procedures agreed upon by the client and its auditor and by the service organisation and its auditor.

4 Reporting

FAST FORWARD   The auditor's report is the sole responsibility of the auditor.

The auditor is always **solely responsible** for the audit opinion. He must be assured that he has gained sufficient, appropriate advice to have an opinion on the financial statements, he must then express his opinion.

It would therefore be inappropriate to refer to the work of others in his final report. His thoughts on the work of others should, however, be adequately documented in the audit file.

5 Staff issues

5.1 External audit staff issues

FAST FORWARD   Audit partners should use appropriate audit staff for each assignment. They should also undertake direction, supervision and review.

When planning the audit the partner or manager must decide how many staff are to be allocated to the assignment, how experienced (which grade) and whether any of them will require special knowledge, skills or experience.

5.1.1 Example

The client may undertake complicated leasing transactions, so an auditor with some experience of leasing would be required.

The partner will look at the staffing of the audit in previous years and he will need to decide whether that level of staffing was acceptable. He might judge this by looking at the amount of overtime worked last year and whether the budgeted cost was over or under run. This must be gauged with reference to any unexpected problems which arose in the previous year and whether they are likely to recur.

The audit partner is in charge of the audit and it is his opinion that will be given in the audit report.

This can be achieved by:

- Good audit planning which is communicated properly to audit staff
- Allocating work to appropriate members of staff
- Supervising work done by keeping in contact with the audit team
- Reviewing the audit file prior to expressing an opinion

5.2 Internal audit staff issues

FAST FORWARD

> A suitably qualified head of internal audit should be appointed to manage the resources of the department. He should also ensure the ongoing training needs of the department are met.

The internal audit department should have a well-qualified head who should 'plan, control and motivate the resources available to him'. Staff with 'varying types and level of skills' should be employed, including specialists, such as IT specialists.

The head of internal audit should also ensure the ongoing training needs of his department are met so that they can carry out their duties.

Chapter Roundup

- External auditors may make use of work internal audit have done when carrying out external audit procedures.
- External auditors may make use of the work of an expert when carrying out audit procedures.
- There may be special circumstances for an auditor when the client makes use of a service organisation.
- The auditor's report is the sole responsibility of the auditor.
- Audit partners should use appropriate audit staff for each assignment. They should also undertake direction, supervision and review.
- A suitably qualified head of internal audit should be appointed to manage the resources of the department. He should also ensure the ongoing training needs of the department are met.

Quick Quiz

1 An effective internal audit function may eliminate the need for external audit procedures.

True ☐

False ☐

2 Name **four** things the external audit function may consider when evaluating the work of internal audit.

1 ....

2 ....

3 ....

4 ....

3 Complete the definitions using the words given below.

An .... is a person or firm possessing ...., knowledge and .... in a particular field other than auditing.

A .... is an organisation that provides .... to another organisation.

services	special	expert	experience	service	skills	organisation

4 The auditor may not use the work of an expert employed by the organisation being audited.

True ☐

False ☐

5 If the auditor relies on the work of an expert or service organisation, he may refer to that person/organisation in his report and share responsibility with them.

True ☐

False ☐

6 There are four criteria for assessing the internal audit function. Name two.

1 ....2 ....

Answers to Quick Quiz

1   False

2   Have the internal auditors had sufficient and adequate technological training to carry out the work?

Are the internal auditors proficient?

Is the work of assistants properly supervised, reviewed and documented?

Has sufficient, appropriate audit evidence been obtained to afford a reasonable basis for the conclusions reached?

Are the conclusions reached appropriate, given the circumstances?

Are any reports produced by internal audit consistent with the result of the work performed?

Have any unusual matters or exceptions arising and disclosed by internal audit been resolved properly?

Are any amendments to the external audit programme required as a result of the matters identified by internal audit?

Has the work of internal audit been sufficiently tested by the external auditor to confirm its adequacy?

3   expert, special skill, experience
service organisation, services

4   False

5   False

6   (1)   Organisational status
(2)   Scope of function
(3)   Technical competence
(4)   Due professional care

Now try the question below from the Exam Question Bank

Number	Level	Marks	Time
Q8	Examination	20	36 mins

Internal control and audit risk evaluation

Topic list	Syllabus reference
1 Gaining an understanding of control systems	5
2 Limitations of accounting and control systems	5
3 Assessing the risks of material misstatement	5
4 Acting on control risk assessment	5
5 Internal controls in a computerised environment	5
6 Recording of accounting and control systems	5

Introduction

In a modern audit the auditor seeks to rely on internal controls in order to reduce the amount of testing of final balances.

The evaluation of a client's system is essential as the auditor gains an understanding of the entity, as we outlined in Chapter 7. In this chapter, we shall look at some of the detailed requirements of ISA 315 with regard to internal controls, and shall also set out control issues the auditor may come across. The auditors will assess the risks of material misstatement arising and, as we discussed in Chapter 6, may respond to those risks by carrying out tests of controls.

We shall examine the detailed controls that businesses operate in Chapters 10 and 11, and the tests that the auditors may carry out. You should bear in mind the principles discussed in this chapter when considering the controls needed over specific accounting areas.

Study guide

12 – Internal control I

- Describe the objectives of internal control systems and the responsibility for internal control systems in the context of organisational objectives
- Describe the importance of internal control to auditors
- Describe and illustrate the limitations of internal control systems in the context of fraud and error
- Explain the need to modify the audit plan in the light of the results of tests of control
- Distinguish between tests of controls and substantive tests

Exam guide

There is likely to be a question on internal controls in the exam. Remember exam questions can cover the controls that ought to be operating, or how auditors should test the controls that are in place.

1 Gaining an understanding of control systems

> **FAST FORWARD**
>
> The auditors must **understand** the **accounting system** and **control environment** in order to determine the audit approach.

> **Key term**
>
> **Internal control** is the process designed and effected by those charged with governance, management, and other personnel to provide reasonable assurance about the achievement of the entity's objectives with regard to reliability of financial reporting, effectiveness and efficiency of operations and compliance with applicable laws and regulations…designed and implemented to address identified business risks that threaten achievement of any of these objectives.

ISA (UK and Ireland) 315 *Understanding the entity and its environment and assessing the risks of material misstatements* deals with the whole area of controls. It requires that auditors '**obtain an understanding of internal control relevant to the audit**'. The ISA states that internal control has five elements:

- The control environment
- The entity's risk assessment process
- The information system (including related business processes/communication)
- Control activities
- Monitoring of controls

In obtaining an understanding of internal control, the auditor must gain an understanding of the **design** of the internal control (is it capable of effectively preventing or detecting and correcting material misstatements?) and the **implementation** of that control (has it been operated correctly in the year?).

1.1 Control environment

Control environment is the framework within which controls operate. The control environment is very much determined by the management of a business.

> **Key term**
>
> **Control environment** includes the governance and management functions and the attitudes, awareness and actions of those charged with governance and management concerning the entity's internal control and its importance in the entity.

A strong control environment does not, by itself, ensure the effectiveness of the overall internal control system, but can be a positive factor when assessing the risks of material misstatement. A weak control environment can undermine the effectiveness of controls.

Aspects of the control environment (such as **management attitudes** towards control) will nevertheless be a significant factor in determining **how controls operate**. Controls are more likely to operate well in an environment where they are treated as being important. In addition consideration of the control environment will mean considering whether certain controls (internal auditors, budgets) actually exist.

The ISA requires auditors to 'obtain an understanding of the control environment'. In evaluating the design of the entity's control environment, the auditor should consider the following elements:

CONTROL ENVIRONMENT	
Communication and enforcement of integrity and ethical values	Essential elements which influence the effectiveness of the design, administration and monitoring of controls
Commitment to competence	Management's consideration of the competence levels for particular jobs and how those levels translate into requisite skills and knowledge
Participation of those charged with governance	Independence from management, their experience and stature, the extent of their involvement and scrutiny of activities, the information which they receive, the degree to which difficult questions are raised and pursued with management and their interaction with internal and external auditors
Management's philosophy and operating style	Management's approach to taking and managing business risks, and management's attitudes and actions toward financial reporting, information processing and accounting functions and personnel
Organisational structure	The framework within which an entity's activities for achieving its objectives are planned, executed, controlled and reviewed
Assignment of authority and responsibility	How authority and responsibility for operating activities are assigned and how reporting relationships and authorization hierarchies are established
Human resource policies and practices	Recruitment, orientation, training, evaluating, counselling, promoting, compensating and remedial actions

The auditor should see whether control environment elements have been implemented by a combination of inquiries and other risk assessment procedures:

- Observation
- Inspection

1.2 Entity's risk assessment process

The ISA says 'the auditor should obtain an understanding of the entity's process for identifying business risks relevant to financial reporting objectives and deciding about actions to address those risks, and the results thereof'. Factors to consider include how management:

- Identifies business risks relevant to financial reporting
- Estimates the significance of the risks
- Assesses the likelihood of their occurrence
- Decides upon actions to manage business risks

If the entity has a good risk management process, this should assist the auditor in determining the risks of material misstatement.

1.3 Information system

The auditor is required to consider the information system relevant to financial reporting objectives, including the accounting system. The ISA sets out detailed requirements for the auditor to 'obtain an understanding of the information system, including the related business processes, relevant to financial reporting, including the following areas:

- The classes of transactions in the entity's operations that are significant to the financial statements (FS)

- The procedures, within both IT and manual systems, by which those transactions are initiated, recorded, processed and reported in the FS

- The related accounting records, whether electronic or manual, supporting information, and specific accounts in the FS, in respect of initiating, recording, processing and reporting transactions

- How the information system captures events and conditions, other than classes of transactions, that are significant to the financial statements

- The financial reporting process used to prepare the entity's financial statements, including significant accounting estimates and disclosures'

So the auditor needs to understand the whole financial reporting system, including how items such as depreciation (not a transaction) are reported, how the use of journals is controlled, how incorrect processing of transactions is controlled (for example, by use of suspense accounts).

In addition, the ISA says that 'the auditor should understand how the entity communicates financial reporting roles and responsibilities and significant matters relating to financial reporting'.

1.4 Control activities

Key term

> **Control activities** are those policies and procedures in addition to the control environment which are established to achieve the entity's specific objectives.

Control activities include those designed to **prevent** or to **detect** and **correct errors**. Examples include those relating to authorization, performance reviews, information processing, physical controls, segregation of duties.

Examples of specific control activities	
Approval and control of documents	Transactions should be approved by an appropriate person.
	For example, overtime should be approved by departmental managers.
Controls over computerised applications	The ISA requires the auditor to 'obtain an understanding of how the entity has responded to risks arising from IT'. We shall look at computer controls later in this chapter.
Checking the arithmetical accuracy of records	For example, checking to see if individual invoices have been added up correctly.
Maintaining and reviewing control accounts and trial balances	Control accounts bring together transactions in individual ledgers. Trial balances bring together unusual transactions for the organisation as a whole.
	Preparing these can highlight unusual transactions or accounts.

Examples of specific control activities	
Reconciliations	Reconciliations involve comparison of a specific balance in the accounting records with what another source says the balance should be. Differences between the two figures should only be reconciling items. For example, a bank reconciliation.
Comparing the results of cash, security and inventory counts with accounting records	For example, a physical count of petty cash. The balance shown in the cash book should be the same amount as is in the tin.
Comparing internal data with external sources of information	For example, comparing records of goods despatched to customers with customers' acknowledgement of goods that have been received.
Limiting physical access to assets and records	Only authorised personnel should have access to certain assets (particularly valuable or portable ones). For example, ensuring that the stock store is only open when the store personnel are there and is otherwise locked. This can be a particular problem in computerised systems.

1.4.1 Segregation of duties

Segregation implies a **number of people** being involved in the accounting process. This makes it more difficult for fraudulent transactions to be processed (since a number of people would have to collude in the fraud), and it is also more difficult for accidental errors to be processed (since the more people are involved, the more checking there can be). Segregation should take place in various ways:

(a) **Segregation of function.** The key functions that should be segregated are the **carrying out** of a transaction, **recording** that transaction in the accounting records and **maintaining custody** of assets that arise from the transaction.

(b) The various **steps** in carrying out the transaction should also be segregated. We shall see how this works in practice when we look at the major control cycles in Chapters 10 and 11.

(c) The **carrying out** of various **accounting operations** should be segregated. For example the same staff should not record transactions and carry out the reconciliations at the period-end.

1.5 Monitoring of controls

The ISA says 'the auditor should obtain an understanding of the major types of activities that the entity uses to monitor internal control over financial reporting, including those related to those control activities relevant to the audit, and how the entity initiates corrective actions to its controls'.

In many organisations, as we discussed in Chapter 4, the role of monitoring controls fall to an internal audit department. As we discussed in Chapter 8, the auditors may make the use of the work of internal auditors in carrying out their own work.

1.6 Confirming understanding

In order to confirm their understanding of the control systems, auditors will often carry out 'walk-through tests'. This is where they pick up a transaction and follow it through the system to see whether all the controls they anticipate should be in existence were in operation with regard to that transaction.

1.7 Small companies – the problem of control

Many of the controls which would be relevant to a large enterprise are neither practical nor appropriate for the small enterprise. For these the most important form of internal control is generally the **close involvement** of the **directors or proprietors**. However, that very involvement will enable them to **override controls** and, if they wish, to **exclude transactions** from the records.

Auditors can have difficulties not because there is a general lack of controls but because the evidence available as to their operation and the completeness of the records is insufficient.

Segregation of duties will often appear inadequate in enterprises having a small number of staff. Similarly, because of the scale of the operation, organisation and management controls are likely to be rudimentary at best.

The onus is on the proprietor, by virtue of his day-to-day involvement, to compensate for this lack. This involvement should encompass physical, authorisation, arithmetical and accounting checks as well as supervision.

However it is important to stress that in a well run small company there will be a system of internal control. In any case, all companies must comply with the provisions of the Companies Act concerning the maintenance of a proper accounting system.

Where the manager of a small business is not himself the owner, he may not possess the same degree of commitment to the running of it as an owner-manager would. In such cases, the auditors will have to consider the adequacy of controls exercised by the shareholders over the manager in assessing internal control.

2 Limitations of accounting and control systems

FAST FORWARD ▶ There are always inherent limitations to internal controls.

Any internal control system can only provide the directors with **reasonable assurance** that their objectives are reached, because of **inherent limitations**. These include:

- The **costs** of control **not outweighing** their **benefits**
- The **potential** for **human error**
- **Collusion** between employees
- The possibility of **controls** being **by-passed** or **overridden** by management
- Controls being **designed to cope** with **routine** and **not non-routine transactions**

These factors show why auditors cannot obtain all their evidence from tests of the systems of internal control. The key factors in the limitations of controls system are **human error** and **potential for fraud**.

The safeguard of segregation of duties can help deter fraud. However, if employees decide to perpetrate frauds in harness, or management commit fraud by overriding systems, the accounting system will not be able to prevent such frauds.

This is one of the reasons that auditors need to be alert to the possibility of fraud, the subject of ISA 240, which was discussed in Chapter 7.

3 Assessing the risks of material misstatement

FAST FORWARD ▶ The auditors must assess the adequacy of the systems as a basis for the financial statements and must identify risks of material misstatements.

Auditors are only concerned with assessing policies and procedures which are relevant to financial statement assertions. Auditors:

- **Assess the adequacy** of the accounting system as a basis for preparing the accounts
- **Identify** the types of **potential misstatements** that could occur in the accounts
- **Consider factors** that affect the **risk of misstatements**
- **Design appropriate audit procedures**

We have discussed the process of assessing the risks of material misstatement in Chapter 7. The assessment of the controls of an entity will have an impact on that risk assessment.

Risks arising from **poor control environments** are unlikely to be confined to particular assertions in the financial statements, and, if severe, may even raise questions about whether the financial statements are capable of being audited, that is, if control risk is so high that audit risk cannot be reduced to an acceptable level.

On the other hand, some **control procedures** may be closely connected to an assertion in financial statements, for example, controls over the inventory count are closely connected with the assertions of existence and completeness of inventory in the financial statements.

3.1 Where substantive procedures alone do not provide sufficient evidence

We already mentioned in Chapter 7 that there may be occasions where substantive procedures alone are not sufficient to address the risks arising. Where such risks exist, auditors must **evaluate the design** and **determine the implementation** of the controls, that is by **controls testing**.

This is most likely to be the case in a system which is highly computerised and which does not require much manual intervention.

4 Acting on control risk assessment

FAST FORWARD

If the auditors believe the system of controls is strong, they may choose to test controls to assess whether they can rely on the controls having operated effectively.

4.1 Tests of control

Remember

Tests of control are performed to obtain audit evidence about the effectiveness of the:

- Design of the accounting and internal control systems, ie whether they are suitably designed to prevent or detect and correct material misstatements; and

- Operation of the internal controls throughout the period.

Tests of controls are distinguished from substantive tests which are designed to detect material misstatements in the financial statements. This distinction was outlined in Chapter 6.

Some procedures which were not designed or performed as tests of controls may qualify as such and may be used to support a control risk assessment as less than high.

Tests of control may include the following.

(a)   **Inspection of documents** supporting controls or events to gain audit evidence that internal controls have operated properly, eg verifying that a transaction has been authorised

        (b)   **Inquiries about internal controls** which leave no audit trail, eg determining who actually performs each function not merely who is supposed to perform it

        (c)   **Reperformance of control procedures**, eg reconciliation of bank accounts, to ensure they were correctly performed by the entity

        (d)   **Examination of evidence of management views**, eg minutes of management meetings

        (e)   Testing of internal controls operating on **computerised systems** or over the overall information technology function, eg access controls

        (f)   **Observation of controls.** Auditors will consider the manner in which the control is being operated

Auditors should consider:

- **How** controls were applied
- The **consistency** with which they were applied during the period
- **By whom** they were applied

Deviations in the operation of controls (caused by change of staff etc) may increase control risk and tests of control may need to be modified to confirm effective operation during and after any change.

The use of CAATs (Computer Assisted Audit Techniques) may be appropriate.

In a continuing engagement, the auditor will be aware of the accounting and internal control systems through work carried out previously but will need to update the knowledge gained and consider the need to obtain further audit evidence of any changes in control.

4.2 Revision of risk assessment

The auditors may find that the evidence they obtain from controls testing indicates that controls did not operate as well as they expected. If the evidence contradicts the original risk assessment, the auditors will have to amend the further procedures they have planned to carry out.

In particular, if controls testing reveals that controls have not operated effectively throughout the year, the auditor may have to extend substantive testing.

4.3 Communication of weaknesses

Significant weaknesses on internal controls should be communicated in writing with those charged with governance. (See Chapter 20.) The issues which might arise to be reported are discussed in Chapters 10 and 11.

Question	Internal control systems

An internal control system has been described as comprising 'the control environment and control activities. It includes all the policies and procedures (internal controls) adopted by the directors and management of an entity to assist in achieving their objective of ensuring, as far as practicable, the orderly and efficient conduct of its business, including adherence to internal policies, the safeguarding of assets, the prevention and detection of fraud and error, the accuracy and completeness of the accounting records, and the timely preparation of reliable financial information'.

Explain the meaning and relevance to the auditors giving an opinion on financial statements of each of the management objectives above.

Answer

The auditors' objective in evaluating and testing internal controls is to determine the degree of reliance which they may place on the information contained in the accounting records. If they obtain reasonable assurance by means of tests of controls that the internal control system is effective in ensuring the completeness and accuracy of the accounting records and the validity of the entries therein, they may limit the extent of their substantive procedures.

(a)   *'The orderly and efficient conduct of its business'*

An organisation which is efficient and conducts its affairs in an orderly manner is much more likely to be able to supply the auditors with sufficient appropriate audit evidence on which to base their audit opinion. More importantly, the level of inherent and control risk will be lower, giving extra assurance that the financial statements do not contain material errors.

(b)   *'Adherence to internal policies'*

Management is responsible for setting up an effective system of internal control and management policy provides the broad framework within which internal controls have to operate. Unless management does have a pre-determined set of policies, then it is very difficult to imagine how the company could be expected to operate efficiently. Management policy will cover all aspects of the company's activities and will range from broad corporate objectives to specific areas such as determining selling prices and wage rates.

Given that the auditors must have a sound understanding of the company's affairs generally, and of specific areas of control in particular, then the fact that management policies are followed will make the task of the auditors easier in that they will be able to rely more readily on the information produced by the systems established by management.

(c)   *'Safeguarding of assets'*

This objective may relate to the physical protection of assets (for example locking monies in a safe at night) or to less direct safeguarding (for example ensuring that there is adequate insurance cover for all assets). It can also be seen as relating to the maintenance of proper records in respect of all assets.

The auditors will be concerned to ensure that the company has properly safeguarded its assets so that they can form an opinion on the existence of specific assets and, more generally, on whether the company's records can be taken as a reliable basis for the preparation of financial statements. Reliance on the underlying records will be particularly significant where the figures in the financial statements are derived from such records rather than as the result of physical inspection.

(d)   *'Prevention and detection of fraud and error'*

The directors are responsible for taking reasonable steps to prevent and detect fraud. They are also responsible for preparing financial statements which give a true and fair view of the entity's affairs. However, the auditors must plan and perform their audit procedures and evaluate and report the results thereof, recognising that fraud or error may materially affect the financial statements. A strong system of internal control will give the auditors some assurance that frauds and errors are not occurring, unless management are colluding to overcome that system.

(e)   *'Accuracy and completeness of the accounting records'/'timely preparation of reliable financial information'*

This objective is most clearly related to statutory requirements relating to both management and auditors. The company has an obligation under the Companies Act 1985 to maintain proper accounting records. The auditors must form an opinion on whether the company has fulfilled this obligation and also conclude whether the financial statements are in agreement with the underlying records.

5 Internal controls in a computerised environment

There are special considerations for auditors when a system is computerised.

The internal controls in a computerised environment includes both manual procedures and procedures designed into computer programs. Such manual and computer control procedures comprise two types of control.

Key terms

General IT controls aim to establish a framework of overall control over the computer information system's activities to provide a reasonable level of assurance that the overall objectives of internal controls are achieved.

Application controls are the specific controls over the relevant accounting applications maintained by the computer. The purpose of application controls is to establish specific control procedures over the accounting applications in order to provide reasonable assurance that all transactions are authorised and recorded, and are processed completely, accurately and on a timely basis.

5.1 General controls

GENERAL CONTROLS	
Development of computer applications	Standards over **systems design, programming and documentation**
	Full **testing procedures** using test data
	Approval by **computer users** and **management**
	Segregation of duties so that those responsible for design are not responsible for testing
	Installation procedures so that data is not corrupted in transition
	Training of staff in new procedures and availability of adequate documentation
Prevention or detection of unauthorised changes to programs	**Segregation of duties**
	Full records of program **changes**
	Password protection of programs so that access is limited to computer operations staff.
	Restricted access to **central computer** by locked doors, keypads
	Maintenance of programs logs
	Virus checks on software: use of anti-virus software and policy prohibiting use of non-authorised programs or files
	Back-up copies of programs being taken and stored in other locations
	Control copies of programs being preserved and regularly **compared** with **actual programs**
	Stricter controls over certain programs (utility programs) by use of **read only memory**

GENERAL CONTROLS	
Testing and documentation of program changes	Complete **testing procedures**
	Documentation standards
	Approval of changes by computer users and management
	Training of staff using programs
Controls to prevent wrong programs or files being used	**Operation controls** over programs
	Libraries of programs
	Proper job scheduling
Controls to prevent unauthorised amendments to data files	See section below on real-time systems
Controls to ensure continuity of operation	**Storing extra copies** of programs and data files off site
	Protection of equipment against fire and other hazards
	Back-up power sources
	Emergency procedures
	Disaster recovery procedures eg availability of back-up computer facilities.
	Maintenance agreements and **insurance**

The auditors will wish to test some or all of the above general IT controls, having considered how they affect the computer applications significant to the audit.

General IT controls that relate to some or all applications are usually interdependent controls, ie their operation is often essential to the effectiveness of application controls. As application controls may be useless when general controls are ineffective, it will be more efficient to review the design of **general IT controls first,** before reviewing the application controls.

The purpose of application controls is to establish **specific control procedures** over the accounting applications in order to provide reasonable assurance that all transactions are authorised and recorded, and are processed completely, accurately and on a timely basis. Application controls include the following.

5.2 Application controls

APPLICATION CONTROLS	
Controls over **input**: **completeness**	Manual or programmed agreement of control totals
	Document counts
	One for one checking of processed output to source documents
	Programmed matching of input to a expected input control file
	Procedures over resubmission of rejected controls
Controls over **input**: **accuracy**	Programmes to check data fields (for example value, reference number, date) on input transactions for plausibility:
	• Digit verification (eg reference numbers are as expected)
	• Reasonableness test (eg VAT to total value)
	• Existence checks (eg customer name)
	• Character checks (no unexpected characters used in reference)
	• Necessary information (no transaction passed with gaps)
	• Permitted range (no transaction processed over a certain value)

APPLICATION CONTROLS		
	Manual scrutiny of output and reconciliation to source	
	Agreement of control totals (manual/programmed)	
Controls over **input: authorisation**	Manual checks to ensure information input was • Authorised • Input by authorised personnel	
Controls over **processing**	Similar controls to input must be completed when input is completed, for example, batch reconciliations. Screen warnings can prevent people logging out before processing is complete	
Controls over **master files and standing data**	One to one checking Cyclical reviews of all master files and standing data Record counts (number of documents processed) and hash totals (for example, the total of all the payroll numbers) used when master files are used to ensure no deletions Controls over the deletion of accounts that have no current balance	

Control over input, processing, data files and output may be carried out by IT personnel, users of the system, a separate control group and may be programmed into application software. The auditors may wish to test the following application controls.

TESTING OF APPLICATION CONTROLS	
Manual controls exercised by the user	If manual controls exercised by the user of the application system are capable of providing reasonable assurance that the system's output is complete, accurate and authorised, the auditors may decide to limit tests of control to these manual controls.
Controls over system output	If, in addition to manual controls exercised by the user, the controls to be tested use information produced by the computer or are contained within computer programs, such controls may be tested by examining the system's output using either manual procedures or CAATs. Such output may be in the form of magnetic media, microfilm or printouts. Alternatively, the auditor may test the control by performing it with the use of CAATs.
Programmed control procedures	In the case of certain computer systems, the auditor may find that it is not possible or, in some cases, not practical to test controls by examining only user controls or the system's output. The auditor may consider performing tests of control by using CAATs, such as test data, reprocessing transaction data or, in unusual situations, examining the coding of the application program.

As we have already noted, general IT controls may have a pervasive effect on the processing of transactions in application systems. If these general controls are not effective, there may be a risk that misstatements occur and go undetected in the application systems. Although weaknesses in general IT controls may preclude testing certain IT application controls, it is possible that manual procedures exercised by users may provide effective control at the **application level**.

Exam focus point | The examiner expects you to be comfortable with a computerised scenario.

6 Recording of accounting and control systems

The auditors must keep a record of the client's systems which must be updated each year.

There are several techniques for recording the assessment of control risk, that is, the system. One or more may be used depending on the complexity of the system.

- Narrative notes
- Flowcharts
- Questionnaires (for example, ICQ)
- Checklists

Whatever method of recording the system is used, the record will usually be retained on the permanent file and updated each year. Your syllabus focuses on the use of questionnaires.

We can look at two types of questionnaire here, each with a different purpose.

- **Internal Control Questionnaires (ICQs)** are used to ask whether controls exist which meet specific control objectives.

- **Internal Control Evaluation Questionnaires (ICEQs)** are used to determine whether there are controls which prevent or detect specified errors or omissions.

6.1 Internal Control Questionnaires (ICQs)

The major question which internal control questionnaires are designed to answer is 'How good is the system of controls?'

Where strengths are identified, the auditors will perform work in the relevant areas. If, however, weaknesses are discovered they should then ask:

- What errors or irregularities could be made possible by these weaknesses?

- Could such errors or irregularities be material to the accounts?

- What substantive procedures will enable such errors or irregularities to be discovered and quantified?

Although there are many different forms of ICQ in practice, they all conform to the following basic principles:

(a) They comprise a list of questions designed to determine whether desirable controls are present.

(b) They are formulated so that there is one to cover each of the major transaction cycles.

Since it is the primary purpose of an ICQ to evaluate the system rather than describe it, one of the most effective ways of designing the questionnaire is to phrase the questions so that all the answers can be given as 'YES' or 'NO' and a 'NO' answer indicates a weakness in the system. An example would be:

Are purchase invoices checked to goods received notes before being passed for payment?   YES/NO/Comments

A 'NO' answer to that question clearly indicates a weakness in the company's payment procedures.

The ICQ questions below dealing with goods inward provide additional illustrations of the ICQ approach.

Goods inward

(a) Are supplies examined on arrival as to quantity and quality?

(b) Is such an examination evidenced in some way?

(c) Is the receipt of supplies recorded, perhaps by means of goods inwards notes?

(d) Are receipt records prepared by a person independent of those responsible for:

    (i) Ordering functions

    (ii) The processing and recording of invoices

(e) Are goods inwards records controlled to ensure that invoices are obtained for all goods received and to enable the liability for unbilled goods to be determined (by pre-numbering the records and accounting for all serial numbers)?

(f) (i) Are goods inward records regularly reviewed for items for which no invoices have been received?

    (ii) Are any such items investigated?

(g) Are these records reviewed by a person independent of those responsible for the receipt and control of goods?

6.2 Internal Control Evaluation Questionnaires (ICEQs)

In recent years many auditing firms have developed and implemented an evaluation technique more concerned with assessing whether specific errors (or frauds) are possible rather than establishing whether certain desirable controls are present.

This is achieved by reducing the control criteria for each transaction stream down to a handful of key questions (or control questions). The characteristic of these questions is that they concentrate on the significant errors or omissions that could occur at each phase of the appropriate cycle if controls are weak. The nature of the key questions may best be understood by reference to the examples on the following pages.

Internal control evaluation questionnaire: control questions

The sales (revenue) cycle

Is there reasonable assurance that:

(a) Sales are properly authorised?

(b) Sales are made to reliable payers?

(c) All goods despatched are invoiced?

(d) All invoices are properly prepared?

(e) All invoices are recorded?

(f) Invoices are properly supported?

(g) All credits to customers' accounts are valid?

(h) Cash and cheques received are properly recorded and deposited?

(i) Slow payers will be chased and that bad and doubtful debts will be provided against?

(j) All transactions are properly accounted for?

(k) Cash sales are properly dealt with?

(l) Sundry sales are controlled?

(m) At the period end the system will neither overstate nor understate trade accounts receivable?

Internal control evaluation questionnaire: control questions

The purchases (expenditure) cycle

Is there reasonable assurance that:

(a)   Goods or services could not be received without a liability being recorded?

(b)   Receipt of goods or services is required in order to establish a liability?

(c)   A liability will be recorded:

    (i)   Only for authorised items

    (ii) At the proper amount?

(d)   All payments are properly authorised?

(e)   All credits due from suppliers are received?

(f)   All transactions are properly accounted for?

(g)   At the period end liabilities are neither overstated nor understated by the system?

(h)   The balance at the bank is properly recorded at all times?

(i)   Unauthorised cash payments could not be made and that the balance of petty cash is correctly stated at all times?

Wages and salaries

Is there reasonable assurance that:

(a)   Employees are only paid for work done?

(b)   Employees are paid the correct amount (gross and net)?

(c)   The right employees actually receive the right amount?

(d)   Accounting for payroll costs and deductions is accurate?

Stock

Is there reasonable assurance that:

(a)   Stock is safeguarded from physical loss (eg fire, theft, deterioration)?

(b)   Stock records are accurate and up to date?

(c)   The recorded stock exists?

(d)   The recorded stock is owned by the company?

(e)   The cut off is reliable?

(f)   The costing system is reliable?

(g)   The stock sheets are accurately compiled?

(h)   The stock valuation is fair?

Fixed tangible assets

Is there reasonable assurance that:

(a)   Recorded assets actually exist and belong to the company?

(b)   Capital expenditure is authorised and reported?

(c)   Disposals of fixed assets are authorised and reported?

(d)   Depreciation is realistic?

(e)   Fixed assets are correctly accounted for?

(f)   Income derived from fixed assets is accounted for?

Internal control evaluation questionnaire: control questions

Investments

Is there reasonable assurance that:

(a)	Recorded investments belong to the company and are safeguarded from loss?
(b)	All income, rights or bonus issues are properly received and accounted for?
(c)	Investment transactions are made only in accordance with company policy and are appropriately authorised and documented?
(d)	The carrying values of investments are reasonably stated?

Management information and general controls

Is the nominal ledger satisfactorily controlled?

Are journal entries adequately controlled?

Does the organisation structure provide a clear definition of the extent and limitation of authority?

Are the systems operated by competent employees, who are adequately supported?

If there is an internal audit function, is it adequate?

Are financial planning procedures adequate?

Are periodic internal reporting procedures adequate?

Each key control question is supported by detailed control points to be considered. For example, the detailed control points to be considered in relation to key control question (b) for the expenditure cycle (Is there reasonable assurance that receipt of goods or services is required to establish a liability?) are as follows.

(1)	Is segregation of duties satisfactory?
(2)	Are controls over relevant master files satisfactory?
(3)	Is there a record that all goods received have been checked for:
	• Weight or number?
	• Quality and damage?
(4)	Are all goods received taken on charge in the detailed inventory ledgers:
	• By means of the goods received note?
	• Or by means of purchase invoices?
	• Are there, in a computerised system, sensible control totals (hash totals, money values and so on) to reconcile the inventory system input with the payables system?
(5)	Are all invoices initialled to show that:
	• Receipt of goods has been checked against the goods received records?
	• Receipt of services has been verified by the person using it?
	• Quality of goods has been checked against the inspection?
(6)	In a computerised invoice approval system are there print-outs (examined by a responsible person) of:
	• Cases where order, GRN and invoice are present but they are not equal ('equal' within predetermined tolerances of minor discrepancies)?
	• Cases where invoices have been input but there is no corresponding GRN?
(7)	Is there adequate control over direct purchases?

(8)	Are receiving documents effectively cancelled (for example cross-referenced) to prevent their supporting two invoices?

Alternatively, ICEQ questions can be phrased so that the weakness which should be prevented by a key control is highlighted, such as the following.

Question	Answer	Comments or explanation of 'yes' answer
Can goods be sent to unauthorised suppliers?		

In these cases a 'yes' answer would require an explanation, rather than a 'no' answer.

6.3 Advantages and disadvantages of questionnaires

ICQs: advantages

(a) If drafted thoroughly, they can ensure **all controls** are **considered.**

(b) They are **quick** to **prepare.**

(c) They are **easy** to **use** and **control.**

ICQs: disadvantages

(a) The client may be able to **overstate controls.**

(b) They may contain a large number of **irrelevant controls.**

(c) They may not include **unusual controls**, which are nevertheless effective in particular circumstances.

(d) They can give the impression that all controls are of **equal** weight. In many systems one NO answer (for example lack of segregation of duties) will cancel out a string of YES answers.

ICEQs: advantages

(a) Because they are drafted in terms of **objectives** rather than specific controls, they are easier to apply to a variety of systems than **ICQs.**

(b) Answering ICEQs should enable auditors to **identify the key controls** which they are most likely to test during control testing.

(c) ICEQs can **highlight areas of weakness** where extensive substantive testing will be required.

ICEQs: disadvantage

They can be **drafted vaguely**, hence **misunderstood** and important controls not identified.

Question   **Segregation of duties**

Explain the importance of segregation of duties

Answer

Segregation of duties is important because the more people that are involved in all the stages of processing a transaction, the more likely it is that fraud or error by a single person will be identified. In addition the more people that are involved, the less the chances of fraudulent collusion between them.

Chapter Roundup

- The auditors must **understand** the **accounting system** and **control environment** in order to determine the audit approach.

- There are always inherent limitations to internal controls.

- The auditors must assess the adequacy of the systems as a basis for the financial statements and must identify risks of material misstatements.

- If the auditors believe the system of controls is strong, they may choose to test controls to assess whether they can rely on the controls having operated effectively.

- There are special considerations for auditors when a system is computerised.

- The auditors must keep a record of the client's systems which must be updated each year.

Quick Quiz

1   Complete the definition taking the words given below.

………….. …………………. includes the governance and management functions and the……………..,
…………………. and …………. of those charged with …………… and management concerning the
entity's internal ……… and its ………………. in the entity.

| attitudes | importance | control | environment | awareness | governance | actions | control |

2   Name two **key** inherent limitations of an internal control system

1   ……………………………………………

2   ……………………………………………

3   Put the controls below in the correct category

Application controls	General controls

one to one checking	virus checks	hash totals
segregation of duties	passwords	program libraries
review of master files	training	controls over account deletions
back-up copies	record counts	back-up power source

4   Which of the following is not a test of control?

A   Inspection of documents
B   Reperformance of control procedures
C   Observation of controls
D   Verification of value to invoice

5   After the controls have been assessed, the audit plan may be modified.

True   ☐

False   ☐

Answers to Quick Quiz

1 Control environment, attitude, awareness, action, governance, control, importance

2 Human error

Possibility of staff colluding in fraud

3

Application controls	General controls
one to one checking	virus checks
hash totals	program libraries
review of master files	segregation of duties
record counts	passwords
	controls over account deletion
	training
	back-up power source
	back-up copies

4 D

5 True

Now try the question below from the Exam Question Bank

Number	Level	Marks	Time
Q9	Examination	20	36 mins

Part C
Tests of controls

10

Tests of controls: sales, purchases and wages

Topic list	Syllabus reference
1 The sales system	5
2 The purchases and expenses system	5
3 The wages system	5
4 Smaller entities	5

Introduction

We have mentioned tests of controls in the last chapter and have considered methods of sample selection and evaluation. In this chapter we will look at **how tests of controls** might be **applied in practice**. We will examine each major component of an average accounting system.

In Chapter 9 we stated that the auditors must ascertain the accounting system and the system of internal control. The auditors will then decide which controls, if any, they wish to rely on and plan **tests of controls** to obtain the audit evidence as to whether such reliance can be warranted. For each of the systems listed above we will look at the system **objectives** the auditors will bear in mind while assessing the internal controls and give examples of common controls. We shall then go on to look at a 'standard' programme of tests of controls.

In this chapter we deal with **sales, purchases** and **wages and salaries**. These areas are the areas that are most commonly tested in auditing exams.

Study guide

13 – Internal control II – Revenue, purchases and stock

- Describe, illustrate and analyse how internal controls systems over revenue, purchases and stock cycles operate in both large and small entities

- Describe and illustrate the use by auditors of internal control checklists for revenue, purchases and stock transaction cycles

- Describe and tabulate tests of control of revenue, purchases and stock for inclusion in a work program

- Explain and illustrate how structural and operational weaknesses in revenue, purchases and stock systems should be reported to management and how recommendations should be made

15 – Internal control IV – Payroll

- Describe, illustrate and analyse how internal control systems over the payroll transaction cycle operate in both large and small entities

- Describe and illustrate the use by auditors of internal control checklists for the payroll transaction cycle

- Describe and tabulate tests of control of payroll for inclusion in a work program

- Explain and illustrate how structural and operational weaknesses in payroll systems should be reported to management and how recommendations should be made

Note. For items 13-16, an understanding of IT issues and computer controls is required.

Exam guide

The controls relating to receipts from sales were tested in the pilot paper. You should be aware of the links between the transaction cycles and the balance sheet – in the pilot paper, sales systems and debtors.

1 The sales system   Pilot paper, 12/02

FAST FORWARD

The tests of controls in the **sales system** will be based around:

- **Selling** (authorisation)
- **Goods outwards** (custody)
- **Accounting** (recording)

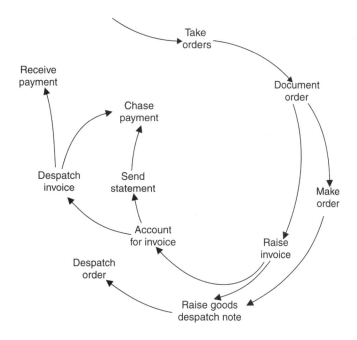

1.1 Control objectives

Area	Objectives
Ordering and granting of credit	• **Goods** and **services** are **only supplied** to **customers** with **good credit ratings** • **Customers** are encouraged to **pay promptly** • **Orders** are **recorded correctly** • **Orders** are **fulfilled**
Dispatch and invoicing	• All **dispatches** of goods are **recorded** • All **goods and services** sold are **correctly invoiced** • All **invoices** raised **relate to goods and services supplied** by the business • **Credit notes** are only given for **valid reasons**
Recording, accounting and credit control	• All sales that have been **invoiced** are **recorded** in the general and sales ledgers • All **credit notes** that have been **issued** are **recorded** in the general and sales ledgers • All **entries** in the sales ledger are **made** to the **correct** sales ledger **accounts** • **Cut-off** is applied correctly to the sales ledger • Potentially **doubtful debts** are **identified**

1.2 Controls

Area	Controls
Ordering and credit approval process	• **Segregation** of duties; credit control, invoicing and inventory dispatch • **Authorisation** of **credit terms** to customers – References/credit checks obtained – Authorisation by senior staff – Regular review • **Authorisation** for changes in **other customer data** – Change of address supported by letterhead – Deletion requests supported by evidence balances cleared/customer in liquidation

Area	Controls
	• **Orders** only **accepted** from **customers** who have no credit problems • **Sequential numbering** of blank pre-printed order documents • **Correct prices quoted** to **customers** • **Matching** of **customer orders** with production orders and dispatch notes and querying of orders not matched • **Dealing** with **customer queries**
Dispatches and invoice preparation	• **Authorisation** of **dispatch** of **goods** – Dispatch only on sales order – Dispatch only to authorised customers – Special authorisation of dispatches of goods free of charge or on special terms • **Examination** of **goods outwards** as to quantity, quality and condition • **Recording** of **goods outwards** • **Agreement** of **goods outwards records** to **customer orders**, **dispatch notes** and **invoices** • **Prenumbering** of dispatch notes and delivery notes and regular checks on sequence • **Condition** of **returns checked** • Recording of goods returned on **goods returned notes** • **Signature** of **delivery notes** by customers • Preparation of invoices and credit notes – **Authorisation** of **selling prices**/use of **price lists** – **Authorisation** of **credit notes** – **Checks on prices, quantities, extensions** and totals on invoices and credit notes – **Sequential numbering** of blank invoices/credit notes and regular sequence checks • **Stock records updated** • **Matching** of sales **invoices** with **dispatch** and **delivery notes** and sales orders • **Regular review** for **dispatch notes** not matched by invoices
Recording and credit problems	• **Segregation of duties**: recording sales, maintaining customer accounts and preparing statements • **Recording** of **sales invoices** sequence and **control** over **spoilt invoices** • **Matching** of **cash receipts** with **invoices** • **Retention** of **customer remittance advices** • **Separate recording** of **sales returns, price adjustments** etc • **Cut-off procedures** to ensure goods dispatched and not invoiced (or vice versa) are properly dealt with the correct period • Regular **preparation** of **trade debtors statements** • **Checking** of **trade debtors statements** • **Safeguarding** of **trade debtors statements** so that they cannot be altered before dispatch

Area	Controls
	• **Review** and **follow-up** of **overdue accounts**
	• **Authorisation** of **writing off** of **bad debts**
	• **Reconciliation** of **sales ledger control account**
	• **Analytical review** of sales ledger and profit margins

1.3 Tests of controls

Area	Test of controls
Ordering and granting of credit	• **Check** that **references** are being **obtained** for **all new customers** • **Check** that all **new accounts** on the sales ledger have been **authorised** by senior staff • **Check** that **orders** are only **accepted** from customers who are **within** their **credit terms** and **credit limits** • **Check** that **customer orders** are being **matched** with **production orders** and **dispatch notes**

Dispatches and invoices	• Verify details of **trade sales** or goods dispatched notes with **sales invoices** checking
	  – **Quantities**
	  – **Prices** charged with official price lists
	  – **Trade discounts** have been properly dealt with
	  – **Calculations** and **additions**
	  – **Entries** in sales day book are correctly **analysed**
	  – **VAT**, where chargeable, has been properly **dealt with**
	  – **Postings** to sales ledger
	• Verify details of trade sales with **entries in stock records**
	• Verify **non-routine** sales (scrap, non current assets etc) with:
	  – **Appropriate supporting evidence**
	  – **Approval** by authorised officials
	  – **Entries** in **plant register**
	• Verify **credit notes** with:
	  – **Correspondence** or other supporting evidence
	  – **Approval** by authorised officials
	  – **Entries** in **stock records**
	  – **Entries** in **goods returned records**
	  – **Calculations** and **additions**
	  – **Entries** in **day book**, checking these are correctly analysed
	  – **Postings** to **sales ledger**
	• **Test numerical sequence** of **dispatch notes** and **enquire** into **missing numbers**
	• **Test numerical sequence** of **invoices** and **credit notes**, **enquire** into **missing numbers** and **inspect copies** of those cancelled
	• **Test numerical sequence** of **order forms** and enquire into missing numbers
	• **Check** that **dispatches of goods free of charge** or on **special terms** have been **authorised** by management

Area	Test of controls
Recording of and accounting for sales	**Sales day book** • **Check entries** with **invoices** and **credit notes** respectively • **Check additions** and **cross casts** • **Check postings** to **sales ledger control account** • **Check postings** to **sales ledger** **Sales ledger** • **Check** entries in a **sample of accounts** to sales day book • **Check additions** and **balances** carried down • **Note** and **enquire** into **contra entries** • Check that **control accounts** have been **regularly reconciled** to total of sales ledger balances • **Scrutinise accounts** to see if credit limits have been observed • **Check** that **trade debtors statements** are **prepared** and **sent out regularly** • **Check** that **overdue accounts** have been **followed up** • **Check** that **all bad debts written off** have been **authorised** by management

Exam focus point

In the exam you may be asked:

(a)   What controls are appropriate for a specific situation?
(b)   What are the major weaknesses in the system given in the question?
(c)   What are the consequences of the failure or non-existence of controls?
(d)   What tests would auditors use on the controls given in the question?

If you are asked about appropriate controls or weaknesses, remember the **objectives** for the accounting area. Controls should be in place to **fulfil** the **objectives** given, weaknesses will mean that the objectives are not fulfilled. You should also consider the **documentation** and **staff** involved in each area.

You should give enough detail about the controls you suggest to enable a non-accountant to implement the controls.

You should use a similar thought process when deciding how to test the controls. Think of the **objectives** of the system; assess how the controls given **fulfil** those **objectives**; and set out tests which demonstrate whether the controls are working. Remember that different types of test can be used to test different controls. For example inspection can be used to test whether different documents are being compared or documents are being properly authorised. Computation can be used to check invoices have been properly completed or reconciliations correctly made.

The examiner may ask you to describe or compile

• An internal control questionnaire/checklist
• A work plan

relating to internal control. An example of each of these was given in Chapters 9 and 7 respectively.

Question

What tests of control can give auditors assurance that the company's system of control ensures that sales are completely recorded?

Answer

Tests of control over completeness of recording of sales include:

(a)   Sequence tests on sales orders, dispatch notes, invoices and credit notes to ensure that there are no missing numbers or two documents with the same number

(b)   Comparisons of dispatch notes with order and invoices, checking documents are cross-referenced to each other

(c)   Checking posting of sales day book to sales ledger control account and sales ledger

(d)   Checking control account reconciliations have been carried out and have been reviewed by senior staff

(e)   Controls over computerised input including:

    (i)   Control totals
    (ii)   Checking of output to source documents
    (iii) Procedure over resubmission of rejected inputs

Question

You are the auditor of Arcidiacono Stationery, and you have been asked to suggest how audit work should be carried out on the sales system.

Arcidiacono Stationery Ltd sells stationery to shops. Most sales are to small customers who do not have a sales ledger account. They can collect their purchases and pay by cash. For cash sales:

(a)   The customer orders the stationery from the sales department, which raises a pre-numbered multi-copy order form.

(b)   The dispatch department make up the order and give it to the customer with a copy of the order form.

(c)   The customer gives the order form to the cashier who prepares a hand-written sales invoice.

(d)   The customer pays the cashier for the goods by cheque or in cash.

(e)   The cashier records and banks the cash.

Required

(a)   State the weaknesses in the cash sales system.
(b)   Describe the systems based tests you would carry out to check the controls over the system.

Answer

(a)   **Weaknesses in the cash system**

    (i)   The physical location of the dispatch department and the cashier are not mentioned here, but there is a risk of the customer taking the goods without paying. The customer should pay the cashier on the advice note and return for the goods, which should only be released on sight of the paid invoice.

(ii)   There is a failure in segregation of duties in allowing the cashier to both complete the sales invoice and receive the cash as he could perpetrate a fraud by replacing the original invoice with one of lower value and keeping the difference.

(iii)   No-one checks the invoices to make sure that the cashier has completed them correctly, for example by using the correct prices and performing calculations correctly.

(iv)   The completeness of the sequence of sales invoices cannot be checked unless they are pre-numbered sequentially and the presence of all the invoices is checked by another person. The order forms should also be pre-numbered sequentially.

(v)   There is also no check that the cashier banks all cash received, ie this is a further failure of segregation of duties.

If the sales department prepared and posted the invoices and also posted the cash for cash sales to a sundry sales account, this would solve some of the internal control problems mentioned above. In addition, the sales department could run a weekly check on the account to look for invoices for which no cash had been received. These could then be investigated.

All of these weaknesses, and possible remedies, should be reported to management.

(b)   **Tests**

(i)   Select a sample of order forms issued to customers during the year. Trace the related sales invoice and check that the details correlate (date, unit amounts etc). The customer should have signed for the goods and this copy should be retained by the dispatch department.

(ii)   For the sales invoices discovered in the above test, I would check that the correct order form number is recorded on the invoice, that the prices used are correct (by reference to the prevailing price list) and that the castings and cross-castings (ie arithmetic) is correct.

(iii)   I will then trace the value of the sales invoices to the cash book and from the cash book that the total receipts for the day have been banked and appear promptly on the bank statement.

(iv)   I would check that the sales invoices have been correctly posted to a cash or sundry sales account. For any sales invoices missing from this account (assuming they are sequentially numbered), I will trace the cancelled invoice and check that the cancelled invoice was initialled by the customer and replaced by the next invoice in sequence.

(v)   Because of the weaknesses in the system I would carry out the following sequence checks on large blocks of order forms/invoices, eg four blocks of 100 order forms/invoices.

(1)   Check all order forms present; investigate those missing.

(2)   Check sales invoices raised for all order forms.

(3)   Check all sales invoices in a sequence have been used; investigate any missing.

(4)   Cash for each sales invoice has been entered into the cash book.

Using the results of the above tests I would decide whether the system for cash sales has operated without material fraud or error. If I am not satisfied that it has then I will consider qualifying my audit report on the grounds of limitation of scope.

2 The purchases and expenses system   12/01

The tests of controls in the **purchases system** will be based around:

- **Buying** (authorisation)
- **Goods** inwards (custody)
- **Accounting** (recording)

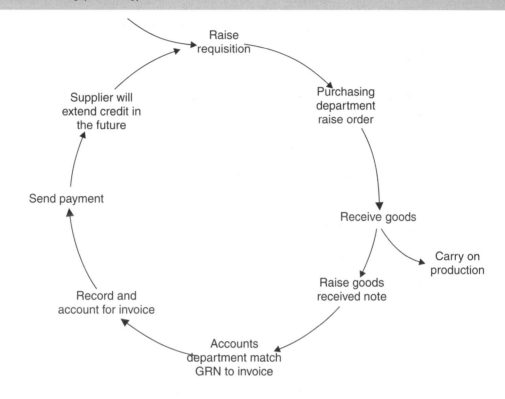

2.1 Control objectives

Area	Objectives
Ordering	• All **orders for goods and services** are properly **authorised**, and are for **goods and services** that are actually **received** and are for the company • Orders are only made to **authorised suppliers** • Orders are made at **competitive prices**
Receipt and invoices	• All goods and services received are used for the **organisation's purposes**, and not private purposes • Goods and services are **only accepted if** they have been **ordered**, and the **order** has been **authorised** • All **goods** and **services received** are accurately **recorded** • **Liabilities** are **recognised** for all **goods and services** that have been **received** • All **credits** to which business is due are **claimed** and **received** • **Receipt** of **goods** and **services** is **necessary** to establish a **liability to be recorded**
Accounting	• All **expenditure** is for goods that are **received** • All **expenditure** is **authorised**

Area	Objectives
	• All **expenditure** that is made is **recorded** correctly in the general and purchase ledger
	• All **credit notes** that are received are **recorded** in the general and purchase ledger
	• All **entries** in the **purchase ledger** are **made** to the **correct purchase ledger accounts**
	• **Cut-off** is **applied correctly** to the purchase ledger

2.2 Controls

Area	Controls
Ordering	• **Segregation** of duties; requisition and ordering
	• **Central policy** for choice of suppliers
	• Evidence required of **requirements** for purchase before purchase authorised (re-order quantities and re-order levels)
	• **Order forms** prepared only when a **pre-numbered purchase requisition** has been **received**
	• **Authorisation** of order forms
	• **Prenumbered order forms**
	• **Safeguarding** of **blank order forms**
	• **Review** for **orders not received** or invoiced
	• **Monitoring** of **supplier terms** and taking advantage of favourable conditions (bulk order, discount)
Goods and invoices received	• **Examination** of goods inwards – Quality – Quantity – Condition
	• **Recording arrival** and **acceptance** of goods (prenumbered goods received notes)
	• **Comparison** of **goods received notes** with **purchase orders**
	• **Referencing** of supplier invoices; numerical sequence and supplier reference
	• **Checking** of **suppliers' invoices** – Prices, quantities, accuracy of calculation – Comparison with order and goods received note
	• **Recording return of goods** (pre-numbered goods returned notes)
	• Procedures for **obtaining credit notes** from suppliers
Accounting for purchases	• **Segregation** of **duties**: accounting and checking functions
	• Prompt **recording of purchases** and **purchase returns** in day books and ledgers
	• **Regular maintenance** of **purchase ledger**
	• **Comparison** of **supplier statements** with **purchase ledger balances**
	• **Authorisation** of **payments** – Authority limits

Area	Controls
	− Confirmation that goods have been received, accord with purchase order, and are properly priced and invoiced • **Review** of **allocation** of expenditure • **Reconciliation** of **purchase ledger** control account to total of purchase ledger balances • **Cut-off** accrual of goods received notes not matched by purchases at year-end

2.3 Tests of control

A most important test of controls is for auditors to check that all **invoices** are **supported** by authorised **purchase invoices** and **purchase orders**. The officials who approve the invoices should be operating within laid-down **authority limits**.

Area	Tests of controls

Receipts of goods and invoices	• Check invoices for goods, raw materials are:
	    − **Supported** by **goods received notes** and **inspection notes**
	    − **Entered** in **stock records**
	    − **Priced correctly** by checking to **quotations**, **price lists** to see the price is in order
	    − **Properly referenced** with a number and supplier code
	    − **Correctly coded** by type of expenditure
	    Trace entry in **record of goods returned** etc and see credit note duly received from the supplier, for invoices not passed due to defects or discrepancy
	• For invoices of all types:
	    − **Check calculations** and **additions**
	    − **Check entries in purchase day book** and verify that they are correctly **analysed**
	    − **Check posting** to **purchase ledger**
	• For credit notes:
	    − **Verify** the **correctness** of credit received with correspondence
	    − **Check entries** in **stock records**
	    − **Check entries** in **record of returns**
	    − **Check entries** in **purchase day book** and verify that they are correctly analysed
	    − **Check postings** to **purchase ledger**
	• Check for **returns** that **credit notes** are duly **received** from the suppliers
	• Test **numerical sequence** and enquire into missing numbers of:
	    − Purchase requisitions − Purchase orders
	    − Goods received notes − Goods returned notes
	    − Suppliers' invoices
	• **Obtain explanations** for **items** which have been **outstanding** for a long time:
	    − Unmatched purchase requisitions
	    − Purchase orders

Area	Tests of controls
	– Goods received notes (if invoices not received) – Unprocessed invoices

Recording of purchases	• Verify that invoices and credit notes recorded in the purchase day book are:
	  – **Initialled** for prices, calculations and extensions
	  – **Cross-referenced** to purchase orders, goods received notes etc
	  – **Authorised** for payment
	• **Check additions**
	• **Check postings** to general ledger accounts and control account
	• **Check postings** of entries to purchase ledger
	Purchase ledger
	• For a sample of accounts recorded in the purchase ledger
	  – **Test check entries** back into books of prime entry
	  – **Test check additions** and **balances** forward
	  – **Note** and **enquire** into all contra entries
	• Confirm **control account balancing** has been regularly carried out during the year
	• **Examine control account** for unusual entries

Question

Purchase controls

Derek, a limited liability company, operates a computerised purchase system. Invoices and credit notes are posted to the bought ledger by the bought ledger department. The computer subsequently raises a cheque when the invoice has to be paid.

Required

List the controls that should be in operation:

(a)   Over the addition, amendment and deletion of suppliers, ensuring that the standing data only includes suppliers from the company's list of authorised suppliers

(b)   Over purchase invoices and credit notes, to ensure only authorised purchase invoices and credit notes are posted to the purchase ledger

Answer

(a)   Controls over the standing data file containing suppliers' details will include the following. These should prevent fraud by the creation of a fictitious supplier.

    (i)   All amendments/additions/deletions to the data should be authorised by a responsible official. A standard form should be used for such changes.

    (ii)   The amendment forms should be input in batches (with different types of change in different batches), sequentially numbered and recorded in a batch control book so that any gaps in the batch numbers can be investigated. The output produced by the computer should be checked to the input.

    (iii)   A listing of all such adjustments should automatically be produced by the computer and reviewed by a responsible official, who should also check authorisation.

    (iv)   A listing of suppliers' accounts on which there has been no movement for a specified period (6 months, 12 months) should be produced to allow decisions to be made about possible deletions, thus ensuring that the standing data is current. The buying department manager might also recommend account closures on a periodic basis.

(v)   Users should be controlled by use of passwords. This can also be used as a method of controlling those who can amend data.

(vi)   Periodic listings of standing data should be produced in order to verify details (for example addresses) with suppliers' documents (invoices/ statements).

(b)   The input of authorised purchase invoices and credit notes should be controlled in the following ways.

(i)   Authorisation should be evidenced by the signature of the responsible official (say the Chief Accountant). In addition, the invoice or credit note should show initials to demonstrate that the details have been agreed: to a signed GRN; to a purchase order; to a price list; for additions and extensions.

(ii)   There should be adequate segregation of responsibilities between the posting function, inventory custody and receipt, payment of suppliers and changes to standing data.

(iii)   Input should be restricted by use of passwords linked to the relevant site number.

(iv)   A batch control book should be maintained, recording batches in number sequence. Invoices should be input in batches using pre-numbered batch control sheets. The manually produced invoice total on the batch control sheet should be agreed to the computer generated total. Credit notes and invoices should be input in separate batches to avoid one being posted as the other.

(v)   A program should check calculation of VAT at standard rate and total (net + VAT = gross) of invoice. Non-standard VAT rates should be highlighted.

(vi)   The input of the supplier code should bring up the supplier name for checking by the operator against the invoice.

(vii)   Invoices for suppliers which do not have an account should be prevented from being input. Any sundry suppliers account should be very tightly controlled and all entries reviewed in full each month.

(viii) An exception report showing unusual expense allocation (by size or account) should be produced and reviewed by a responsible official. Expenses should be compared to budget and previous years.

(ix)   There should be monthly reconciliations of purchase ledger balances to suppliers' statements by someone outside the purchasing (accounting) function.

Question   Tests of controls

You have recently been appointed auditor of Dryden Manufacturing, a limited liability company, and are commencing the audit of the purchases system for the year ended 31 December 20X6. The company has about 200 employees and generally has sufficient staff for there to be a proper division of duties for internal control purposes.

Required

For the audit of the company's purchases system:

(a)   Describe how you would evaluate the controls, and how your audit tests would be affected by the results of this evaluation;

(b)   List the audit tests you would perform (your answer should include consideration of:

(i)   The number of items you would select for testing

(ii)   The basis of selecting the items

(iii)   What action you would take if errors are found, and you should consider the effect of the size and frequency of errors)

(c)   Describe the general form of your conclusions on the results of testing the purchase system and how these conclusions may influence your work at the final audit.

Answer

(a)   Many large audit firms now use a standard method of internal control evaluation questionnaire (ICEQ) based on key control questions. The characteristics of this system are usually as follows.

(i)   It is concerned only with the primary or key controls.

(ii)   The format of the questionnaires leads to a detailed assessment of each of the primary control areas.

(iii)   The ICEQ schedules can normally be linked and cross-referenced to the flowcharts, ICQs or other systems records.

(iv)   It encourages the audit staff to design their tests to suit the particular needs of each client's systems. In other words, it ensures that time is not wasted in performing 'standard' audit programme tests that are not relevant to the circumstances, and that there is a direct link between the evaluation of the system of internal control and the tests carried out.

One method of constructing an ICEQ could be by listing under each major control question the answers of the detailed questions relating to that control which appear in the ICQ and then answering the major question on the basis of the subsidiary questions.

It is also important that against each major control question in the ICEQ there should be space for the auditors to cross-reference their answer to the action they have taken (eg modifying the audit programme or advising the client of weaknesses). An ICEQ will be useless unless the appropriate action is taken as a result of the evaluation.

(b)   The audit tests necessary in relation to the purchases system will depend very much upon the auditors' evaluation of the strengths of the system. Assuming there to be a sound system of internal control in operation, then it will be necessary to carry out a programme of both tests of controls and substantive procedures and these will be spread over the interim and final audit visits. The sample size will depend on:

(i)   The level of tolerable error, the error that the auditor is prepared to tolerate and still conclude that the objectives of the tests have been achieved. For tests of control the level is likely to be low.

(ii)   The level of sampling risk. The more I am relying on the tests, the lower will be the level of sampling risk I am prepared to tolerate, and the higher the sample size will be.

(iii)   The level of control risk. The lower the level, the lower will be the sample size.

Samples should be selected using a method that ensures samples chosen are representative of the population. Random sampling would be one such method.

Typically the majority of the tests of control will be carried out on the occasion of the interim audit and should cover tests on the following.

(i)   Sequence of purchase orders
(ii)   Approval of purchase orders
(iii)   Adherence to authority limits

(iv)   Sequence of goods received records
(v)   Sequence of goods returned records
(vi)   Authorisation of adjustments to purchase ledger balances
(vii) Serial numbering of purchase orders
(viii) Sequence of purchase invoices
(ix)   Correlation of purchase invoices with purchase orders and goods received records
(x)   Correlation of credit notes with goods returned records
(xi)   Checking of castings and extensions on purchase invoices
(xii) Coding of purchase invoices for accounting classification purposes
(xiii) Correct segregation of VAT
(xiv) Initialling of purchase invoice 'grid' for work done
(xv)   Approval of purchase invoices for processing into accounting system

Since the main aim of the testing at the interim stage is to ensure that the company's laid down procedures are being properly applied, it will be necessary to follow up an error on a transaction of £5 in the same way as an error in a transaction of £50,000. Where errors are found further testing will usually be necessary in the area of weakness to confirm whether the error is isolated or recurring. If the errors persist, then management should be informed of the facts and the matters should be noted in the interim comments letter sent by the auditors to the client.

(c)   If the results of the auditors' tests on the purchases system are satisfactory they may conclude that it will produce reliable accounting records and this in turn will mean that they may keep substantive testing at the year end to a minimum. If, however, the tests of control reveal weaknesses in the system then at the final audit, the auditors will have to carry out a more extensive programme of substantive tests.

3 The wages system

12/03

FAST FORWARD

Key controls over **wages** cover:

- **Documentation** and **authorisation** of staff changes
- **Calculation** of wages and salaries
- **Payment** of wages
- **Authorisation** of **deductions**

3.1 Control objectives

Area	Objectives
Setting of wages and salaries	• **Employees** are **only paid** for **work** that they have **done** • **Gross pay** has been **calculated correctly** and **authorised**
Recording of wages and salaries	• **Gross** and **net pay** and **deductions** are **accurately recorded** on the payroll • **Wages and salaries paid** are **recorded correctly** in the **bank** and **cash records** • **Wages and salaries** are **correctly recorded** in the **general ledger**
Payment of wages and salaries	• The **correct employees** are **paid**
Deductions	• All **deductions** have been **calculated correctly** and are **authorised** • The **correct amounts** are **paid** to the **taxation authorities**

3.2 Controls

While in practice separate arrangements are generally made for dealing with wages and salaries, the considerations involved are broadly similar and for convenience the two aspects are here treated together.

Area	Controls
General arrangements	Responsibility for the preparation of pay sheets should be delegated to a suitable person, and adequate staff appointed to assist him. The extent to which the staff responsible for preparing wages and salaries may perform other duties should be clearly defined. In this connection full advantage should be taken where possible of the division of duties, and checks available where automatic wage-accounting systems are in use.
Setting of wages and salaries	<ul><li>**Staffing** and **segregation of duties**</li><li>**Maintenance of personnel records** and regular checking of wages and salaries to details in personnel records</li><li>**Authorisation**<ul><li>– Engagement and discharge of employees</li><li>– Changes in pay rates</li><li>– Overtime</li><li>– Non-statutory deductions (for example pension contributions)</li><li>– Advances of pay</li></ul></li><li>**Recording** of **changes** in **personnel** and **pay rates**</li><li>**Recording** of hours worked by **timesheets**, **clocking** in and out arrangements</li><li>**Review** of hours worked</li><li>**Recording** of **advances** of **pay**</li><li>**Holiday pay** arrangements</li><li>**Answering queries**</li><li>**Review** of wages against **budget**</li></ul>
Payment of cash wages	<ul><li>**Segregation of duties**<ul><li>– Cash sheet preparation</li><li>– Filling of pay packets</li><li>– Distribution of wages</li></ul></li><li>**Authorisation** of **wage cheque** cashed</li><li>**Custody** of cash<ul><li>– Encashment of cheque</li><li>– Security of pay packets</li><li>– Security of transit</li><li>– Security and prompt banking of unclaimed wages</li></ul></li><li>**Verification of identity**</li><li>**Recording** of distributions</li></ul>
Payment of salaries	<ul><li>**Preparation** and **authorisation** of cheques and bank transfer lists</li><li>Comparison of **cheques** and **bank transfer list** with **payroll**</li><li>**Maintenance** and **reconciliation** of wages and salaries bank account</li></ul>
Wages and salaries	<ul><li>**Bases** for **compilation** of payroll</li><li>**Preparation**, **checking** and **approval** of payroll</li><li>Dealing with **non-routine matters**</li></ul>

Area	Controls
Deductions from pay	• **Maintenance** of **separate employees' records**, with which pay lists may be compared as necessary
	• **Reconciliation** of **total pay** and **deductions** between one pay day and the next
	• **Surprise cash counts**
	• **Comparison** of actual pay totals with **budget estimates** or standard costs and the investigation of variances
	• **Agreement** of **gross earnings** and **total tax deducted** with taxation returns

3.3 Tests of controls

Appropriate arrangements should be made for dealing with statutory and other authorised deductions from pay, such as taxation, pension fund contributions, and savings held in trust. A primary consideration is the establishment of adequate controls over the **records** and **authorising** deductions.

Area	Tests of controls
Setting of wages and salaries	Auditors should check that the **wages** and **salary summary** is approved for payment. They should confirm that procedures are operating for **authorising changes** in **rates of pay**, overtime, and holiday pay.
	A particular concern will be joiners and leavers. Auditors will need to obtain evidence that staff only start being paid when they join the company, and are removed from the payroll when they leave the company. They should check that the **engagement** of **new employees** and **discharges** have been **confirmed in writing**.
	Auditors will also wish to check calculations of wages and salaries. This test should be designed to check that the client is carrying out **checks** on **calculations** and also to provide substantive assurance that **wages** and **salaries** are being **calculated correctly**.
	For wages, this will involve checking **calculation** of **gross pay** with:
	• Authorised rates of pay
	• Production records. See that production bonuses have been authorised and properly calculated
	• Clock cards, time sheets or other evidence of hours worked. Verify that overtime has been authorised
	For salaries, auditors should **verify that gross salaries and bonuses are in accordance with personnel records, letters of engagement** etc and that increases in pay have been properly authorised.
Payment of wages and salaries	*If wages are paid in cash*
	• **Arrange to attend** the **pay-out** of wages to confirm that the official procedures are being followed
	• Before the wages are paid **compare payroll** with **wage packets** to ensure all employees have a wage packet
	• **Examine receipts** given by employees; **check unclaimed wages** are recorded in unclaimed wages book
	• **Check** that **no employee receives more than one wage packet**
	• **Check entries** in the **unclaimed wages book** with the entries on the payroll

Area	Tests of controls
	• **Check that unclaimed wages** are **banked regularly** • **Check** that unclaimed wages books shows **reasons** why wages are unclaimed • **Check pattern** of **unclaimed wages** in unclaimed wages book; variations may indicate failure to record *Holiday pay* • **Verify** a sample of **payments** with the **underlying records** and **check** the **calculation** of the amounts paid For salaries, auditors should check that comparisons are being made between payment records and they should themselves **examine paid cheques** or a **certified copy** of the **bank list** for employees paid by cheque of banks transfer.
Recording of wages and salaries	A key control auditors will be concerned with will be the reconciliation of wages and salaries. For wages, there should have been reconciliations with: • The **previous week's payroll** • **Clock cards/time sheets/job cards** • **Costing analyses, production budgets** The total of **salaries** should be **reconciled** with the **previous week/month** or the **standard payroll.** In addition auditors should confirm that important calculations have been checked by the clients and re-perform those calculations. These include checking for wages for a number of weeks: • **Additions** of **payroll sheets** • **Totals** of **wages sheets** selected to summary • **Additions** and **cross-casts** of summary • **Postings** of **summary** to **general ledger** (including control accounts) • **Casts** of **net cash column** to cash book For salaries they include checking for a number of weeks/months: • **Additions of payroll sheets** • **Totals of salaries sheets** to **summary** • **Additions** and **cross-casts** of **summary** • **Postings** of **summary** to **general ledger** (including control accounts) • **Total** of **net pay column** to cash book
Deductions	Auditors should **check** the **calculations** of **taxation** and **non-statutory deductions.** For PAYE and NI they should carry out the following tests: • **Scrutinise** the **control accounts** maintained to see **appropriate deductions** have been **made** • **Check** that the **payments** to the **taxation** bodies are **correct** They should check other deductions to appropriate records. For voluntary deductions, they should see the authority completed by the relevant employees.

Question

The following questions have been selected from an internal control questionnaire for wages and salaries.

Internal control questionnaire – wages and salaries

		Yes	No
1	Does an appropriate official authorise rates of pay?		
2	Are written notices required for employing and terminating employment?		
3	Are formal records such as time cards used for time keeping?		
4	Does anyone verify rates of pay, overtime hours and computations of gross pay before the wage payments are made?		
5	Does the accounting system ensure the proper recording of payroll costs in the financial records?		

Required

(a) Describe the internal control objective being fulfilled if the controls set out in the above questions are in effect.

(b) Describe the audit tests which would test the effectiveness of each control and help determine any potential material error.

(c) Identify the potential consequences for the company if the above controls were not in place.

You may answer in columnar form under the headings:

ICQ question	Internal control objective	Audit tests	Consequences

Answer

	ICQ question	Internal control objective	Audit tests	Consequences
1	Does an appropriate official authorise rates of pay?	Employees are paid amounts authorised	Test rates of pay from payroll to schedule of authorised pay rates (personnel files, board minutes etc)	Incorrect rates of pay could lead to over/under statement of profit
2	Are written notices required for employing and terminating employment?	All employees paid through payroll exist	Check a sample of employees from payroll files for authorisation of employment or termination

Check details for cheque or credit transfer salary payments to personnel files | Payroll may include fictitious employees |

	ICQ question	Internal control objective	Audit tests	Consequences
3	Are formal records such as time cards used for time keeping?	Employees are only paid for work done	Review time records to ensure they are properly completed and controlled Observe procedures for time recording Check time records where absences are recorded to payroll to ensure they have been accounted for Review the wages account and investigate any large or unusual amounts	Overstatement of payroll costs. Employees over/under paid
4	Does anyone verify rates of pay, overtime hours and computation of gross pay before wage payments are made?	Employees are paid the correct amount	Examine payroll for evidence of verification Recompute gross pay (including overtime) Check wage rates to authorised schedule	Misstatement of payroll costs
5	Does the accounting system ensure the proper recording of payroll costs in the financial records?	Payroll costs are properly recorded	Check posting of payroll costs to the nominal ledger	Misstatement of payroll costs

4 Smaller entities

FAST FORWARD

Segregation of duties is a particularly important control in smaller entities.

4.1 Minimum business controls

The control systems in smaller entities are often not as sophisticated as those in larger entities. The particular area that can be a concern for smaller entities with few staff is **segregation of duties**. It can be impossible to adequately share duties between staff when there are only one or two staff.

Having established in Chapter 9 that proprietor involvement is the key to internal control in the small enterprise, we need next to be rather more precise and identify the types of control relevant to each principal accounting area. These controls can be referred to as **'minimum business controls'**.

It is important to appreciate that such controls will not, and **cannot, be evaluated and relied on** by the auditors as in a 'systems' audit approach, but they do **provide overall comfort** to the auditors, particularly when determining whether to seek to rely on management assurances as to the completeness of the accounting records.

The following checklist provides illustrative examples of minimum control standards.

Area and objective	Question
Mail (Cash receipts are complete)	• Is all mail received and opened by the proprietor? • If the proprietor does not himself open the mail, is it opened by a person not connected with the accounts and read by him before it is distributed to the staff?
Receipts (Cash receipts are complete)	• Are all cheques and postal orders received by post counted by the proprietor before they are passed to the cashier? • Are all cheques and postal orders crossed to the company's branch of its bankers 'Not negotiable – account payee only'. • Are cash sales and credit sale receipts over the counter controlled by locked cash register tapes which only the proprietor can open? • Does the proprietor reconcile the cash register totals with the cash sales receipts daily? • Is the person performing the duties of cashier barred any responsibility concerning the sales, purchase or nominal ledgers?
Banking (Cash payments are complete)	• Is all cash received banked intact at intervals of not more than three days? • Does the proprietor reconcile all monies received with the copy paying-in slips at regular intervals?
Payments (Cash payments are complete)	• Are all payments except sundry expenses made by cheques? • Does the proprietor sign all cheques? • Are cheques signed by the proprietor only after he has satisfied himself that: – He has approved and cancelled all vouchers supporting the payment? – All cheques are crossed not negotiable and account payee only? – All cheque numbers are accounted for? • Are petty cash expenses controlled by the imprest system? • Does the proprietor review all expenses and initial the petty cash book before reimbursing the cashier?
Bank statements (Cash/cheques safeguarded against theft and liabilities not paid twice)	• Are bank statements and paid cheques sent direct to the proprietor and opened only by him? • Does the proprietor scrutinise all paid cheques to ensure that he has signed them all before he passes them to the cashier? • Does the proprietor: – Prepare a bank reconciliation each month? or – Review in detail a reconciliation produced by the cashier?
Orders (Purchases are for the business only)	• Are all purchase orders issued: – Serially numbered by the printer? – Pre-printed duplicate order forms? • Does the proprietor approve all orders?
Receipt of goods (Only ordered goods are accepted)	Are delivery notes: • Checked with goods? • Compared with the copy order? • Compared with the invoice?

Area and objective	Question
Wages (Wages are paid to correct employees in correct amount)	• Is a separate cheque drawn for the exact amount to pay wages and tax? • Does the proprietor either prepare or examine the wages records before signing the cheque? • Does the proprietor initial the wages records after his examination? • Does the proprietor oversee the distribution of the wages packets or does he distribute them himself?

Debtors
 	
(Credit is extended to creditworthy customers and debt is chased)
	• If credit is granted to customers does the proprietor:
	  – Authorise every extension of credit to a customer?
	  – Approve credit limits for each customer?
	• Does the proprietor authorise all:
	  – Write offs of bad debts?
	  – Sales returns and allowances?
	  – Discounts other than routine cash discounts?
	• Does the proprietor receive a monthly list of **trade debtors**, showing the age of the debts?
	• Are all authorisations by the proprietor evidenced by his initials?

Goods outwards
 	
(Dispatches are recorded, invoiced and accounted for)
	• Are pre-numbered dispatch notes prepared for all goods leaving the premises?
	• Are all dispatch notes:
	  – Accounted for?
	  – Cross referenced with invoices and credit notes?
	• Is the proprietor satisfied that all goods leaving the premises have been accounted for?

Stock (Stock is kept secure and valued properly)	Does the proprietor scrutinise stock regularly to: • Keep abreast of what is in stock? • Discover obsolete items? • Discover damaged articles? • Ensure that stock levels are kept under control?

Although the above types of control are desirable and feasible, they are nevertheless relatively informal. Consequently evidence of their performance tends to be lacking and they may indeed be overridden as there is no check on the proprietor himself.

Exam focus point

> In the exam, run the following checklist through your mind when approaching questions about controls in smaller entities.
>
> Are you being logical?
>
> • Consider the number of staff the entity is likely to employ.
> • Remember, top management or the owners are likely to be involved on a day to day level
> • Bear in mind a general rule: The smaller the entity, the fewer the daybooks and ledgers...

Chapter Roundup

- The tests of controls in the **sales system** will be based around:

  - **Selling** (authorisation)
  - **Goods outwards** (custody)
  - **Accounting** (recording)

- The tests of controls in the **purchases system** will be based around:

  - **Buying** (authorisation)
  - **Goods inwards** (custody)
  - **Accounting** (recording)

- Key controls over **wages** cover:

  - **Documentation** and **authorisation** of staff changes
  - **Calculation** of wages and salaries
  - **Payment** of wages
  - **Authorisation** of **deductions**

- Segregation of duties is a particularly important control in smaller entities.

Quick Quiz

1   Complete the table, putting the sales system control considerations under the correct headings.

Ordering/credit approval	Dispatch/invoicing	Recording/accounting

   (a)   All sales that have been invoiced have been put in the general ledger
   (b)   Orders are fulfilled
   (c)   Cut off is correct
   (d)   Goods are only supplied to good credit risks
   (e)   Goods are correctly invoiced
   (f)   Customers are encouraged to pay promptly

2   Name five controls relating to the ordering and granting of credit process.

   1   ....
   2   ....
   3   ....
   4   ....
   5   ....

3   When checking sales invoicing the auditor should verify ...., ...
   ,............... and ...., ..., correct analysis in the sales ledger
   and correct posting and that VAT has been dealt with.

4   Complete the table, putting the purchase system control considerations under the correct headings.

Ordering	Receipts/invoices	Accounting

(a)   Orders are only made to authorised suppliers

(b)   Liabilities are recognised for all goods and services received

(c)   Orders made at competitive prices

(d)   All expenditure is authorised

(e)   Cut off is correctly applied

(f)   Goods and services are only accepted if there is an authorised order

5   (a)   Name four examples of purchase documentation on which numerical sequence should be checked

         1   ....

         2   ....

         3   ....

         4   ....

     (b)   Why is numerical sequence checked?

6   Name 6 procedures auditors should carry out if wages are paid in cash.

     1   ....

     2   ....

     3   ....

     4   ....

     5   ....

     6   ....

Answers to Quick Quiz

1

Ordering/credit approval	Dispatch/invoicing	Recording/accounting
(b) (d) (f)	(e)	(a) (c)

2
- **Segregation** of duties; credit control, invoicing and inventory dispatch

- **Authorisation** of **credit terms** to customers

    – References/credit checks obtained
    – Authorisation by senior staff
    – Regular review

- **Authorisation** for changes in **other customer data**

    – Change of address supported by letterhead
    – Deletion requests supported by evidence balances cleared/customer in liquidation

- **Orders** only **accepted** from **customers** who have no credit problems

- **Sequential numbering** of blank pre-printed order documents

- **Correct prices quoted** to **customers**

- **Matching** of **customer orders** with production orders and dispatch notes and querying of orders not matched

- **Dealing** with **customer queries**

3 quantities, prices, calculations, additions, discounts

4

Ordering	Receipts/invoices	Accounting
(a) (c)	(b) (f)	(d) (e)

5 (a) (1) purchase requisitions, (2) purchase orders, (3) goods received notes, (4) goods returned notes, (5) suppliers invoices

  (b) Sequence provides a control that sales are complete. Missing documents should be explained, or cancelled copies available.

6
- **Arrange to attend** the **pay-out** of wages to confirm that the official procedures are being followed

- Before the wages are paid **compare payroll** with **wage packets** to ensure all employees have a wage packet

- **Examine receipts** given by employees; **check unclaimed wages** are recorded in unclaimed wages book

- **Check** that **no employee receives more than one wage packet**

- **Check entries** in the **unclaimed wages book** with the entries on the payroll

- **Check that unclaimed wages** are **banked regularly**

- **Check** that unclaimed wages books shows **reasons** why wages are unclaimed

- **Check pattern** of **unclaimed wages** in unclaimed wages book; variations may indicate failure to record

- **Verify** a sample of holiday pay **payments** with the **underlying records** and **check** the **calculation** of the amounts paid

Now try the question below from the Exam Question Bank

Number	Level	Marks	Time
Q10	Examination	20	36 mins

Tests of controls: other areas

Introduction

This chapter completes the tests of controls topic begun in Chapter 10. Other 'specialised' companies may have different systems, for example a share dealing system in a bank.

Controls over **cash and bank balances** cannot be seen in complete isolation from controls over the sales, purchases and wages cycle. In this chapter we concentrate on controls over and testing of the safe **custody and recording** of cash. You should note in particular the emphasis on prompt recording of receipts and payments, and prompt banking of cash and cheques received. Bear in mind also when you work through the section on bank and cash that controlling cheque receipts and payments is significantly easier than controlling cash receipts and payments.

For **stock**, there should be **proper security arrangements** and **prompt recording**. You should note however the other aspects of control of stock, particularly reviews of the condition of stock, and stock holding policies designed to ensure that the business is not holding too much or too little stock. These controls interest auditors since they may impact upon how stock is valued. We shall discuss valuation of stock further in Chapter 14.

For **fixed assets,** it is vital that there are controls in place to ensure that capital items are capitalised as assets and revenue items are charged to the profit and loss account.

Introduction (continued)

Note that weakness reporting is covered in the section on management letters in Chapter 20.

Lastly in this chapter we shall look at some of the wider **operational cycles** of interest to internal auditors, which were touched on in Chapter 4, and the aims and operations of controls in these cycles. We shall also consider tests of control which **internal auditors** might carry out on them.

Study guide

13 – Internal control II (See Chapter 10)

14 – Internal control III – Revenue expenditure and capital expenditure

- Describe, illustrate and analyse how internal control systems over revenue and capital expenditure transaction cycles operate in both large and small entities

- Describe and illustrate the use by auditors of internal control checklists for revenue and capital expenditure transaction cycles

- Describe and tabulate tests of control of revenue and capital expenditure for inclusion in a work program

- Explain and illustrate how structural and operational weaknesses in revenue and capital expenditure systems should be reported to management and how recommendations should be made

16 – Internal control V – Bank and cash

- Describe, illustrate and analyse how internal control systems over the bank and cash transaction cycle operate in both large and small entities

- Describe and illustrate the use by auditors of internal control checklists for the bank and cash transaction cycle

- Describe and tabulate tests of control of bank and cash for inclusion in a work program

- Explain and illustrate how structural and operational weaknesses in bank and cash systems should be reported to management and how recommendations should be made

Exam guide

Controls testing and substantive testing could both be examined in a question on a specific balance sheet area.

1 The cash system   6/02

FAST FORWARD ▶▶   Controls over cash receipts and payments should prevent fraud or theft.

1.1 Control objectives

- **All monies received** are **recorded**
- **All monies received** are **banked**
- **Cash and cheques** are **safeguarded** against loss or theft
- **All payments** are **authorised**, **made** to the **correct payees** and **recorded**
- **Payments** are **not made twice** for the same liability

1.2 Controls

Key controls over **receipts** include:

- Proper **post-opening** arrangements
- **Prompt recording**
- **Prompt banking**
- **Reconciliation** of records of cash received and banked

A further important control is **regular independent bank reconciliations**

Controls over the **completeness** of **recording** of cash receipts are particularly important. If these controls are inadequate, there may be insufficient audit evidence available when the auditor carries out substantive procedures.

Segregation of duties is also important. The person responsible for receiving and recording cash when it arrives in the post should not be the same as the person responsible for banking it. Ideally the cash book should be written up by a further staff member, and a fourth staff member should reconcile the various records of amounts received.

Controls: Cash at bank and in hand – receipts	
Segregation of duties between the various functions listed below is particularly important.	
Recording of receipts by post	• **Safeguards** to **prevent interception of mail** between receipt and opening • Appointment of **responsible person** to supervise mail • **Protection** of **cash and cheques** (restrictive crossing) • **Amounts received listed** when post opened • **Post stamped** with date of receipt

Recording of cash sales and collections	• **Restrictions** on **receipt of cash** (by cashiers only, or by salesmen etc)
	• **Evidencing** of receipt of cash
	  – Serially numbered receipt forms
	  – Cash registers incorporating sealed till rolls
	• **Clearance** of cash offices and registers
	• **Agreement of cash collections with till rolls**
	• **Agreement of cash collections with bankings and** cash and sales **records**
	• **Investigation** of cash shortages and surpluses

General controls over recording	• Prompt **maintenance of records** (cash book, ledger accounts)
	• **Limitation** of **duties** of receiving cashiers
	• **Holiday arrangements**
	• **Giving** and **recording** of **receipts**
	  – Retained copies
	  – Serially numbered receipts books
	  – Custody of receipt books
	  – Comparisons with cash records and bank paying in slips

Banking	• **Daily bankings** • **Make-up** and **comparison** of **paying-in** slips against initial receipt records and cash book • **Banking** of receipts **intact**/control of disbursements

Controls: Cash at bank and in hand – receipts	
Safeguarding of cash and bank accounts	• **Restrictions** on **opening new bank accounts**
	• **Limitations** on **cash floats** held
	• **Restrictions** on **payments** out of **cash received**
	• **Restrictions** on **access** to cash registers and offices
	• **Independent checks** on cash floats
	• **Surprise cash counts**
	• **Custody** of **cash** outside **office hours**
	• **Custody** over **supply** and issue of cheques
	• **Preparation** of **cheques** restricted
	• **Safeguards** over **mechanically signed cheques**/cheques carrying printed signatures
	• **Restrictions** on issue of **blank** or **bearer** cheques
	• **Safeguarding** of **IOUs**, cash in transit
	• **Insurance arrangements**
	• **Control of funds** held in trust for employees
	• **Bank reconciliations**
	– Issue of bank statements
	– Frequency of reconciliations by independent person
	– Reconciliation procedures
	– Treatment of longstanding unpresented cheques
	– Stop payment notice
	– Sequence of cheque numbers
	– Comparison with cash books

FAST FORWARD

Key controls over **payments** include:

- **Restriction of access** to cash and cheques
- Procedures for **preparation and authorisation** of payments

Controls: Cash at bank and in hand – payments	
The arrangements for controlling payments will depend to a great extent on the nature of business transacted, the volume of payments involved and the size of the company.	
Cheque and cash payments generally	The cashier should generally not be concerned with keeping or writing-up books of account other than those recording disbursements nor should he have access to, or be responsible for the custody of, securities, title deeds or negotiable instruments belonging to the company.
	The person responsible for preparing cheques or traders' credit lists should not himself be a cheque signatory. Cheque signatories in turn should not be responsible for recording payments.
Cheque payments	• **Cheque requisitions**
	– Appropriate supporting documentation
	– Approval by appropriate staff
	– Presentation to cheque signatories

Controls: Cash at bank and in hand – payments	
	– Cancellation (crossing/recording cheque number on requisition)
	• **Authority** to sign cheques

	– Signatories should not also approve cheque requisitions
	  – Limitations on authority to specific amounts
	  – Number of signatories
	  – Prohibitions over signing of blank cheques

	• **Prompt dispatch** of signed **cheques**
	• **Obtaining** of paid **cheques** from **banks**
	• Payments **recorded promptly** in **cash book** and **general** and **purchase ledger**
Cash payments	• **Authorisation** of **expenditure**
	• **Cancellation** of **vouchers** to ensure they cannot be paid
	• **Limits** on **disbursements**
	• **Rules** on **cash advances** to employees, IOUs and cheque cashing

1.3 Tests of controls

Note that as well as testing controls over receipts, auditors are also obtaining evidence to support the assertion that sales and receipts are **completely recorded**.

Area	Tests of control

Receipts received by post	• **Observe procedures** for **post opening** are being followed
	• **Observe** that **cheques** received by post are immediately **crossed** in the company's favour of the company
	• For items entered in the rough cash book (or other record of cash, cheques etc received by post), **trace entries** to:
	  – **Cash book**
	  – **Paying-in book**
	  – **Counterfoil** or carbon copy receipts
	• **Verify amounts entered** as **received** with remittance advices or other supporting evidence

Cash sales, branch takings	• For a sample of cash sales summaries/branch summaries from different locations:
	  – **Verify with till rolls** or copy cash sale notes
	  – **Check to paying-in slip** date-stamped and initialled by the bank
	  – **Verify that takings** are banked intact daily
	  – **Vouch expenditure** out of takings

Collections	• For a sample of items from the original collection records:
	  – **Trace amounts** to **cash book** via collectors' cash sheets or other collection records
	  – **Check entries** on **cash sheets** or collection records with collectors' receipt books
	  – **Verify** that **goods delivered** to travellers/salesmen have been regularly **reconciled** with sales and inventories in hand
	  – **Check numerical sequence** of collection records

Area	Tests of control

Receipts cash book	• For cash receipts for several days throughout the period:
	  – **Check to entries in rough cash book**, receipts, branch returns or other records
	  – **Check to paying-in slips** obtained direct from the bank, observing that there is no delay in banking monies received
	  – **Check additions of paying-in slips**
	  – **Check additions of cash book**
	  – **Check postings to the sales ledger**
	  – **Check postings** to the **general ledger**, including control accounts
	• **Scrutinise the cash book** and **investigate items** of a **special** or **unusual nature**.

Payments cash book (authorisation)	• For a sample of payments:
	  – **Compare** with paid cheques to ensure payee agrees
	  – **Note** that **cheques** are **signed** by the **persons authorised** to do so within their authority limits
	  – **Check to suppliers' invoices** for goods and services. Verify that supporting documents are signed as having been **checked** and **passed for payment** and have been stamped 'paid'
	  – **Check to suppliers' statements**
	  – **Check** to **other documentary evidence**, as appropriate (agreements, authorised expense vouchers, wages/salaries records, petty cash books etc)

Payments cash book (recording)	• For a sample of weeks:
	  – **Check the sequence of cheque numbers** and enquire into missing numbers
	  – **Trace transfers** to other bank accounts, petty cash books or other records, as appropriate
	  – **Check additions**, including extensions, and balances forward at the beginning and end of the months covering the periods chosen
	  – **Check postings** to the **purchase ledger**
	  – **Check postings** to the **general ledger**, including the control accounts

When checking that bank and cash are **secure**, auditors should consider the security arrangements over blank cheques. Bank reconciliations are also a very important control and auditors should carry out the following tests on these.

Area	Tests of control
Bank reconciliations	• For a period which includes a reconciliation date **reperform reconciliation** (see Chapter 16) • **Verify** that **reconciliations have been prepared** at **regular intervals** throughout the year • **Scrutinise reconciliations for unusual items**

Petty cash	• For a sample of payments:
	  – **Check** to supporting vouchers
	  – **Check** whether they are properly **approved**
	  – **See** that **vouchers** have been **marked and initialled** by the cashier to prevent their re-use

Area	Tests of control
	• For a sample of weeks: – **Trace amounts** received to **cash books** – **Check additions** and **balances carried** forward – **Check postings** to the **nominal ledger**

Exam focus point

Questions about the sales or purchases systems may also require consideration of controls over receipts or payments.

2 The stock system

FAST FORWARD

Stock controls are designed to ensure safe custody.

The stock system can be very important in an audit because of the high value of stock or the complexity of its audit. It is closely connected with the sales and purchases systems covered in Chapter 10.

2.1 Control objectives

Area	Objectives
Recording	• All **stock movements** are **authorised** and **recorded** • **Stock records** only **include items** that **belong** to the client • **Stock records include stock** that **exists** and is **held** by the client • **Stock quantities** have been **recorded correctly** • **Cut-off procedures** are **properly applied** to stock
Protection of stock	• **Stock** is **safeguarded** against loss, pilferage or damage
Valuation of stock	• The **costing system values stock correctly** • **Allowance** is **made** for **slow-moving**, **obsolete** or **damaged stock**
Stock-holding	• **Levels** of **stock held** are **reasonable**

2.2 Controls

FAST FORWARD

Important controls over stock include restriction of access, documentation and authorisation of movements, regular **independent stock counting** and **review of stock condition**.

Area	Controls
Recording of stock	• **Segregation** of duties; custody and recording of inventories • **Reception, checking** and **recording** of goods inwards • **Stock issues supported** by **appropriate documentation** • **Maintenance** of **stock records** – Stock ledgers – Bin cards – Transfer records

Area	Controls

Protection of stock	• **Precautions** against **theft, misuse** and **deterioration**
	   – Restriction of access to stores
	   – Controls on stores environment (right temperature, precautions against damp etc).
	 • **Security** over **stock** held by third parties, and third party stock held by entity
	 • **Stock-taking** (see also Chapter 14).
	   – Regular stock counts
	   – Fair coverage so that all stock is counted at least once a year
	   – Counts by independent persons
	   – Recording
	   – Cut-off for goods in transit and time differences
	   – Reconciliation of stock count to book records and control accounts

Valuation of stock	• **Computation** of **stock valuation**
	   – Accords with SSAP 9
	   – Checking of calculations
	 • **Review** of **condition** of stock
	   – Treatment of slow-moving, damaged and obsolete stock
	   – Authorisation of write-offs
	 • **Accounting** for **scrap** and **waste**

Stock holding	• **Control** of **stock levels**
	   – Maximum stock limits
	   – Minimum stock limits
	   – Re-order quantities and levels
	 • Arrangements for dealing with **returnable containers**

2.3 Tests of controls

Most of the testing relating to stock has been covered in the purchase and sales testing outlined in Chapter 10. Auditors will primarily be concerned at this stage with ensuring that the business keeps track of stock. To confirm this, checks must be made on how stock **movements** are **recorded** and how **stock** is **secured**.

Area	Tests of control
Stock movements	• **Select** a sample of **stock movements records** and **agree** to **goods received** and **goods dispatched notes** • **Confirm** that **movements** have been **authorised** as **appropriate** • **Select** a sample of **goods received** and **goods dispatched** notes and agree to **stock movement records** • **Check sequence** of stock records

Other tests that auditors are likely to perform	• **Test** check **stock counts** carried out from time to time (eg monthly) during the period and confirm:
	   – **All discrepancies** between **book** and **actual** figures have been fully investigated
	   – **All discrepancies** have been **signed off** by a senior manager

Area	Tests of control
	– **Obsolete, damaged or slow-moving goods** have been **marked accordingly** and written down to net realisable value
	• **Observe security arrangements** for stock
	• **Consider environment** in which stock are held

Auditors will carry out extensive tests on the **valuation** of stock at the substantive testing stage (see Chapter 14).

Question

Cash-control weaknesses

Jonathan is the sole shareholder of Furry Lion Stores, a company which owns five stores in the west of England. The stores mainly stock food and groceries, and four of the stores have an off-licence as well.

Each store is run by a full-time manager and three or four part-time assistants. Jonathan spends on average ½ a day a week at each store, and spends the rest of his time at home, dealing with his other business interests.

All sales are for cash and are recorded on till rolls which the manager retains. Shop manager wages are paid monthly by cheque by Jonathan. Wages of shop assistants are paid in cash out of the takings.

Most purchases are made from local wholesalers and are paid for in cash out of the takings. Large purchases (over £250) must be made by cheques signed by the shop manager and countersigned by Jonathan.

Shop managers bank surplus cash once a week, apart from a float in the till.

All accounting records including the cash book, wages and sales tax records are maintained by the manager. Jonathan reviews the weekly bank statements when he visits the shops. He also has a look at inventories to see if stock levels appear to be about right. All invoices are also kept in a drawer by a manager and marked with a cash book reference, and where appropriate a cheque number when paid.

Required

Discuss the weaknesses in the control systems of Furry Lion Stores, and how the weaknesses can be remedied.

Answer

Weaknesses in the system, and their remedies, are as follows.

Stock

The shops do not appear to have any stock movement records. This would appear to breach the Companies Act s 221 requirement for the company to maintain proper accounting records. Jonathan has also only a very approximate indication of stock levels. Hence it will be difficult to detect whether stock levels are too high, or too low with a risk of running out of stock. Theft of stock would also be difficult to detect. The company should therefore introduce stock movement records, detailing values and volumes.

In addition regular stock counts should be made either by Jonathan or by staff from another shop. Discrepancies between the stock records and the actual stock counted should be investigated.

Cash controls

Too much cash appears to be held on site. In addition the fact that most payments appear to be for cash may mean inadequate documentation is kept. The level of cash on site can be decreased by daily rather than weekly bankings. In addition the need for cash on site can be decreased by paying wages by cheque, and by paying all but the smallest payments by cheque.

The cash book should obviously still be maintained but cheque stubs should also show details of amounts paid. The cash book should be supported by invoices and other supporting documentation, and should be cross-referenced to the general ledger (see below).

Cash reconciliations

There is no indication of the till-rolls that are kept being reconciled to cash takings.

There should be a daily reconciliation of cash takings and till rolls; this should be reviewed if not performed by the shop manager.

Bank reconciliations

There is no mention of bank reconciliations taking place.

Bank reconciliations should be carried out at least monthly by the shop manager, and reviewed by the owner.

Purchases

There is no formal system for recording purchases. Invoices do not appear to be filed in any particular way. It would be difficult to see whether accounting records were complete, and hence it would be difficult to prepare a set of accounts from the accounting records available.

In addition the way records are maintained means that accounts would have to be prepared on a cash basis, and not on an accruals basis.

A purchase day book should be introduced. Invoices should be recorded in the purchase day book, and filed in a logical order, either by date received or by supplier.

General ledger

There is no general ledger, and again this means that annual accounts cannot easily be prepared (and also management accounts).

A general ledger should be maintained with entries made from the cash book, wages records and purchase day book. This will enable accounts to be prepared on an accruals basis.

Supervision

Jonathan does not take a very active part in the business, only signing cheques over £250, and visiting the shops only half a day each week. This may mean that assets can easily go missing, and Jonathan cannot readily see whether the business is performing as he would wish.

Jonathan should review wage/sales tax/cash book reconciliations. Management accounts should also be prepared by shop managers for Jonathan.

Tutorial note. This question deals with controls that are possible given the circumstances of the business. Greater segregation of duties does not appear to be possible as the shops are small, and Jonathan cannot spend more time at the shops (although he can use his time more productively by reviewing reconciliations).

3 Revenue and capital expenditure 12/01, 6/03

FAST FORWARD ▶▶ Most of the key controls over capital and revenue expenditure are the general purchase controls, covered in Chapter 10.

The nature of a balance sheet and profit and loss account means that it is important to classify capital and revenue expenditure correctly, or profit will be over or understated. You should know the distinction between them from your 2.5 studies.

The controls and tests outlined below are often considered and performed during the audit of fixed assets (see Chapter 13) as this is where the main issue of capitalisation occurs.

3.1 Control objectives

Area	Objective
Authorisation	• All expenditure is authorised
Recording	• All expenditure is classified correctly in the financial statements as capital or revenue expenditure

3.2 Controls

FAST FORWARD

> It is important that expenditure is recorded correctly, so that profit/loss and assets/liabilities are not misstated.

Area	Controls
Ordering	• Orders for capital items should be authorised • Order should be requisitioned on appropriate (different to revenue) documentation
Invoices	• Invoices should be approved by the person who authorised the order • They should be marked with the appropriate general ledger code
Recording	• All the standard controls over purchases are relevant here • Capital items should be written up in the fixed asset register • The fixed asset register should be reconciled regularly to the general ledger

3.3 Tests of controls

FAST FORWARD

> It may not be cost-effective to test controls in this area.

If the ordering documentation is different for capital purchases, all the standard purchase control tests should be carried out. If the documentation is not different, the auditor should enquire as to the client's system for recording and filing capital invoices.

It is likely that capital purchases in the year will be fewer than standard purchases in the year and if the invoices are not segregated it may not be cost efficient to test the controls over this area.

Alternative substantive procedures include:

Procedure	Description
Analytical review	• General review between current and prior year figures to ascertain any unexplained differences • Review of sensitive codes in the general ledger such as repairs or maintenance • Review of the movements on the fixed asset codes • Compare budgeted capital purchases with actual capital purchases

Procedure	Description
Enquiry and review	• Discuss the level of capital purchases in the year with the purchasing manager • Review the board minutes for authorisation of capital purchases

These substantive tests are often carried out as part of the substantive audit of fixed assets.

The auditor should be aware of the risks attaching to the audit of this area. As test of controls might be cost-ineffective, control risk in this area is higher than would have been if they were tested.

Inherent risk can also be high in this area. Capital and revenue expenditure is treated differently for the purposes of tax, and if the client is sensitive to their tax bill, there may be motivation to account creatively.

4 Internal audit: relevant cycles   12/03

FAST FORWARD

> The **internal auditors are interested in the risks arising to the company in certain cycles,** not simply the risks of errors arising in the financial statements.

In Chapter 4 we discussed some of the operational cycles that internal auditors might be interested in. These are likely to be of lesser interest to the external auditor, particularly where the cycle does not directly impact on the financial statements.

In this section we shall consider some of the matters which will affect the work of the internal auditors, in particular, aims of controls in the cycles, the controls themselves, and how the auditor will test those controls.

4.1 Procurement

We have already noted that many of the controls in this cycle will be the same as in the purchases cycle which the external auditor is interested in. However, as the scope of the internal auditor goes beyond the financial statements, consider these additional factors which he will be interested in.

A procurement system is likely to have many systems within it (for example, tendering, placing orders, checking goods inwards), which the internal auditor would probably approach separately.

Procurement system	
Control objectives	• The business has goods and services when it needs them • The business does not pay too much for those goods and services • The business does not make short-term savings on goods and services which lead to longer term inflated costs • Employees or suppliers do not defraud the company
Controls	• The business always invites tenders for goods and services • Research is conducted on potential suppliers before they are invited to tender • Requirements for goods and services are always put in writing • Use is made of discounting and calculations of long term costs where service is for a prolonged period • No transaction carried out with employees and connected persons
Tests of control	• A sample of contracts can be reviewed to confirm research and tender process • A sample of invoices checked back to written requisition • For a sample of long term contracts, check long term calculations exist and are correct • Review central database of suppliers to ensure that none are connected parties

Exam focus point

> As usual, there could be various tests of these controls. If required in an exam to suggest tests of controls, you should consider what the objective of the control is, and how you could prove that that objective is being met.
>
> Remember however, that only internal audit would be interested in some of these controls features. In principle, for example, the external auditors are not too concerned if the company pays more than it should do for its goods and services, so long as what it does pay is recorded properly in the financial statements.

4.2 Marketing

Similarly to procurement, 'marketing' covers a wide range of systems, including research, advertising, promotions, sales, after-sales.

Marketing system	
Control objectives	• Customer demand should be understood and met • Customers should be made aware of products • Products are competitive, not hampered by pricing or promotion tactics • Goods are sold for valuable consideration
Controls	Some of the controls will be similar to those discussed in the sales cycle in Chapter 10. However, think again that the internal auditor is interested in objectives beyond the scope of the financial systems. The following controls might be used to meet the above objectives: • Market research should be commissioned or carried out • Actual sales should be compared to budgets • Advertising is targeted • Promotions are timed to coincide with periods historically linked with sales, eg Christmas • Competitor prices are monitored • Terms and conditions are made known to customers • Credit checks are made
Tests of control	Some of the tests, particularly those in relation to credit, will be the same as those discussed in the sales system in Chapter 10.

Question   Marketing – tests of control

Try to think up some ways of testing the controls listed above.

Answer

Potential tests of control include:

- Review company policy on commissioning market research
- For a sample of major promotions, check that research was commissioned and used
- Check that actual sales are compared to budget sales and that variances are investigated
- For a sample of major promotions, ensure that timing has been considered and documented
- Ensure that records are maintained of competitor pricing policy
- Review terms and conditions to ensure that they comply with company policy
- Check as sample of contracts/sales to ensure terms and conditions were highlighted

You may have thought of other tests of controls, this list is not definitive. Check that your answers prove that the objective you had in mind is being tested.

4.3 Treasury

Treasury system	
Control objectives	• Money is available to the company when it is required • Risks in relation to foreign currency and interest rates are managed effectively • Transactions do not lose the company money over time • Exposures are highlighted and reported on, on a timely basis
Controls	• Cash flow forecasting • Arrangements with the bank in the event of cash emergencies • Contingency plans available • Clear policy on tolerated risk • Regular review of investment • Frequent two-way communication
Tests of controls	• Reviewing cash flow forecasts • Reading correspondence with the bank • Reading contingency plans and assessing them for realism • Discuss review of investments with investment managers • Seek evidence of such reviews being made (reports, memos) • Seek evidence of communication

4.4 Human resources

Human resources system	
Control objectives	• Sufficiently qualified and capable staff are available when required • There is no significant over-reliance on key personnel • Staff are paid the correct remuneration on a timely basis • Staff are contented and not prone to industrial action or seeking alternative employment • Employment laws are complied with • The human resource is handled considerately
Controls	• The business has a long term human requirement plan • Salary is benchmarked against the market • Performance of staff is regularly and formally appraised • Staff are given adequate training • Key personnel are not put at risk together • Long term succession planning is undertaken • Payroll controls as discussed in Chapter 10 • Relationships with trade unions are well maintained • Human resources managers receive training in employment law
Tests of control	• Obtain a copy of the long term human resource plan and review it • Obtain evidence that the HR department monitors pay levels in the market • Review of appraisal procedure, check that a sample of employees have had appraisals

Human resources system	
	• Review training records to ensure that training is in accordance with company policy
	• Review long term succession plan and any 'apprenticing' schemes are in operation
	• Review training procedures within department by discussion with staff

Exam focus point

As you considered each of these cycles more carefully, you will have seen the strong links that they have with the income and asset cycles that the external auditor is interested in. You will also have seen that the internal auditor is interested in risks arising to the company, whereas the external auditor is more interested in risks of errors in the financial statements.

In the exam, you could be asked the difference between the internal and external auditors interest in internal controls. Remember that the difference is in the objectives each is interested in, and the controls and the tests follow on from that. You might want to re-read the following sections in conjunction with one another, to see how the objectives of the internal auditors (or the company) extend further than the external auditors in each case:

- Purchases/procurement
- Sales/marketing
- Cash/treasury
- Payroll/human resources

Chapter Roundup

- Controls over cash receipts and payments should prevent fraud or theft.

- Key controls over **receipts** include:
    - Proper **post-opening** arrangements
    - **Prompt recording**
    - **Prompt banking**
    - **Reconciliation** of records of cash received and banked

- A further important control is **regular independent bank reconciliations**

- Key controls over **payments** include:
    - **Restriction of access** to cash and cheques
    - Procedures for **preparation and authorisation** of payments

- **Stock controls** are designed to ensure safe custody.

- Important controls over stock include restriction of access, documentation and authorization of movements, regular **independent stock counting** and **review of stock condition**.

- Most of the key controls over capital and revenue expenditure are the general purchase controls, covered in Chapter 10.

- It is important that expenditure is recorded correctly, so that profit/loss and assets/liabilities are not misstated.

- It may not be cost-effective to test controls in this area.

- The **internal auditors are interested in the risks arising to the company in certain cycles,** not simply the risks of errors arising in the financial statements.

Quick Quiz

1 Name the five key aims of controls of the cash system.

1 ....

2 ....

3 ....

4 ....

5 ....

2 Give five examples of tests to be performed on the cash payments book.

1 ....

2 ....

3 ....

4 ....

5 ....

3 Three important controls over the protection of stock are:

- Restriction of access to stores
- Regular stock counts
- Reconciliation of book stock to physical stock

True ☐

False ☐

4 Give two examples of **substantive procedures** that can be used to test capital and revenue expenditure.

Answers to Quick Quiz

1 • **All monies received** are **recorded**
   • **All monies received** are **banked**
   • **Cash and cheques** are **safeguarded** against loss or theft
   • **All payments** are **authorised**, **made** to the **correct payees** and **recorded**
   • **Payments** are **not made twice** for the same liability

2 For a sample of payments:

   • **Compare** with paid cheques to ensure payee agrees

   • **Note** that **cheques** are **signed** by the **persons authorised** to do so within their authority limits

   • **Check** to **suppliers' invoices** for goods and services. Verify that supporting documents are signed as having been **checked** and **passed for payment** and have been stamped 'paid'

   • **Check** to **suppliers' statements**

   • **Check** to **other documentary evidence**, as appropriate (agreements, authorised expense vouchers, wages/salaries records, petty cash books etc)

3 True

4 **Analytical review**

   • General review between current and prior year figures to ascertain any unexplained differences
   • Review of sensitive codes in the general ledger such as repairs or maintenance
   • Review of the movements on the fixed asset codes
   • Compare budgeted capital purchases with actual capital purchases

   Enquiry and review

   • Discuss the level of capital purchases in the year with the purchasing manager
   • Review the board minutes for authorisation of capital purchases

Now try the question below from the Exam Question Bank

Number	Level	Marks	Time
Q11	Examination	20	36 mins

Part D
Substantive testing

The substantive audit

12

Topic list	Syllabus reference
1 Substantive testing	6
2 Directional testing	6
3 Analytical procedures	6
4 Accounting estimates	6
5 Opening balances and comparatives	6

Introduction

Having looked at tests of control in detail, we now move onto substantive testing of the main balance sheet areas. In Chapters 13-17 we shall consider substantive testing in each of the major audit areas. In this chapter however we consider general auditing issues that affect substantive tests generally, directional testing, analytical review and the audit of estimates.

Analytical review impacts upon the whole audit process. We mentioned briefly in Chapter 7 that auditors are required to carry out analytical procedures when **planning** an audit; this chapter goes into more detail about how analytical procedures are used as substantive procedures and as a key part of the **overall review** of the final accounts. The purpose of analytical review at this stage is to answer the question 'Do the figures make sense?'

In the second part of this chapter we examine **accounting estimates**. We have mentioned in previous chapters that judgement has to be used in accounting for several figures in the accounts. Often these judgements depend on uncertain future events – what percentage of outstanding customers will fail to pay their debts, or for how much will inventory which has been in the warehouse eventually sell.

Since there may be a range of plausible answers to questions such as these, estimates can cause problems for auditors. We shall see that there are a number of possible ways in which estimates can be tested, and auditors will often wish to use a combination of procedures to obtain the required assurance.

Lastly we look at the work that the auditor has to do on **opening balances and comparatives**. Substantiating the opening position is a key feature of any substantive audit.

Study guide

17 – Other audit and review evidence I

- Describe and illustrate how analytical procedures are used as substantive procedures
- Explain the problems associated with the audit and review of accounting estimates

Exam guide

This chapter forms a basis for the next six chapters, so the topics covered here are likely to be examined in that context.

1 Substantive testing

FAST FORWARD

Auditors need to obtain **sufficient and appropriate audit evidence** to support the financial statement assertions. Substantive procedures aim to obtain that evidence.

1.1 Types of audit tests

Substantive procedures are tests to obtain audit evidence to detect material misstatements in the financial statements. They are generally of two types:

- Analytical procedures
- Other substantive procedures such as tests of detail of transactions and balances, review of minutes of directors' meetings and enquiry.

The types of substantive tests carried out to obtain evidence about various financial statement assertions are outlined in the table below.

Audit objective	Typical audit tests
Completeness	(a) Review of post balance sheet items (b) Cut off (c) Analytical review (d) Confirmations (e) Reconciliations to control account (f) Sequence checks (g) Review of reciprocal populations
Rights and obligations	(a) Checking invoices for proof that item belongs to the company (b) Confirmations with third parties
Valuation and allocation	(a) Checking to invoices (b) Recalculation (c) Confirming accounting policy consistent and reasonable (d) Review of post balance sheet payments and invoices (e) Expert valuation
Existence	(a) Physical verification (b) Third party confirmations (c) Cut off testing
Occurrence	(a) Inspection of supporting documentation (b) Confirmation from directors that transactions relate to business (c) Inspection of items purchased

PROFESSIONAL EDUCATION

Audit objective	Typical audit tests
Accuracy	(a) Re-calculation of correct amounts (b) Third party confirmation (c) Analytical review
Classification	(a) Check compliance with law and accounting standards (b) True and fair override invoked

Use the following model for drawing up an audit plan:

- **Agree opening balances** with **previous year's working papers**
- **Review general ledger** for unusual records
- **Check client schedules to/from accounting records** to ensure completeness
- Carry out **analytical review**
- **Test transactions in detail**
- **Test balances in detail**
- **Review presentation** and **disclosure** in accounts.

Exam focus point

Auditing exams require a good knowledge of how the **financial statement assertions** determine audit objectives, and the procedures for obtaining audit evidence. Students should be aiming to produce a description of procedures that could be followed by an inexperienced staff member.

2 Directional testing

FAST FORWARD

Substantive tests are designed to discover errors or omissions.

Broadly speaking, substantive procedures can be said to fall into two categories:

- Tests to discover **errors** (resulting in over– or under-statement)
- Tests to discover **omissions** (resulting in under-statement)

We have already mentioned over– and under-statement in previous chapters, but such matters are particularly relevant in the next few chapters.

2.1 Tests designed to discover errors

These tests will start with the **accounting records** in which the transactions are recorded and check from the entries to supporting documents or other evidence. Such tests should detect any over-statement and also any under-statement through causes other than omission.

 Case Study

Test for errors

If the test is designed to ensure that sales are priced correctly, the test would begin with a sales invoice selected from the sales ledger. Prices would then be checked to the official price list.

2.2 Tests designed to discover omissions

These tests must start from **outside the accounting records** and then check back to those records. Understatements through omission will never be revealed by starting with the account itself as there is clearly no chance of selecting items that have been omitted from the account.

 Case Study

Tests for omission

If the test is designed to discover whether all raw material purchases have been properly processed, the test would start, say, with goods received notes, to be checked to the stock records or purchase ledger.

2.3 Directional testing

For most systems auditors would include tests designed to discover both errors and omissions. The type of test, and direction of the test, should be recognised before selecting the test sample. If the sample which tested the accuracy and validity of the sales ledger were chosen from a file of sales invoices then it would not substantiate the fact that there were no errors in the sales ledger.

Directional testing is particularly appropriate when testing the financial statement assertions of existence, completeness, rights and obligations, and valuation.

The concept of directional testing derives from the principle of double-entry bookkeeping, in that for every **debit** there is a **corresponding credit**, (assuming that the double entry is complete and that the accounting records balance). Therefore, any **misstatement** of a **debit entry** will result in either a corresponding **misstatement** of a **credit entry** or a **misstatement** in the opposite direction, of **another debit entry**.

By designing audit tests carefully the auditors are able to use this principle in drawing audit conclusions, not only about the debit or credit entries that they have directly tested, but also about the corresponding credit or debit entries that are necessary to balance the books.

Tests are therefore designed in the following way.

Test item	Example
Test **debit items** (expenditure or assets) for overstatement by selecting debit entries recorded in the nominal ledger and checking value, existence and ownership	If a fixed asset entry in the nominal ledger of £1,000 is selected, it would be overstated if it should have been recorded at anything less than £1,000 or if the company did not own it, or indeed if it did not exist (eg it had been sold or the amount of £1,000 in fact represented a revenue expense)
Test **credit items** (income or liabilities) for understatement by selecting items from appropriate sources independent of the nominal ledger and ensuring that they result in the correct nominal ledger entry	Select a goods dispatched note and check that the resultant sale has been recorded in the nominal ledger sales account. Sales would be understated if the nominal ledger did not reflect the transaction at all (completeness) or reflected it at less than full value (say if goods valued at £1,000 were recorded in the sales account at £900, there would be an understatement of £100).

A test for the overstatement of an asset simultaneously gives comfort on understatement of other assets, overstatement of liabilities, overstatement of income and understatement of expenses.

Question

Directional audit

Fill in the blank spaces.

(a)   Based on double-entry bookkeeping, it can be seen from the matrix that assets can only be *understated* by virtue of:

    (i)   Other assets being _____; or

    (ii)   Liabilities being _____; or

    (iii)   Income being _____; or

    (iv)   Expenses being _____.

(b)   Similarly, liabilities can only be *overstated* by virtue of:

    (i)   Assets being _____; or

    (ii)   Other liabilities being _____; or

    (iii)   Income being _____; or

    (iv)   Expenses being _____.

Answer

(a)	(i)	Overstated	(b)	(i)	Overstated
	(ii)	Understated		(ii)	Understated
	(iii)	Understated		(iii)	Understated
	(iv)	Overstated		(iv)	Overstated

So, by performing the primary tests, the auditors obtain audit assurance in other audit areas. Successful completion of the primary tests will therefore result in them having tested all account areas both for overstatement and understatement.

The **major advantage** of the directional audit approach is its **cost-effectiveness.**

(a)   Assets and expenses are tested for overstatement only, and liabilities and income for understatement only, that is, items are not tested for both overstatement and understatement.

(b)   It audits directly the more likely types of transactional misstatement, that is, unrecorded income and improper expense (arising intentionally or unintentionally).

3 Analytical procedures

6/02, 6/03

Analytical procedures are used at all stages of the audit.

3.1 Nature and purpose of analytical procedures

Key term

Analytical procedures consist of the analysis of significant ratios and trends including the resulting investigations of fluctuations and relationships that are inconsistent with other relevant information or which deviate from predictable amounts.

ISA (UK and Ireland) 520 *Analytical procedures* states 'the auditor should apply analytical procedures as risk assessment procedures to obtain an understanding of the entity and its environment and in the overall review at the end of the audit'. In addition to the uses of analytical procedures above, they may also be used as substantive procedures, to obtain audit evidence directly.

The ISA states that analytical procedures include:

(a)   The consideration of comparisons with:

- **Similar information** for prior periods

- **Anticipated results** of the entity, from budgets or forecasts

- **Predictions** prepared by the auditors

- **Industry information**, such as a comparison of the client's ratio of sales to trade accounts receivable with industry averages, or with the ratios relating to other entities of comparable size in the same industry.

(b)   Those between elements of financial information that are expected to conform to a predicted pattern based on the entity's experience, such as the relationship of gross profit to sales.

(c)   Those between financial information and relevant non-financial information, such as the relationship of payroll costs to number of employees.

A variety of methods can be used to perform the procedures discussed above, ranging from **simple comparisons** to **complex analysis** using statistics, on a company level, branch level or individual account level. The choice of procedures is a matter for the auditors' professional judgement.

3.2 Analytical procedures in planning the audit   12/05

FAST FORWARD

> During **planning** analytical procedures should be used as a means of **understanding the business** and **identifying audit risk**.

As we have discussed, analytical procedures should be used at the risk assessment stage. Possible sources of information about the client include:

- Interim financial information
- Budgets
- Management accounts
- Non-financial information
- Bank and cash records
- Sales tax returns
- Board minutes
- Discussions or correspondence with the client at the year-end

Auditors may also use specific industry information or general knowledge of current industry conditions to assess the client's performance.

As well as helping to determine the nature, timing and extent of other audit procedures, such analytical procedures may also indicate aspects of the business of which the auditors were previously unaware. Auditors are looking to see if developments in the client's business have had the expected effects. They will be particularly interested in changes in audit areas where problems have occurred in the past.

Exam focus point

> In December 2005 candidates were given prior year and budget figures for a client, with associated information, and asked to prepare the overall audit strategy. It was necessary to perform a little simple analytical review in order to comment on risk areas.

3.3 Analytical procedures as substantive procedures

When using analytical procedures as **substantive tests**, auditors should consider the information available, assessing its **availability, relevance** and **comparability**.

The ISA states that auditors must decide whether using available analytical procedures as substantive procedures will be effective and efficient in **reducing detection risk** for specific financial statement assertions. Auditors may efficiently use analytical data produced by the entity itself, provided they are satisfied that it has been properly prepared.

There are a number of factors which the auditors should consider when using analytical procedures as substantive procedures.

Factors to consider	Example
The **objectives** of the analytical procedures and the extent to which their results are reliable	Analytical procedures may be a good indicator of whether a population is complete
The degree to which information can be **analysed**	Analytical procedures may be more effective when applied to financial information on individual sections of an operation
The **availability of information**	Financial: budgets or forecasts Non-financial: eg the number of units produced or sold
The **reliability** of the information available	Whether budgets are prepared with sufficient care
The **relevance of the information** available	Whether budgets are established as results to be expected rather than as goals to be achieved
The **source of the information available**	Independent sources are generally more reliable than internal sources
The **comparability of the information** available	Broad industry data may need to be supplemented to be comparable with that of an entity that produces and sells specialised products
The **knowledge gained during previous audits**	The effectiveness of the accounting and internal control systems The types of problems giving rise to accounting adjustments in prior periods

Auditors will also consider the plausibility and predictability of the relationships being tested. Some relationships are strong, for example between selling expenses and sales in business where the sales force is mainly paid by commission.

Other factors should be considered when determining the reliance that the auditors should place on the results of analytical procedures.

Reliability factors	Example
Materiality of the items involved	When inventory balances are material, auditors do not solely rely on analytical procedures
Other audit procedures directed towards the same financial statements assertions	Other procedures auditors undertake in reviewing the collectability of accounts receivable, such as the review of subsequent cash receipts, may confirm or dispel questions arising from the application of analytical procedures to an aged profile of customers' accounts
The **accuracy** with which the expected results of analytical procedures can be predicted	Auditors normally expect greater consistency in comparing the relationship of gross profit to sales from one period to another than in comparing discretionary expenses, such as research or advertising

Reliability factors	Example
The **frequency** with which a relationship is observed	A pattern repeated monthly as opposed to annually
Assessment of **inherent** and **control risks**	If internal controls over sales order processing is weak, and control risk is high, auditors may rely more on tests of individual transactions or balances than analytical procedures

Auditors will need to consider testing the controls, if any, over the **preparation** of **information** used in applying analytical procedures. When such controls are effective, the auditors will have greater confidence in the reliability of the information, and therefore in the results of analytical procedures.

The **controls** over **non-financial information** can often be tested in conjunction with tests of **accounting-related controls**. For example, in establishing controls over the processing of sales invoices, a business may include controls over unit sales recording. In these circumstances the auditors could test the controls over the recording of unit sales in conjunction with tests of the controls over the processing of sales invoices.

Reliance on the results of analytical procedures depends on the auditors' assessment of the **risk** that the procedures may identify relationships (between data) as expected, whereas a material misstatement exists (ie the relationships, in fact, do not exist).

3.4 Analytical procedures as part of the overall review

FAST FORWARD

Analytical procedures at the **final stage** of an audit help auditors decide whether the accounts are consistent with their knowledge of the business.

The ISA states that 'the auditor should apply analytical procedures at or near the end of the audit when forming an overall conclusion as to whether the financial statements as a whole are consistent with the auditor's understanding of the entity'.

The conclusions from these analytical procedures should corroborate the conclusions formed from other audit procedures on parts of the financial statements. The auditor should consider whether the assertions made are consistent with the auditors' understanding of the entity, or, in particular, whether they reveal new factors or undue influence by those charged with governance. However, these analytical procedures may highlight areas which require further investigation and audit.

3.5 Investigating significant fluctuations or unexpected relationships

FAST FORWARD

Auditors must investigate **significant fluctuations** and **unexpected relationships**.

The ISA says 'when analytical procedures identify significant fluctuations or relationships that are inconsistent with other relevant information or that deviate from predicted patterns, the auditor should investigate and obtain adequate explanations and appropriate corroborative evidence'. Investigations will start with **enquiries** of management and then corroboration of management's responses:

(a) By **comparing** them with the auditors' knowledge of the entity's business and with other evidence obtained during the course of the audit

(b) If the analytical procedures are being carried out as substantive procedures, by **undertaking additional audit procedures** where appropriate to confirm the explanations received

If explanations cannot be given by management, or if they are insufficient, the auditors must determine which further audit procedures to undertake to explain the fluctuation or relationship.

3.6 Practical techniques

When carrying out analytical procedures, auditors should remember that every industry is different and each company within an industry differs in certain respects.

Ratio analysis can be a useful technique. However ratios mean very little when used in isolation. They should be calculated for previous periods and for comparable companies. This may involve a certain amount of initial research, but subsequently it is just a matter of adding new statistics to the existing information each year. The permanent file should contain a section with summarised accounts and the chosen ratios for prior years.

In addition to looking at the more usual ratios the auditors should consider examining other ratios that may be relevant to the particular clients' business, such as revenue per passenger mile for an airline operator client, or fees per partner for a professional office.

Other analytical techniques include:

(a) **Examining related accounts** in conjunction with each other. Often revenue and expense accounts are related to balance sheet accounts and comparisons should be made to ensure relationships are reasonable.

(b) **Trend analysis**. Sophisticated statistical techniques (beyond the scope of this paper) can be used to compare this period with previous periods.

(c) **Reasonableness test**. These involve calculating the **expected value** of an item and comparing it with its actual value, for example, for the straight-line depreciation.

(Cost + Additions − Disposals) × Depreciation % = Change in Profit and loss account

Important accounting ratios	• Gross profit margins, in total and by product, area and months/quarter (if possible) • Debtors ratio (average collection period) • Stock turnover ratio (turnover divided into cost of sales) • Current ratio (current assets to current liabilities) • Quick or acid test ratio (liquid assets to current liabilities) • Gearing ratio (debt capital to equity capital) • Return on capital employed (profit before tax to total assets less current liabilities)
Related items	• Creditors and purchases • Stocks and cost of sales • Fixed assets and depreciation, repairs and maintenance expense • Intangible assets and amortisation • Loans and interest expense • Investments and investment income • Debtors and bad debt expense • Debtors and sales

Other areas for consideration
• **Examine changes** in **products, customers and levels** of **returns**
• **Assess** the effect of **price and mix changes** on the cost of sales
• **Consider** the effect of **inflation, industrial disputes, changes in production methods** and **changes in activity** on the charge for wages
• **Obtain explanations** for all **major variances** analysed using a standard costing system. Particular attention should be paid to those relating to the over or under absorption of overheads since these may, inter alia, affect inventory valuations

Other areas for consideration
• **Compare trends in production and sales** and assess the effect on any provisions for obsolete inventories
• **Ensure** that **changes in the percentage labour or overhead content** of production costs are also reflected in the inventory valuation.

• **Review other expenditure**, comparing:
  – Rent with annual rent per rental agreement
  – Rates with previous year and known rates increases
  – Interest payable on loans with outstanding balance and interest rate per loan agreement
  – Hire or leasing charges with annual rate per agreements
  – Vehicle running expenses to vehicles
  – Other items related to activity level with general price increase and change in relevant level of activity (for example telephone expenditure will increase disproportionately if export or import business increases)
  – Other items not related to activity level with general price increases (or specific increases if known)

• **Review** profit and loss account for **items** which may have been **omitted** (eg scrap sales, training levy, special contributions to pension fund, provisions for dilapidation etc).

• **Ensure expected variations** arising from the following have occurred:
  – Industry or local trends
  – Known disturbances of the trading pattern (for example strikes, depot closures, failure of suppliers)

Certain of the comparisons and ratios measuring liquidity and longer-term capital structure will assist in evaluating whether the company is a going concern, in addition to contributing to the overall view of the accounts. We shall see in Chapter 17 however, that there are factors other than declining ratios that may indicate going concern problems.

The working papers must contain the completed results of analytical procedures. They should include:

- The outline **programme** of the work
- The summary of **significant figures** and relationships for the period
- A summary of **comparisons** made with budgets and with previous years
- Details of all **significant fluctuations** or **unexpected relationships** considered
- Details of the **results of investigations** into such fluctuations/relationships
- The audit **conclusions** reached
- **Information considered** necessary for assisting in the **planning** of subsequent audits

<table>
<tr><td>Exam focus
point</td><td>In the exam you may be given a set of figures and:

(a)   Asked to calculate changes, key ratios etc and hence identify significant areas of the accounts
(b)   Asked what audit work will be required on these significant areas

When analysing figures, make sure that the points which you make are consistent with each other. Factors that indicate possible going concern problems are particularly important.

Mention of analytical procedures will generally be worth a couple of marks in any question on substantive testing. However you will not get any marks just for saying 'perform analytical procedures'; you will need to give details of the procedures that should be performed.</td></tr>
</table>

3.7 Analytical procedures in a review

As we mentioned in Chapter 1, analytical procedures have a key role in a review where significant use is made of analytical review and enquiries of client staff.

4 Accounting estimates

When auditing **accounting estimates** auditors should:

- Test the management process
- Use an independent estimate
- Review subsequent events

in order to assess whether the estimates are reasonable.

4.1 The nature of accounting estimates

ISA (UK and Ireland) 540 *Audit of accounting estimates* provides guidance on the audit of accounting estimates contained in financial statements, stating 'auditors should obtain sufficient appropriate audit evidence regarding accounting estimates'.

Key term

An **accounting estimate** is an approximation of the amount of an item in the absence of a precise means of measurement.

The ISA gives these examples.

- Allowances to reduce inventories and receivables to their estimated realisable value
- Provisions to allocate the cost of long-term assets over their estimated useful lives
- Accrued revenue
- Provision for a loss from a lawsuit
- Losses on construction contracts in progress
- Provision to meet warranty claims

Directors and management are responsible for making accounting estimates included in the financial statements. These estimates are often made in conditions of uncertainty regarding the outcome of events and involve the use of judgement. The risk of a material misstatement therefore increases when accounting estimates are involved.

Audit evidence supporting accounting estimates is **generally less than conclusive** and so auditors need to exercise greater judgement than in other areas of an audit.

Accounting estimates may be produced as part of the routine operations of the accounting system, or may be a non-routine procedure at the period end. Where, as is frequently the case, a **formula** based on past experience is used to calculate the estimate, it should be reviewed regularly by management (eg actual vs estimate in prior periods).

If there is no objective data to assess the item, or if it is surrounded by uncertainty, the auditors should consider the implications for their report.

4.2 Audit procedures

Auditors should gain an understanding of the procedures and methods used by management to make accounting estimates to gain evidence of whether estimates are reasonable given the circumstances and appropriately disclosed if necessary. It will also aid the auditors' planning of their own procedures.

This ISA says that 'the auditor should adopt one or a combination of the following approaches in the audit of an accounting estimate:

(a) Review and test the process used by management or the directors to develop the estimate

(b) Use an independent estimate for comparison with that prepared by management or the directors or

(c) Review subsequent events which confirm the estimate made.'

4.2.1 Review and testing the process

The auditors will carry out the following steps.

• **Consider whether data** is accurate, complete and reliable
• **Seek appropriate evidence from outside client** (for example, industry sales projections to confirm internal estimates of future sales orders)
• **Check** whether **data is appropriately analysed** and **projected** (for example, age analysis of accounts receivable)
• **Evaluate** whether **base used** for assumptions is **appropriate**   • **Evaluate** whether **assumptions** are **reasonable** in light of **prior period results**

• **Consider** whether **formulae** used remain **appropriate**
 • Consider whether **assumptions** are **consistent**
   – With those used for other accounting estimates
   – With management's plans
 • **Consider** whether **expert opinion** is required if estimates are complex

• **Test calculations** involved in the estimate considering:
   – Complexity of calculation
   – Procedures and methods used by the client
   – Materiality of estimate

• **Compare previous estimates** with actual results, aiming to obtain evidence about:
   – General reliability of the client's estimating procedures
   – Whether adjustments to estimating formulae will be required
   – Whether differences between previous estimates and actual figures ought to be disclosed

• Consider management's approval procedures, confirming it is performed by the **appropriate level of management** and **evidenced**

4.2.2 Use of an independent estimate

The auditors may seek evidence from sources outside the entity. Such an estimate (made or obtained by the auditors) may be compared with the accounting estimate. The auditors should evaluate the data, consider the assumptions and test the calculation procedures used to develop the independent estimate. Prior period independent assessments and actual results could also be compared.

4.2.3 Review of subsequent events

The auditors should review transactions or events after the period end which may reduce or even remove the need to test accounting estimates (as described above).

4.3 Evaluation of results of audit procedures

'The auditor should make a final assessment of the reasonableness of the accounting estimate based on the auditor's understanding of the entity and its environment and whether the estimates are consistent with other audit evidence obtained during the audit.'

Auditors must assess the differences between the amount of an estimate supported by evidence and the estimate calculated by management. If the auditors believe that the difference is unreasonable then an adjustment should be made. If the directors or management refuse to revise the estimate, then the difference is considered a misstatement and will be treated as such.

5 Opening balances and comparatives

FAST FORWARD

Auditors should ensure that the opening balances and comparatives are fairly stated.

5.1 Audit procedures

Key term

Opening balances are those account balances which exist at the beginning of the period. Opening balances are based upon the closing balances of the prior period and reflect the effects of:

- Transactions of prior periods
- Accounting policies applied to the prior period

ISA (UK and Ireland) 510 *Initial Engagements – Opening Balances and continuing engagements – opening balances* provides guidance on opening balances

- When the financial statements of an entity are audited for the first time
- When the financial statements for the prior period were audited by another auditor

It states that 'for initial audit engagements, the auditor should obtain sufficient appropriate audit evidence that:

(a)   The opening balances do not contain misstatements that materially affect the current period's financial statements

(b)   The prior period's closing balances have been correctly brought forward to the current period or, when appropriate, have been restated and

(c)   Appropriate accounting policies are consistently applied or changes in accounting policies have been properly accounted for and adequately disclosed.'

For continuing engagements, the auditor should also obtain sufficient appropriate audit evidence for these matters.

Appropriate and sufficient audit evidence is required on the opening balances and this depends on matters such as the following.

- The **accounting policies** followed by the entity

- Whether the **prior period's financial statements were audited** and, if so, whether the auditors' report was modified

- The **nature of the accounts** and the risk of their misstatement in the current period's financial statements

- The **materiality** of the opening balances relative to the current period's financial statements

The auditor must consider whether **opening balances reflect the application of appropriate accounting policies** and that those policies are **consistently applied** in the current period's financial statements.

When there are any changes in the accounting policies or application thereof, the auditor should consider whether they are appropriate and properly accounted for and adequately disclosed.

When the prior period's financial statements were audited by another auditor, the current auditor may be able to obtain sufficient appropriate audit evidence regarding opening balances by **reviewing** the predecessor auditor's **working papers**. In these circumstances, the current auditor would also consider the professional competence and independence of the predecessor auditor.

If the prior period's audit report was **modified**, the auditor would pay particular attention in the current period to the matter which resulted in the modification.

Before communicating with the predecessor auditor, the current auditor must consider the relevant parts of IFAC's *Code of Ethics for Professional Accountants*.

When the prior period's financial statements were not audited or when the auditor is not able to be satisfied by using the procedures described above, the auditor must perform other procedures such as those discussed below.

For **current assets and liabilities** some audit evidence can usually be obtained as part of the current period's audit procedures. For example, the **collection** (payment) of opening **accounts receivable** (accounts payable) during the current period will provide some audit evidence of their existence, rights and obligations, completeness and valuation at the beginning of the period.

In the case of **stock**, however, it is more difficult for the auditor to be satisfied as to stock on hand at the beginning of the period. Therefore, additional procedures will usually be necessary such as:

- **Observing a current physical stock count** and reconciling it back to the opening stock quantities
- **Testing the valuation** of the opening stock items
- **Testing gross profit** and cut-off

A combination of these procedures may provide sufficient appropriate audit evidence.

For **non-current assets and liabilities**, the audit will ordinarily examine the records underlying the opening balances. In certain cases, the auditor may be able to obtain confirmation of opening balances with third parties, eg, for long-term debt and investments. In other cases, the auditor may need to carry out additional audit procedures.

5.2 Audit conclusion and reporting

The auditor should qualify or disclaim his opinion if he cannot obtain sufficient, appropriate information about whether opening balances are fairly stated.

If the opening balances contain misstatements which could materially affect the current period's financial statements, the auditor should inform management, and any predecessor auditor. If the effect is now properly accounted for/disclosed the auditor should modify his opinion.

The report will also be modified if **accounting policies** are **not consistently applied**.

If the prior period auditor's report was modified, the auditor should **consider the effect on the current period's financial statements**. For example, if there was a scope limitation, such as one due to the inability to determine opening inventory in the prior period, the auditor may not need to qualify or disclaim the current period's audit opinion.

The ISA finishes 'however, if a modification regarding the prior period's financial statements remains relevant and material to the current period's financial statements, the auditor should modify the current auditor's report accordingly'.

5.3 What are comparatives?

ISA 710 *Comparatives* establishes standards and provides guidance on the auditors' responsibilities regarding comparatives. It states 'the auditor should determine whether the comparatives comply in all material respects with the financial reporting framework applicable to the financial statements being audited', and 'the auditor should obtain sufficient appropriate audit evidence that amounts derived from the preceding period's financial statements are free from material misstatements and are appropriately incorporated in the financial statements for the current period'.

Comparatives are presented differently under different countries' financial reporting frameworks. Generally comparatives can be defined as **corresponding amounts** and **other disclosures** for the preceding financial reporting period(s), presented for comparative purposes. Because of these variations in countries' approach to comparatives, the ISA refers to the following frameworks and methods of presentation.

Key terms

> **Corresponding figures** are amounts and other disclosures for the preceding period included as part of the current period financial statements, which are intended to be read in relation to the amounts and other disclosures relating to the current period (referred to as 'current period figures'). These corresponding figures are not presented as complete financial statements capable of standing alone, but are an integral part of the current period financial statements intended to be read only in relationship to the current period figures. These are usually used in UK and Ireland.
>
> **Comparative financial statements** are amounts and other disclosures of the preceding period included for comparison with the financial statements of the current period, but do not form part of the current period financial statements.

Comparatives are presented in compliance with the relevant financial reporting framework. The essential audit reporting differences are that:

- For **corresponding figures**, the auditors' report only refers to the financial statements of the current period.

- For **comparative financial statements**, the auditors' report refers to each period that financial statements are presented.

Audit procedures performed on **corresponding figures** are usually limited to checking that the corresponding figures have been correctly reported and are appropriately classified. Auditors must assess whether:

(a) **Accounting policies** used for the corresponding figures are **consistent** with those of the current period or whether appropriate adjustments and/or disclosures have been made.

(b) **Corresponding figures agree** with the **amounts** and other disclosures presented in the prior period or whether appropriate adjustments and/or disclosures have been made.

'In the UK and Ireland, the auditor should obtain sufficient appropriate audit evidence that:

(a) The accounting policies used for the corresponding amounts are consistent with those of the current period and appropriate adjustments and disclosures have been made where this is not the case;

(b) The corresponding amounts agree with the amounts and other disclosures presented in the preceding period and are free from errors in the context of the financial statements of the current period; and

(c) Where corresponding amounts have been adjusted as required by relevant legislation and accounting standards, appropriate disclosures have been made.'

If the auditors become aware of a possible material misstatement in the corresponding figures when performing the current period audit, then they must perform any necessary additional procedures.

'When the comparatives are presented as corresponding figures, the auditor should issue an audit report in which the comparatives are not specifically identified because the auditor's opinion is on the current period financial statements as a whole, including the corresponding figures.'

The auditor's report will only make any specific reference to corresponding figures if there was a modification in the prior year.

The auditors are effectively required to follow the same procedures on the **comparative financial statements** as noted above for corresponding figures. The ISA says 'the auditor should obtain sufficient appropriate audit evidence that the comparative financial statements meet the requirements of the applicable financial reporting framework'.

When the comparatives are presented as comparative financial statements, the auditor should issue a report in which the comparatives are specifically identified because the auditor's opinion is expressed individually on the financial statements of each period presented.'

The auditors may therefore express a **modified opinion** or include an **emphasis of matter** paragraph with respect to one or more financial statements for one or more period, whilst issuing a different report on the other financial statements.

Question   Opening balances and comparatives

Auditing standards have been issued on opening balances for initial engagements and comparatives, and one of the matters considered is where one firm of auditors takes over from another firm. You have recently been appointed auditor of Lowdham Castings, a limited liability company which has been trading for about thirty years, and are carrying out the audit for the year ended 30 September 20X6. The company's turnover is about £500,000 and its normal profit before tax is about £30,000. Comparatives are shown as corresponding figures only.

Required

Discuss your responsibilities in relation to the comparatives included in the accounts for the year ended 30 September 20X6. You should also consider the information you would require from the retiring auditors.

Answer

Consideration of the financial statements of the preceding period is necessary in the audit of the current period's financial statements in relation to three main aspects.

(a)   *Opening position:* obtaining satisfaction that those amounts which have a direct effect on the current period's results or closing position have been properly brought forward.

(b)   *Accounting policies:* determining whether the accounting policies adopted for the current period are consistent with those of the previous period.

(c)   *Comparatives:* determining that the comparatives are properly shown in the current period's financial statements.

The auditors' main concern will therefore be to satisfy themselves that there were no material misstatements in the previous year's financial statements which may have a bearing upon their work in the current year.

The new auditors do not have to 're-audit' the previous year's financial statements, but they will have to pay more attention to them than would normally be the case where they had themselves been the auditors in the earlier period. A useful source of audit evidence will clearly be the previous auditors, and, with the client's permission, they should be contacted to see if they are prepared to co-operate. Certainly, any known areas of weakness should be discussed with the previous auditors and it is also possible that they might be prepared to provide copies of their working papers (although there is no legal or ethical provision which requires the previous auditors to co-operate in this way).

Chapter Roundup

- Auditors need to obtain **sufficient and appropriate audit evidence** to support the financial statement assertions. Substantive procedures aim to obtain that evidence.

- Substantive tests are designed to discover errors or omissions.

- Analytical procedures are used at all stages of the audit.

- During planning analytical procedures should be used as a means of understanding the business and identifying audit risk.

- When using analytical procedures as **substantive tests**, auditors should consider the information available, assessing its **availability, relevance** and **comparability**.

- Analytical procedures at the **final stage** of an audit help auditors decide whether the accounts are consistent with their knowledge of the business.

- Auditors must investigate **significant fluctuations** and **unexpected relationships**.

- When auditing **accounting estimates** auditors should:

  - Test the management process
  - Use an independent estimate
  - Review subsequent events

  in order to assess whether the estimates are reasonable.

- Auditors should ensure that the opening balances and comparatives are fairly stated.

Quick Quiz

1   Link the type of account with the purpose of the primary test in directional testing.

    (a)   Assets   (i)   Overstatement
    (b)   Liabilities   (ii)   Overstatement
    (c)   Income   (iii)   Understatement
    (d)   Expense   (iv)   Understatement

2   Name four sources of analytical information which can be used at the planning stage of the audit.

    1   ....

    2   ....

    3   ....

    4   ....

3   Identify the significant relationships in the list of items below

    (a)   creditors   (b)   interest   (c)   purchases   (d)   sales
    (e)   amortisation (f)   loans   (g)   debtors   (h)   intangibles

4   Complete the definition.

    An accounting estimate is an .... of the .... of an item in the absence of a .... of measurement.

5   Give three examples of an accounting estimate.

    1   ....

    2   ....

    3   ....

6   Auditors are responsible for making accounting estimates to be used in the accounts.

    True   ☐

    False   ☐

7   Give three steps in the review and testing stage of auditing accounting estimates.

    1   ....

    2   ....

    3   ....

8   The audit report covers the corresponding figures as well as the current year figures.

    True   ☐

    False   ☐

BPP
PROFESSIONAL EDUCATION

Answers to Quick Quiz

1.   (a) (i)
   (b) (iii)
   (c) (ii)
   (d) (iv)

2. • Interim financial information
   • Budgets
   • Management accounts
   • Non-financial information
   • Bank and cash records
   • Sales tax returns
   • Board minutes
   • Discussions or correspondence with the client at the year-end

3.   (a) (c)
   (b) (f)
   (d) (g)
   (e) (h)

4. approximation, amount, precise means

5. From:
   • Allowances to reduce inventories and receivables to their estimated realisable value
   • Provisions to allocate the cost of long-term assets over their estimated useful lives
   • Accrued revenue
   • Provision for a loss from a lawsuit
   • Losses on construction contracts in progress
   • Provision to meet warranty claims

6. False

7. From:
   • **Consider whether data** is **accurate, complete and reliable**
   • **Seek appropriate evidence from outside client** (for example, industry sales projections to confirm internal estimates of future sales orders)
   • **Check** whether **data is appropriately analysed** and **projected** (for example, age analysis of accounts receivable)
   • **Evaluate** whether **base used** for assumptions is **appropriate**
   • **Evaluate** whether **assumptions** are **reasonable** in light of **prior period results**
   • **Consider** whether **formulae** used remain **appropriate**
   • Consider whether **assumptions** are **consistent**
     – With those used for other accounting estimates
     – With management's plans
   • **Consider** whether **expert opinion** is required if estimates are complex
   • **Test calculations** involved in the estimate considering:
     – Complexity of calculation
     – Procedures and methods used by the client
     – Materiality of estimate

- **Compare previous estimates** with actual results, aiming to obtain evidence about:

    - General reliability of the client's estimating procedures

    - Whether adjustments to estimating formulae will be required

    - Whether differences between previous estimates and actual figures ought to be disclosed

- Consider management's approval procedures, confirming it is performed by the **appropriate level of management** and **evidenced**

8   True

Now try the question below from the Exam Question Bank

Number	Level	Marks	Time
Q12	Introductory	n/a	30 mins

Fixed assets

Topic list	Syllabus reference
1 Tangible fixed assets	6
2 Other fixed assets	6

Introduction

The final audit will concentrate on the balance sheet to a great extent. The following chapters cover the audit of the key balance sheet areas.

Although each audit client is different, most of the assets in this and the next three chapters will be present in the final accounts. The importance of each balance sheet component will vary from client to client.

The chapter highlights the key objectives for each major component. You must understand what **objectives** the various audit tests are designed to achieve. Objectives of particular significance for tangible fixed assets are **rights and obligations** (that is ownership), **existence and valuation**. You should note it is generally necessary to carry out different tests on ownership and existence.

Valuation is the other important assertion. The auditors will concentrate on testing any valuations made during the year, and also whether other values appear reasonable given asset usage and condition. A very important aspect of testing valuation is reviewing depreciation rates.

A topic we covered in an earlier chapter, using the work of an expert, may well be important in the audit of fixed assets. We covered this in Chapter 8. You should refer back to your notes in this subject.

Study guide

22 – Other audit and review evidence VI – Fixed assets and long-term liabilities

- Describe and tabulate for inclusion in a work program the substantive procedures used in obtaining evidence in relation to fixed assets and long-term liabilities and the related income instatement entries

- Explain the purpose of substantive procedures in relation to financial statement assertions concerning fixed assets and long-term liabilities

Note: long term liabilities are dealt with in Chapter 17.

Exam guide

Exam questions on any balance sheet area may either focus on:

- Audit work required
- Accounting treatment problems
- Both the above

Tangible fixed assets are often financed by long term loans (for instance a mortgage or lease). Therefore these areas could be examined together. In December 2005, audit procedures in relation to depreciation were examined.

1 Tangible fixed assets   **Pilot paper**

FAST FORWARD

Key areas when testing **tangible fixed assets** are:

- **Confirmation** of ownership
- **Inspection** of fixed assets
- **Valuation** by third parties
- **Adequacy** of **depreciation** rates

1.1 Internal control considerations

The **fixed asset register** is a very important aspect of the internal control systems. It enables assets to be identified, and comparisons between the general ledger, fixed asset register and the assets themselves provide **evidence** that the assets are **completely recorded**.

Another significant control is procedures over acquisitions and disposals, that acquisitions are properly **authorised**, and **disposals** are **authorised** and **proceeds accounted for**.

Other significant aspects are:

- **Security arrangements** over fixed assets are **sufficient**.
- **Fixed assets** are **maintained properly.**
- **Depreciation** is **reviewed every year.**
- **All income** is **collected** from **income-yielding assets.**

1.2 Audit procedures

AUDIT PLAN: TANGIBLE FIXED ASSETS	

COMPLETENESS	• **Obtain** or **prepare** a **summary** of tangible fixed assets showing how:
	  – **Gross book value**
	  – **Accumulated depreciation**
	  – **Net book value**
	reconcile with the **opening position**.
	• **Compare fixed assets** in the general ledger with the **fixed assets register** and **obtain explanations** for **differences**
	• **Check** whether **assets** which **physically exist** are **recorded** in **fixed asset register**
	• If a fixed asset register is not kept, **obtain** a **schedule** showing the original costs and present depreciated value of major fixed assets
	• **Reconcile** the **schedule** of fixed assets with the **general ledger**

EXISTENCE	• **Confirm** that the **company physically inspects** all items in the fixed asset register each year
	• **Inspect assets,** concentrating on high value items and additions in year. Confirm items inspected:
	  – Exist
	  – Are in use
	  – Are in good condition
	  – Have correct serial numbers
	• **Review records** of **income yielding assets**
	• **Reconcile** opening and closing **vehicles** by numbers as well as amounts

VALUATION	• **Verify valuation** to valuation certificate
	• **Consider reasonableness** of **valuation**, reviewing:
	  – Experience of valuer
	  – Scope of work
	  – Methods and assumptions used
	  – Valuation bases are in line with accounting standards
	• **Check revaluation** surplus has been **correctly calculated**
	• Check valuations of all assets that have been revalued have been **updated regularly** (full valuation every five years and an interim valuation in year three generally)
	• Check that client has **recognised** in the **profit and loss account** revaluation losses which relate to clear consumption of economic benefits or which take the valuation below depreciated historical cost, and client has **recognised all other gains and losses** in **statement of total recognised gains and losses**

AUDIT PLAN: TANGIBLE FIXED ASSETS	
VALUATION (Depreciation)	• **Review depreciation** rates applied in relation to: – Asset lives – Residual values – Replacement policy – Past experience of gains and losses on disposal – Consistency with prior years and accounting policy – Possible obsolescence • **Check depreciation** has been **charged on all assets** with a limited useful life • For **revalued assets**, ensure that the charge for **depreciation** is **based** on the **revalued amount** • **Check calculation** of depreciation rates • **Compare ratios** of depreciation to fixed assets (by category) with: – Previous years – Depreciation policy rates • **Ensure no further depreciation** provided on **fully depreciated assets** • **Check** that **depreciation policies and rates are disclosed** in the accounts
(Insurance)	• **Review insurance policies** in force for all categories of tangible fixed assets and consider the adequacy of their insured values and check expiry dates
RIGHTS AND OBLIGATIONS	• **Verify title** to land and buildings by inspection of: – Title deeds – Land registry certificates – Leases • Obtain a certificate from solicitors/bankers: – **Stating purpose** for which the deeds are being held (custody only) – **Stating deeds** are **free** from **mortgage** or **lien** • **Inspect registration documents** for vehicles held, checking that they are in client's name • **Confirm** all vehicles used for the **client's business** • **Examine documents** of **title** for other assets (including purchase invoices, architects' certificates, contracts, hire purchase or lease agreements)
(Charges and commitments)	• **Review for evidence** of charges in statutory books and by company search • **Review leases** of leasehold properties to ensure that company has fulfilled covenants therein • **Examine invoices received after year-end, orders and minutes** for evidence of capital commitments

Inspection of a building's title deeds does not give audit evidence about **existence** and if there is doubt that a building actually exists, the auditors should physically inspect it.

Exam focus point

Make sure you do not confuse the tests for **ownership** and the tests for **existence** in the exam.

AUDIT PLAN: TANGIBLE FIXED ASSETS	
ADDITIONS	These tests are to confirm **rights and obligations**, **valuation** and **completeness**

	• **Verify additions** by inspection of architects' certificates, solicitors' completion statements, suppliers' invoices etc.
	• **Check capitalisation** of **expenditure** is correct by considering for fixed assets additions and items in relevant expense categories (repairs, motor expenses, sundry expenses) whether:
	  – Capital/revenue distinction is correctly drawn
	  – Capitalisation is in line with consistently applied company policy
	• **Check purchases** have been **properly allocated** to correct fixed asset accounts
	• **Check purchases** have been **authorised** by directors/senior management by reviewing board minutes
	• **Ensure** that appropriate **claims** have been made for **grants**, and grants received and receivable have been received
	• **Check additions** have been **recorded** in fixed asset register and general ledger

SELF CONSTRUCTED ASSETS	These tests are to confirm **valuation** and **completeness**

	• **Verify material** and **labour** costs and **overheads** to invoices, wage records etc
	• **Ensure expenditure** has been **analysed correctly** and **properly charged** to capital
	• Expenditure should be capitalised if it:
	  – **Enhances** the **economic benefits** of the asset in excess of its previously assessed standard of performance
	  – **Replaces or restores a component** of the assets that has been treated separately for depreciation purposes, and depreciated over its useful economic life
	  – Relates to a **major inspection** or **overhaul** that restores the economic benefits of the assets that have been consumed by the entity, and have already been reflected in depreciation
	• **Check no profit element** has been included in costs
	• Check **finance costs** have been **capitalised** or not capitalised on a consistent basis, and costs capitalised in period do not exceed total finance costs for period

DISPOSALS	These tests are to confirm **rights and obligations**, **completeness**, **occurrence** and **accuracy**.
	• **Verify disposals** with supporting documentation, checking transfer of title, sales price and dates of completion and payment • **Check calculation** of profit or loss • **Check** that **disposals** have been **authorised** • **Consider** whether **proceeds** are **reasonable** • If the asset was **used as security**, ensure **release from security** has been correctly made
CLASSIFICATION AND UNDERSTAND-ABILITY	• Review fixed asset disclosures in the financial statements to ensure they meet FRS 15 criteria.

| Question | Non-current assets |

You are the manager in charge of the audit of Puppy, a building and construction company, and you are reviewing the fixed asset section of the current audit file for the year ended 30 September 20X5. You find the following five matters which the audit senior has identified as problem areas. He is reviewing the company's proposed treatment of the five transactions in the accounts and is not sure that he has yet carried out sufficient audit work.

The five matters are as follows.

(a) During the year Puppy built a new canteen for its own staff at a cost of £450,000. This amount has been included in buildings as at 30 September 20X5.

(b) Loose tools included in the financial statements at a total cost of £166,000 are tools used on two of the construction sites on which Puppy operates. They are classified as fixed assets and depreciated over two years.

(c) A dumper truck, previously written off in the company's accounting records has been refurbished at a cost of £46,000 and this amount included in plant and machinery as at 30 September 20X5.

(d) The company's main office block has been revalued from £216,000 to £266,000 and this amount included in the balance sheet as at 30 September 20X5.

(e) A deposit of £20,000 for new equipment has been included under the heading plant and machinery although the final instalment of £35,000 was not paid over until 31 October 20X5 which was the date of delivery of the plant.

You are required, for each of the above matters to:

(a) Comment on the acceptability of the accounting treatment and disclosure as indicated above.
(b) Outline the audit work and evidence required to substantiate the assets.

| Answer |

(a) *Acceptability of accounting treatment and disclosure*

(i) *New staff canteen.* The costs of building a new staff canteen can quite properly be capitalised and treated as part of buildings in the balance sheet as work has produced future economic benefits (FRS 15). The company's normal depreciation policy should be applied, subject only to the canteen being completed and in use at the year end.

(ii) *Loose tools.* Loose tools tend to have a very limited life and individually not to be material in value. For these reasons any capitalisation policy must be extremely prudent. The acceptability of this accounting treatment would depend on the policy in previous years and normal practice within the industry.

(iii) *Dumper truck.* The refurbishment costs have obviously extended the useful life of this asset and it therefore seems reasonable to capitalise the expenditure. Depreciation should be charged on the refurbishment costs over the estimated remaining useful life.

(iv) *Revaluation of office block.* The revaluation of property is acceptable, but the auditors will need to ensure that the company complies with a number of disclosure requirements. A note to the accounts should give details of the revaluation and the name of the valuer. The surplus on revaluation should be transferred to a separate non-distributable reserve in the balance sheet as part of shareholders' funds. In addition any other assets of a similar nature to this should also be revalued.

(v)   *Deposit for new equipment.* As the equipment was not actually in the company's possession and use at the year end, the deposit should not have been shown as plant and machinery, but rather as a payment on account. If the amount was considered to be material a note to the accounts should give details of this prepayment.

(b)   The audit work and evidence required to substantiate each of the assets referred to in (a) above would be as follows.

(i)   *New staff canteen*

(1)   Physically confirm existence of the asset.

(2)   Confirm title to building by reference to central registry certificate.

(3)   Ascertain and confirm the details of any security granted over the asset, ensuring that this is properly recorded and disclosed.

(4)   Test the detailed costings of the building and obtain explanations for any material variances from the original budget. Particular care should be taken in assessing the reasonableness of any overheads included as an element of cost.

(5)   Review the depreciation policy for adequacy and consistency.

(ii)   *Loose tools*

(1)   Visit the two sites where the loose tools are used to confirm the existence and condition of a sample of them.

(2)   Vouch the cost and ownership of the loose tools to purchase invoices and the company's asset register.

(3)   Confirm the company's estimate of a two year life for these assets.

(4)   Review control procedures for safe custody of the loose tools.

(5)   Review the company's policy with regard to scrapping and/or sale of tools no longer required to ensure that any proceeds are properly recorded and the assets register appropriately updated and tools are completely recorded.

(iii)   *Dumper truck*

(1)   Inspect the truck to confirm its existence and to gain evidence of its valuation by reviewing its condition and the fact that it is still being used.

(2)   If the vehicle is used at all on public roads then the vehicle registration document should be inspected as some evidence of title.

(3)   Inspect the insurance policy for the truck as evidence of valuation.

(4)   Vouch the expenditure on refurbishment to suppliers' invoices or company's payroll records where any of the work has been done by the client's own staff.

(5)   Review the depreciation policy and assess for reasonableness by discussion with management and past experience of similar vehicles.

(iv)   *Revaluation of office block*

(1)   Inspect the building to confirm its existence and state of repair.

(2)   Examine documents of title to confirm ownership.

(3)   Enquire about any charges on the building and confirm that these have been properly recorded and disclosed.

(4)   Review the valuer's certificate and agree to the amount used in the financial statements, with consideration also being given to his qualifications, experience and reputation.

(5)   Assess the reasonableness of the valuation by comparison with any similar properties which may have recently changed hands on the open market.

(v)   *Deposit for new equipment*

(1)   Agree the payment of the deposit to the contract for purchase of the equipment.

(2)   Confirm the existence of the plant following its delivery on 31 October 20X5 as it is unlikely that the audit work will have been completed by that date.

2 Other fixed assets

 Key assertions for other fixed assets are existence and valuation.

The key assertions relating to intangibles are **existence** (not so much 'do they exist?', but 'are they genuinely assets?') and **valuation**. They will therefore be audited with reference to criteria laid down in the financial reporting standards. As only purchased goodwill or intangibles or intangibles with a readily ascertainable market value can be capitalised, **audit evidence should be available** (purchase invoices or specialist valuations). Audit of **amortisation** will be similar to the audit of depreciation.

AUDIT PLAN: OTHER FIXED ASSETS	
Goodwill	• Agree the consideration to sales agreement
	• Check that asset valuation is reasonable
	• Agree that the calculation is correct
	• Review the impairment review
	• Ensure valuation of goodwill is reasonable/there has been no impairment not adjusted
Intangibles	• Agree purchased intangibles to purchase documentation
	• Review specialist valuation of intangibles and ensure they are reasonable
	• Review amortisation calculations and ensure they are correct
Research and development costs	• Check that capitalised development costs conform to SSAP 13 criteria
	• Confirm feasibility and viability by reference to budgets
	• Check amortisation calculations, to ensure it commences with production/is reasonable

Chapter Roundup

- Key areas when testing **tangible fixed assets** are:
    - **Confirmation** of ownership
    - **Inspection** of fixed assets
    - **Valuation** by third parties
    - **Adequacy** of **depreciation** rates
- Key assertions for other fixed assets are existence and valuation.

Quick Quiz

1   Complete the control procedures.

    (a)   Acquisitions are properly ....

    (b)   Disposals are .... and proceeds ....

    (c)   Security .... over fixed assets are ....

    (d)   .... is reviewed ....

2   Complete the table, showing which tests are designed to provide evidence about which financial statement assertion.

Completeness	Existence
Valuation	Rights and obligations

    (a)   Inspect assets

    (b)   Verify to valuation certificate

    (c)   Refer to title deeds

    (d)   Compare assets in ledger to fixed asset register

    (e)   Review depreciation rates

    (f)   Verify material on self-constructed asset to invoices

    (g)   Examine invoices after the year end

    (h)   Review repairs in general ledger

3   Name two tests to confirm rights and obligations concerning charges and commitments.

    1 ....

    2 ....

Answers to Quick Quiz

1 (a) authorised
   (b) authorised, accounted for
   (c) arrangements, sufficient
   (d) depreciation, every year

2

Completeness	Existence
(d) Compare assets in ledger to register (h) Review repairs in general ledger	(a) Inspect assets
Valuation	**Rights and obligations**
(b) Verify to valuation certificate (e) Review valuation rates (f) Verify material on self-constructed assets to invoice	(c) Refer to title deeds (g) Examine invoices after the year end

3 • **Review for evidence** of charges in statutory books and by company search

   • **Review leases** of leasehold properties to ensure that company has fulfilled covenants therein

   • **Examine invoices received after year-end, orders and minutes** for evidence of capital commitments

Now try the question below from the Exam Question Bank

Number	Level	Marks	Time
Q13	Examination	20	36 mins

Stock

Introduction

No balance sheet audit area creates more potential problems for the auditors than that of stock.

Closing stock does not normally form an integrated part of the double entry bookkeeping system and hence a misstatement (under or overstatement) may not be detected from tests in other audit areas.

The four main elements of the audit of stock (completeness, existence, rights and obligations (ownership) and valuation) require careful consideration.

The auditor's attendance at the stock count is a particularly important part of the audit of stock. This is because the stock count gives evidence about the **existence** of stock, the **completeness** of stock (auditors check it is all counted and included) and review of the condition of the stock at the stock count is also an important part of assessing whether stock has been correctly **valued**.

Study guide

19 – Other audit and review evidence III – Stock

- Explain the importance of stock
- Describe stock counting procedures
- Explain cut-off
- Describe and tabulate for inclusion in a work program the substantive procedures used in obtaining evidence in relation to stock, including the auditor's attendance at stock counting
- Explain the purpose of substantive procedures, including direct confirmation of stock held by third parties, in relation to financial statement assertions concerning stock

Exam guide

As stock is often the most difficult area in practice for auditors it is also very important in exams. Questions could be on any area covered in this chapter, or a combination of them. The stock count and valuation were both covered in the Pilot paper and, more recently, in the December 2005 exam.

1 Regulatory aspects of stock

FAST FORWARD
> The **valuation** and **disclosure** rules for stock are laid down in SSAP 9.

1.1 SSAP 9 Stocks and work in progress

Key terms

> **Cost** is defined by SSAP 9 as comprising all costs of purchase and other costs incurred in bringing stock to its present location and condition.
>
> **Net realisable value** is the estimated selling price in the ordinary course of business, less the estimated costs of completion and the estimated costs necessary to make the sale.

Production costs (costs of conversion) include:

    (a)   Costs specifically attributable to units of production

    (b)   Production overheads

    (c)   Other overheads attributable to bringing the product or service to its present location and condition

2 The physical stock count   Pilot paper, 6/03

FAST FORWARD
> Physical stock count procedures are vital as they provide evidence which cannot be obtained elsewhere or at any other time about the quantities and conditions of stocks and work in progress.

Exam focus point

> You **must** have a thorough knowledge of audit procedures before, during and after the physical stock count.

2.1 The stock count

Responsibilities in relation to stock	
Management	Ensure stock figure in accounts • Represents stock that **exists** • Includes all stock **owned** Ensure accounting records include **statements of physical stock count**
Auditors	**Obtain sufficient audit evidence** about stock figure from • Stock records • Stock control systems • Results of physical stock counts • Test counts by auditors **Attend physical stock count** if stock is material and evidence of existence is provided by management stock counts

A business may count stock by one or a combination of the following methods.

(a) **Physical stock counts** at the **year-end**

From the viewpoint of the auditor this is often the best method.

(b) **Physical stock counts before** or **after** the **year-end**

This will provide audit evidence of varying reliability depending on:

(i) The **length of time** between the physical stock count and the year-end; the greater the time period, the less the value of audit evidence

(ii) The **business's system** of **internal controls**

(iii) The **quality of records** of **stock movements** in the period between the physical stock count and the year-end

(c) **Perpetual stock** where management has a programme of stock-counting throughout the year

If perpetual stock is used, auditors will check that management:

(a) Ensures that all stock lines are counted at least once a year.

(b) Maintains **adequate stock records** that are kept up-to-date. Auditors may compare sales and purchase transactions with stock movements, and carry out other tests on the stock records, for example checking casts and classification of stock.

(c) Has **satisfactory procedures** for **stock counts** and **test-counting**. Auditors should confirm the stock count arrangements and instructions are as rigorous as those for a year-end stock count by reviewing instructions and observing counts. Auditors will be particularly concerned with **cut-off**, that there are no stock movements whilst the count is taking place, and stock records are updated up until the time of the stock counts.

(d) **Investigates** and **corrects** all **material differences**. Reasons for differences should be recorded and any necessary corrective action taken. All corrections to stock movements should be **authorised** by a manager who has not been involved in the detailed work; these procedures are necessary to guard against the possibility that stock records may be adjusted to conceal shortages. Auditors should check that the procedures are being operated.

AUDIT PLAN: PERPETUAL STOCK COUNT

- Attend one of the stock counts (to observe and confirm that instructions are being adhered to)
- **Follow up** the **stock counts attended** to compare quantities counted by the auditors with the stock records, obtaining and verifying explanations for any differences, and checking that the client has reconciled count records with book stock records
- **Review** the **year's stock counts** to confirm the extent of counting, the treatment of discrepancies and the overall accuracy of records (if matters are not satisfactory, auditors will only be able to gain sufficient assurance by a full count at the year-end)
- Assuming a full count is not necessary at the year-end, **compare** the **listing of stock with the detailed stock records**, and carry out other procedures (**cut-off, analytical review**) to gain further comfort

---

Attendance at an stock count gives evidence of the **existence** and apparent **ownership** of stock. It also gives evidence of the **completeness** of stock, as do the follow up tests to ensure all stock sheets were included in the final count.

2.2 Planning attendance at stock count

FAST FORWARD

Before the physical stock count the auditors should ensure audit **coverage** of the **count** is **appropriate**, and that the client's **count instructions** have been reviewed.

PLANNING STOCK COUNT	
Gain knowledge	**Review** previous year's **arrangements**
	Discuss with **management stock count arrangements** and **significant changes**
Assess key factors	The **nature** and **volume** of the **stock**
	Risks relating to stock
	The **identification** of **high value items**
	Method of accounting for stock
	Location of stock and how it affects stock control and recording
	Internal control and **accounting systems** to identify potential areas of difficulty
Plan procedures	**Ensure** a **representative selection** of **locations**, **stock** and **procedures** are covered
	Ensure sufficient attention is given to **high value items**
	Arrange to obtain from **third parties confirmation** of stock they hold
	Consider the need for **expert help**

REVIEW OF STOCK COUNT INSTRUCTIONS	
Organisation of count	**Supervision** by senior staff including senior staff not normally involved with stock
	Tidying and **marking** stock to help counting
	Restriction and **control** of the production process and stock movements during the count
	Identification of damaged, obsolete, slow-moving, third party and **returnable** stock
Counting	**Systematic counting** to ensure all stock is counted
	Teams of **two counters**, with one counting and the other checking or two **independent counts**

REVIEW OF STOCK COUNT INSTRUCTIONS	
Recording	**Serial numbering, control** and **return** of all stock sheets
	Stock sheets being **completed** in **ink** and **signed**
	Information to be recorded on the **count records** (location and identity, count units, quantity counted, conditions of items, stage reached in production process)
	Recording of **quantity, conditions** and **stage of production** of **work-in-progress**
	Recording of last numbers of **goods inwards** and **outwards** records and of internal transfer records
	Reconciliation with **stock records** and **investigation** and correction of any **differences**

2.3 Attendance at stock count

FAST FORWARD

> During the count the auditors should **check the count** is being carried out according to instructions, carry out **test counts**, and watch for **third party** and **slow moving stocks** and **cut-off problems**.

AUDIT PLAN: ATTENDANCE AT STOCK COUNT

- **Check** the **client's staff** are following instructions as this will help to ensure the count is complete and accurate
- **Make test counts** to ensure procedures and internal controls are working properly
- **Ensure** that the **procedures** for **identifying damaged, obsolete** and **slow-moving** stock operate properly; the auditors should obtain information about the stocks' condition, age, usage and in the case of work in progress, its stage of completion to ensure that it is later valued appropriately
- **Confirm** that **stock held** on behalf of **third parties** is separately identified and accounted for so that stock is not overstated
- **Conclude** whether the **count** has been **properly carried out** and is sufficiently reliable as a basis for determining the existence of stocks
- **Consider** whether any **amendment** is necessary to subsequent **audit procedures**
- **Gain** an **overall impression** of the levels and values of stocks held so that the auditors may, in due course, judge whether the figure for stock appearing in the financial statements is reasonable

When carrying out test counts the auditors should select items from the count records and from the physical stock and check one to the other, to confirm the accuracy of the count records. The auditors should concentrate on high value stock. If the results of the test counts are not satisfactory, the auditors may request stock be recounted.

The auditors' working papers should include:

- Details of their **observations** and **tests**
- The manner in which **points** that are **relevant** and **material** to the stock being counted or measured have been dealt with by the client
- Instances where the **client's procedures** have **not been satisfactorily carried out**
- **Items for subsequent testing**, such as photocopies of (or extracts from) rough stock sheets
- **Details** of the **sequence** of **stock sheets**
- The **auditors' conclusions**

2.4 After the stock count

FAST FORWARD

After the count the auditors should check that **final stock sheets** have been **properly compiled** from count records and that **book stock** has been **appropriately adjusted**.

After the count, the matters recorded in the auditors' working papers at the time of the count or measurement should be followed up. Key tests include the following.

AUDIT PLAN: FOLLOWING UP THE STOCK COUNT

- **Trace items** that were **test counted** to final stock sheets
- **Check all count** records have been **included** in final stock sheets
- **Check final stock sheets** are **supported by** count records
- **Ensure** that **continuous stock records** have been **adjusted** to the amounts physically counted or measured, and that differences have been investigated
- **Confirm cut-off** by using details of the last serial number of goods inward and outwards notes; and of movements during the count
- **Check replies** from **third parties** about stock held by or for them
- **Confirm** the client's final **valuation** of stock has been calculated correctly
- **Follow up queries** and **notifying problems** to management

Question

Stock count

In connection with your examination of the financial statements of Camry Products, a limited company, for the year ended 31 March 20X9, you are reviewing the plans for a physical stock count at the company's warehouse on 31 March 20X9. The company assembles domestic appliances, and stock of finished appliances, unassembled parts and sundry stock are stored in the warehouse which is adjacent to the company's assembly plant. The plant will continue to produce goods during the stock count until 5pm on 31 March 20X9. On 30 March 20X9, the warehouse staff will deliver the estimated quantities of unassembled parts and sundry stock which will be required for production for 31 March 20X9; however, emergency requisitions by the factory will be filled on 31 March. During the stock count, the warehouse staff will continue to receive parts and sundry stock, and to dispatch finished appliances. Appliances which are completed on 31 March 20X9 will remain in the assembly plant until after the count has been completed.

Required

(a) List the principal procedures which the auditors should carry out when planning attendance at a company's physical stock count.

(b) Describe the procedures which Camry Products should establish in order to ensure that all stock items are counted and that no item is counted twice.

Answer

(a) In planning attendance at a physical stock count the auditors should:

    (i) Review previous year's audit working papers and discuss any developments in the year with management.

    (ii) Obtain and review a copy of the company's count instructions.

    (iii) Arrange attendance at count planning meetings, with the consent of management.

(iv) Gain an understanding of the nature of the stock and of any special problems this is likely to present, for example liquid in tanks, scrap in piles.

(v) Consider whether expert involvement is likely to be required as a result of any circumstances noted in (iv) above.

(vi) Obtain a full list of all locations at which stocks are held, including an estimate of the amount and value of stocks held at different locations.

(vii) Using the results of the above steps, plan for audit attendance by appropriately experienced audit staff at all locations where material stocks are held, subject to other factors (for example rotational auditing, reliance on internal controls).

(viii) Consider the impact of internal controls upon the nature and timing of attendance at the count.

(ix) Ascertain whether stocks are held by third parties and if so make arrangements to obtain written confirmation of them or, if necessary, to attend the count.

(b) Procedures to ensure a complete count and to prevent double-counting are particularly important in this case because movements will continue throughout the count.

(i) Clear instructions should be given as to procedures, and an official, preferably not someone normally responsible for stocks, should be given responsibility for organising the count and dealing with queries.

(ii) Before the count, all locations should be tidied and stock should be laid out in an orderly manner.

(iii) All stock should be clearly identified and should be marked after being counted by a tag or indelible mark, so that it is evident that it has been counted.

(iv) Prenumbered sheets should be issued to counters and should be accounted for at the end of the count.

(v) Counters should be given responsibility for specific areas of the warehouse. Each area should be subject to a recount.

(vi) A separate record should be kept of all goods received or issued during the day (for example by noting the GRN or dispatch note numbers involved).

(vii) Goods received on the day should be physically segregated until the count has been completed.

(viii) Similarly, goods due to be dispatched on the day should be identified in advance and moved to a special area or clearly marked so that they are not inadvertently counted in stock as well as being included in sales.

3 Cut-off

FAST FORWARD

Auditors should check **cut-off** by noting the **serial numbers** of items received and dispatched just before and after the year-end, and subsequently checking that they have been included in the **correct period**.

3.1 The importance of cut-off

Cut-off is most critical to the accurate recording of transactions in a manufacturing enterprise at particular points in the accounting cycle as follows:

- The **point** of **purchase** and **receipt** of **goods** and **services**
- The **requisitioning** of **raw materials** for production
- The **transfer** of **completed work-in-progress** to finished goods
- The **sale** and **dispatch** of **finished goods**

3.2 Audit procedures

The auditors should consider whether management has instituted adequate cut-off procedures: procedures intended to ensure that movements into, within and out of stocks are properly identified and reflected in the accounting records.

Purchase invoices should be recorded as liabilities only if the goods were received prior to the count. A schedule of 'goods received not invoiced' should be prepared, and items on the list should be accrued for in the accounts.

Sales cut-off is generally more straightforward to achieve correctly than purchases cut-off. Invoices for goods dispatched after the count should not appear in the profit and loss accounts for the period.

Prior to the physical stock count management should make arrangements for cut-off to be properly applied.

(a) Appropriate systems of recording of receipts and dispatches of goods are in place, and also a system for documenting materials requisitions. Goods received notes (GRNs) and goods dispatched notes (GDNs) should be sequentially pre-numbered.

(b) Final GRN and GDN and materials requisition numbers are noted. These numbers can then be used to check subsequently that purchases and sales have been recorded in the current period.

(c) Arrangements should be made to ensure that the cut-off arrangement for stocks held by third parties are satisfactory.

There should ideally be no movement of stock during the count. Preferably, receipts and dispatches should be suspended for the full period of the count. It may not be practicable to suspend all deliveries, in which case any deliveries which are received during the count should be segregated from other stock and carefully documented.

AUDIT PLAN: CUT-OFF	

Stock count	• Record **all movement notes** relating to the period, including:
	
	  – All interdepartmental requisition numbers
	  – The last goods received notes(s) and dispatch note(s) prior to the count
	  – The first goods received notes(s) and dispatch note(s) after the count
	
	• **Observe** whether **correct cut-off procedures** are being **followed** in the dispatch and receiving areas.
	
	• **Discuss procedures** with **company staff performing** the **count** to ensure they are understood
	
	• **Ensure** that **no goods finished** on the day of the count are **transferred** to the warehouse

AUDIT PLAN: CUT-OFF	
Final audit	• **Match up** the **goods received notes** with **purchase invoices** and ensure the **liability** has been **recorded** in the **correct period** (only goods received before the year end should be recorded as purchases) • **Match up** the **goods dispatched notes** to **sales invoices** and ensure the **income** has been **recorded** in the **correct period** (only goods dispatched before the year end should be recorded as sales) • **Match up** the **requisition notes** to the **work in progress** figures for the receiving department to ensure correctly recorded

Question   Cut-off

Using the information in the last Question above, describe the audit procedures you would carry out at the time of the physical stock count in order to ensure that cut-off is correct.

Answer

In order to ensure that cut-off of stock is correct, the following procedures should be carried out.

(a)   Make a record during the count attendance of all movement notes relating to the period, including:

    (i)   All interdepartmental requisition numbers

    (ii)   The last goods received note and dispatch note prior to the count

    (iii)   The first goods received note and dispatch note after the count. This information can be used for subsequent cut-off tests

(b)   Observe whether correct cut-off procedures are being followed in the dispatch and receiving areas. Discuss procedures with company staff performing the count to ensure they are understood

(c)   Ensure that no goods finished on the day of the count are transferred to the warehouse

4 Stock valuation   Pilot paper, 12/02, 12/05

> **FAST FORWARD**
>
> Auditing the valuation of stock includes:
> - Checking the **allocation of overheads** is appropriate
> - Confirming stock is carried at the **lower** of **cost** and **net realisable value**

4.1 Assessment of cost and net realisable value

Exam focus point

Valuation of stock is a very popular exam topic in auditing exams. You must know the audit work needed to confirm valuation of stock when overheads have been absorbed, and to confirm stock is stated at the lower of cost and net realisable value.

Knowledge of the requirements of SSAP 9 is essential and you should refer back to your Paper 2.5 notes if you are still unsure about this area.

Auditors must understand how the company determines the cost of an item for stock valuation purposes. Cost should include an appropriate proportion of overheads, in accordance with SSAP 9.

There are several ways of determining cost. Auditors must ensure that the company is **applying** the method **consistently** and that each year the method used **gives** a **fair approximation** to cost. They may need to support this by additional procedures:

- **Reviewing price** changes near the year end
- **Ageing the stock** held
- **Checking gross profit** margins to reliable management accounts

4.1.1 Valuation of raw materials and brought in components

The auditors should check that the correct prices have been used to value raw materials and brought in components valued at actual costs by **referring** to **suppliers' invoices**. The valuation may include unrealised profit if stock valued at the latest invoice price. Reference to suppliers' invoice will also provide the auditors with assurance as regards ownership.

If standard costs are used, auditors should **check** the **basis** of the **standards**, **compare standard costs** with **actual costs** and **confirm** that **variances** are being **treated appropriately**.

4.1.2 Valuation of work in progress and finished goods (other than long-term contract work in progress)

'Cost' comprises the cost of purchase plus the costs of conversion. The cost of conversion comprises:

- Costs specifically attributable to units of production

- Production overheads

- Other overheads attributable to bringing the product or service to its present location and condition

4.2 Audit procedures

The audit procedures will depend on the methods used by the client to value work in progress and finished goods, and on the adequacy of the system of internal control.

The auditors should consider what tests they can carry out to check the reasonableness of the valuation of finished goods and work in progress. **Analytical procedures** may assist comparisons being made with items and categories from the previous year's summaries. If the client has a computerised accounting system, the auditors may be able to request an exception report listing, for example, all items whose value has changed by more than a specified amount. A reasonableness check will also provide the auditors with assurance regarding completeness.

4.2.1 Cost

AUDIT PLAN: STOCK PRODUCTION COSTS	
For materials:	• **Check** the **valuation** of raw materials to **invoices** and **price lists**
	• **Confirm appropriate basis** of **valuation** (eg FIFO) is being used
	• **Confirm correct quantities** are being used when calculating raw material value in work in progress and finished goods
For labour costs:	• **Check labour costs** to **wage records**
	• **Review standard labour costs** in the light of actual costs and production;
	• **Check labour hours** to **time summaries**

The auditors should ensure that the client includes a proportion of overheads **appropriate** to **bringing** the **stock** to its **present location and condition**. The basis of overhead allocation should be:

- Consistent with prior years
- Calculated on the normal level of production activity

Thus, overheads arising from **reduced levels of activity**, **idle time** or **inefficient production** should be written off to the profit and loss account, rather than being included in stock.

AUDIT PLAN: ALLOCATION OF OVERHEADS

(a) All **abnormal conversion** costs (such as idle capacity) must be **excluded**.

(b) Where **firm sales contracts** have been entered into for the provision of goods or services to customer's specification, **design, marketing and selling costs** incurred before manufacture may be **included**.

(c) Overheads are **classified by function** when being allocated (eg whether they are a function of production, marketing, selling or administration).

(d) The costs of **general management**, as distinct from functional management, are not directly related to current production and are, therefore, **excluded**.

(e) The allocation of costs of **central service departments** should depend on the function or functions that the department is serving. **Only** those costs that can reasonably be allocated to the **production function** should be **included**.

(f) In determining what constitutes **'normal'** activity the following factors need to be considered:

　(i) The volume of production which the production facilities are **designed to achieve**

　(ii) The **budgeted level of activity** for the year under review and for the ensuing year

　(iii) The **level of activity achieved** both in the **year under review** and in **previous years**

Although temporary changes in the load of activity may be ignored, persistent variation should lead to revision of the previous norm.

Difficulty may be experienced if the client operates a system of total overhead absorption. It will be necessary for those overheads that are of a general, non-productive nature to be identified and excluded from the valuation.

4.2.2 Cost vs NRV

Auditors should **compare cost and net realisable value** for each item of stock. Where this is impracticable, the comparison may be done by group or category.

Net realisable value is likely to be less than cost when there has been:

- An **increase in costs** or a fall in selling price
- **Physical deterioration**
- **Obsolescence** of products
- A **marketing decision** to manufacture and sell products at a loss
- **Errors in production or purchasing**

AUDIT PLAN: STOCK – COST V NRV

- **Review and test the client's system** for **identifying slow-moving**, obsolete or damaged stock

- **Follow up** any **such items** that were **identified** at the **stock count**, ensuring that the client has made adequate provision to write down the items to net realisable value

- **Examine stock records** to identify slow-moving items (it may be possible to incorporate into a computer audit program certain tests and checks such as listing items whose value or quantity has not moved over the previous year)

> **AUDIT PLAN: STOCK – COST V NRV**
>
> - **Examine the prices** (per sales invoices) at which finished goods have been sold after the year-end and ascertain whether any finished goods items need to be reduced below cost
> - **Review quantities of goods sold after the year end** to determine that year end stock has, or will be, realised
> - If significant quantities of finished goods stock remain unsold for an unusual time after the year-end, **consider the need to make appropriate provision**

For work in progress, the **ultimate selling price** should be **compared** with the **carrying value** at the year end plus **costs** to be **incurred** after the year end to bring work in progress to a finished state.

Question

Cost v NRV

Your firm is the auditor of Arnold Electrical, a limited liability company, and you have been asked to audit the valuation of the company's stock at 31 May 20X1 in accordance with SSAP 9. Arnold Electrical operates from a single store and purchases domestic electrical equipment from wholesalers and manufacturers and sells them to the general public. These products include video and audio equipment, washing machines, refrigerators and freezers. In addition, it sells small items such as electrical plugs, tapes for video recorders, records and compact discs.

A full physical stock count was carried out at the year end, and you are satisfied that the stock was counted accurately and there are no cut-off errors. Because of the limited time available between the year end and the completion of the audit, the company has valued the stock at cost by recording the selling price and deducting the normal gross profit margin. Stock which the company believes to be worth less than cost has been valued at net realisable value. The selling price used is that on the item in the store when it was counted.

The stock has been divided into three categories.

(a) Video and audio equipment: televisions, video recorders, video cameras and audio equipment
(b) Domestic equipment: washing machines, refrigerators and freezers
(c) Sundry stock: electrical plugs, magnetic tapes and compact discs

The normal gross profit margin for each of these categories has been determined and this figure has been used to calculate the cost of the stock (by deducting the gross profit margin from the selling price). In answering the question you should assume there are no sales taxes.

Required

(a) List and describe the audit work you will carry out to check that stock has been correctly valued at cost.

(b) List and describe the audit work you will carry out to:

    (i) Find stock which should be valued at net realisable value
    (ii) Check that net realisable value is correct

(c) List and describe the other work you will perform to check that the stock value is accurate.

Note. In answering the question you are only required to check that the price per unit of the stock is correct. You should assume that the stock quantities are accurate and there are no purchases or sales cut-off errors.

Answer

(a) This method of valuation at cost is permitted by SSAP 9, but it is usually applied to large retail concerns which stock thousands of low value items, for example supermarket chains. This method is only permitted when it can be shown that it gives a reasonable approximation of the actual cost.

The following tests should be performed to ensure that the stock is correctly valued at cost.

(i) Obtain a schedule of the client calculations of the gross profit margins. Check the mathematical accuracy and consider the reliability of all sources of information used in the calculation.

(ii) Where the normal overall gross margin has been used, check the reasonableness of the figure by comparing it to the monthly management accounts for the year and last year's published accounts.

Test a sample of items to make sure that gross profit does not vary too much across all items of stock (which is unlikely for Arnold Electrical). The test will compare selling price to purchase price.

(iii) If a weighted average gross margin has been used, check that the weighting is correct in terms of the proportion of each type of product in closing stock.

(iv) Select a sample of high value lines and check the reasonableness of the gross profit estimate by calculating the gross profit for each of those lines. Sales price will be compared to stock sheets and to sales prices in the shop at the year end. Cost will be checked by examining purchase invoices. The weighted average profit margin for the selected lines can then be calculated and compared to the gross margin applied to the whole stock. *(Note.* High value lines may consist of individual items with a high selling price, or a large number of low value items.)

(v) Overvaluation of slow moving stock is possible when the prices of those items are affected by inflation. To check this, examine the stock sheets for any slow moving items (or ask the management of the company or use my own observation). Compare the value of the stock at the end of the accounting period to cost according to purchase invoices. If an overvaluation has occurred it should be quantified.

(vi) Check whether any goods were being offered for sale at reduced prices at the year end. If the reduced price is greater than cost, the use of an average gross profit percentage will cause stock to be undervalued. This undervaluation must be quantified. If full selling price was used in the calculation then the problem will not arise. Check a sample of stock items to sales invoices issued around the year end to make sure that the correct price was used in the costing calculation.

(b) (i) Stock which may be worth less than cost will include:

(1) Slow moving stock
(2) Obsolete or superseded stock
(3) Seconds and items that have been damaged
(4) Stocks which are being, or are soon likely to be, sold at reduced prices
(5) Discontinued lines

Finished goods where the selling price is less than cost will be valued at net realisable value. This is defined as the actual or estimated selling price less costs to completion and marketing, selling and distribution expenses.

To identify stocks which may be worth less than cost the following work will be carried out.

(1) Examine the computerised stock control system and list items showing an unacceptably low turnover rate. An unacceptable rate of turnover may be different for different items, but stock representing more than six months' sales is likely to qualify.

(2) Check the stock printout for items already described as seconds or recorded as damaged.

(3) Discuss with management the current position regarding slow moving stocks and their plans and expectations in respect of products that may be discontinued. The standard system must be carefully considered and estimates obtained of the likely selling price of existing stocks. The most likely outcome regarding the use and value of discontinued components must be decided.

(4) At the physical stock count, look for stock which is dusty, inaccessible and in general not moving and mark on the stock sheets.

(5) Find out whether any lines are unreliable and therefore frequently returned for repairs as these may be unpopular.

(6) Check with the trade press or other sources to see whether any of the equipment is out of date.

(ii) Determining the net realisable value of stocks is a difficult task and involves management judging how much stock can be sold and at what price, together with deciding whether to sell off raw materials and components separately or to assemble them into finished products. Each separate type of stock item should be considered separately in deciding on the level of prudent provision.

To determine the net realisable value of the stocks the following tests should be carried out.

(1) Find the actual selling prices from the latest sales invoice. For items still selling, invoices will be very recent, but for slow moving and obsolete items the invoiced prices will be out of date and allowance will have to be made for this (probably a reduction in estimating the most likely sale price of the stock concerned).

(2) Estimate the value of marketing, selling and distribution expenses using past figures for the types of finished goods concerned as a base. I would update and check for reasonableness against the most recent accounting records.

(3) Discuss with management what selling prices are likely to be where there is little past evidence. Costs to completion will be questioned where these are difficult to estimate and where there are any unusual assembly, selling or distribution problems.

(c) The following procedures would also be performed to check the value of stock at the year end.

(i) Compare current results with prior year(s). This would include gross profit margins, sales and turnover. Marked variations from the current year's results should be investigated.

(ii) Consider the effects of new technology and new fashions. The electrical appliance business will be exposed to obsolescence problems. Quantify any necessary write down.

(iii) Compare selling prices to those charged elsewhere. If the prices elsewhere are lower, than the distortion in selling price might affect the value of the stock of Arnold Electrical. Alternatively, if prices elsewhere are higher, then the company's prices may occasionally fall below cost. Again, any adjustment discovered to be necessary must be quantified.

(iv) Compare the valuation of stock this year to that at the end of last year. This will be particularly useful for lines held at both dates. If the values are comparable, taking account of inflation, then the current valuation is more likely to be correct.

(v) Sale prices should be checked as long after the year end as possible, to make sure that prices were not kept artificially high over the year end and then reduced at a later date. Stock turnover should also be examined on this same basis.

Chapter Roundup

- The **valuation** and **disclosure** rules for stock are laid down in SSAP 9.

- Physical stock count procedures are vital as they provide evidence which cannot be obtained elsewhere or at any other time about the quantities and conditions of inventories and work in progress.

- Before the physical stock count the auditors should ensure audit **coverage** of the **count** is **appropriate**, and that the client's **count instructions** have been reviewed.

- During the count the auditors should **check the count** is being carried out according to instructions, carry out **test counts**, and watch for **third party** and **slow moving stocks** and **cut-off problems.**

- After the count the auditors should check that **final stock sheets** have been **properly compiled** from count records and that **book stock** has been appropriately adjusted.

- Auditors should check **cut-off** by noting the **serial numbers** of items received and dispatched just before and after the year-end, and subsequently checking that they have been included in the correct period.

- Auditing the valuation of stock includes:

  - Checking the **allocation of overheads** is appropriate
  - Confirming inventories are carried at the lower of **cost** and **net realisable value**

Quick Quiz

1 Complete the definition, using the words given below.

   .... is defined by SSAP ...... comprising all costs of .... and other costs incurred in bringing the inventories to their .... and ....

9	purchase	condition	present	cost	location

2 Name three methods of stock counting

   1 ....

   2 ....

   3 ....

3 When should the following stock counting tests take place?

   (a) Check client staff are following instructions

   (b) Review previous year's stock count arrangements

   (c) Assess method of accounting for stocks

   (d)   Trace counted items to final stock sheets

   (e)   Check replies from third parties about stock held for them

   (f)   Conclude as to whether stock count has been properly carried out

   (g)   Gain an overall impression of levels and values of stock

   (h)   Consider the need for expert help

BEFORE	DURING	AFTER

4   Name four points in the accounting cycle when cut off is critical.

   1   ....

   2   ....

   3   ....

   4   ....

5   Give four occasions when the net realisable value of stock is likely to fall below cost.

   1   ....

   2   ....

   3   ....

   4   ....

Answers to Quick Quiz

1   Cost, 9, purchase, present location, condition

2
- Year end
- Pre/post year end
- Continuous

3   (a) DURING   (b) BEFORE   (c) BEFORE   (d) AFTER

         (e) AFTER   (f) DURING   (g) DURING   (h) BEFORE

4
- The **point** of **purchase** and **receipt** of **goods** and **services**
- The **requisitioning** of **raw materials** for production
- The **transfer** of **completed work-in-progress** to finished goods
- The **sale** and **dispatch** of **finished goods**

5   From:

- An **increase in costs** or a fall in selling price
- **Physical deterioration**
- **Obsolescence** of products
- A **marketing decision** to manufacture and sell products at a loss
- **Errors in production or purchasing**

Now try the question below from the Exam Question Bank

Number	Level	Marks	Time
Q14	Examination	20	36 mins

15

Debtors and prepayments

Topic list	Syllabus reference
1 Trade debtors	6
2 Bad debts	6
3 Sales	6
4 Prepayments	6

Introduction

Debtors will generally be a material figure on a company's balance sheet, and must therefore be given due weight.

You should make sure that you are fully conversant with the 'standard' procedures such as the confirmation of **debtors**. The debtors confirmation is primarily designed to test the client's entitlement to receive the debt, not the customer's ability to pay. Auditors also need to consider **cut-off** for debtors.

Study guide

18 – Other audit and review evidence II – Debtors and prepayments

- Describe and tabulate for inclusion in a work program the substantive procedures, including direct confirmation of debtors, used in obtaining evidence in relation to debtors and prepayments, and the related profit and loss account entries

- Explain the purpose of substantive procedures in relation to financial statement assertions concerning debtors and prepayments

Exam guide

Debtors were examined in conjunction with sales system controls in the pilot paper.

1 Trade debtors   12/01

FAST FORWARD

A **confirmation** of **debtors** is a major procedure, usually achieved by direct contact with customers.

1.1 Debtors listing and aged analysis

Much of the auditors' detailed work will be based on a selection of accounts debtors' balances chosen from a listing of sales ledger balances, prepared by the client or auditors. Ideally the list should be aged, showing the period or periods of time money has been owed. The following substantive procedures check the **completeness** and **accuracy** of a client-prepared list.

- **Check** the **balances** from the **individual sales ledger accounts** to the **list of balances** and vice versa

- **Check** the **total** of the **list** to the **sales ledger control account**

- **Cast** (that is, add up) the **list of balances** and the **sales ledger control account**

- **Confirm** whether **list of balances reconciles** with the **sales ledger control account**

1.2 Confirmation of debtors

1.2.1 Objectives of confirmation

Part of ISA (UK and Ireland) 501 *External confirmations* covers confirmation of debtors. This states that, when it is reasonable to expect customers to respond, the auditors should ordinarily plan to obtain direct confirmation of debtors to individual entries in an account balance.

The verification of trade debtors by direct communication is therefore the normal means of providing audit evidence to satisfy the objective of checking whether customers exist and owe *bona fide* amounts to the company (**existence and rights and obligations**).

Confirmation will produce for the current audit file a written statement from each respondent that the amount owed at the date of the confirmation is correct. This is, *prima facie*, reliable audit evidence, being from an independent source and in 'documentary' form. The confirmation of debtors on a test basis should not be regarded as replacing other normal audit checks, such as the testing in depth of sales transactions, but the results may influence the scope of such tests.

1.2.2 Timing

Ideally the confirmation should take place immediately after the year-end and hence cover the year-end balances to be included in the balance sheet. However, time constraints may make it impossible to achieve this ideal.

In these circumstances it may be acceptable to carry out the confirmation **prior to the year-end** provided that confirmation is no more than three months before the year-end and internal controls are strong.

1.2.3 Client's mandate

Confirmation is essentially an act of the **client**, who alone can authorise third parties to divulge information to the auditors.

The ISA outlines what the auditors' response should be when management refuse permission for the auditors to contract third parties for evidence. Note that this applies to all such external confirmations, not just trade debtors circularisations.

The ISA says 'when the auditor seeks to confirm certain balances or other information, and management requests the auditor not to do so, the auditor should consider whether there are valid grounds for such a request and obtain evidence to support the validity of management's requests. If the auditor agrees to management's request not to seek external confirmation regarding a particular matter, the auditor should apply alternative procedures to obtain sufficient appropriate evidence regarding that matter. If the auditor does not accept the validity of management's request and is prevented from carrying out the confirmations, there has been a limitation on the scope of the auditor's work and the auditor should consider the possible impact on the auditor's report'.

1.2.4 Positive v negative confirmation

When confirmation is undertaken the method of requesting information from the customer may be either 'positive' or 'negative'.

- Under the **positive** method the customer is requested to confirm the accuracy of the balance shown or state in what respect he is in disagreement.

- Under the **negative** method the customer is requested to reply if the amount stated is disputed.

The positive method is generally preferable as it is designed to encourage definite replies from those contacted.

The negative method may be used if the client has good internal control, with a large number of small accounts. In some circumstances, say where there is a small number of large accounts and a large number of small accounts, a combination of both methods, as noted above, may be appropriate.

A specimen 'positive' confirmation letter is shown below.

The statements will normally be prepared by the client's staff, from which point the auditors, as a safeguard against the possibility of fraudulent manipulation, must maintain strict control over the checking and dispatch of the statements.

Precautions must also be taken to ensure that undelivered items are returned, not to the client, but to the auditors' own office for follow-up by them.

MANUFACTURING CO LIMITED
15 South Street
London

Date

Messrs   (customer)

In accordance with the request of our auditors, Messrs Arthur Daley & Co, we ask that you kindly confirm to them directly your indebtedness to us at (insert date) which, according to our records, amounted to £.......... as shown by the enclosed statement.

If the above amount is in agreement with your records, please sign in the space provided below and return this letter direct to our auditors in the enclosed stamped addressed envelope.

If the amount is not in agreement with your records, please notify our auditors directly of the amount shown by your records, and if possible detail on the reverse of this letter full particulars of the difference.

Yours faithfully,

For Manufacturing Co Limited

Reference No: ....

....

(Tear off slip)

The amount shown above is/is not * in agreement with our records as at

Account No   ....   Signature   ....

Date   ....   Title or position ....

* The position according to our records is shown overleaf.

Notes

- The letter is on the client's paper, signed by the client.
- A copy of the statement is attached.
- The reply is sent directly to the auditor in a pre-paid envelope.

1.2.5 Sample selection

Auditors will normally only contact a sample of debtors. If this sample is to yield a meaningful result it must be based upon a complete list of all debtors. In addition, when constructing the sample, the following classes of account should receive special attention:

- **Old unpaid accounts**
- **Accounts written off** during the period under review
- **Accounts with credit balances**
- **Accounts settled by round sum payments**

Similarly, the following should not be overlooked:

- **Accounts with nil balances**
- **Accounts which** have been **paid** by the date of the examination

1.2.6 Follow up procedures

Auditors must follow up **customer disagreements** and **failure by customers** to **respond**.

Auditors will have to carry out further work in relation to those debtors who:

- **Disagree** with the **balance stated** (positive and negative confirmation)
- **Do not respond** (positive confirmation only)

In the case of disagreements, the customer response should have identified specific amounts which are disputed.

REASONS FOR DISAGREEMENTS
There is a **dispute** between the client and the customer. The reasons for the dispute would have to be identified, and provision made if appropriate against the debt.
Cut-off problems exist, because the client records the following year's sales in the current year or because goods returned by the customer in the current year are not recorded in the current year. Cut-off testing may have to be extended (see below).
The customer may have sent the **monies before** the year-end, but the monies were **not recorded** by the client as receipts until **after** the year-end. Detailed cut-off work may be required on receipts.
Monies received may have been posted to the **wrong account** or a cash-in-transit account. Auditors should check if there is evidence of other mis-posting. If the monies have been posted to a cash-in-transit account, auditors should ensure this account has been cleared promptly.
Customers who are also suppliers may **net off balances** owed and owing. Auditors should check that this is allowed.
Teeming and lading, stealing monies and **incorrectly posting** other receipts so that no particular customer is seriously in debt is a fraud that can arise in this area. If auditors suspect teeming and lading has occurred, detailed testing will be required on cash receipts, particularly on prompt posting of cash receipts.

When the positive request method is used the auditors must follow up by all practicable means those debtors who **fail to respond**. Second requests should be sent out in the event of no reply being received within two or three weeks and if necessary this may be followed by telephoning the customer, with the client's permission.

After two, or even three, attempts to obtain confirmation, a list of the outstanding items will normally be passed to a responsible company official, preferably independent of the sales accounting department, who will arrange for them to be investigated.

1.2.7 Additional procedures where confirmation is carried out before year-end

The auditors will need to carry out the following procedures where their confirmation is carried out before the year-end.

- **Review** and **reconcile entries** on the **sales ledger control account** for the intervening period
- **Verify sales entries** from the control account by checking sales day book entries, copy sales invoices and dispatch notes
- **Check** that **appropriate credit entries** have been made for goods returned notes and other evidence of returns/allowances to the sales ledger control account
- Select a sample from the cash received records and **ensure** that **receipts** have been **credited** to the control account

- **Review** the **list of balances** at the **confirmation** date and year end and **investigate** any **unexpected movements** or lack of them (it may be prudent to send further confirmation requests at the year end to material debtors where review results are unsatisfactory)

- **Carry out analytical review** procedures, comparing debtors' ratios at the confirmation date and year-end

- **Carry out** year end **cut-off tests**, in addition to any performed at the date of the confirmation (see below)

1.2.8 Non purchase ledger accounting

Certain entities operate systems, often computerised, which make it impossible for them to confirm the balance on their account.

Typically in these circumstances their 'purchase ledger' is merely a list of unpaid invoices in date order.

However, given sufficient information the customer will be able to confirm that any given invoice is outstanding. Hence the auditors can contact such enterprises, but they will need to break down the total on the account into its constituent outstanding invoices.

Confirmation letters should nevertheless state the full balance so that the customer has the option of confirming the balance and also has the opportunity to object if he thinks the total appears incorrect.

1.2.9 Evaluation and conclusions

All confirmations, regardless of timing, must be properly recorded and evaluated. All **balance disagreements** and **non-replies** must be **followed up** and their effect on total debtors evaluated.

Differences arising that merely represent **invoices** or **cash in transit** (normal timing differences) generally do not require adjustment, but disputed amounts, and errors by the client, may indicate that further substantive work is necessary to determine whether material adjustments are required.

1.3 Alternative procedures

If it proves impossible to get confirmations from individual customers, alternative procedures include the following.

AUDIT PLAN: DEBTORS – ALTERNATIVE PROCEDURES

- **Check receipt of cash** after date
- **Verify valid purchase** orders if any
- **Examine the account** to see if the balance outstanding represents specific invoices and **confirm** their **validity**
- **Obtain explanations** for **invoices remaining unpaid** after subsequent ones have been paid
- **Check** if the **balance** on the account is **growing**, and if so, why
- **Test company's control** over the issue of **credit notes** and the **write-off of bad debts**

2 Bad debts

FAST FORWARD ▶▶ The **recoverability** of **debts** can be tested by a combination of methods.

A significant test of bad debts will be reviewing the **cash received** after date. This will provide evidence of collectability of debts (and hence **valuation**). It also provides some evidence of correctness of title (**rights and obligations**), although ideally it should be carried out as well as a debtors' confirmation (which is the main test on rights and obligations).

AUDIT PLAN: BAD DEBTS

- **Confirm necessity/adequacy** of allowance against **write-off** of specific debts by review of correspondence, solicitors' debt collection, agencies' letters, liquidation statements

- **Examine customer files** on **overdue debts**, and **assess** whether **provision** is required in the circumstances

- **Consider** whether **amounts owed** may be **not recovered** where there has been:
  - Round sum payments on account
  - Invoices unpaid after subsequent invoices paid

- **Review customer files/correspondence** from solicitors and **debtors confirmation results** for evidence of potential bad debts

- **Confirm general provisions** for bad debts considering:
  - How well previous year's provision predicted actual bad debts
  - Whether calculation correct
  - Whether formula used is reasonable and consistent with previous years
  - Exclusion of debtors against whom specific allowance is made

- **Examine credit notes** issued after the year-end for **provisions** that should be made against current period balances

- **Check accuracy** of **aged customer analysis** by comparing analysis with dates on invoices and **matching cash receipts** against outstanding invoices

- **Investigate** and **consider need for provision against unusual features** on aged customer analysis, such as:
  - Unapplied credits
  - Unallocated cash

- **Investigate** and **consider need for provision against unusual items** in the sales ledger, such as:
  - Journal entries transferring balances from one account to another
  - Journal entries that clear post year-end trade account debtors balances
  - Balances not made up of specific invoices
  - Sales ledger accounts with significant adjustments or credit notes

Auditors should also consider the collectability of material **customer** balances other than those contained in the sales ledger. Auditors should request certificates of loan balances from employees and others, and inspect the authority if necessary.

3 Sales

FAST FORWARD

Sales is a material figure often audited by analytical review as it should have predictable relationships with other figures in the financial statements.

Debtors will often be tested in conjunction with sales. Auditors are seeking to obtain evidence that sales pertain to the entity (occurrence), and are **completely** and **accurately recorded**. This will involve carrying out certain procedures to test for **completeness** of sales and also testing **cut-off.**

In June 2005, there were 10 marks available for setting out the tests to check completeness and accuracy of sales for a particular company. The question asked candidates to explain the **reason** for each test, so as you are working through any audit test in this book, make sure you understand why each course of action is being recommended. You should practice questions like these. This question is in your Practice and Revision Kit.

3.1 Completeness and occurrence of sales

Analytical review is likely to be important when testing completeness. A client is likely to have a great deal of information about company sales and should be able to explain any fluctuations and variances. Auditors should consider the following.

- The **level of sales** over the year, compared on a month-by-month basis with the previous year
- The effect on sales value of **changes in quantities** sold
- The effect on sales value of **changes in products** or **prices**
- The level of **goods returned, sales allowances** and **discounts**
- The **efficiency of labour** as expressed in sales or profit per tax per employee

In addition auditors must record reasons for changes in the **gross profit margin** ($\frac{\text{Gross profit}}{\text{Turnover}} \times 100\%$).

Analysis of the gross profit margin should be as detailed as possible, ideally broken down by **product area** and **month or quarter**.

As well as analytical review, auditors may feel that they need to carry out a directional test on **completeness of recording** of individual sales in the accounting records. To do this, auditors should start with the documents that first record sales (**goods dispatched notes** or **till rolls** for example), and trace sales recorded in these through intermediate documents such as sales summaries to the **sales ledger**.

Auditors must ensure that the population of documents from which the sample is originally taken is itself complete, by checking for example the **completeness** of the **sequence** of goods dispatched notes.

You must remember the direction of this test. Since we are checking the completeness of recording of sales in the sales ledger, we cannot take a sample from the ledger since the sample cannot include what has not been recorded.

3.2 Other sales tests

If on the other hand, the auditors suspect that sales may have been **invalidly** recorded, and have not **occurred**, then the sample will be taken from the **sales ledger** and **confirmed** to **supporting documentation** (orders, dispatch notes etc).

AUDIT PLAN: SALES – ACCURACY
• Check the **pricing calculations** and **additions** on invoices
• Check whether **discounts** have been **properly calculated**
• Check whether **tax** has been **added appropriately**

Other tests that may be carried out on sales include:

- **Trace debits** in the **sales account** to credit notes
- **Check casting** of **sales ledger accounts** and **sales ledger control account**
- **Review reconciliations** of sales ledger control account and other relevant reconciliations (for example till rolls) and investigate unusual items

3.3 Sales cut-off

We can now turn to the requirement to confirm that sales cut-off is satisfactory and hence sales are completely recorded. During the stock count the auditors will have obtained details of the last serial numbers of goods outward notes issued before the commencement of the stock count.

AUDIT PLAN: SALES CUT OFF

- **Check goods dispatched** and **returns inwards** notes around year-end to ensure:
- **Invoices** and **credit notes** are **dated** in the **correct period**
- **Invoices** and **credit notes** are **posted** to the **sales ledger** and **general ledger** in the correct period
- **Reconcile entries** in the **sales ledger control account** around the **year-end** to daily batch invoice totals ensuring batches are posted in correct year
- **Review sales ledger control account** around year-end for **unusual items**
- **Review material after-date invoices, credit notes** and **adjustments** and ensure that they are properly treated as following year sales

---

3.4 Goods on sale or return

Care should be exercised to ensure that goods on sale or return are properly treated in the accounts. Except where the client has been notified of the sale of the goods they should be reflected in the accounts as **stock** at cost and not as debtors, otherwise profits may be incorrectly anticipated.

4 Prepayments

FAST FORWARD

Prepayments may also be tested by analytical review.

The auditors will be concerned primarily that prepayments **exist** and have been **completely** and **accurately** included on the balance sheet at the appropriate **value**.

AUDIT PLAN: PREPAYMENTS

- **Verify prepayments** by reference to the cash book, expense invoices, correspondence and so on (existence and rights and obligations, valuation)
- **Check calculations** of prepayments (accuracy, valuation)
- **Review** the **detailed profit and loss account** to ensure that all likely prepayments have been provided for (completeness)
- **Review** the **prepayments** for **reasonableness** by comparing with prior years and using analytical procedures where applicable

---

Question

Debtors

Sherwood Textiles, a listed company, manufactures knitted clothes and dyes these clothes and other textiles. You are carrying out the audit of the accounts of the company for the year ended 30 September 20X6 which show a turnover of about £10 million, and a profit before tax of about £800,000.

You are attending the final audit in December 20X6 and are commencing the audit of trade debtors, which are shown in the draft accounts at £2,060,000.

The interim audit (tests of control) was carried out in July 20X6 and it showed that there was a good system of internal control in the sales system and no serious errors were found in the audit tests. The company's sales ledger is maintained on a computer, which produces at the end of each month:

(i)   A list of transactions for the month

(ii)   An aged list of balances

(iii)   Open item statements which are sent to customers. (*Note.* Open item statements show all items which are outstanding on each account, irrespective of their age.)

Required

(a)   List and briefly describe the audit tests you would carry out to verify trade debtors at the year end. You are not required to describe how you would carry out a direct confirmation of debtors.

(b)   Describe the audit work you would carry out on the following replies to a debtors' circularisation:

(i)   Balance agreed by customer

(ii)   Balance not agreed by customer

(iii)   Customer is unable to confirm the balance because of the form of records kept by the customer

(iv)   Customer does not reply to the confirmation letter

Answer

(a)   The auditors will carry out the following tests on the list of balances.

(i)   Check the balances from the individual sales ledger accounts to the list of balances and vice versa.

(ii)   Check the total of the list to the sales ledger control account.

(iii)   Cast the list of balances and the sales ledger control account.

Other general tests auditors will carry out will be to:

(i)   Agree the opening balance on the sales ledger control account to ensure that last year's audit adjustments were recorded.

(ii)   Scrutinise ledger balances for unusual entries.

(iii)   Carry out analytical procedures considering particularly changes in debtors' collection period and in age profile of debtors.

The determination of whether the company has made reasonable provision for bad and doubtful debts, will be facilitated as the company produces an aged listing of balances.

Auditors will carry out the following procedures to check bad debts.

(i)   Debts against which specific provision has been made (and debts written off) should be examined in conjunction with correspondence, lawyers'/debt collection agencies' letters, liquidators' statements and so on, and their necessity or adequacy confirmed.

(ii)   A general review of relevant correspondence may reveal debts where a provision is warranted, but has not been made.

(iii)   Where specific and/or general provisions have been determined using the aged analysis, the auditors should ensure that the analysis has been properly prepared by comparing the analysis with the dates on invoices and matching cash receipts against outstanding invoices. They should check the reasonableness and consistency of any formula used to calculate general provisions.

(iv) Additional tests that should be carried out on individual balances will include the ascertainment of the subsequent receipt of cash, paying particular attention to round sum payments on account, examination of specific invoices and, where appropriate, goods received notes, and enquiry into any invoices that have not been paid when subsequent invoices have been paid.

(v) Excessive discounts should be examined, as should journal entries transferring balances from one account to another and journal entries that clear customer balances after the year end.

(vi) Credit notes issued after the year end should be reviewed and provisions checked where they refer to current period sales;

In order to check cut-off and hence completeness, the auditors should, during the physical stock count, have obtained details of the last serial numbers of goods outwards issued before the commencement of the count. The following substantive procedures are designed to test that goods taken into stock are not also treated as sales in the year under review and, conversely, goods despatched are treated as sales in the year under review and not also treated as stock.

(i) Check goods outwards and returns inwards notes around year end to ensure that:

    (1) Invoices and credit notes are dated in the correct period; and

    (2) Invoices and credit notes are posted to the sales ledger and nominal ledger in the correct period.

(ii) Reconcile entries in the sales ledger control around the year end to daily batch invoice totals ensuring batches are posted in correct year.

(iii) Review sales ledger control account around year end for unusual items.

(iv) Review material after date invoices and ensure that they are properly treated as following year sales.

(b) The verification of trade debtors by direct communication is the normal means of providing audit evidence to prove that debtors represent bona fide amounts due to the company existence and rights and obligations.

The audit work required on the various replies to a debtors' circularisation would be as follows.

(i) *Balances agreed by customer*

Where the balance has been agreed by the customer all that is required would be to ensure that the debt does appear to be collectable. This would be achieved by reviewing cash received after date or considering the adequacy of any provision made for a long outstanding debt.

(ii) *Balances not agreed by customer*

All balance disagreements must be followed up and their effect on total debtors evaluated. Differences arising that merely represent invoices or cash in transit (which are normal timing differences) generally do not require adjustment, but disputed amounts, and errors by the client, may indicate that further substantive work is necessary to determine whether material adjustments are required.

(iii)   *Customer is unable to confirm the balance because of the form of records he or she maintains*

Certain companies, often computerised, operate systems which make it impossible for them to confirm the balance on their account. Typically in these circumstances their purchase ledger is merely a list of unpaid invoices. However, given sufficient information the customer will be able to confirm that any given invoice is outstanding. Hence the auditors can circularise such enterprises successfully, but they will need to break down the total on the account into its constituent outstanding invoices.

(iv)   *Customer does not reply to confirmation letter*

When the positive request method is used the auditors must follow up by all practicable means those customers who fail to respond. Second requests should be sent out in the event of no reply being received within two or three weeks and if necessary this may be followed by telephoning the customer with the client's permission.

After two, or even three attempts to obtain confirmation, a list of the outstanding items will normally be passed to a responsible company official, preferably independent of the sales department, who will arrange for them to be investigated.

Alternative audit procedures might include the following.

(1)   Check receipt of cash after date.

(2)   Verify valid purchase orders, if any.

(3)   Examine the account to see if the balance represents specific outstanding invoices.

(4)   Obtain explanations for invoices remaining unpaid after subsequent ones have been paid.

(5)   See if the balance on the account is growing, and if so, why.

(6)   Test the company's control over the issue of credit notes and the write-off of bad debts.

Chapter Roundup

- A **confirmation** of **debtors** is a major procedure, usually achieved by direct contact with customers.

- Auditors must follow up **customer disagreements** and **failure by customers** to **respond**.

- The **recoverability** of **debts** can be tested by a combination of methods.

- Sales is a material figure often audited by analytical review as it should have predictable relationships with other figures in the financial statements.

- Prepayments may also be tested by analytical review.

Quick Quiz

1   The negative method of debtors confirmation should only be used if the client has a good internal control and a small number of large debtors accounts.

True   ☐

False   ☐

2   Name four types of account which should receive special attention when picking a sample for debtors confirmation.

1   ....

2   ....

3   ....

4   ....

3   Complete the following tests which aim to confirm the valuation of bad debts.

(a)   Confirm adequacy of provision by reviewing correspondence with

(i)   ....

(ii)   ....

(b)   Examine .... issued after the year end for provisions that should be made against current period balances.

4   Name three things that can be considered when undertaking analytical review on sales.

1   ....

2   ....

3   ....

5   Give two examples of tests to verify prepayments

1   ....

2   ....

Answers to Quick Quiz

1   False

2   From:

- **Old unpaid accounts**
- **Accounts written off** during the period under review
- **Accounts with credit balances**
- **Accounts settled by round sum payments**
- **Accounts with nil balances**
- **Accounts which** have been **paid** by the date of the examination

3   (a)   customers, solicitors
    (b)   credit notes

4   1   Level of sales, month by month
    2   Price
    3   Goods returned

5   1   Verify by reference to invoices, cash book correspondence
    2   Check calculations

Now try the question below from the Exam Question Bank

Number	Level	Marks	Time
Q15	Examination	20	36 mins

16

Bank and cash

Topic list	Syllabus reference
1 Bank	6
2 Cash	6

Introduction

Work on bank and cash will concentrate on completeness and accuracy of balances. The audit of cash book transactions has been considered in the chapters on sales, purchases and wages cycles, and fixed asset additions and disposals.

Study guide

21 – Other audit and review evidence V – Bank and cash

- Describe and tabulate for inclusion in a work program the substantive procedures, including bank confirmation reports used in obtaining evidence in relation to bank and cash, and the related profit and loss account entries

- Explain the purpose of substantive procedures in relation to financial statement assertions concerning bank and cash

Exam guide

Bank reconciliation testing is often the most important in practice, and so may be where exam questions are focused.

1 Bank   6/02

FAST FORWARD

> **Bank balances** are usually **confirmed directly with the bank** in question.

1.1 Bank confirmation procedures

The audit of bank balances will need to cover **completeness, existence, rights and obligations and valuation**. All of these elements can be audited directly through the device of obtaining third party confirmations from the client's banks and reconciling these with the accounting records, having regard to cut-off. The auditors should update details of bank accounts held.

This type of audit evidence is valuable because it comes directly from an **independent source** and, therefore, provides greater assurance of reliability than that obtained solely from the bank's own records. The bank letter is mentioned as a source of external third party evidence in ISA (UK and Ireland) 505 *External Confirmations*.

1.2 Confirmation requests

FAST FORWARD

> The bank letter can be used to ask a variety of questions, including queries about outstanding interests, contingent liabilities and guarantees.

The auditors should decide from which bank or banks to request confirmation, have regard to such matters as **size of balance**, **volume of activity**, **degree of reliance** on **internal control**, and **materiality** within the context of the financial statements.

The auditors should determine which of the following approaches is the most appropriate in seeking confirmation of balances or other information from the bank:

- **Listing balances** and other information, and requesting confirmation of their accuracy and completeness, or

- **Requesting details of balances** and other information, which can then be compared with the requesting bank's records

In determining which of the above approaches is the most appropriate, the auditors should weigh the **quality** of **audit evidence** they require in the particular circumstances against the **practicality** of obtaining a reply from the confirming bank.

Difficulty may be encountered in obtaining a satisfactory response even where the client company submits information for confirmation to the confirming bank. It is important that a response be sought for **all** confirmation requests. Auditors should not usually request a response only if the information submitted is incorrect or incomplete.

1.2.1 Preparation and dispatch of requests and receipt of replies

Control over the content and dispatch of confirmation requests is the responsibility of the auditors. However, it will be necessary for the request to be authorised by the client entity. Replies should be returned directly to the auditors and to facilitate such a reply, a pre-addressed envelope should be enclosed with the request.

1.2.2 Content of confirmation requests

The form and content of a confirmation request letter will depend on the purpose for which it is required and on local practices.

The most commonly requested information is in respect of balances due to or from the client entity on **current, deposit, loan and other accounts**. The request letter should provide the account description number and the type of currency for the account.

It may also be advisable to request information about **nil balances** on accounts, and accounts which were closed in the twelve months prior to the chosen confirmation date. The client entity may ask for confirmation not only of the balances on accounts but also, where it may be helpful, other information, such as the maturity and interest terms, unused facilities, lines of credit/standby facilities, any offset or other rights or encumbrances, and details of any collateral given or received.

The client entity and its auditors are likely to request confirmation of **contingent liabilities**, such as those arising on guarantees, comfort letter, bills and so on.

Banks often hold **securities** and other items in safe custody on behalf of customers. A request letter may thus ask for confirmation of such items held by the confirming bank.

The procedure is simple but important.

(a) The banks will require **explicit written authority** from their client to disclose the information requested.

(b) The **auditors' request** must **refer** to the **client's letter** of authority and the date thereof. Alternatively it may be countersigned by the client or it may be accompanied by a specific letter of authority.

(c) In the case of joint accounts, **letters of authority** signed by all **parties** will be necessary.

(d) Such **letters** of **authority** may either **give permission** to the bank to disclose information for a specific request or grant permission for an indeterminate length of time.

(e) The request should **reach** the **branch manager** at least **two weeks in advance** of the client's **year-end** and should state both that year-end date and the previous year-end date.

(f) The **auditors** should themselves **check** that the bank response covers all the information in the standard and other responses.

1.3 Cut-off

Care must be taken to ensure that there is no **window dressing**, by checking **cut-off** carefully. Window dressing in this context is usually manifested as an attempt to overstate the liquidity of the company by:

(a) Keeping the cash book open to take credit for **remittances actually received** after the year end, thus enhancing the balance at bank and reducing receivables

(b)   **Recording cheques paid in** the period under review which are not actually despatched until after the year end, thus decreasing the balance at bank and reducing creditors

A combination of (a) and (b) can contrive to present an artificially healthy looking current ratio.

With the possibility of (a) above in mind, where lodgements have not been cleared by the bank until the new period the auditors should **examine the paying-in slip** to ensure that the amounts were actually paid into the bank on or before the balance sheet date.

As regards (b) above, where there appears to be a particularly **large number of outstanding cheques** at the year-end, the auditors should check whether these were **cleared within** a **reasonable time** in the new period. If not, this may indicate that despatch occurred after the year-end.

AUDIT PLAN: BANK

- **Obtain standard bank confirmations** from each bank with which the client conducted business during the audit period
- **Check arithmetic** of bank reconciliation
- **Trace cheques shown as outstanding** from the bank reconciliation to the cash book prior to the year-end and to the **after date bank statements** and **obtain explanations** for any **large or unusual items** not cleared at the time of the audit
- **Compare cash book(s)** and **bank statements** in detail for the last month of the year, and **check items outstanding** at the reconciliation date to bank reconciliations
- **Review bank reconciliation** previous to the year-end bank reconciliation and check that **all items** are **cleared** in the last period or **taken forward** to the year-end bank reconciliation
- **Obtain satisfactory explanations** for **all items** in the **cash book** for which there are **no corresponding entries** in the **bank statement** and vice versa
- **Verify contra items** appearing in the cash books or bank statements with original entry
- **Verify** by checking pay-in slips that **uncleared bankings** are **paid in** prior to the year end
- **Examine all lodgements** in respect of which payment has been refused by the bank; ensure that they are cleared on representation or that other appropriate steps have been taken to effect recovery of the amount due
- **Verify balances** per the **cash book** according to the **bank reconciliation** with **cash book, bank statements and general ledger**
- **Verify** the **bank balances** with reply to **standard bank letter** and with the **bank statements**
- **Scrutinise** the cash book and bank statements before and after the balance sheet date for **exceptional entries** or **transfers** which have a material effect on the balance shown to be in hand
- **Identify** whether any **accounts** are **secured** on the **assets** of the company
- **Consider** whether there is a **legal right** of **set-off** of overdrafts against positive bank balances
- **Determine** whether the **bank accounts** are **subject** to any **restrictions**

Note. Auditors should ensure that all cheques are dispatched immediately after signature and entry in the cash book. Examine the interval between dates of certain of the larger cheques in the cash book and payment by the bank since this may indicate that cheques were dispatched after the year-end (window dressing).

2 Cash

Cash balances should be **checked** if they are material or irregularities are suspected.

Cash balances/floats are often individually immaterial but they may require some audit emphasis because of the opportunities for fraud that could exist where internal control is weak and because in total they may be material.

However in enterprises such as hotels, the amount of cash in hand at the balance sheet date could be considerable; the same goes for retail organisations. Cash counts may be important for internal auditors, who have a role in fraud **prevention**.

Auditors will be concerned that the cash **exists**, is **complete** and belongs to the company (**rights and obligations**).

Where the auditors determine that cash balances are potentially material they may conduct a cash count, ideally at the balance sheet date. Rather like attendance at an stock court, the conduct of the count falls into three phases: planning, the count itself and follow up procedures.

2.1 Planning

Planning is an essential element, for it is an important principle that all cash balances are counted at the same time as far as possible. Cash in this context may include unbanked cheques received, IOUs and credit card slips, in addition to notes and coins.

As part of their planning procedures the auditors will hence need to determine the **locations** where cash is held and which of these locations warrant a count.

Planning decisions will need to be recorded on the current audit file including:

- The **precise time** of the count(s) and location(s)
- The **names** of the **audit staff** conducting the counts
- The **names** of the **client staff** intending to be present at each location

Where a location is not visited it may be expedient to obtain a letter from the client confirming the balance.

2.2 Cash count

The following matters apply to the count itself.

- All cash/petty **cash books** should be **written up** to date in ink (or other permanent form at the time of the count.

- All **balances** must be **counted** at the **same time**.

- All **negotiable securities** must be **available** and **counted** at the time the cash balances are counted.

- At **no time** should the **auditors** be left **alone** with the cash and negotiable securities.

- **All cash** and securities **counted** must be **recorded** on working papers subsequently filed on the current audit file. Reconciliations should be prepared where applicable (for example imprest petty cash float).

AUDIT PLAN: CASH COUNT

- **Count cash balances** held and agree to petty cash book or other record:
  - Count all balances simultaneously
  - All counting to be done in the presence of the individuals responsible
  - Enquire into any IOUs or cashed cheques outstanding for unreasonable periods of time
- **Obtain certificates** of cash in hand from responsible officials
- **Confirm** that bank and cash **balances** as reconciled above are **correctly stated** in the accounts

Follow up

- Check **certificates of cash-in-hand** are **obtained** as appropriate.
- Verify **unbanked cheques/cash receipts** have subsequently been **paid in** and agree to the bank reconciliation.
- Ensure **IOUs** and cheques cashed for employees have been **reimbursed.**
- Check **IOUs or cashed cheques outstanding** for **unreasonable periods** of time have been provided for.
- Verify the **balances** as **counted** are **reflected** in the **accounts** (subject to any agreed amendments because of shortages and so on).

 Question

(a) Explain the importance of the bank letter and describe the procedures used to obtain confirmations from the bank.

(b) Describe how you would check a client's bank reconciliation.

Answer

(a) The bank letter is important because it is independent confirmation of a number of important matters in the client's financial statements. It confirms cash and bank balances which may well be a significant asset. It also provides confirmation of customer's assets held as security, customers' other assets held (as custodian) and contingent liabilities. Auditors also ask the bank to give details of other banks and branches that the respondent bank is aware have a relationship with the client.

Audit procedures

(i) Obtain written authority from the client to the bank to disclose the necessary information.

(ii) Send a bank letter in standard form to the bank in sufficient time for it to arrive at least two weeks before the year-end. The letter should state both the year-end date and the previous year-end date, and should refer to the client's granting of authority.

(iii) If additional information over and above what is in the standard letter is requested, send a separate letter requesting that information.

(iv) When confirmation is received from the bank, check that the bank have answered all the questions in the letter.

(v) Follow up all points disclosed in the bank letter.

(b) The following procedures should be carried out.

(i) Obtain standard bank confirmations from each bank with which the client conducted business during the period.

(ii) Check arithmetic of bank reconciliation.

(iii)   Trace cheques shown as outstanding from the bank reconciliation to the cash book prior to the year-end and to the after date bank statements and obtain explanations for any large or unusual items not cleared at the time of the audit.

(iv)   Verify by checking pay-in slips that uncleared bankings are paid in prior to the year end, and check uncleared bankings are cleared quickly after the year-end.

(v)   Verify balances per cash book according to the reconciliation with cash book and general ledger.

(vi)   Verify the bank balances with reply to standard bank letter and with the bank statements.

(vii)   Scrutinise the cash book and bank statements before and after the balance sheet date for exceptional entries or transfers which have a material effect on the balance shown to be in hand.

(viii) Identify whether any accounts are secured on the assets of the company.

(ix)   Consider whether there is a legal right of set-off of overdrafts against positive bank balances.

(x)   Determine whether the bank accounts are subject to any restrictions.

Chapter Roundup

- **Bank balances** are usually **confirmed directly with the bank** in question.

- The bank letter can be used to ask a variety of questions, including queries about outstanding interests, contingent liabilities and guarantees.

- **Cash balances** should be **checked** if they are material or irregularities are suspected.

Quick Quiz

1   Summarise the procedure for obtaining confirmation from a client's bank.

1   ....

2   ....

3   ....

4   ....

5   ....

6   ....

2   Complete these two of the audit tests performed to verify the bank reconciliation.

(a)   Trace cheques shown as outstanding on the .... to the ....
.... prior to the year end and ....
....

(b)   Obtain satisfactory explanations for all items in the .... for which there is no corresponding entry in the .... and ....
....

3   Give two examples of business where cash floats could be considerable.

   1   ....

   2   ....

4   What planning matters relating to a cash count should be recorded in the current audit file?

   1   ....

   2   ....

   3   ....

Answers to Quick Quiz

1   (1)   The banks will require **explicit written authority** from their client to disclose the information requested.

   (2)   The **auditors' request** must **refer** to the **client's letter** of authority and the date thereof. Alternatively it may be countersigned by the client or it may be accompanied by a specific letter of authority.

   (3)   In the case of joint accounts, **letters of authority** signed by all **parties** will be necessary.

   (4)   Such letters of authority may either give **permission** to the bank to disclose information for a **specific request** or grant permission for an **indeterminate length of time.**

   (5)   The request should **reach** the **branch manager** at least **two weeks in advance** of the client's **year-end** and should state both that year-end date and the previous year-end date.

   (6)   The **auditors** should themselves **check** that the bank **answers all the questions** and, where the reply is not received direct from the bank, be responsible for establishing the authenticity of the reply.

2   bank reconciliations, cash book, after date bank statements, bank statements, cash book, bank reconciliation

3   hotels
   retail operations

4   Time of count
   Names of client staff attending
   Names of audit staff attending

	Now try the question below from the Exam Question Bank		
Number	**Level**	**Marks**	**Time**
Q16	Examination	20	36 mins

Liabilities and capital

Topic list	Syllabus reference
1 Trade creditors and purchases	6
2 Accruals	6
3 Long-term liabilities	6
4 Provisions and contingencies	6
5 Capital and other issues	6

Introduction

Some of the liability components of the balance sheet are technically quite difficult in that they are regulated by local legislation. This mainly applies to share capital and reserves which we examine in Section 5. In the rest of this chapter we will try to avoid the more complex legalistic aspects of these items and concentrate on the fundamental auditing procedures involved.

In the case of other liabilities, direct confirmation for verification purposes is quite rare and other procedures are normally used. This can be one of the most sensitive areas of the audit as it affects the company's liquidity and gearing ratios and these may be closely related to bank borrowing covenants or debenture agreements. Testing for **understatement** and **completeness** is particularly important.

Auditing provisions can be complex due to the complexity of the accounting for them.

Section 5 discusses three areas which, although only tenuously related, are often bracketed together for audit purposes. The audit objectives are to ascertain that:

(a) **Share capital** has been **properly classified** and **disclosed** in the financial statements and **changes** properly **authorised**.

(b) **Movements** on reserves have been properly **authorised** and, in the case of statutory reserves, **only used** for **permitted purposes**.

(c) **Statutory records** have been **properly maintained** and returns properly and expeditiously dealt with.

Study guide

20 – Other audit and review evidence IV – Current liabilities and accruals

- Describe and tabulate for inclusion in a work program the substantive procedures used in obtaining evidence in relation to current liabilities and accruals, and the related profit and loss account entries

- Explain the purpose of substantive procedures, including supplier statement reconciliations and direct confirmation of creditors, in relation to financial statement assertions concerning current liabilities and accruals

22 – Other audit and review evidence VI – Fixed assets and long term liabilities (See Chapter 13)

Exam guide

As long-term liabilities are often used to finance fixed assets, these could be examined jointly. Trade creditors could be examined in conjunction with purchase controls.

1 Trade creditors and purchases   12/02

FAST FORWARD

The largest figure in **current liabilities** will normally be **trade creditors** generally checked by comparison of **suppliers' statements** with **purchase ledger accounts.**

1.1 Completeness

As with debtors, creditors are likely to be a material figure in the balance sheet of most enterprises. The purchases cycle tests of controls will have provided the auditors with some assurance as to the completeness of liabilities.

Auditors should however be particularly aware, when conducting their balance sheet work, of the possibility of **understatement** of **liabilities** to improve liquidity and profits (by understating the corresponding purchases). The primary objective of their balance sheet work will be to ascertain whether **liabilities** existing at the year-end have been **completely** and **accurately recorded**.

As regards **trade creditors**, this primary objective can be subdivided into two detailed objectives.

- Is there a **satisfactory cut-off** between goods received and invoices received, so that purchases and trade creditors are recognised in the correct year?

- Do trade creditors represent the **bona fide** amounts due by the company?

Before we ascertain how the auditors design and conduct their tests with these objectives in mind, we need to establish the importance, as with debtors, of the list of balances.

1.2 Trade creditors listing

The list of balances will be one of the principal sources from which the auditors will select their samples for testing. The listing should be extracted from the purchase ledger by the client. The auditors will carry out the following substantive tests to verify that the extraction has been properly performed.

- **Check** from the **purchase ledger accounts** to the **list of balances** and *vice versa*
- **Reconcile** the **total** of the list with the **purchase ledger control account**
- **Cast** the **list** of balances and the purchase ledger control account

The client should also prepare a detailed schedule of trade and sundry accrued expenses.

1.3 Completeness, rights and obligations and existence of trade creditors

The most important test when considering **trade creditors** is comparison of suppliers' statements with purchase ledger balances.

When selecting a sample of creditors to test, auditors must be careful not just to select suppliers with large year-end balances. Remember, it is errors of **understatement** that auditors are primarily interested in when reviewing creditors, and errors of understatement could occur equally in creditors with low or nil balances as with high.

When comparing **supplier statements** with **year-end purchase ledger balances**, auditors should include within their sample creditors with nil or negative purchase ledger balances. Auditors should be particularly wary of low balances with major suppliers. Remember the client has no incentive to record liabilities before being invoiced.

You may be wondering as we normally carry out a debtors confirmation whether we would also circularise suppliers. The answer is generally no.

The principal reason for this lies in the nature of the purchases cycle: third party evidence in the form of suppliers' invoices and even more significantly, **suppliers' statements**, are part of the standard documentation of the cycle. The auditors will hence concentrate on these documents when designing and conducting their tests.

FAST FORWARD

A **direct confirmation of trade creditors** might be appropriate, although they are relatively rare in practice.

In the following circumstances the auditors may, however, determine that a confirmation is necessary. In these cases confirmation requests should be sent out and processed in a similar way to accounts receivable confirmation requests. 'Positive' replies will be required where:

- **Suppliers' statements** are, for whatever reason, **unavailable** or **incomplete**.
- **Weaknesses in internal** control or the nature of the client's business make possible a material misstatement of liabilities that would not otherwise be picked up.
- It is thought that the **client** is **deliberately** trying to **understate creditors**.
- The **accounts** appear to be **irregular** or if the nature or size of balances or transactions is abnormal.

Exam focus point

Testing suppliers' statements is frequently examined in auditing exams.

1.4 Other creditors   12/05

Companies may have other creditors and the audit tests carried out on them will vary according to what the nature of that account is. Remember that you are primarily testing for understatement. Consider if you can obtain third party evidence about the balance. You may have to think laterally about the specific balance.

Exam focus point

In December 2005 there was a question about underpayment of VAT (for which there was an outstanding creditors balance). The answer focused on the controls that operated around recording VAT and why they had failed. However, it was also necessary to ascertain what the payable should be by reference to the sales invoices on which the tax has been charged.

1.5 Purchases and expenses

When testing purchases and expenses, auditors are testing whether they are for **valid** reasons, that goods and services purchased have provided benefits to the company. They are also checking for **accuracy of recording** so again **cut-off** procedures will be important.

1.5.1 Occurrence and completeness of purchases

As with sales, **analytical procedures** will be important. Auditors should consider:

- The **level of purchases and expenses** over the year, compared on a month-by-month basis with the previous year

- The effect on value of purchases of **changes in quantities purchased**

- The effect on purchases value of changes in **products** purchased (for example a change in ingredients), or **prices of products**

- How the **ratio of trade creditors to purchases** compares with previous figures

- How the **ratio of trade creditors to stock** compares with previous years' figures

---

AUDIT PLAN: PURCHASES – COMPLETENESS AND OCCURRENCE

- Check **purchases and other expenses recorded** in the **purchase or general ledger or cash book** to supporting documentation (books of prime entry, invoices, delivery notes) considering whether:
  - **Purchases and expenses are valid** (invoices addressed to the client, for goods and services ordered by the client, for the purposes of the business)
  - **Purchases** and expenses have been **allocated** to the correct **purchase or general ledger** account
- Consider **reasonableness of deductions** from purchases or expenses by reference to subsequent events
- Check whether **valid debts** are **recorded** in **purchase ledger** by checking **credit notes**

One important expense is obviously wages and salaries which we consider below.

1.5.2 Purchases cut-off (completeness)

The procedures applied by the auditors will be designed to ascertain whether:

- **Goods received** for which **no invoice** has been **received** are **accrued**

- **Goods received** which have been **invoiced** but **not yet posted** are **accrued.**

- **Goods returned** to suppliers **prior** to the **year-end** are **excluded** from **inventory** and **trade creditors**

At the year-end stock count the auditors will have made a note of the last serial numbers of goods received notes. Suggested substantive procedures are as follows.

AUDIT PLAN: PURCHASES CUT OFF

- **Check from goods received notes** with serial numbers before the year-end to ensure that invoices are either:
  - Posted to purchase ledger prior to the year-end, or
  - Included on the schedule of accruals
- **Review the schedule of accruals** to ensure that goods received after the year-end are not accrued

AUDIT PLAN: PURCHASES CUT OFF

- **Check from goods returned notes prior to year-end** to ensure that **credit notes** have been **posted** to the purchase ledger prior to the year-end or accrued

- **Review large invoices** and **credit notes** included after the year-end to ensure that they refer to the following year

- **Review outstanding purchase orders** for indications of any purchases completed but not invoiced

- **Reconcile daily batch invoice totals** around the year-end to purchase ledger control ensuring batches are posted in the correct year

- **Review** the **control account** around the year-end for **any unusual items**

1.5.3 Purchase of goods subject to reservation of title clauses

Under certain transactions, the seller may retain legal ownership of goods passed to a 'purchaser'. The requirements are known as 'reservation of title'.

In UK cases, particularly the *Romalpa* case, it is suggested that a reservation of title clause will only be upheld if it states that the seller has a charge over the goods and the goods, any products made from them and any sale proceeds are kept separately and are readily identifiable.

AUDIT PLAN PURCHASES (RESERVATION OF TITLE)

- **Ascertain** how the **client identifies suppliers selling** on terms which **reserve title** by enquiry of those responsible for purchasing and the board

- **Review** and test the **procedures** for **quantifying** or **estimating** the **liabilities**

- **Consider** whether **disclosure** is **sufficient** by itself if the directors have decided quantification is impractical

- **Consider** the adequacy of the **disclosures** in the accounts

- **Review the terms of sale** of **major suppliers** to confirm that liabilities not provided for do not exist or are immaterial

2 Accruals

Auditors should review **after-date invoices and payments**, and consider whether anything else that would have been expected has not been accrued.

2.1 Sundry accruals

Checking the completeness and valuation of sundry accruals is an area that lends itself to **analytical procedures** and reconciliation techniques.

A variety of sources can indicate possible accruals. These include **last year's accruals**, **expense items** where an accrual would be expected, and **invoices received** and **cash paid** after the year-end.

Auditors should also use their **knowledge of the business** to consider whether there are accruals which they would expect to be there, but which may not be invoiced or paid until long after the year-end.

AUDIT PLAN: PURCHASES ACCRUALS

- Check that **accruals** are **fairly calculated** and **verify** by reference to **subsequent payments** and **supporting documentation**
- **Review the profit and loss account** and **prior years' figures** and consider liabilities inherent in the trade to **ensure** that all **likely accruals have been provided**
- **Scrutinise payments** made **after year-end** to ascertain whether any payments made should be accrued
- **Consider basis** for **round sum accruals** and ensure it is consistent with prior years
- **Ascertain** why any **payments on account** are being **made** and **ensure** that the **full liability is provided**
- **Income tax**. Normally this should represent one month's deductions. Check amount paid to taxation authorities by inspecting receipted annual declaration of tax paid over, or returned cheque
- **Sales tax**. Check reasonableness to next return. **Verify last amount paid in year** per cash book to return

2.2 Wages and salaries

Although auditors may test other expenses solely by analytical review, they may carry out more detailed testing on wages and salaries, partly because of the consequences of failure to deduct income tax correctly.

Analytical procedures will nonetheless be used to give some assurance on wages and salaries. Auditors should consider:

- **Wages and salaries levels** month-by-month with **previous years**
- **Effect on wages and salaries of rate changes** during the year
- **Average wage** per month **over the year**
- **Sales/profits** per **employee**
- **Payroll proof in total** (Pay rise × staff changes × staff mix)

AUDIT PLAN: WAGES AND SALARIES CREDITOR	
OCCURRENCE	• **Check individual remuneration** per payroll to **personnel records, records of hours** worked, **salary agreements** etc
	• **Confirm existence** of **employees** on payroll by meeting them, attending wages payout, inspecting personnel and tax records, and confirmation from managers
	• **Check benefits** (pensions) on payroll to **supporting documentation**
ACCURACY	• **Check accuracy of calculation of remuneration**
	• **Check** whether **calculation** of **statutory deductions** is **correct**
	• **Check validity** of **other deductions** (pension contributions, share save etc) by agreement to supporting documentation (personnel files, conditions of pension scheme) and **check accuracy** of **calculation** of other deductions
COMPLETENESS	• **Check casts** of **payroll records**
	• **Confirm** payment of **net pay** per payroll records to **cheque** or **bank transfer** summary
	• **Agree net pay** per cash book to **payroll**
	• **Scrutinise payroll** and **investigate unusual items**

Question

You have been assigned to the audit of Carter Brandon Co (CBC), and you are drafting the audit programme for creditors, accruals and provisions for the year ended 31 December 20X7.

The company operates from a site in West Wendon. All raw materials are received in the stores and all deliveries are checked to the delivery note and purchase order. The stores supervisor raises a goods received note and is also responsible for raising credit requests if there are any problems with the raw materials delivered.

When the purchase ledger department staff receive the purchase invoices, they match them to the relevant goods received notes and purchase orders, and post them to the computerised purchase ledger. Suppliers are paid on the last day of each month.

Other creditors and accruals consist of tax, wages and other statutory deductions, accruals and time-apportioned expenses such as electricity and telephone.

The company has two significant provisions in its accounts. The first is a new provision in 20X7 for £100,000 that relates to a legal action brought by a competitor who claims their manufacturing process has been illegally copied.

The second provision was set up in the accounts of 20X6 and relates to sums required to be spent on urgent repairs to the factory foundations. The provision in the 20X6 accounts was £60,000. Although £51,000 was spent on repairs to the foundations during 20X7, the directors are proposing that the provision in the balance sheet of the 20X7 accounts should increase to £75,000.

Required

Describe the audit work you will carry out:

(a)   To compare suppliers' statements with balances recorded on the purchase ledger
(b)   To check that purchases cut-off has been applied correctly
(c)   To confirm that other creditors and accruals have been accurately stated.

Answer

(a)   The audit work I will carry out to check suppliers' statements to the balances on the purchase ledger is as follows.

Select a sample of balances and **compare suppliers' statements with purchase ledger balances**. The extent of the sample will depend on the results of tests of controls and assessment of the effectiveness of controls within the purchases system (ie if the system of control is strong I will check fewer items).

Select the **sample on a random basis**. Selection of only large balances or those with many transactions will not yield an appropriate sample as I am looking for understatement of liabilities. Nil and negative balances will also need to be included in the sample.

If **no statement** was **available** for the supplier, I would ask for **confirmation** of the balance **from the supplier**.

If the balance **agrees exactly**, no further work needs to be carried out.

Where differences arise these need to be categorised as either in-transit items or other (including disputed) items.

In transit items

In-transit items will be either goods or cash.

If the difference relates to goods in transit, I would **ascertain** whether the **goods** were **received** before the year end by reference to the GRN and that they are included in year end stock and purchase accruals. If not, a cut-off error has occurred and should be investigated.

If the goods were received after the year end, the difference with the suppliers' accounts is correct.

Similarly, cash in transit would arise where the payment to the supplier was made by cheque before the year end but was not received by him until after the year end. The **date** the **cheque** was **raised** and its subsequent **clearing** through the bank account after the year end should be **verified by checking the cash book** and the post year end bank statements.

However, if the cheque clears after the year end date, it may indicate that the cheque, though raised before the year end was not sent to the supplier until after the year end. The relevant amount should be added back to year end creditors and to the end of year bank balance.

Other items

Differences which do not arise from in-transit items need to be investigated and **appropriate adjustments** made where necessary.

These differences may have arisen due to **disputed invoices**, where for example the client is demanding credit against an invoice which the supplier is not willing to agree. The client may decide not to post the invoice to the supplier account as he does not consider it to be a liability of the company. However, differences may also arise because **invoices** have been **held back** in order to reduce the level of year-end creditors.

If significant unexplained differences are discovered it may be necessary to **extend** my **testing**. There may also be a problem if sufficient suppliers' statements are not available. Alternative procedures, eg a circularisation may then be required.

(b)   The audit work I would carry out to verify that purchases cut-off has been correctly carried out at the year end is as follows.

   (i)   From my notes taken at the stock count I will have the **number** of the **last GRN** that was issued before the year end.

   (ii)   **Select a sample** of GRNs issued in the period immediately before and immediately after the year end. The period to be covered would be at least two weeks either side of the year end.

   (iii)   **Concentrate** my sample on **high value items**, and more on those GRNs from before the year end as these represent the greatest risk of cut-off error.

   (iv)   **Check** that the **GRNs** have a **correct number**, according to the last GRN issued in the year and whether the **goods** were **received before or after the year end**.

   (v)   For **GRNs** issued **before the year end**, check whether the **stock** has been included in the year end **stock** total. In addition, I will check whether that the **creditor** is either **included** in **trade creditors** or **purchase accruals**.

   (vi)   For **GRNs** issued **after the year end**, to ensure that the **stock** is **included** in the stock records **after the year end**. In addition, I will need to **check** to the **purchase ledger** to ensure that the relevant **invoice** has been **posted** to the supplier account after the year end.

(c)   The audit work I will carry out to ensure that other creditors and accruals are correctly stated is as follows.

   (i)   **Assess the system of control** instituted by management to identify and quantify accruals and creditors.

(ii)   From the client's sundry creditors and accruals listing, **check** that **accruals** are **calculated correctly** and verify them by reference to subsequent payments. **Check** that **all time apportionments** have been made correctly (for example, for electricity).

(iii)   **Taxation balances**

(1)   **Check** the **amount paid to the tax authorities**. The balance at the year end would normally represent one month's deductions and can be verified to the payroll records. The payment should be traced from the cash book to the payment book (if used) and subsequent bank statements.

(2)   For the sales tax balance, **review** for **reasonableness** to the **next return**. I would also **ensure** that the **payment** for the **previous return** was for the **correct** amount and had cleared through the bank.

(iv)   **Review the profit and loss account** and **prior year figures** (for any accruals which have not appeared this year or which did not appear last year) and consider liabilities inherent in the trade (eg weekly wages) to ensure that all likely accruals have been provided.

(v)   **Scrutinise payments** made after the year end to ascertain whether any payments made should be accrued. This will include consideration of any payments relating to the current year which are made a long time after the year-end.

(vi)   **Consider and document** the basis for **round sum accruals** and ensure it is consistent with prior years.

(vii)   **Ascertain** why any **payments on account** are being made and **ensure** that the full **liability** is **provided**.

(viii) **Accrued interest** and basic **charges on loans** or overdrafts can be **agreed** to the **bank letter** received for audit purposes.

3 Long-term liabilities

FAST FORWARD

Long-term liabilities are usually **authorised** by the **board** and should be **well documented**.

We are concerned here with long-term liabilities comprising debentures, loan stock and other loans **repayable** at a date **more than one year after the year-end**.

Auditors will primarily try and determine:

- **Completeness**: whether all long-term liabilities have been disclosed

- **Accuracy**: whether interest payable has been calculated correctly and included in the correct accounting period

- **Classification and understandability**: whether long-term loans and interest have been correctly disclosed in the financial statements

The major complication for the auditors is that debenture and loan agreements frequently contain conditions with which the company must comply, including restrictions on the company's total borrowings and adherence to specific borrowing ratios.

AUDIT PLAN: LONG TERM LIABILITIES

- **Obtain/prepare schedule of loans** outstanding at the balance sheet date showing, for each loan: name of lender, date of loan, maturity date, interest date, interest rate, balance at the end of the period and security
- **Compare opening balances** to previous year's papers
- **Test the clerical accuracy** of the analysis
- **Compare balances** to the **general ledger**
- **Check name** of **lender** etc, to **register** of **debenture holders** or equivalent (if kept)
- **Trace additions** and **repayments** to **entries** in the **cash book**
- **Confirm repayments** are in accordance with **loan agreement**
- **Examine cancelled cheques** and **memoranda of satisfaction** for **loans repaid**
- **Verify** that **borrowing limits** imposed either by Articles or by other agreements are **not exceeded**
- **Examine signed Board minutes** relating to **new borrowings/repayments**
- **Obtain direct confirmation** from **lenders** of the amounts outstanding, accrued interest and what security they hold
- **Verify interest charged** for the period and the adequacy of accrued interest
- **Confirm assets charged** have been **entered** in the **register of charges** and **notified** to the **Registrar**
- **Review restrictive covenants** and provisions relating to default:
  - **Review** any **correspondence** relating to the loan
  - **Review confirmation** replies for non-compliance
  - If a **default appears** to exist, **determine** its **effect**, and schedule findings
- **Review minutes, cash book** to **check** if all **loans have been recorded**

4 Provisions and contingencies   12/02, 6/03

FAST FORWARD

> The accounting provisions for provisions and contingencies are complex and that can make them difficult to audit.

4.1 Accounting issues

Key terms

A **provision** is a liability of uncertain timing or amount

A **liability** is a present obligation of the enterprise arising from past events, the settlement of which is expected to result in an outflow from the enterprise of resources embodying economic benefits.

An **obligating event** is an event that creates a legal or constructive obligation that results in an enterprise having no realistic alternative to settling that obligation.

A **legal obligation** is an obligation that derives from:

(a)   A contract (through its explicit or implicit terms),
(b)   Legislation, or
(c)   Other operation of law.

A **constructive obligation** is an obligation that derives from an enterprise's actions where

(a)   By an established pattern of past practice, published policies and sufficiently specific current statement, the enterprise has indicated to other parties that it will accept certain responsibilities, and

(b)   As a result, the enterprise has created a valid expectation on the part of those other parties that it will discharge those responsibilities.

A **contingent liability** is:

(a)   A possible obligation that arises from past events and whose existence will be confirmed only by the occurrence or non-occurrence of one or more uncertain future events not wholly within the control of the enterprise, or

(b)   A present obligation that arises from past events but is not recognised because:

    (i)   It is not probable that an outflow of resources embodying economic benefits will be required to settle the obligation, or

    (ii)   The amount of the obligation cannot be measured with sufficient reliability.

A **contingent asset** is a possible asset that arises from past events and whose existence will be confirmed only by the occurrence or non-occurrence of one or more uncertain future events not wholly within the control of the enterprise.

Under FRS 12, an entity should not recognise a **contingent asset** or a **contingent liability**. However if it becomes probable that an outflow of future economic benefits will be required for a previous contingent liability, a provision should be recognised. A contingent asset should not be accounted for unless its realisation is virtually certain; if an inflow of economic benefits has become probable, the asset should be disclosed.

The standard provides a table summarising when contingent assets and liabilities are to be recognised.

PROVISIONS AND CONTINGENT LIABILITIES		
Where, as a result of past events, there may be a outflow of resources embodying future economic benefits in settlement of (a) a present obligation or (b) a possible obligation whose existence will be confirmed by the occurrence or non-occurrence of one or more uncertain future events not wholly within the enterprise's control, and		
there is a present obligation that probably requires an outflow of resources,	there is a possible obligation or a present obligation that may, but probably will not, require an outflow of resources,	there is a possible obligation or a present obligation where the likelihood of an outflow of resources is remote,
a provision is recognised and disclosures are required for the provision.	no provision is recognised but disclosures are required for the contingent liability.	no provision is recognised and no disclosure is required.

A contingent liability also arises in the extremely rare case **where there is a liability** that cannot be recognised because it cannot be **measured reliably**. Disclosures are required for the contingent liability.

CONTINGENT ASSETS		
Where, as a result of past events, there is a possible asset whose existence will be confirmed by the occurrence or non-occurrence of one or more uncertain future events not wholly within the enterprise's control, and		
the inflow of economic benefits is virtually certain,	the inflow of economic benefits is probable but not virtually certain,	the inflow is not probable,
the asset is not contingent.	no asset is recognised but disclosures are required.	no asset is recognised and no disclosure is required.

Examples of the principal types of contingencies disclosed by companies are:

- **Guarantees**
    - For other group companies
    - Of staff pension schemes
    - Of completion of contracts

- **Discounted bills of exchange**

- **Uncalled liabilities** on shares or loan stock

- **Lawsuits** or claims pending

- **Options** to purchase assets

4.2 Obtaining audit evidence of contingencies

Part of ISA (UK and Ireland) 501 *Audit evidence – additional considerations for specific items* covers contingencies relating to litigation and legal claims, which will represent the major part of audit work on contingencies. Litigation and claims involving the entity may have a material effect on the financial statements, and so will require adjustment to/disclosure in those financial statements.

'The auditor should carry out procedures in order to become aware of any litigation and claims involving the entity which may have a material effect on the financial statements.' Such procedures would include the following.

AUDIT PLAN: PROVISIONS/CONTINGENCIES

- **Make appropriate inquiries of management** including obtaining representations
- **Review board minutes** and correspondence with the entity's lawyers
- **Examine legal expense** account
- **Use any information** obtained regarding the entity's business including information obtained from discussions with any in-house legal department

'When litigation or claims have been identified or when the auditor believes they may exist, the auditor should seek direct communication with the entity's lawyers.' This will help to obtain sufficient appropriate audit evidence as to whether potential material litigation and claims are known and management's estimates of the financial implications, including costs, are reliable.

The ISA discusses the form the letter to the entity's lawyer should take. 'The letter, which should be prepared by management and sent by the auditor, should request the lawyer to communicate directly with the auditor.'

If it is thought unlikely that the lawyer will respond to a general enquiry, the letter should specify the following.

(a) A list of **litigation and claims**

(b) **Management's assessment** of the outcome of the litigation or claim and its estimate of the financial implications, including costs involved

(c) A request that the **lawyer confirm the reasonableness** of management's assessments and provide the auditor with further information if the list is considered by the lawyer to be incomplete or incorrect

The auditors must consider these matters up to the date of their report and so a further, updating letter may be necessary.

A meeting between the auditors and the lawyer may be required, for example where a complex matter arises, or where there is a disagreement between management and the lawyer. Such meetings should take place only with the permission of management, and preferably with a management representative present.

'If management refuses to give the auditor permission to communicate with the entity's lawyers, this would be a scope limitation and should ordinarily lead to a qualified opinion or a disclaimer of opinion.'

If the lawyer refuses to respond as required and the auditor can find no alternative sufficient evidence, a limitation of scope may lead to a qualified opinion or a disclaimer of opinion.

AUDIT PLAN: PROVISIONS/CONTINGENCIES

- **Obtain details** of all **provisions** which have been included in the **accounts** and all **contingencies** that have been disclosed
- **Obtain** a **detailed analysis** of all **provisions** showing opening balances, movements and closing balances
- **Determine** for each material provision **whether** the **company** has a **present obligation** as a result of past events by:
  - **Review** of **correspondence** relating to the item
  - **Discussion** with the **directors**. Have they created a valid expectation in other parties that they will discharge the obligation?
- **Determine** for each material provision **whether** it is **probable** that a **transfer of economic benefits** will be required to settle the obligation by:
  - **Checking** whether any **payments** have been **made** in the post balance sheet period in respect of the item
  - **Review of correspondence** with solicitors, banks, customers, insurance company and suppliers both pre and post year end
  - **Sending** a **letter** to the **solicitor** to obtain their views (where relevant)
  - **Discussing** the **position** of similar **past provisions** with the directors. Were these provisions eventually settled?
  - **Considering** the **likelihood** of **reimbursement**
- **Recalculate** all **provisions** made
- **Compare** the **amount provided** with any post year end payments and with any amount paid in the past for similar items
- In the event that it is not possible to estimate the amount of the **provision**, check that this **contingent liability** is **disclosed** in the accounts
- **Consider** the **nature** of the **client's business**. Would you expect to see any other provisions eg warranties?
- Consider adequacy of disclosure of **provisions, contingent assets** and **contingent liabilities**

You should appreciate that the problems of accounting for contingencies makes their audit difficult.

5 Capital and other issues

FAST FORWARD

The main concern with **share capital, reserves** and **company books** is that the company has complied with the law.

5.1 Share (equity) capital, reserves and distributions

The issued share capital as stated in the accounts must be **agreed** in total with the **share register**. An examination of transfers on a test basis should be made in those cases where a company handles its own registration work. Where the registration work is dealt with by independent registrars, auditors will normally examine the reports submitted by them to the company, and obtain from them at the year-end a certificate of the share capital in issue.

Auditors should check carefully whether clients have complied with local legislation about share issues or purchase of own shares. Auditors should take particular care if there are any movements in reserves that cannot be distributed, and should **confirm** that these movements are **valid**.

AUDIT PLAN: CAPITAL AND RELATED ISSUES	
SHARE EQUITY CAPITAL	• **Agree** the **authorised share capital** with the statutory documents governing the company's constitution • **Agree changes** to **authorised share capital** with **properly authorised resolutions**
ISSUE OF SHARES	• **Verify any issue** of share capital or other changes during the year with general and board **minutes** • **Ensure issue or change** is within the **terms** of the **constitution**, and directors possess appropriate authority to issue shares • **Confirm** that **cash** or **other consideration** has been **received** or **debtor(s) is included** as called up share capital not paid

TRANSFER OF SHARES	• **Verify transfers of shares** by reference to:
	  – Correspondence
	  – Completed and stamped transfer forms
	  – Cancelled share certificates
	  – Minutes of directors' meeting
	
	• **Check the balances** on **shareholders' accounts** in the register of members and the total list with the amount of issued share capital in the general ledger

DIVIDENDS	• **Agree dividends** paid and proposed to **authority** in minute books and **check calculation** with **total share capital** issued to ascertain whether there are any outstanding or unclaimed dividends • **Check dividend payments** with **documentary evidence** (say, the returned dividend warrants) • **Check** that **dividends do not contravene** the distribution provisions of the legislation • Check that **imputed tax** has been accounted for to the taxation authorities and correctly treated in the accounts

AUDIT PLAN: CAPITAL AND RELATED ISSUES	
RESERVES	• **Check movements on reserves** to **supporting authority**
	• **Ensure that movements on reserves do not contravene** the **legislation** and the company's constitution
	• **Confirm** that the **company** can **distinguish** those reserves at the balance sheet date that are **distributable** from those that are **non-distributable**
	• **Ensure appropriate disclosures** of movements on reserves are made in the company's accounts

5.2 Statutory books

Incorporated entities in all countries will be governed by some kind of local or national company legislation. Certain minimum standards of record-keeping will be normally required. In particular legislation may require specific records to be kept of share movements, minutes of management meetings, directors/management shareholdings in the company and so on.

AUDIT PLAN: STATUTORY BOOKS	
REGISTER OF MEMBERS OF GOVERNING BOARD/ COMMITTEE	• **Update permanent file** giving details of **board members**
	• **Verify** any **changes** with the **minutes** and ensure that the necessary details have been filed at any central registry (if required by local legislation)
REGISTER OF MANAGERS'/ DIRECTORS' INTERESTS IN SHARES AND DEBENTURES	• **Ensure** that **managers'/directors' interests** are **noted** on the permanent file for cross-referencing to accounts
	• **Ensure** that **shareholdings comply** with the **company's constitution**
MINUTE BOOKS	• **Obtain photocopies** or **prepare extracts** from the **minute books** of meetings concerning financial matters, cross-referencing them to appropriate working papers
	• **Ensure** that **extracts** of **agreements** referred to in the minutes are **prepared** for the permanent file
	• **Note the date** of the last **minute reviewed**
	• **Check** that **meetings** have been **properly convened** and that quorums attended them
REGISTER OF INTERESTS IN SHARES (if applicable)	• **Scrutinise register** and verify that *prima facie* it appears to be in order
	• **Ensure** that **significant interests** are **noted on** the permanent file
REGISTER OF CHARGES	• **Update permanent file schedule** from the register
	• **Ensure** that **any assets** which are **charged** as security for loans from third parties are **disclosed** in the accounts
	• **Obtain confirmation** that there are **no charges** to be recorded if no entries are recorded in the register
	• **Consider carrying out company search** at Central Registry to verify the accuracy of the register

AUDIT PLAN: STATUTORY BOOKS	

ACCOUNTING RECORDS	• Consider whether the accounting records are adequate to:
	
	  – **Show** and **explain** the **company's transactions**
	
	  – **Disclose** with **reasonable accuracy**, at any time, the **financial position** of the **company**
	
	  – **Comply** with **local legislation** by recording money received and expended, assets and liabilities, year-end inventory and physical inventory count, sales and purchases
	
	  – **Enable** the **managers/directors** to ensure that the **accounts give a true and fair view** or **present fairly**

GENERAL LEDGER AND JOURNALS	• **Check opening balances** in general ledger to **previous year's audited** accounts • **Check additions** of **general ledger accounts** • **Review general ledger accounts** and ensure significant transfers and unusual items are *bona fide* • **Review the journal** and ensure that significant entries are **authorised** and properly **recorded** • **Check extraction** and **addition** of **trial balance** (if prepared by the client)
RETURNS	• **Check that regulatory returns** have been **filed** properly
MANAGERS'/ DIRECTORS' SERVICE CONTRACTS	• **Inspect copies** of directors' service contracts or memoranda • **Verify** that **long-term service contracts** have been **approved in general meeting**

5.3 Directors' emoluments

The auditors may have a duty to include in their report the required disclosure particulars of directors' emoluments and transactions with directors, if these requirements have not been complied with in the accounts.

The auditors will have carried out an evaluation of salaries payroll procedures, including the system in operation for directors' salaries, earlier in the audit. At the year end, they can probably concentrate on limited substantive work designed to ensure that the final **figures** in the **accounting records** are **complete** and the disclosure requirements in respect of directors have been complied with.

AUDIT PLAN: DIRECTORS' EMOLUMENTS

• **Ascertain** whether **monies payable or benefits** in kind provided have been **properly approved** in accordance with the company's memorandum and articles of association and that they are not prohibited by legislation
 	
• **Confirm** that all **monies payable** and **benefits receivable** in relation to the current accounting period have been **properly accounted for**, unless the right to any of these has been waived by inspecting:
  – Salary records
  – Service contracts
  – Board minutes
  – Other relevant records
 	
• **Consider** whether the **most common types of benefit** (company cars or cheap loans) may have been **omitted**
 	
• **Review directors' service contracts**

AUDIT PLAN: DIRECTORS' EMOLUMENTS
• **Review** the **company's procedures** to ensure that **all directors advise** the board of all disclosable **emoluments**
• **Review** the **procedures** for ensuring that any **payments made to former directors** of the company are **identified** and **properly disclosed**
• **Consider** the **need** for any **amounts** included in directors' remuneration to be **further disclosed** in accordance with legislation

Chapter Roundup

- The largest figure in **current liabilities** will normally be **trade creditors** generally checked by comparison of **suppliers' statements** with **purchase ledger accounts.**

- A **direct confirmation of trade creditors** might be appropriate, although they are relatively rare in practice.

- Auditors should review **after-date invoices and payments**, and consider whether anything else that would have been expected has not been accrued.

- **Long-term liabilities** are usually **authorised** by the board and should be well documented.

- The accounting provisions for provisions and contingencies are complex and that can make them difficult to audit.

- The main concern with **share capital, reserves** and **company books** is that the company has complied with the law.

Quick Quiz

1   What are the two primary objectives of balance sheet work on liabilities?

    1   ....

    2   ....

2   Nil balances should not be included in a supplier statement test.

    True   ☐

    False   ☐

3   Give two instances where trade creditors confirmation is required.

    1   ....

    2   ....

4   Give four things auditors should consider when carrying out analytical review on wages and salaries.

    1   ....

    2   ....

    3   ....

    4   ....

5   Complete the definition

Long-term liabilities comprise ...., ...-......................... and other loans .... at a date .... a year .... the year end.

6   What are the audit objectives relating to share capital?

1   ....

2   ....

3   ....

7   Name three audit procedures in relation to minutes of director's meetings

1   ....

2   ....

3   ....

8   Name three sources of information on director's emoluments.

1   ....

2   ....

3   ....

Answers to Quick Quiz

1   To ensure (1) completely and (2) accurately recorded

2   False

3   1   Supplier statements are unavailable
     2   Weak internal controls

4   1   Salary rate changes
     2   Average wage by month over the year
     3   Sale/employee
     4   Payroll proof in total

5   debentures, loan-stock, repayable, more than, after.

6   Share capital has been (1) properly classified and (2) disclosed in the financial statements and changes are (3) properly authorised

7   1   Obtain photocopies of minutes relating to FS items
     2   Ensure that extracts of agreements in minutes are copied to permanent audit file
     3   Note the date of the last minute reviewed
     4   Check that meetings have been properly convened/attended

8   1   Salary records
     2   Service contracts
     3   Board minutes

Now try the question below from the Exam Question Bank

Number	Level	Marks	Time
Q17	Examination	20	36 mins

Audit reviews and finalisation

Topic list	Syllabus reference
1 Going concern	6
2 Subsequent events	6
3 Management representations	6
4 Overall review of financial statements	6
5 Other information in documents containing audited financial statements	6
6 Completion of the audit	6

Introduction

This chapter will consider the reviews that take place to complete the audit.

There are two key reviews

- Going concern
- Subsequent events

These are both important disclosure issues in the financial statements. If the disclosures are not correct, this will impact on the auditors' report.

In Chapter 12, in the context of accounting estimates, we discussed how there are some items in financial statements where facts or knowledge is confined to management. In the final stages of the audit, the auditor must consider this evidence, and obtain written representations from directors where necessary.

Accountancy knowledge is particularly important in this chapter. Auditors need to be able to interpret accounts understand the requirements of specific accounting standards.

These procedures are extremely important; failure to carry them out can lead to the gravest consequences for the auditors. Given this fact, they tend to be fairly standard in most audit approaches.

Study guide

24 – Going concern reviews

- Explain the importance of going concern reviews
- Describe the procedures to be applied in performing going concern reviews
- Describe the disclosure requirements in relation to going concern issues
- Describe the reporting implications of the findings of going concern reviews

25 – Audit finalisation and the final review

Describe and explain the:

- Quality of management representations as audit evidence

- Circumstances in which obtaining management representations is necessary and the matters on which representations are commonly obtained

- Purpose of the subsequent events review

- Procedures to be undertaken in performing a subsequent events review

- Importance of the overall review of evidence obtained

- Problems associated with the application of accounting treatments

- Significance of unadjusted differences

Exam guide

All the reviews are very important to the audit, but particularly going concern. This is highly examinable. It was examined in December 2003 and June 2005. Letters of representation were examined in December 2002 and June 2005. The examiner said recently that audit areas where a consideration of the future is required (for example, going concern and subsequent events) are dealt with badly in exams, so expect him to examine them again.

1 Going concern   12/03, 6/05

FAST FORWARD

Auditors must consider the **future plans** of directors and any signs of **going concern problems** which may be noted throughout the audit.

1.1 The going concern basis

Key term

Under the '**going concern assumption**' an entity is ordinarily viewed as continuing in business for the foreseeable future with neither the intention nor the necessity of liquidation, ceasing trading or seeking protection from creditors pursuant to laws or regulations. Accordingly assets and liabilities are recorded on the basis that the entity will be able to realise its assets and discharge its liabilities in the normal course of business'.

ISA (UK and Ireland) 570 *Going concern* states that 'when planning and performing audit procedures and in evaluating the results thereof, the auditor should consider the appropriateness of management's use of the going concern assumption in the preparation of the financial statements', and 'consider any relevant disclosures in the financial statements'.

When preparing accounts, **management** should make an explicit **assessment** of the entity's ability to continue as a going concern. Most accounting frameworks require management to do so.

When management are making the assessment, the following factors should be considered.

- The **degree of uncertainty** about the events or conditions being assessed increases significantly the further into the future the assessment is made.

- Judgements are made on the basis of the **information available** at the time.

- Judgements are affected by the **size** and **complexity** of the entity, the **nature** and **condition** of the business and the **degree** to which it is **affected** by **external factors**.

The following list gives examples of possible indicators of going concern problems.

(a) **Financial indications**

- Net liabilities or net current liability position

- Necessary borrowing facilities have not been agreed

- Fixed-term borrowings approaching maturity without realistic prospects of renewal or repayment, or excessive reliance on short-term borrowings

- Major debt repayment falling due where refinancing is necessary to the entity's continued existence

- Major restructuring of debt

- Indications of withdrawal of financial support by creditors

- Negative operating cash flows indicated by historical or prospective financial statements

- Adverse key financial ratios

- Substantial operating losses or significant deterioration in the value of assets used to generate cash flows

- Major losses or cash flow problems which have arisen since the balance sheet date

- Arrears or discontinuance of dividends

- Inability to pay creditors on due dates

- Inability to comply with terms of loan agreements

- Reduction in normal terms of credit by suppliers

- Change from credit to cash-on-delivery transactions with suppliers

- Inability to obtain financing for essential new product development or other essential investments

- Substantial sale of fixed assets not intended to be replaced

(b) **Operating indications**

- Loss of key management without replacement

- Loss of key staff without replacement

- Loss of a major market, franchises, license, or principal supplier

- Labour difficulties or shortages of important supplies

- Fundamental change in the market or technology to which the entity is unable to adapt adequately

- Excessive dependence on a few product lines where the market is depressed

- Technical developments which render a key product obsolete

(c) **Other indications**

- Non-compliance with capital or other statutory requirements

- Pending legal proceedings against the entity that may, if successful, result in judgements that could not be met

- Changes in legislation or government policy

- Issues which involve a range of possible outcomes so wide that an unfavourable result could affect the appropriateness of the going concern basis

Exam focus point

A question on going concern might ask you to identify signs that a particular client may not be a going concern.

The significance of such indications can often be **mitigated** by other factors.

(a) The effect of an entity being unable to make its normal debt repayments may be counterbalanced by management's plans to maintain **adequate cash flows** by alternative means, such as by disposal of assets, rescheduling of loan repayments, or obtaining additional capital.

(b) The loss of a principal supplier may be mitigated by the availability of a suitable alternative source of supply.

1.2 Auditors' responsibilities

FAST FORWARD

When reporting on the accounts, auditors should consider whether the going concern basis is **appropriate,** and whether **disclosure** of going concern problems is **sufficient**.

Auditors are responsible for **considering**:

- The **appropriateness** of the **going concern assumption**

- The **existence** of **material uncertainties** about the going concern assumption that need to be disclosed in the accounts

- Whether there are **adequate disclosures** in the financial statements concerning going concern

- Whether the entity can continue in operational existence in the foreseeable future

'In obtaining a understanding of the entity, the auditor should consider whether there are events or conditions and related business risks which may cast significant doubt on the entity's ability to continue as a going concern. The auditor should remain alert for evidence of events or conditions and related business risks which may cast doubt on the entity's ability to continue as a going concern in performing audit procedures throughout the audit. If such events or conditions are identified, the auditor should, in addition to performing the procedures in Paragraph 26 [of the ISA], consider whether they affect the auditor's assessments of the risk of material misstatement.'

Management may already have made a preliminary assessment of going concern. If so, the auditors would review potential problems management had identified, and management's plans to resolve them. Alternatively auditors may identify problems as a result of discussions with management. Auditors should evaluate management's assessment.

1.2.1 Procedures

The audit procedures will be based on the directors' deliberations and the information they used. The auditors must assess whether the audit evidence is sufficient and appropriate and whether they agree with the directors' judgement. They should consider:

- The nature of the entity (its size and the complexity of its circumstances, for instance)
- Whether the information relates to future events, and if so how far into the future those events lie

A lengthy appendix to the ISA gives examples of how auditors might apply the ISA in different circumstances.

The ISA states 'the auditors should assess the adequacy of the means by which the directors have satisfied themselves that:

(a) It is appropriate for them to adopt the going concern basis in preparing the financial statements; and

(b) The financial statements include such disclosures, if any, relating to going concern as are necessary for them to give a true and fair view.

For this purpose:

(i) The auditors should make enquiries of the directors and examine appropriate available financial information; and

(ii) Having regard to the future period to which the directors have paid particular attention in assessing going concern, the auditors should plan and perform procedures specifically designed to identify any material matters which could indicate concern about the entity's ability to continue as a going concern'.

The auditors' approach includes a **preliminary assessment**, when the overall audit plan is being developed, of the risk that the entity may be unable to continue as a going concern. The auditors should consider:

(a) **Whether the period** to which the directors have paid particular attention in assessing going concern is **reasonable** in the client's circumstances

(b) The **systems**, or other means (formal or informal), **for timely identification of warnings of future risks** and uncertainties the entity might face

(c) **Budget and/or forecast information** (cash flow information in particular) produced by the entity, and the quality of the systems (or other means, formal or informal) in place for producing this information and keeping it up to date

(d) Whether the **key assumptions** underlying the budgets and/or forecasts appear appropriate in the circumstances, including consideration of:
    - Projected profit
    - Forecast levels of working capital
    - The completeness of forecast expenditure
    - Whether the client will have sufficient cash at periods of maximum need
    - The financing of capital expenditure and long-term plans

(e) The **sensitivity of budgets and/or forecasts** to variable factors both within the control of the directors and outside their control

(f) Any **obligations, undertakings or guarantees** arranged with other entities (in particular, lenders, suppliers and group companies)

(g)   The **existence, adequacy and terms of borrowing facilities**, and supplier credit

(h)   The **directors' plans** for resolving any matters giving rise to the concern (if any) about the appropriateness of the going concern basis. In particular, the auditors may need to consider whether:

- The plans are realistic

- There is a reasonable expectation that the plans are likely to resolve any problems foreseen

- The directors are likely to put the plans into practice effectively

The auditors' and directors' procedures can be very simple in some cases, particularly in the case of smaller companies, where budgets and forecasts are not normally prepared and no specific systems are in place to monitor going concern matters.

The auditors will usually:

- Obtain confirmations of the existence and terms of bank facilities
- Make their own assessment of the intentions of the bankers relating thereto

These procedures will become more important if (for example) there is a **low margin** of **financial resources** available to the entity, correspondence between the bankers and the entity reveals that the **last renewal** of facilities was **agreed with difficulty** and a **significant deterioration in cash flow** is projected. If the auditors cannot satisfy themselves then, in accordance with the audit reporting standard, they should consider whether the relevant matters need to be:

- **Disclosed in the financial statements** in order that they give a true and fair view
- **Referred to in the auditors' report** (by explanatory paragraph or qualified opinion)

The ISA states 'the auditors should determine and document the extent of their concern (if any) about the entity's ability to continue as a going concern. In determining the extent of their concern, the auditors should take account of all relevant information of which they have become aware during their audit'.

If management's assessment covers a period of **less than twelve months** from the balance sheet date, the auditor should ask management to extend its assessment period to twelve months from the balance sheet date. If the period used is less than one year, and this is not disclosed in the financial statements, the auditors should disclose this fact in their audit report.

Management should not need to make a detailed assessment, and auditors carry out detailed procedures, if the entity has a **history of profitable operations** and **ready access** to **financial resources.**

'The auditor should inquire of management as to its knowledge of events or conditions beyond the period of assessment used by management that may cast significant doubt on the entity's ability to continue as a going concern.'

Because the time period is some way into the future, the indications of potential going concern problems would have to be significant. Auditors do not have to carry out specific procedures to identify potential problems which may occur after the period covered by management's assessment. However they should be alert during the course of the audit for any **indications** of future problems.

When there is a significant delay in approving the accounts, auditors should consider whether this is due to doubts about the going concern status of the business. The delay may prompt the auditors to perform additional procedures on going concern.

1.2.2 Audit procedures where the entity's going concern status is doubtful   6/05

The ISA says 'when events or conditions have been identified which may cast significant doubt on the entity's ability to continue as a going concern, the auditor should:

(a)   **Review management's plans for future actions** based on its going concern assessment;

(b) **Gather sufficient appropriate audit evidence** (see list of procedures below) to confirm or dispel whether or not a material uncertainty exists through carrying out procedures considered necessary, including considering the effects of any plans of management and other mitigating factors; and

(c) **Seek written representations from management** regarding its plans for future action.'

In other words, if circumstances exist which indicate that the entity is not a going concern, the auditors must proactively test whether it is or not. Clearly important areas to focus this testing on will be cashflow and bank – the company is unlikely to be able to carry on if it does not have sufficient cash to carry out its operations.

Specifically, auditors may need **written representations** concerning:

- The assessment of those charged with governance that the company is a going concern
- Any relevant disclosures in the financial statements

When questions arise on the appropriateness of the going concern assumption, some of the normal audit procedures carried out by the auditors may take on an **additional significance** (for example, the audit of bank, as the company's financial resources are critical). Auditors may also have to carry out **additional procedures** or to update information obtained earlier. The ISA lists various procedures which the auditors should carry out in this context.

- **Analyse and discuss cash flow**, profit and other relevant forecasts with management
- **Analyse and discuss** the entity's latest available **interim financial statements** (or management accounts)
- **Review the terms of debentures and loan agreements** and determine whether they have been breached
- **Read minutes** of the meetings of shareholders, the board of directors and important committees for reference to financing difficulties
- **Enquire** of the entity's lawyer regarding **litigation and claims**
- **Confirm the existence, legality and enforceability** of arrangements to provide or maintain financial support with related and third parties
- **Assess** the **financial ability** of such parties to **provide additional funds**
- **Consider the entity's position** concerning unfulfilled customer orders
- **Review events after the period end** for items affecting the entity's ability to continue as a going concern

The auditors should **discuss** with management its **plans** for **future action**, for example plans to liquidate assets, borrow money or restructure debt, reduce or delay expenditure or increase capital, and assess whether these are feasible and are likely to improve the situation.

When analysis of cash flow is a significant factor, auditors should consider:

- The **reliability** of the **system** for generating the information
- Whether there is **adequate support** for the assumptions underlying the forecast
- How **recent forecasts** have **differed** from **actual results**

The bank letter which the auditor has obtained will contain useful information in relation to a company's going concern status, for example, the overdraft facility extended to the company. The auditor should review correspondence with the bank to assess the state of the relationship between the bank and the company as this will be very important if the company is having financial problems.

Going concern status is likely to be an area that will feature in a management representation letter (see section 3).

1.3 Impact on financial statements

'Based on the audit evidence obtained, the auditor should determine if, in the auditors' judgement, a material uncertainty exists related to events or conditions that alone or in aggregate, may cast significant doubt on the entity's ability to continue as a going concern.' An uncertainty will be material if it has so great a potential impact as to require clear disclosure of its nature and implications in the accounts. The accounts should:

(a)   **Adequately describe** the **principal events or conditions** that give rise to the uncertainty about continuance as a going concern, and management's plans to deal with the situation

(b)   **State clearly** that a **material uncertainty exists** and therefore the entity may be unable to realize its assets and discharge its liabilities in the normal course of business

1.3.1 Emphasis of matter

'If adequate disclosure is made in the financial statements, the auditor should express an unqualified opinion but modify the auditor's report by adding an emphasis of a matter paragraph that highlights the existence of a material uncertainty relating to an event or condition that may cast significant doubt on the entity's ability to continue as a going concern and draws attention to the note in the financial statements that discloses the matters.'

The auditor's report will be considered in detail in Chapter 19. The ISA gives an example of an emphasis of matter paragraph in such circumstances.

> 'Without qualifying our opinion we draw attention to Note X in the financial statements which indicates that the company incurred a net loss of zzz during the year ended December 31, 20X1 and, as of that date, the company's current liabilities exceeded its total assets by zzz. These conditions, along with other matters as set forth in Note X, indicate the existence of a material uncertainty which may cast significant doubt about the company's ability to continue as a going concern.'

This paragraph would be sub-headed "Going concern" for clarity. If there is a significant level of concern about the entity's ability to continue in the foreseeable future, the following needs to be disclosed as a minimum.

(a)   A statement that the financial statements have been prepared on the going concern basis

(b)   A statement of the pertinent factors

(c)   The nature of the concern

(d)   A statement of the assumptions adopted by those charged with governance, which should be clearly distinguishable from the pertinent facts

(e)   (Where appropriate and applicable) A statement regarding the plans of those charged with governance for resolving the matters giving rise to the concern; and

(f)   Details of any relevant actions by those charged with governance

1.3.2 Disclaimer of opinion

The auditors may express a disclaimer of opinion if for example there are multiple material uncertainties. The ISA says 'if adequate disclosure is not made in the financial statements, the auditor should express a qualified or adverse opinion, as appropriate. The report should include specific reference to the fact that there is a material uncertainty which may cast significant doubt about the company's ability to continue as a going concern'.

1.3.3 Adverse opinion

'If in the auditors' judgement, the entity will not be able to continue as a going concern, the auditor should express an adverse opinion if the financial statements have been prepared on a going concern basis.' This applies whatever the level of disclosure in the accounts.

If a basis other than the going concern basis is used, and the auditors consider it appropriate, they can issue an unqualified opinion with an emphasis of matter paragraph.

1.3.4 Limitation of scope

'If management is unwilling to make or extend its assessment when requested to do so by the auditor, the auditor should consider the need to modify the auditor's report as a result of the limitation on the scope of the auditor's work.' The auditors may be able to obtain sufficient alternative evidence even if management's assessment is inadequate.

2 Subsequent events   12/03, 12/05

FAST FORWARD

Auditors should consider the effect of **subsequent events** (after the balance sheet date) on the accounts.

'Subsequent events' include:

- Events occurring between the period end and the date of the auditor's report
- Facts discovered after the date of the auditor's report

ISA (UK and Ireland) 560 *Subsequent events* begins by stating that: 'The auditor should consider the effect of subsequent events on the financial statements and on the auditor's report.' You should remember from your Paper 2.5 studies that FRS 21 *Events after the balance sheet date* deals with the treatment in financial statement of events, both favourable and unfavourable, occurring after the period end. There are two types of event:

- Those that provide further evidence of conditions that existed at the period end
- Those that are indicative of conditions that arose subsequent to the period end

Exam focus point

Knowing the details of FRS 21 is vital in this area. In December 2005, 6 marks were available for assessing which of a given list of events were adjusting or non-adjusting.

2.1 Procedures

FAST FORWARD

Auditors have a responsibility to **review subsequent events** before they sign their audit report, and may have to take action if they become aware of subsequent events between the date they sign their audit report and the date the financial statements are laid before members.

2.1.1 Events occurring up to the date of the auditor's report

'The auditor should perform procedures designed to obtain sufficient appropriate audit evidence that all events up to the date of the auditor's report that may require adjustment of, or disclosure in, the financial statements have been identified.'

These procedures should be applied to any matters examined during the audit which may be susceptible to change after the year end. They are in addition to tests on specific transactions after the period end, eg cut-off tests.

The ISA lists procedures to identify subsequent events which may require adjustment or disclosure. They should be performed as near as possible to the date of the auditors' report.

335

PROCEDURES TESTING SUBSEQUENT EVENTS	
Enquiries of management	Status of items involving **subjective judgement**/accounted for using preliminary data
	Whether there are any new **commitments**, borrowings or guarantees
	Whether there have been any:
	• **Sales** or destruction of **assets**
	• **Issues** of **shares/debentures** or changes in business structure
	• **Developments** involving **risk areas, provisions** and **contingencies**
	• **Unusual accounting adjustments**
	• **Major events** (eg going concern problems) affecting appropriateness of accounting policies for estimates
Other procedures	**Review** management procedures for identifying subsequent events to ensure that such events are identified
	Read minutes of general board/committee meetings and enquire about unusual items
	Review latest accounting records and financial information and budgets and forecasts
	Obtain evidence concerning any litigation or claims from the company's solicitors (only with client permission)

Reviews and updates of these procedures may be required, depending on the length of the time between the procedures and the signing of the auditors' report and the susceptibility of the items to change over time. 'When the auditor becomes aware of events which materially affect the financial statements, the auditor should consider whether such events are properly accounted for and adequately disclosed in the financial statements.'

2.1.2 Facts discovered after the date of the auditor's report but before the financial statements are issued

The financial statements are the management's responsibility. They should therefore inform the auditors of any material subsequent events between the date of the auditors' report and the date the financial statements are issued. The auditors do **not** have any obligation to perform procedures, or make enquires regarding the financial statements **after** the date of their report.

'When, after the date of the auditor's report but before the financial statements are issued, the auditor becomes aware of a fact which may materially affect the financial statements, the auditor should consider whether the financial statements need amendment, should discuss the matter with the management and should take action appropriate in the circumstances.'

When the financial statements are amended, the auditors should **extend the procedures** discussed above to the **date of their new report**, carry out any other appropriate procedures and issue a new audit report dated the day it is signed.

The situation may arise where the statements are not amended but the auditors feel that they should be. The ISA says 'when management does not amend the financial statements in circumstances where the auditor believes they need to be amended and the auditor's report has not been released to the entity, the auditor should express a qualified opinion or an adverse opinion'.

If the auditors' report has already been issued to the entity then the auditors should notify those who are ultimately responsible for the entity (the management or possibly a holding company in a group), not to issue the financial statements or auditors' reports to third parties. If they have already been so issued, the auditors must take steps to prevent the reliance on the auditors' report. The action taken will depend on the auditors' legal rights and obligations and the advice of the auditors' lawyer.

2.1.3 Facts discovered after the financial statements have been issued

Auditors have no obligations to perform procedures or make enquiries regarding the financial statements **after** they have been issued. 'When, after the financial statements have been issued, the auditor becomes aware of a fact which existed at the date of the auditor's report and which, if known at that date, may have caused the auditor to modify the auditor's report, the auditor should consider whether the financial statements need revision, should discuss the matter with management, and should take the action as appropriate in the circumstances.'

The ISA gives the appropriate procedures which the auditors should undertake when management revises the financial statements.

(a) **Carry out the audit procedures** necessary in the circumstances

(b) **Review the steps taken by management** to ensure that anyone in receipt of the previously issued financial statements together with the auditors' report thereon is informed of the situation

(c) **Issue a new report** on the revised financial statements

'The new auditor's report should include an emphasis of a matter paragraph referring to a note to the financial statements that more extensively discusses the reason for the revision of the previously issued financial statements and to the earlier report issued by the auditor.'

> In our opinion, the revised financial statements give a true and fair view (or 'present fairly, in all material respects'), as at the date the original financial statements were approved, of the financial position of the company as of December 31, 20X1, and of the results of its operations and its cash flows for the year then ended in accordance with [relevant national legislation].
>
> In our opinion the original financial statements for the year to December 31, 20X1, failed to comply with [relevant national standards or legislation].
>
> Date   AUDITOR
> Address

Where local regulations allow the auditor to restrict the audit procedures on the financial statements to the effects of the subsequent event which caused the revision, the new auditor's report should contain a statement to that effect.

Where the management does **not** revise the financial statements but the auditors feel they should be revised, or if the management does not intend to take steps to ensure anyone in receipt of the previously issued financial statements is informed of the situation, then the auditors should consider steps to take, on a timely basis, to prevent reliance on their report. The actions taken will depend on the auditors' legal rights and obligations (eg to contact the shareholders directly) and legal advice received.

In the UK, 'after the financial statements have been issued' includes the period after the financial statements have been issued but before they have been laid before members. Therefore, as auditors in the UK have a right to make statements at the AGM, they can use this right to prevent reliance on their report.

3 Management representations   12/02

FAST FORWARD

Representations from management should generally be restricted to matters that cannot be verified by other audit procedures.

3.1 Representations

The auditors receive many representations during the audit, both unsolicited and in response to specific questions. Some of these representations may be critical to obtaining sufficient appropriate audit evidence. Representations may also be required for general matters, eg full availability of accounting records. ISA 580 *Management representations* says 'the auditor should obtain appropriate representations from management'.

> **Management** comprises officers and those who also perform senior managerial functions.

3.2 Acknowledgement by management of their responsibility for the financial statements

'The auditor should obtain audit evidence that management acknowledges its responsibility for the fair presentation of the financial statements in accordance with the applicable financial reporting framework and has approved the financial statements.'

'In the UK and Ireland, the auditors should obtain evidence that those charged with governance acknowledge their collective responsibility for the preparation of the financial statements and have approved the financial statements'.

This is normally done when the auditors receive a signed copy of the financial statements which incorporate a relevant statement of responsibilities. Alternatively, the auditors may obtain such evidence from:

- **Relevant minutes of meetings** of the board of directors or similar body, or by attending such a meeting

- A **written representation** from management

They should also obtain written representations that management acknowledges its responsibility for the design and implementation of internal control and that it believes the effects of uncorrected misstatements aggregated by the auditors during the audit is immaterial.

3.3 Representations by management as audit evidence

FAST FORWARD

> Any representations should be **compared** with other evidence and their **sufficiency** assessed.

In addition to representations relating to responsibility for the financial statements, the auditors may wish to rely on management representations as audit evidence. The ISA says 'the auditor should obtain written representations from management on matters material to the financial statements when other sufficient appropriate audit evidence cannot be reasonably expected to exist'.

Written confirmation of oral representations avoids confusion and disagreement. Such matters should be discussed with those responsible for giving the written confirmation, to ensure that they understand what they are confirming. Written confirmations are normally required of appropriately senior management. Only matters which are material to the financial statements should be included.

When the auditors receive such representations they should:

(a) Seek **corroborative audit evidence** from sources inside or outside the entity

(b) **Evaluate** whether the **representations** made by management appear reasonable and are consistent with other audit evidence obtained, including other representations

(c) **Consider whether the individuals** making the representations can be expected to be **well-informed** on the particular matters

The ISA then makes a very important point. 'Representations by management cannot be a substitute for other audit evidence that the auditor could reasonably expect to be available ... if the auditor is unable to obtain sufficient appropriate audit evidence regarding a matter which has, or may have, a material effect on the financial statements and such audit evidence is expected to be available, this will constitute a limitation in the scope of the audit, even if a representation from management has been received on the matter.'

There are instances where management representations *may* be the only audit evidence available.

- **Knowledge of the facts is confined to management**, eg the facts are a matter of management intention.

- The **matter is principally one of judgement or opinion**, eg the trading position of a particular customer.

There may be occasions when the representations received do not agree with other audit evidence obtained. The ISA says 'if a representation by management is contradicted by other audit evidence, the auditor should investigate the circumstances and, when necessary, consider whether it casts doubt on the reliability of other representations made by management.'

Investigations of such situations will normally begin with further enquires of management; the representations may have been misunderstood or, alternatively, the other evidence misinterpreted. If explanations are insufficient or unforthcoming, then further audit procedures may be required.

3.3.1 Examples of paragraphs in a management representation letter

- There have been no irregularities involving management or employees who have a significant role in the accounting and internal control systems or that could have a material effect on the financial statements.

- The financial statements are free of material misstatement, including omissions.

- We have no plans or intentions that may materially alter the carrying value or classification of assets and liabilities reflected in the financial statements.

- We have no plans to abandon lines of product or other plans or intentions that will result in any excess or obsolete stock, and no stock is stated at an amount in excess of net realisable value.

- The company has satisfactory title to all assets and there are no liens or encumbrances on the company's assets, except for those that are disclosed in Note X to the financial statements.

- We have recorded or disclosed, as appropriate, all liabilities, both actual and contingent, and have disclosed in Note X to the financial statements all guarantees that we have given to third parties.

- Other than ... described in Note X to the financial statements, there have been no events subsequent to period end which require adjustment of or disclosure in the financial statement or notes thereto.

> • The ... claim by XYZ company has been settled for the total sum of XXX which has been properly accrued in the financial statements. No other claims in connection with litigation have been or are expected to be received.

> The exam in June 2005 contained a requirement to draft some paragraphs for a management representation letter.

3.4 Documentation of representations by management

The auditors should include in audit working papers evidence of management's representations in the form of a summary of oral discussions with management or written representations from management.

A written representation is better audit evidence than an oral representation and can take the form of:

- A **representation letter** from management

- A **letter from the auditors** outlining the auditors' understanding of management's representations, duly acknowledged and confirmed by management

- **Relevant minutes** of meetings of the board of directors or similar body or a signed copy of the financial statements (note)

Note

The ISA goes on to say 'A signed copy of the financial statements for a company may be sufficient evidence of the directors' acknowledgement of their collective responsibility for the preparation of the financial statements where it incorporates a statement to that effect. A signed copy of the financial statements, however, is not, by itself, sufficient appropriate evidence to confirm other representations given to the auditor as it does not, ordinarily, clearly identify and explain the specific, separate representations'.

3.4.1 Basic elements of a management representation letter

A management representation letter should:

- Be **addressed** to the **auditors**
- **Contain specified information**
- Be **appropriately dated** and **signed** by those with specific relevant knowledge

The letter will usually be **dated** on the **day the financial statements are approved**, but if there is any significant delay between the representation letter and the date of the auditors' report, then the auditors should consider the need to obtain further representations.

A management representation letter is usually signed by the members of management who have **primary responsibility** for the entity and its financial aspects (ie the senior executive officer and the senior financial officer) based on the best of their knowledge and belief.

3.5 Actions if management refuses to provide representations

'If management refuses to provide a representation that the auditor considers necessary, this constitutes a scope limitation report and the auditor should express a qualified opinion or a disclaimer of opinion.' In these circumstances, the auditors should consider whether it is appropriate to rely on other representations made by management during the audit.

However, before the audit report is qualified, the auditors should discuss the matter with the directors to find out why they don't want to sign the letter and to see if they fully understand the importance of the letter to the auditors. The auditors should try and persuade the directors to sign the letter.

Question   Management representations

Management representations are an important source of audit evidence. These representations may be oral or written, and may be obtained either on an informal or formal basis. The auditors will include information obtained in this manner in their audit working papers where it forms part of their total audit evidence.

Required

(a)   Explain the nature and role of the letter of representation.

(b)   Explain why it is important for the auditors to discuss the contents of the letter of representation at an early stage of the audit.

(c)   Explain why standard letters of representation are becoming less frequently used by the auditing profession.

Answer

(a)   The letter of representation is a letter normally signed by appropriate directors or managers, normally on behalf of the whole board. Such a letter contains representations relating to matters which are material to the financial statements but concerning which knowledge of the facts is confined to management, or where the directors have used judgement or opinion in the preparation of the financial statements.

The precise scope and content of the letter of representation should be appropriate to the particular audit. An example of a typical situation in which representations may be required would be a case in which an employee's legal claim is settled out of court and the directors are asked to set out in writing their view that no further similar claims are expected to be paid. An absence of independent corroborative evidence and the fact that judgement on the part of directors is involved indicates the need for written evidence of the judgement in the letter of representation.

Representations are not a substitute for other necessary audit work, and they do not relieve the auditors of any of their responsibilities. Even where written representations are obtained, the auditors need to decide whether in the circumstances these representations, together with other audit evidence obtained, are sufficient to justify an unqualified opinion on the financial statements.

However, written representations by the directors do form part of the total audit evidence, and form part of the auditors' working papers.

One function which the letter of representation may also serve, although it is subsidiary to its central purposes, is that such a letter may act as a reminder to the directors and management of their responsibilities. For example, the letter will remind them of their responsibilities with regard to the truth and fairness of the accounts, and of their responsibility for statements made orally to the auditors but only recorded in writing in the letter of representation.

(b)   The letter of representation should not be seen as an afterthought in the audit process, even though the letter should be finally approved and signed on a date as close as possible to the date of the audit report and after all other audit work has been completed.

Discussion of the contents of the letter early in the audit is an important part of the audit planning process. It makes the auditors aware at an early stage of the areas in which representations may be required. It also acts as prior warning to management of errors. This may usefully give management a chance to think carefully about the nature of any representations which are likely to be required in writing, and may encourage directors to become more fully aware of their responsibilities in relation to such written confirmations.

If discussion of the contents of the representation letter are left until the last stages of the audit, senior management may justifiably object that, the matters covered by the letter ought to have been raised earlier by the auditors. Management might object that if this had been done there would have been an opportunity to assemble appropriate corroborative evidence and thus avoid the need for written representations by the directors. Such objections may be made especially where audit deadlines are tight, which is often the case for companies which are part of a group. Lengthy discussions of judgmental matters on which representations are being sought may, if left until the end of the audit process, detract from a good working relationship between the auditors and client management, and in extreme cases management may become reluctant to comply with the auditors' requests.

(c)   Some audit firms make use of a standard form of letter of representation. The principal merit of using a standard letter is that, by using a standard for all audit work in the firm, the firm has more assurance that staff on each audit will have considered all of the typical kinds of matter on which written representations are normally sought from clients. Audit staff may benefit from using such a standard letter as a checklist of possible matters to include in a draft letter to discuss with management. However, in all cases there will be a need to 'tailor' the standard letter to suit the needs of the particular audit engagement. This may involve adapting paragraphs of a standard letter, or adding new paragraphs to cover matters special to the assignment. Instead of using a full standardised letter, some firms make use of 'specimen paragraphs' to be included in draft letters of representation. Such specimen paragraphs offer the advantage of suggesting appropriate wording dealing with common matters on which representations are required. Given the judgmental nature of many such matters, careful wording is important.

As with all standardised audit documentation, there remains the danger that standardisation may encourage a 'mechanical' approach to audit work and this probably explains why many firms are becoming reluctant to use standard forms of letter. Where audit staff fail to use their initiative and imagination, the standard letter may be followed too closely, and important matters may be missed. However, it could be argued that the problem in such cases lies more with a lack of adequate training of audit staff than with the fact that standardised documentation is available.

In presenting a letter of representation to the directors, it is important that the letter is not treated as merely a standard formality. Even if the letter for a particular assignment contains only similar material to that included generally in such letters, and is little different from last year's letter for the same client, each point should be discussed with management in order to encourage the signatories to consider its contents fully.

4 Overall review of financial statements   12/03

FAST FORWARD

The auditors must perform and document an **overall review** of the financial statements before they can reach an opinion.

Once the bulk of the substantive procedures have been carried out, the auditors will have a draft set of financial statements which should be supported by appropriate and sufficient audit evidence. At the beginning of the end of the audit process, it is usual for the auditors to undertake an **overall review** of the financial statements.

This review of the financial statements, in conjunction with the conclusions drawn from the other audit evidence obtained, gives the auditors a reasonable basis for their opinion on the financial statements. It should be carried out by a senior member of the audit team, with appropriate skills and experience.

4.1 Compliance with accounting regulations

The auditors should consider whether:

(a)   The information presented in the financial statements is in accordance with local/national statutory requirements.

(b)   The accounting policies employed are in accordance with accounting standards, properly disclosed, consistently applied and appropriate to the entity.

When examining the **accounting policies**, auditors should consider:

(a)   Policies **commonly adopted in particular industries**

(b)   Policies for which there is **substantial authoritative support**

(c)   Whether any **departures from applicable accounting standards** are necessary for the financial statements to give a true and fair view

(d)   Whether the **financial statements reflect the substance** of the underlying transactions and not merely their form

When compliance with local/national statutory requirements and accounting standards is considered, the auditors may find it useful to use a **checklist**.

4.2 Review for consistency and reasonableness

The auditors should consider whether the financial statements are consistent with their knowledge of the entity's business and with the results of other audit procedures, and the manner of disclosure is fair.

The principal considerations are as follows.

(a)   Whether the financial statements adequately reflect the **information** and **explanations** previously obtained and conclusions previously reached during the course of the audit

(b)   Whether it reveals any **new factors** which may affect the presentation of, or disclosure in, the financial statements

(c)   Whether analytical procedures applied when completing the audit, such as comparing the information in the financial statements with other pertinent data, **produce results** which assist in arriving at the overall conclusion as to whether the financial statements as a whole are consistent with their knowledge of the entity's business (see Chapter 7)

(d)   Whether the **presentation** adopted in the financial statements may have been unduly influenced by the **directors' desire** to present matters in a favourable or unfavourable light

(e)   The potential impact on the financial statements of the **aggregate of uncorrected misstatements** (including those arising from bias in making accounting estimates) identified during the course of the audit and the preceding period's audit, if any

4.3 Problems of accounting treatment

As noted in the previous section auditors review the financial statements to assess whether the **accounting policies are consistently applied**. As you know, FRS 18 requires entities to adopt the **best** policy at all times, which may be at odds with this requirement for consistency.

Auditors should therefore consider whether new accounting policies are appropriate, whether matters in financial statements are consistent with each other, and whether the financial statements give a true and fair view.

4.4 Analytical procedures

In Chapter 12 we discussed how analytical review procedures are used as part of the overall review procedures at the end of an audit.

Remember the areas that the analytical review at the final stage must cover:

- Important accounting ratios
- Related items
- Changes in products/customers
- Price and mix changes
- Wages changes
- Variances
- Trends in production and sales
- Changes in material and labour content of production
- Other profit and loss account expenditure
- Variations caused by industry or economy factors

As at other stages, significant fluctuations and unexpected relationships must be investigated and documented.

5 Other information in documents containing audited financial statements

FAST FORWARD

Auditors may have a statutory responsibility to report inconsistencies between the other information provided to shareholders and the accounts.

5.1 Directors' report

The auditor has a statutory duty to report whether the information given in the directors' report is consistent with the financial statements. The auditors must therefore **read the directors' report**. Information that has been extracted directly from the financial statements should be verified against them.

Some information in the directors' report may be more detailed than the financial statements or prepared on a different basis. Such information must be verified back to the client's accounting records or to auditor working papers.

If the auditor discovers **inconsistencies** between the directors' report and the financial statements, he should seek to resolve them, through discussion with management and those charged with governance.

If the directors' report is inconsistent and the directors will not agree to change it, the audit report should state that it is not consistent.

Example audit report (extracts)

Opinion

In our opinion:

- [opinion on financial statements here ...]

Material inconsistency between the financial statements and the directors' report

In our opinion, the information given in the seventh paragraph of the Business Review in the directors' report is not consistent with the financial statements. That paragraph states without amplification that "the company's trading for the period resulted in a 10% increase in profit over the previous period's profit". The profit and loss account, however, shows that the company's profit for the period included a profit of £Z which did not arise from trading but arose from the disposal of assets of a discontinued operation. Without this profit on the disposal of assets, the company would have reported a profit for the year of £Y, representing a reduction in profit of 25% over the previous period's profit on a like for like basis. Except for this matter, in our opinion the information given in the directors' report is consistent with the financial statements.

5.2 Other information on which auditors are not required to report

ISA 720 *Other information in documents containing audited financial statements and the auditors' statutory reporting responsibility in relation to directors' reports* establishes standards and provides guidance on the auditors' consideration of other information, on which the auditors have **no obligation to report,** in documents containing audited financial statements. It says 'the auditor should read the other information to identify material inconsistencies with the audited financial statements'. If any apparent misstatement or material inconsistencies exist, he should seek to resolve them.

Key terms

Other information is financial and non-financial information *other than* the audited financial statements and the auditors' report, which an entity may include in its annual report, either by custom or statute.

A **material inconsistency** exists when other information contradicts information contained in the audited financial statements. A material inconsistency may raise doubt about the audit conclusions drawn from audit evidence previously obtained and, possibly, about the basis for the auditors' opinion on the financial statements.

Examples of other information are:

- A report by management or the board of directors on operations
- Financial summaries or highlights
- Employment data
- Planned capital expenditures
- Financial ratios
- Name of officers and directors
- Selected quarterly data

Auditors have **no** responsibility to report that other information is properly stated because an audit is only an expression of opinion on the truth and fairness of the financial statements. However, they may be **engaged separately**, or **required by statute**, to report on elements of other information. In any case, the auditors should give consideration to other information as inconsistencies with the audited financial statements may undermine their report.

Some countries require the auditors to apply specific procedures to certain other information, eg required supplementary data and interim financial information. If such other information is omitted or contains deficiencies, the auditors may be required to refer to the matter in their report.

When there is an obligation to report specifically on other information, the auditors' responsibilities are determined by the **nature of the engagement** and by **local legislation** and professional standards. When such responsibilities involve the review of other information, the auditors will need to follow the guidance on **review engagements** in the appropriate ISAs.

5.3 Access to other information

Timely access to other information will be required. The auditors therefore must make arrangements with the client to obtain such information prior to the date of their report. In circumstances where all the other information may not be available prior to that date, the auditors should follow the guidance below.

5.4 Material inconsistencies

'If, on reading the other information, the auditor identifies a material inconsistency, the auditor should determine whether the audited financial statements or the other information needs to be amended. The auditor should seek to resolve the matter by discussion with those charged with governance.

Other information may contain misstatements or inconsistencies with the financial statements and the auditors may be unable to resolve them by discussion with the directors. They may need to use an **emphasis of matter paragraph** within the auditors' report to describe the apparent misstatement or material inconsistency.

If an amendment is necessary in the audited financial statements and the entity refuses to make the amendment, the auditor should express a qualified or adverse opinion.

If an amendment is necessary in the other information and the entity refuses to make the amendment, the auditor should consider including in the auditor's report an emphasis of matter paragraph describing the material inconsistency or taking other actions.'

The actions taken by the auditors will depend on the individual circumstances and the auditors may consider taking legal advice.

5.5 Material misstatements of fact

A 'material misstatement of fact' in other information exists when such information, not related to matters appearing in the financial statement, is incorrectly stated and presented. 'If the auditor becomes aware that the other information appears to include a material misstatement of fact, the auditor should discuss the matter with the entity's management.' He should consider whether the other information needs amending.

When discussing the matter with the entity's management, the auditors may not be able to evaluate the validity of the other information and management's responses to the auditors' enquiries, and would need to consider whether valid differences of judgement or opinion exist.

'When the auditor still considers that there is an apparent misstatement of fact, the auditor should request management to consult with a qualified third party, such as the entity's legal counsel and should consider the advice received.

If the auditor concludes that there is a material misstatement of fact in the other information which management refuses to correct, the auditor should consider taking further appropriate action.'

Such an action could include such steps as notifying those ultimately responsible for the overall direction of the entity and obtaining legal advice.

In the UK, the auditor requests those charged with governance to correct material misstatements of fact in the other information. 'If an amendment is necessary in the other information and the entity refuses to make the amendment, the auditor should consider including in the auditor's report an emphasis of matter paragraph describing the material misstatement.'

The auditor also has a right to be heard on such matters at the AGM, if he sees fit. In addition, the auditor might consider resigning from the engagement and making his statutory statement of circumstances if he feels the situation merits such action.

6 Completion of the audit

FAST FORWARD ▶▶

As part of their completion procedures, auditors should consider whether the **aggregate of uncorrected misstatements** is material.

6.1 Summarising errors

During the course of the audit, errors will be discovered which may be material or immaterial to the financial statements. It is very likely that the client will adjust the financial statements to take account of material and immaterial errors during the course of the audit. At the end of the audit, however, some errors may still be outstanding and the auditors will summarise these **unadjusted errors**.

The summary of errors will not only list errors from the current year, but also those in the previous year(s). This will allow errors to be highlighted which are reversals of errors in the previous year, such as in the valuation of closing/opening inventory. Cumulative errors may also be shown, which have increased from year to year. It is normal to show both the balance sheet and the profit and loss effect, as in the example given here.

SCHEDULE OF UNADJUSTED ERRORS

		20X2 P & L account Dr £	20X2 P & L account Cr £	20X2 Balance sheet Dr £	20X2 Balance sheet Cr £	20X1 P & L account Dr £	20X1 P & L account Cr £	20X1 Balance sheet Dr £	20X1 Balance sheet Cr £
(a)	ABC Ltd debt unprovided	10,470			10,470	4,523			4,523
(b)	Opening/ closing stock under-valued*	21,540			21,540		21,540	21,540	
(c)	Closing stock undervalued		34,105	34,105					
(d)	Opening unaccrued expenses								
	Telephone*		453	453		453			453
	Electricity*		905	905		905			905
(e)	Closing unaccrued expenses								
	Telephone	427			427				
	Electricity	1,128			1,128				
(f)	Obsolete stock write off	2,528			2,528	3,211			3,211
	Total	36,093	35,463	35,463	36,093	9,092	21,540	21,540	9,092
	*Cancelling items	21,540			21,540				
				453	453				
				905	905				
		14,553	34,105	34,105	14,553				

6.2 Evaluating the effect of misstatements

ISA 320 states that 'in evaluating whether of the financial statements are prepared, in all material respects, in accordance with an applicable financial reporting framework, the auditor should assess whether the aggregate of uncorrected misstatements that have been identified during the audit is material'.

The aggregate of uncorrected misstatements comprises:

(a)   **Specific misstatements** identified by the auditors, including the net effect of uncorrected misstatements identified during the audit of the previous period.

(b)   Their **best estimate** of **other misstatements** which cannot be quantified specifically (ie projected errors)

If the auditors consider that the aggregate of misstatements may be material, they must consider reducing audit risk by extending audit procedures or requesting management to adjust the financial statements (which management may wish to do anyway).

'If management refuses to adjust the financial statements and the results of extended audit procedures do not enable the auditor to conclude that the aggregate of uncorrected misstatements is not material, the auditor should consider the appropriate modification to the auditor's report in accordance with ISA 700 *The auditor's report on financial statements.*'

If the aggregate of the uncorrected misstatements that the auditors have identified approaches the materiality level, the auditors should consider whether it is likely that undetected misstatements, when taken with aggregated uncorrected misstatements, could exceed the materiality level. Thus, as aggregate uncorrected misstatements approach the materiality level the auditors should consider reducing the risk by:

(a) **Performing additional audit procedures or**
(b) By **requesting management** to adjust the financial statements for identified misstatements

The schedule will be used by the audit manager and partner to decide whether the client should be requested to make adjustments to the financial statements to correct the errors.

6.3 Completion checklists

Audit firms frequently use checklists which must be signed off to ensure that all final procedures have been carried out, all material amounts are supported by sufficient appropriate evidence, etc.

Chapter Roundup

- Auditors must consider the **future plans** of directors and any signs of **going concern problems** which may be noted throughout the audit.

- When reporting on the accounts, auditors should consider whether the going concern basis is **appropriate,** and whether **disclosure** of going concern problems is **sufficient**.

- Auditors should consider the effect of **subsequent events** (after the balance sheet date) on the accounts.

- Auditors have a responsibility to **review subsequent events** before they sign their audit report, and may have to take action if they become aware of subsequent events between the date they sign their audit report and the date the financial statements are laid before members.

- **Representations from management** should generally be restricted to matters that cannot be verified by other audit procedures.

- Any representations should be **compared** with other evidence and their **sufficiency** assessed.

- The auditors must perform and document an **overall review** of the financial statements before they can reach an opinion.

- Auditors may have a statutory responsibility to report inconsistencies between the other information provided to shareholders and the accounts.

- As part of their completion procedures, auditors should consider whether the **aggregate of uncorrected misstatements** is material.

Quick Quiz

1 Complete the definition, using the words given below.

The .... assumption: the enterprise is ordinarily viewed as .... in business for the .... with neither the .... nor the .... of liquidation, ceasing .... or seeking protection from creditors.

intention	future	going	necessity	continuing	foreseeable	trading	concern

2 Complete the table putting the indicators of an entity's inability to continue as a going concern under the correct headings.

Financial	Operational	Other

(a) Legal proceedings   (c) Loss of key market   (e) Withdrawal of financial
(b) Inability to pay creditors   (d) Loss of key license   support by creditors
                                                 (f) Loss of key management

3 The directors must satisfy themselves that the going concern basis in the financial statements is appropriate.

True ☐

False ☐

4 Name three enquiries that should be made of management to test subsequent events.

1 ....
2 ....
3 ....

5 Name two instances when management representation may be the only audit evidence available.

1 ....
2 ....

6 Name four factors which the auditors should consider when examining accounting policies.

1 ....
2 ....
3 ....
4 ....

7 Give five examples of what areas analytical review at the final stage should cover.

1 ....

2 ....

3 ....

4 ....

5 ....

8 In which two instances might other information in documents containing an audit report be referred to in the audit report?

1 ....

2 ....

9 In evaluating whether the financial statement give a true and fair view, auditors should assess the materiality of the aggregate of uncorrected misstatements.

True ☐

False ☐

Answers to Quick Quiz

1   going concern, continuing, foreseeable future, intention, necessity, trading

2

Financial	Operational	Other
(b) (e)	(c) (d) (f)	(a)

3   True

     From:

     • What the status is of items involving subjective judgement
     • Whether there are any new commitments, borrowings or guarantees
     • Whether any assets have been sold or destroyed
     • Whether any new shares/debentures have been issued
     • Whether there have been any developments in risk areas
     • Any unusual accounting adjustments
     • Any major events

5   (1)   When knowledge of facts is confined to management
     (2)   When the matter is judgement/opinion

6   (1)   Policies **commonly adopted in particular industries**

     (2)   Policies for which there is **substantial authoritative support**

     (3)   Whether any **departures from applicable accounting standards** are necessary for the financial
            statements to give a true and fair view

     (4)   Whether the **financial statements reflect the substance** of the underlying transactions and not
            merely their form

7   From:

     • Important accounting ratios
     • Related items
     • Changes in products/customers
     • Price and mix changes
     • Wages changes
     • Variances
     • Trends in production and sales
     • Changes in material and labour content of production
     • Other profit and loss account expenditure
     • Variations caused by industry or economy factors

8   (1)   There is a material inconsistency
     (2)   There is a material misstatement of fact

9   True

Now try the question below from the Exam Question Bank

Number	Level	Marks	Time
Q18	Examination	20	36 mins

Part E

Reporting

Public reporting

Topic list	Syllabus reference
1 The auditors' report on financial statements	7
2 Modified reports	7
3 The audit report as a means of communication	7

Introduction

The **audit report** is the means by which the external auditors express their opinion on the **truth and fairness** of a company's financial statements. This is for the benefit principally of the shareholders, but also for other users as the audit report is usually kept on public record, with the filed financial statements.

As we saw in Chapter 3, many of the contents of the auditor's report are prescribed by the statute. They are also subject to the professional requirements in the form of ISA (UK and Ireland) 700 *The auditor's report on financial statements*. This makes it extremely different to the private reports auditors produce which we will look at in more detail in Chapter 20.

The difference between this public report and the private report is not an issue of formality. Although other reports do not go on the public record, they are no less formal than the statutory audit report. There are two key differences, however:

- Purpose
- Understandability

The **purpose** of the publicised audit report is, as you know, to report on whether the accounts show a **true and fair view** to the **shareholders.** The private reports are for the purposes of directors and management.

The second issue is that of **understandability**, how the purpose and conclusion of the public report is **communicated** to shareholders. Directors and management work in the business, the report submitted to them may well be more meaningful to them than the audit report is to more isolated shareholders. We discuss communication and the **expectations gap** briefly in Section 3.

You need to be comfortable with all the terms of the audit report (unqualified and modified) and to be able to describe and analyse them.

Study guide

26 – Reporting I

- Describe, illustrate and analyse the format and content of unmodified and modified statutory audit reports

Exam guide

You will not be required to reproduce a full audit report in the exam; however you may be required to describe:

- How the audit report in a specific situation differs from an unqualified audit report, or
- Give extracts from an audit report dealing with uncertainties or disagreements

In December 2001, the requirement was to compare and contrast the audit report and the review report.

1 The auditors' report on financial statements 12/01, 6/05

FAST FORWARD

The auditor is required to produce an audit report containing a number of consistent elements so that users know the audit has been conducted according to recognised standards.

Point to note

The International Federation of Accountants has revised ISA 700, but the APB has not yet adopted the revised ISA. It is listed as a planned future activity. If ISA 700 (revised) becomes examinable for June 2007 candidates, it will be covered in detail in the current issues section of the Practice and Revision Kit.

ISA 700 (UK and Ireland) *The auditor's report on financial statements* establishes standards and provides guidance on the form and content of the auditor's report issued as a result of an audit performed by an independent auditor of the financial statements of an entity. It states that 'the auditor should review and assess the conclusions drawn from the audit evidence obtained as the basis for forming an opinion on the financial statements'.

This evaluation, which we have covered in Chapter 18, involves considering whether the financial statements have been **prepared** in accordance with an **acceptable financial reporting framework** being either IASs or relevant national standards or practices (FRSs in the UK). Auditors may also have to consider whether the financial statements comply with statutory requirements. The ISA says 'the auditor's report should contain a clear written expression of the auditor's opinion on the financial statements'.

1.1 Basic elements of the auditor's report

The example of an unqualified UK audit report was given in Chapter 3. You should refer back to it when working through this section.

The auditor's report includes the following basic elements, usually in the following layout.

    (a)   **Title**
    (b)   **Addressee**
    (c)   **Introductory paragraph** identifying the financial statements audited
    (d)   A statement of management's responsibility for the financial statements
    (e)   A statement of the auditor's responsibility
    (f)   Scope paragraph including a description of the work performed by the auditor
    (g)   **Opinion paragraph** containing an expression of opinion on the financial statements
    (h)   **Date** of the report

| (i) | **Auditor's address** |
| (j) | **Auditor's signature** |

A measure of uniformity in the form and content of the auditor's report is desirable because it helps to promote the reader's understanding and to identify unusual circumstances when they occur.

1.1.1 Title

The title could indicate that the report is by an **independent** auditor to confirm all the relevant ethical standards have been met.

1.1.2 Addressee

The report should be addressed as required by the circumstances. This will be determined by national law, but is likely to be the **shareholders** or **board of directors**.

1.1.3 Introductory paragraph

This should:

- Identify the entity being audited
- State that the financial statements have been audited
- Identify the financial statements being audited (for example, profit and loss account, balance sheet, cash flow statement and the period they cover)
- Specify the date and period covered by the financial statements

The auditor may be able to refer to specific page numbers if the financial statements are contained in a larger report.

1.1.4 Management's responsibility

The report must contain a statement that management is responsible for the presentation of the financial statements. This responsibility includes designing, implementing and maintaining internal controls, selecting appropriate accounting policies and making reasonable accounting estimates.

1.1.5 Auditor's responsibility

The report must state that the auditor is responsible for expressing an opinion on the financial statements. The auditor should distinguish his duties from the relevant responsibilities of those charged with governance, by referring to the summary of the responsibilities of those charged with governance contained elsewhere in the published information. If this information has not been published elsewhere, the auditor should include it in his report. The scope paragraph should explain that the auditor adhered to international standards on auditing and ethical requirements and that the auditor planned and performed the audit so as to obtain reasonable assurance that the financial statements are free from material misstatements.

The report should describe the audit as including:

(a) Examining, on a test basis, evidence to support the financial statement amounts and disclosures

(b) Assessing the accounting principles used in the preparation of the financial statements

(c) Assessing the significant estimates made by management in the preparation of the financial statements

(d) Evaluating the overall financial statement presentation

The ISA continues 'In the UK and Ireland, the accounting principles used in the preparation of financial statements are established by legislation. The auditor should consider whether the accounting policies are appropriate to the reporting entity's circumstances, consistently applied and adequately disclosed'. Lastly in the scope paragraph, 'the report should include a statement by the auditor that the audit provides a reasonable basis for the opinion'.

1.1.6 Auditor's opinion

If the auditor concludes that the financial statements give a true and fair view, he should express an unqualified opinion.

An unqualified opinion states that the financial statements give a true and fair view or present fairly, in all material respects, in accordance with the applicable financial reporting framework. It should clearly indicate the financial reporting framework used, and, if IFRSs are not used, the country of origin of the framework, such as UK accounting standards.

In addition, as discussed in Chapter 18, he must state his opinion whether the directors' report is consistent with the financial statements.

1.1.7 Auditor's signature

The report must contain the signature, whether this is the auditor's own name or the audit firm's name.

1.1.8 Date

The report must be dated, a date after all the audit evidence has been collected. This date shows the completion date of the audit and should not be before management has approved the financial statements.

1.1.9 Address

The location where the auditor practices must be included. This is usually the city where the auditor has his office.

1.2 Framework

An unqualified opinion may be expressed only when the auditor is able to conclude that the financial statements give a true and fair view in accordance with **the identified financial reporting framework.**

An unqualified opinion must only be given when the financial statements **fully** comply with the identified reporting framework.

1.2.1 Auditing framework

The auditor's report may only state that the audit has been conducted in accordance with international standards on auditing when the auditor has complied fully with ISAs.

Similarly, the auditor must **fully comply** with ISAs in order for him to be able to claim that the audit has been conducted in accordance with ISAs.

1.3 Unqualified auditor's report

'An *unqualified opinion* should be expressed when the auditor concludes that the financial statements give a true and fair view (or are presented fairly, in all material respects) in accordance with the applicable financial reporting framework.' An unqualified opinion also indicates implicitly that any **changes in**

accounting principles or in the method of their application, and the effects therefore, have been properly determined and disclosed in the financial statements.

This section has introduced you to the standard unqualified audit reports. The next section looks at how the audit report is affected when problems of varying severity arise in the audit. Before we go on to modifications, look back at the audit report in Chapter 3, and identify all the elements discussed above.

Question   Auditor's report

The following is a series of extracts from an unqualified audit report which has been signed by the auditors of Kiln Ltd.

AUDITORS' REPORT TO THE SHAREHOLDERS OF KILN LIMITED

We have audited *the financial statements on pages .... to ....* which have been prepared under the historical cost convention.

We have conducted our audit *in accordance with Auditing Standards* issued by the Auditing Practices Board. An audit includes examination on a test basis of evidence relevant to the amounts and disclosures in the financial statements.

In our opinion the financial statements give a true and fair view of the state of the company's affairs as at 31 December 20X3 and of its profit for the year then ended and have been properly prepared in accordance with the Companies Act 1985.

Required

Explain the purpose and meaning of the following phrases taken from the above extracts of an unqualified audit report.

(a)   '... the financial statements on pages .... to ....'
(b)   '... in accordance with Auditing Standards.'
(c)   'In our opinion ...'

Answer

(a)   *'...the financial statements on pages 8 to 20...'*

Purpose

The purpose of this phrase is to make it clear to the reader of an audit report the part of a company's annual report upon which the auditors are reporting their opinion.

Meaning

An annual report may include documents such as a chairman's report, employee report, five year summary and other voluntary information. However, under the Companies Act, only the profit and loss account, balance sheet and associated notes are required to be audited in true and fair terms. FRS 1 requires a cash flow statement and FRS 3 requires a statement of total recognised gains and losses which, under auditing standards, are audited in true and fair terms. Thus the page references (for instance, 8 to 20) cover only the profit and loss account, balance sheet, notes to the accounts, cash flow statement and statement of total recognised gains and losses. The directors' report, although examined and reported on (as discussed in Chapter 18) if it contains inconsistencies, is not included in these page references.

(b)   *'...in accordance with Auditing Standards...'*

Purpose

This phrase is included in order to confirm to the reader that best practice, as laid down in Auditing Standards, has been adopted by the auditors in both carrying out their audit and in drafting their audit opinion. This means that the reader can be assured that the audit has been properly conducted, and that should he or she wish to discover what such standards are, or what certain key phrases mean, he or she can have recourse to Auditing Standards to explain such matters.

Meaning

Auditing Standards are those auditing standards prepared by the Auditing Practices Board.

These prescribe the principles and practices to be followed by auditors in the planning, designing and carrying out various aspects of their audit work, the content of audit reports, both qualified and unqualified and so on. Members are expected to follow all of these standards.

(c)   *'In our opinion ...'*

Purpose

Under the Companies Act, auditors are required to report on every balance sheet, profit and loss account or group accounts laid before members and on the directors' report issued with those financial statements. In reporting, they are required to state their opinion on those accounts. Thus, the purpose of this phrase is to comply with the statutory requirement to report an opinion.

Meaning

An audit report is an expression of opinion by suitably qualified auditors as to whether the financial statements give a true and fair view, and have been properly prepared in accordance with the Companies Act. It is not a certificate; rather it is a statement of whether or not, in the professional judgement of the auditors, the financial statements give a true and fair view.

2 Modified reports   12/03

FAST FORWARD

Modified audit reports arise when auditors do not believe that they can state without reservation that the accounts give a true and fair view.

2.1 Modifications to the auditor's report

The ISA goes on to deal with situations where the auditor cannot issue an unqualified opinion. There are two general types of modified opinion:

(a)   **Matters that do not affect the auditor's opinion:** emphasis of matter

(b)   **Matters that do affect the auditor's opinion**

- Qualified opinion
- Disclaimer of opinion
- Adverse opinion

2.2 Matters that do not affect the auditor's opinion

Key term

In certain circumstances, an auditor's report may be modified by adding an **emphasis of matter** to highlight a matter affecting the financial statements which is included in a note to the financial statements that more extensively discusses the matter. The addition of such an emphasis of matter paragraph **does not affect** the auditor's opinion. The auditor may also modify the auditor's report by using an emphasis of matter paragraph(s) to report matters other than those affecting the financial statements.

The paragraph would preferably be included after the opinion paragraph and would ordinarily refer to the fact that the auditor's opinion is not qualified in this respect.

The ISA distinguishes between **going concern matters** and other matters, saying 'the auditor should modify the auditor's report by adding a paragraph to highlight a material matter regarding a going concern problem. The auditor should consider modifying the auditor's report by adding a paragraph if there is a significant uncertainty (other than a going concern problem), the resolution of which is dependent upon future events and which may affect the financial statements.'

Key term

An **uncertainty** is a matter whose outcome depends on future actions or events not under the direct control of the entity but that may affect the financial statements.

The following is an example of an emphasis of matter paragraph.

> **Example 4. Unqualified opinion with emphasis of matter paragraph describing a fundamental uncertainty.**
>
> *Fundamental uncertainty* (insert just before opinion paragraph)
>
> In forming our opinion, we have considered the adequacy of the disclosures made in the financial statements concerning the possible outcome to litigation against B Limited, a subsidiary undertaking of the company, for an alleged breach of environmental regulations. The future settlement of this litigation could result in additional liabilities and the closure of B Limited's business, whose net assets included in the consolidated balance sheet total £... and whose profit before tax for the year is £... . Details of the circumstances relating to this fundamental uncertainty are described in note .... . Our opinion is not qualified in this respect.

An illustration of an emphasis of matter paragraph relating to going concern is set out in ISA 570 *Going concern*.

> Without qualifying our opinion we draw attention to Note X in the financial statements. The Company incurred a net loss of zzz during the year ended December 31, 20X1 and, as of that date, the Company's current liabilities exceeded its total assets by zzz. These factors, along with other matters as set forth in Note X, raise substantial doubt that the Company will be able to continue as a going concern.

This type of paragraph will usually be sufficient to meet the auditor's reporting responsibilities. In extreme cases, however, involving multiple uncertainties that are significant to the financial statements, a **disclaimer of opinion** may be required instead (see below).

The auditor may also modify the report by using an emphasis of matter paragraph for matters which do **not** affect the financial statements. This might be the case if amendment is necessary to other information in a document containing audited financial statements and the entity refuses to make the amendment. An emphasis of matter paragraph could also be used for **additional statutory reporting responsibilities**.

2.3 Matters that do affect the auditor's opinion

An auditor may not be able to express an unqualified opinion when either of the following circumstances exist and, in the auditor's judgement, the effect of the matter is or may be **material** to the financial statements:

(a)   There is a **limitation on the scope** of the auditor's work.

(b)   There is a **disagreement** with management regarding the acceptability of the accounting policies selected, the method of their application or the adequacy of financial statement disclosures.

There are different types and degrees of modified opinion.

- A limitation on scope may lead to a **qualified opinion** or a **disclaimer of opinion**.
- A disagreement may lead to a **qualified opinion** or an **adverse opinion**.

The ISA describes these different modified opinions and the circumstances leading to them as follows. 'A **qualified opinion** should be expressed when the auditor concludes that an unqualified opinion cannot be expressed but that the effect of any disagreement with management, or limitation on scope is not so material and pervasive as to require an adverse opinion or a disclaimer of opinion. A qualified opinion should be expressed as being 'except for the effects of the matter to which the qualification relates.'

A **disclaimer of opinion** should be expressed when the possible effect of a limitation on scope is so material and pervasive that the auditor has not been able to obtain sufficient appropriate audit evidence and accordingly is unable to express an opinion on the financial statements.

An **adverse opinion** should be expressed when the effect of a disagreement is so material and pervasive to the financial statements that the auditor concludes that a qualification of the report is not adequate to disclose the misleading or incomplete nature of the financial statements.'

The concept of materiality was discussed in Chapter 7 and you can now see its fundamental importance in auditing. ISA 700 says 'whenever the auditor expresses an opinion that is other than unqualified, a clear description of all the substantive reasons should be included in the report and, unless impracticable, a quantification of the possible effect(s) on the financial statements'.

This would usually be set out in a **separate paragraph** preceding the opinion or disclaimer of opinion and may include a reference to a more extensive discussion (if any) in a note to the financial statements.

2.3.1 Limitation on scope

There are two circumstances identified by the standard where there might be a limitation on scope.

Firstly, a limitation on the scope of the auditor's work may sometimes be **imposed by the entity** (for example, when the terms of the engagement specify that the auditor will not carry out an audit procedure that the auditor believes is necessary).

However, when the limitation in the terms of a proposed engagement is such that the auditor believes the need to express a disclaimer of opinion exists, the auditor would usually not accept such a limited audit engagement, unless required by statute. Also, a statutory auditor would not accept such an audit engagement when the limitation infringes on the auditor's statutory duties.

Secondly, a scope limitation may be **imposed by circumstances** (for example, when the timing of the auditor's appointment is such that the auditor is unable to observe the counting of physical inventories). It may also arise when, in the opinion of the auditor, the entity's accounting records are inadequate or when the auditor is unable to carry out an audit procedure believed to be desirable. In these circumstances, the auditor would attempt to carry out reasonable alternative procedures to obtain sufficient appropriate audit evidence to support an unqualified opinion.

'Where there is a limitation on the scope of the auditor's work that requires expression of a qualified opinion or a disclaimer of opinion, the auditor's report should describe the limitation and indicate the possible adjustments to the financial statements that might have been determined to be necessary had the limitation not existed.'

The following examples are reports given under a limitation of scope.

Example 8. Qualified opinion: limitation on the auditors' work

(Basis of opinion: extract)

.... or error. However, the evidence available to us was limited because £... of the company's recorded turnover comprises cash sales, over which there was no system of control on which we could rely for the purposes of our audit. There were no other satisfactory audit procedures that we could adopt to confirm that cash sales were properly recorded.

In forming our opinion we also evaluated the overall adequacy of the presentation of information in the financial statements.

Qualified opinion arising from limitation in audit scope

Except for any adjustments that might have been found to be necessary had we been able to obtain sufficient evidence concerning cash sales, in our opinion the financial statements give a true and fair view of the state of the company's affairs as at 31 December 20.. and of its profit (loss) for the year then ended and have been properly prepared in accordance with the Companies Act 1985.

In respect alone of the limitation on our work relating to cash sales:

(a)   we have not obtained all the information and explanations that we considered necessary for the purpose of our audit; and

(b)   we were unable to determine whether proper accounting records had been maintained.

Example 9. Disclaimer of opinion

(Basis of opinion: extract)

.... or error. However, the evidence available to us was limited because we were appointed auditors on (date) and in consequence we were unable to carry out auditing procedures necessary to obtain adequate assurance regarding the quantities and condition of stock and work in progress, appearing in the balance sheet at £... . Any adjustment to this figure would have a consequential significant effect on the profit for the year.

In forming our opinion we also evaluated the overall adequacy of the presentation of information in the financial statements.

Opinion: disclaimer on view given by financial statements

Because of the possible effect of the limitation in evidence available to us, we are unable to form an opinion as to whether the financial statements give a true and fair view of the state of the company's affairs as at 31 December 20.. or of its profit (loss) for the year then ended. In all other respects, in our opinion the financial statements have been properly prepared in accordance with the Companies Act 1985.

In respect of the limitation on our work relating to stock and work-in-progress:

(a)   we have not obtained all the information and explanations that we considered necessary for the purpose of our audit; and

(b)   we were unable to determine whether proper accounting records had been maintained.

2.3.2 Disagreement with management

The auditor may disagree with management about matters such as the acceptability of accounting policies selected, the method of their application, or the adequacy of disclosures in the financial statements. The ISA says 'if such disagreements are material to the financial statements, the auditor should express a qualified or an adverse opinion'.

Look through the following examples.

Example 7. Qualified opinion: disagreement

Qualified opinion arising from disagreement about accounting treatment

Included in the debtors shown on the balance sheet is an amount of £Y due from a company which has ceased trading. XYZ plc has no security for this debt. In our opinion the company is unlikely to receive any payment and full provision of £Y should have been made, reducing profit before tax and net assets by that amount.

Except for the absence of this provision, in our opinion the financial statements give a true and fair view of the state of the company's affairs as at 31 December 20.. and of its profit (loss) for the year then ended and have been properly prepared in accordance with the Companies Act 1985.

Example 10. Adverse opinion

Adverse opinion

As more fully explained in note ... no provision has been made for losses expected to arise on certain long-term contracts currently in progress, as the directors consider that such losses should be off-set against amounts recoverable on other long-term contracts. In our opinion, provision should be made for foreseeable losses on individual contracts as required by Statement of Standard Accounting Practice 9. If losses had been so recognised the effect would have been to reduce the profit before and after tax for the year and the contract work in progress at 31 December 20.. by £.. .

In view of the effect of the failure to provide for the losses referred to above, in our opinion the financial statements do not give a true and fair view of the state of the company's affairs as at 31 December 20.. and of its profit (loss) for the year then ended. In all other respects, in our opinion the financial statements have been properly prepared in accordance with the Companies Act 1985.

Exam focus point

Exam questions on audit reports are often about possible qualifications in specific situations.

 Question   **Modified reports**

During the course of your audit of the fixed assets of Eastern Engineering plc at 31 March 20X4, two problems have arisen.

(a)   The calculations of the cost of direct labour incurred on assets in course of construction by the company's employees have been accidentally destroyed for the early part of the year. The direct labour cost involved is £10,000.

(b)   The company has upwardly revalued a previously unrevalued asset by £25,000 The revaluation has been credited in full to the profit and loss account as exceptional income.

(c)   Other relevant financial information is as follows.

	£
Profit before tax	100,000
Fixed asset additions	133,000
Assets constructed by company	34,000
Fixed asset at net book value	666,667

Required

(a) List the general forms of qualification available to auditors in drafting their report and state the circumstances in which each is appropriate.

(b) State whether you feel that a qualified audit report would be necessary for each of the two circumstances outlined above, giving reasons in each case.

(c) On the assumption that you decide that a qualified audit report is necessary with respect to the treatment of the revaluation, draft the section of the report describing the matter (the whole report is not required).

(d) Outline the auditors' general responsibility with regard to the statement in the directors' report concerning the valuation of land and buildings.

Answer

(a) ISA 700 *Auditors' report on financial statements* suggests that the auditors may need to qualify their audit opinion under one of two main circumstances:

(i) Limitation in scope of the auditors' examination; and

(ii) Disagreement with the treatment or disclosure of a matter in the financial statements (including inherent uncertainties).

For both circumstances there can be two 'levels' of qualified opinion:

(i) *Material but not pervasive,* where the circumstances prompting the uncertainty or disagreement is material but confined to one particular aspect of the financial statements, so that it does not affect their overall value to any potential user;

(ii) The more serious qualification where the extent of the uncertainty or disagreement is such that it will be *pervasive* to the overall view shown by the financial statements, ie the financial statements are or could be misleading.

The general form of qualification appropriate to each potential situation may be seen by the following table.

Circumstance	Material but not pervasive	Pervasive
Limitation of scope	Except for ... might	Disclaimer of opinion
Disagreement	Except for ...	Adverse opinion

(b) Whether a qualification of the audit opinion would be required in relation to either of the two circumstances described in the question would depend on whether or not the auditors considered either of them to be material. An item is likely to be considered as material in the context of a company's financial statements if its omission, misstatement or non-disclosure would prevent a proper understanding of those statements on the part of a potential user. Whilst for some audit purposes materiality will be considered in absolute terms, more often than not it will be considered as a relative term.

(i)   *Loss of records relating to direct labour costs for assets in the course of construction*

The loss of records supporting one of the asset figures in the balance sheet would cause a limitation in scope of the auditors' work. The £10,000, which is the value covered by the lost records, represents 29.4% of the expenditure incurred during the year on assets in course of construction but only 6% of total additions to fixed assets during the year and 1.5% of the year end net book value for fixed assets. The total amount of £10,000 represents 10% of pre-tax profit but, as in relation to asset values, the real consideration by the auditors should be the materiality of any over- or under-statement of assets resulting from error in arriving at the £10,000 rather than the total figure itself.

Provided there are no suspicious circumstances surrounding the loss of these records and the total figure for additions to assets in the course of construction seems reasonable in the light of other audit evidence obtained, then it is unlikely that this matter would be seen as sufficiently material to merit any qualification of the audit opinion. If other records have been lost as well, however, it may be necessary for the auditors to comment on the directors' failure to maintain proper books and records.

(ii)   *Upwards revaluation credited in total to profit and loss account*

The situation here is one of disagreement, since best accounting practice, as laid down by FRS 15, requires that revaluations should be credited to the statement of recognised gains and losses.

This departure from FRS 15 does not seem to be justifiable and would be material to the reported pre-tax profits for the year, representing as it does 22.5% of that figure.

Whilst this overstatement of profit (and corresponding understatement of undistributable reserves) would be material to the financial statements, it is not likely to be seen as pervasive and therefore an 'except for' qualified opinion would be appropriate.

(c)   *Qualified audit report extract*

'As explained in note ... a revaluation of fixed assets of £25,000 has been credited in full to profits instead of being recognised in the statement of total recognised gains and losses as required by FRS 15; the effect of so doing has been to increase profits before and after tax for the year by £25,000.

Except for ...'

(d)   The auditors' general responsibility with regard to the statement in the directors' report concerning the valuation of land and buildings is to satisfy themselves that this is consistent with the treatment and disclosure of this item in the audited financial statements. If the auditors are not satisfied that the directors' report is consistent with the financial statements they will state that it is not so in their opinion.

3 The audit report as a means of communication

FAST FORWARD

The audit report can convey a great deal of information to the reader of financial statements.

3.1 Implied information

Unqualified audit reports may not appear to give a great deal of information. The report says a lot, however, by implication. Remember that the auditors report *by exception*, so an unqualified report tells the user that:

- **Proper accounting** records have been **kept**.
- The **accounts agree** with the **records.**
- The **auditors** have **received** all **necessary information**.
- All **directors' transactions** have been **disclosed**.

The real problem here is that, unfortunately, most users do not know that this is what an unqualified audit report tells them. This issue is also confused by the fact that most users do no understand the responsibilities of either the auditors or the directors in relation to the financial statements.

3.2 Expectations gap

This difference between the actual and the public perception is part of what is called the 'expectations gap', defined as the difference between the apparent public perceptions of the responsibilities of auditors on the one hand (and hence the assurance that their involvement provides) and the legal and professional reality on the other. The question remains: how can we make the **meaning** of an unqualified audit report clear to the user?

The above definition of the expectations gap is not definitive and it is not a 'static phenomenon'. However, we can highlight some specific issues.

(a) **Misunderstandings of the nature of audited financial statements**, for example that:

- The balance sheet provides a fair valuation of the reporting entity.

- The amounts in the financial statements are stated precisely.

- The audited financial statements will guarantee that the entity concerned will continue to exist.

(b) **Misunderstanding as to the type and extent of work undertaken by auditors**.

(c) **Misunderstanding about the level of assurance provided by auditors**, for example that:

- An unqualified auditors' report means that no frauds have occurred in the period.

- The auditors provide absolute assurance that the figures in the financial statements are correct (ignoring the concept of materiality and the problems of estimation).

Different countries have tackled this problem in different ways. The role of auditors has been included in the debate on corporate governance in many Western countries, leading to further rules which are nevertheless voluntary, not mandatory.

Chapter Roundup

- The auditor is required to produce an audit report containing a number of consistent elements so that users know the audit has been conducted according to recognised standards.

- An unqualified opinion may be expressed only when the auditor is able to conclude that the financial statements give a true and fair view in accordance with **the identified financial reporting framework.**

- The auditor's report may only state that the audit has been conducted in accordance with international standards on auditing when the auditor has complied fully with ISAs.

- Modified audit reports arise when auditors do not believe that they can state without reservation that the accounts give a true and fair view.

- The audit report can convey a great deal of information to the reader of financial statements.

Quick Quiz

1   Complete the standard opinion paragraph.

In our opinion the .... give a ....
.... of (or .... , in all ....
respects) the financial position of the company as of December 31 20XX, and of the .... of its
operations and its cash flows for the year then ended in accordance with [FRS or relevant
....] and comply with [relevant .... or
.......................].

2   The statement of directors' responsibilities is always included in the auditors' report.

True   ☐

False   ☐

3   Complete the diagram by filling in the type of report that would be issued in each situation.

FORMING AN OPINION ON FINANCIAL STATEMENTS

4   Draw a matrix showing the different qualified opinions.

5   Give three examples of misunderstandings which contribute to the expectations gap.

1   ....

2   ....

3   ....

Answers to Quick Quiz

1   financial statements, true and fair view, present fairly, material, results, national standards, statute, law.

2   False

3

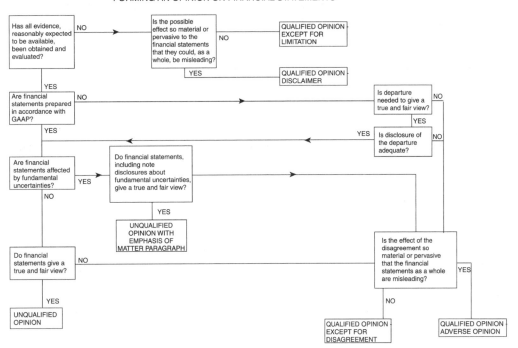

FORMING AN OPINION ON FINANCIAL STATEMENTS

4   QUALIFICATION MATRIX

Nature of circumstances	Material but not pervasive	Pervasive
Disagreement	Except for .. might	Disclaimer of opinion
Limitation in scope	Except for ...	Adverse opinion

Except for . . . might	Auditors disclaim an opinion on a particular aspect of the accounts which is not considered fundamental.
Disclaimer of opinion	Auditors state they are unable to form an opinion on truth and fairness.
Except for	Auditors express an adverse opinion on a particular aspect of the accounts which is not considered fundamental.
Adverse opinion	Auditors state the accounts do not give a true and fair view.

5   1   The nature of the financial statements
    2   The type of extent of work undertaken by auditors
    3   The level of assurance given by auditors

Now try the question below from the Exam Question Bank

Number	Level	Marks	Time
Q19	Examination	20	36 mins

Private reporting

20

Topic list	Syllabus reference
1 External review reports	7
2 Internal audit reports	7
3 Reporting control weakness	7
4 Communication of audit matters with those charged with governance	7

Introduction

In Chapter 19 we looked at the formal statutory audit report to members. In this chapter we will look at the other reports arising from audits and reviews.

We shall look at the guidance, found in ISRE 2400, *Engagements to Review Financial Statements*.

Auditors, both internal and external, also **report to management** about issues arising from audit work undertaken. **External auditors** report on controls and systems issues, and matters connected with accounting policies as a **by-product** of their audit and we will look at the form these reports take in Section 3.

Internal auditors report on the basis of **pre-planned work** with a **variety of objectives.** The work may be **'risk-based'** assessing whether systems an controls are in line with the objectives of the entity, or '**performance-enhancing**' where recommendations might be made in a wider risk context. We discussed these types of audits in Chapter 3. Here, in Section 2, we will look at the reporting process.

Lastly, **external auditors** are **required** by auditing standards to report to **those charged with governance**. We shall investigate what ISA 260 requires in this regard in Section 4.

Study guide

26 – Reporting I

- Identify and report systems weaknesses and their potential effects and make appropriate recommendations to management (eg accounting procedures and financial controls)

27 – Reporting II

Describe, illustrate and analyse the format and content of:

- Internal review reports and other reports dealing with recommendations for the enhancement of business performance

Exam guide

You are unlikely to be asked to draft a report, but might have to outline what points should be included in a report given a particular scenario, or discuss the level of assurance given in such a report, as was the case in June 2005, when four marks were available for discussing negative assurance.

1 External review reports   12/01, 6/05

FAST FORWARD

Assurance on review assignments is given in the form of negative assurance.

1.1 Negative assurance

The concept of an **external review** was introduced in Chapter 1. It is an exercise, similar to an audit, which is designed to give a reduced degree of assurance concerning the proper preparation of a set of financial statements.

Guidance is given in ISRE 2400, *Engagements to Review Financial Statements*. Remember that, as discussed in Chapter 1, negative assurance is given on review assignments. The ISRE says 'the review report should contain a clear written expression of **negative assurance.** The auditor should review and assess the conclusion drawn from the evidence obtained as the basis for the expression of negative assurance.

Based on the work performed, the auditor should assess whether any information obtained during the review indicates that the financial statements do not give a true and fair view (or 'are not presented fairly, in all material respects,') in accordance with the identified financial reporting framework.'

1.2 No matters have come to the attention of the auditor

In this case, the auditor should give a clear expression of negative assurance in his report. An example of an unqualified review report is given in the appendix to the ISRE, and it is reproduced here.

PROFESSIONAL EDUCATION

Form of Unqualified Review Report

REVIEW REPORT TO...

We have reviewed the accompanying balance sheet of ABC Company at December 31, 20XX, and the related statements of income and cash flows for the year then ended. These financial statements are the responsibility of the Company's management. Our responsibility is to issue a report on these financial statements based on our review.

We conducted our review in accordance with the International Standard on Auditing (or refer to relevant national standards or practices) applicable to review engagements. This Standard requires that we plan and perform the review to obtain moderate assurance as to whether the financial statements are free of material misstatement. A review is limited primarily to inquiries of company personnel and analytical procedures applied to financial data and thus provides less assurance than an audit. We have not performed an audit and, accordingly, we do not express an audit opinion.

Based on our review, nothing has come to our attention that causes us to believe that the accompanying financial statements do not give a true and fair view (or 'are not presented fairly, in all material respects,') in accordance with International Accounting Standards.

Date   AUDITOR

Address

1.3 Matters have come to the attention of the auditor

If matters have come to the attention of the auditor, he should **describe those matters**. The matters may have the following effects.

Impact	Effect on report
Material	Express a **qualified** opinion of negative assurance
Pervasive	Express an **adverse** opinion that the financial statements do not give a true and fair view

The auditor may feel there has been a limitation in the scope of the work he intended to carry out for the review. If so, he should **describe the limitation.** The limitation may have the following effects.

Impact	Effect on report
Material to one area	Express a **qualified** opinion of negative assurance due to amendments which might required if the limitation did not exist
Pervasive	Do not provide any assurance

2 Internal audit reports   6/03

FAST FORWARD

The internal auditors' report may take any form as there are no formal reporting requirements for internal review reports.

2.1 Reporting on internal review assignment

Internal audit make reports to directors and management as a result of work performed. These reports are internal to the business and are unlikely to be shared with third parties other than the external auditors.

We looked in detail at the types of assignment internal audit will carry out in Chapter 4. These may be summarised as '**risk-based**', where the internal auditors consider internal and external risks and discuss company operations and systems in place in respect of them or **'performance enhancement'** where internal audit consider risk and strategy on a higher level.

For the most part, as seen in Chapter 4, work is likely to be **risk-based**. Regardless of the nature of the assignment, however, all internal audits are likely to result in a formal report.

There are **no formal requirements** for such reports as there are for the statutory audit. The statutory audit report is a highly stylised document which is substantially the same for any audit. A report from the internal auditors in relation to an assignment can take essentially any form. However, some points should be borne in mind.

There is a generally accepted format for reports in business, which is laid out below. This format makes reports useful to readers as it highlights the conclusions drawn and gives easy reference to the user.

Standard report format

TERMS OF REFERENCE

EXECUTIVE SUMMARY – summarising conclusions drawn from assignment

BODY OF THE REPORT

APPENDICES FOR ANY ADDITIONAL INFORMATION

The report is likely also to be dated, designated as to whether it is draft or final and have a 'distribution list' of directors and management who should read it attached.

Some internal audit reports will be modified as responses are made to it may various members of staff. If this is the case, the report should clearly state which version it is. The distribution list may also be annotated to show who has commented on the report at any time.

2.2 Contents of the report

The **executive summary** of an internal audit report should give the following information.

- Background to the assignment
- Objectives of the assignment
- Major outcomes of the work
- Key risks identified
- Key action points
- Summary of the work left to do

The **main body** of the report will contain the detail; for example the audit tests carried out and their findings, full lists of action points, including details of who has responsibility for carrying them out, the future time-scale and costs.

3 Reporting control weakness   6/03

FAST FORWARD Reports to management can be sent by external auditors after both the interim and final audits.

One of the matters which the external auditors is required to report on by ISA 260 is the area of weaknesses in control systems. Many external auditors produce a report to management as a by-product of an external audit, listing any weaknesses they have found in systems and making recommendations for improvements.

3.1 Communications with management   Pilot paper, 12/01

External auditors should report any weaknesses discovered in the system of internal control to the management of the company. This report usually takes the form of a **letter**, but other types of report are acceptable.

Several ISAs refer to the auditors' relationship with management. Some aspects of this relationship are determined by legal and professional requirements, some by the auditors' own internal procedures and practices.

Communications between auditors and management are important throughout the audit, but may be particularly crucial in the closing stages.

3.1.1 During the audit

During the audit, the auditors will wish to discuss with management various matters including the following.

- An **understanding of the business**

- The **audit plan**

- The **effect of new legislation** or professional standards on the audit

- **Information necessary** for audit risk assessments

- **Explanations, evidence and representations** from management or from a lower level in the organisation

- Any **observations and suggestions** arising from the audit on such matters as operational or administrative efficiencies, business strategies

- **Unaudited information management** is intending to publish with the audited accounts which the auditors consider is inconsistent or appears to be misleading

- **Details of inefficiencies** or delays in the agreed timetable for preparation of the accounts or of workings schedules which delayed the completion of the audit

- Any **significant differences** between the accounts and any management accounts or budgets

- Any **results of the auditors' analytical procedures** of which management may not be aware and may be of benefit to them.

Important points for the auditors to bear in mind are as follows.

(a)   Such discussions are normally conducted during **audit visits** to the client, but may take place at other times.

(b)   When discussions are held for the purpose of obtaining audit evidence, the auditors need to **identify** the **most appropriate person** from whom to obtain audit evidence.

(c)   All **important discussions** with management should be **documented** in the auditors' working papers. Such documentation would include **explanations** and **representations** regarding material transactions.

3.1.2 At the end of the audit

At the end of the audit the auditors will need to discuss with management matters such as the following.

- Any **practical difficulties** encountered in performing the audit

- Any **disagreements** with management relating to the financial statements

375

- **Significant audit adjustments**, whether or not reflected in the financial statements

- **Significant concerns** or problems relating to accounting policies and the disclosure of items in the financial statements that might lead to a modification of the audit report

- Any **irregularities** or suspected non-compliance with laws and regulations which came to the attention of the auditors

- **Significant risks** or exposures faced by the entity such as matters that have the potential to jeopardise the ability of the entity to continue as a going concern

- **Recommendations** (eg regarding internal control matters: see below) that the auditors wish to make as a result of the audit

The auditors should bear the following points in mind.

- The auditors should communicate such matters to the **appropriate level** of management.

- The **communication** may be **oral or written**. If the communication is oral, the auditors document communication in the working papers.

- A **specific meeting** will usually **take place** at the **end of the audit** with the board of directors, audit committee or other senior management.

3.2 Communications on internal control

FAST FORWARD

The primary purpose of the report to management is to inform management of weaknesses in the system of internal controls but the letter can also be used for other purposes.

Recommendations regarding internal control are a by-product of the financial statement audit, not a primary objective, but nonetheless are frequently of great value to a client. The auditors should make management aware, on a timely basis, of material weaknesses in the design or operation of the accounting and internal control systems which have come to the auditors' attention.

When auditors prepare a written communication on internal control matters, the following points are suggested by the statement.

(a)   It should not **include language** that **conflicts** with the **opinion** expressed in the audit report.

(b)   It should state that the **accounting and internal control** system were **considered only** to the **extent necessary** to **determine** the **auditing procedures** to report on the financial statements and not to determine the adequacy of internal control for management purposes or to provide assurances on the accounting and internal control systems.

(c)   It will state that it **discusses only weaknesses** in internal control which have **come to the auditors' attention** as a result of the **audit** and that other weaknesses in internal control may exist.

(d)   It should also include a statement that the **communication is provided for use only** by **management** (or another specific named party).

After the above items and the auditors' suggestions for corrective action are communicated to management, the auditors will usually ascertain the actions taken, including the reasons for those suggestions rejected. The auditors may encourage management to respond to the auditors' comments in which case any response can be included in the report.

The significance of findings relating to the accounting and internal control systems may change with the passage of time. Suggestions from previous years' audits which have not been adopted, if any, should normally be repeated or referred to.

Communication with management by the auditors regarding internal control, or any other matter, does not remove the need for the auditors to consider any effect on the financial statement or the audit nor is it an adequate substitute for an emphasis of matter or qualification.

3.2.1 Specimen letter on internal control

This is an example of a letter on internal controls which demonstrates how the principles described in the previous paragraphs might be put into practice.

Exam focus point

You may be asked to draft paragraphs for a letter on internal controls in the exam.

AB & Co
Certified Accountants
29 High Street

The Board of Directors,
Manufacturing Ltd,
15 South Street

1 April 20X8

Members of the board,

Financial statements for the year ended 31 May 20X8

In accordance with our normal practice we set out in this letter certain matters which arose as a result of our review of the accounting systems and procedures operated by your company during our recent interim audit.

We would point out that the matters dealt with in this letter came to our notice during the conduct of our normal audit procedures which are designed primarily for the purpose of expressing our opinion on the financial statements of your company. In consequence our work did not encompass a detailed review of all aspects of the system and cannot be relied on necessarily to disclose defalcations or other irregularities or to include all possible improvements in internal control.

1   *Purchases: ordering procedures*

Present system

During the course of our work we discovered that it was the practice of the stores to order certain goods from X Co orally without preparing either a purchase requisition or purchase order.

Implication

There is therefore the possibility of liabilities being set up for unauthorised items and at a non-competitive price.

Recommendation

We recommend that the buying department should be responsible for such orders and, if they are placed orally, an official order should be raised as confirmation.

2   *Purchase ledger reconciliation*

Present system

Although your procedures require that the purchase ledger is reconciled against the control account on the nominal ledger at the end of every month, this was not done in December or January.

Implication

The balance on the purchase ledger was short by some £2,120 of the nominal ledger control account at 31 January 20X8 for which no explanation could be offered. This implies a serious breakdown in the purchase invoice and/or cash payment batching and posting procedures.

Recommendation

It is important in future that this reconciliation is performed regularly by a responsible official independent of the day to day purchase ledger, cashier and nominal ledger functions.

3   *Sales ledger: credit control*

Present system

As at 28 February 20X8 trade accounts receivable accounted for approximately 12 weeks' sales, although your standard credit terms are cash within 30 days of statement, equivalent to an average of about 40 days (6 weeks) of sales.

Implication

This has resulted in increased overdraft usage and difficulty in settling some key suppliers accounts on time.

Recommendation

We recommend that a more structured system of debt collection be considered using standard letters and that statements should be sent out a week earlier if possible.

4   Preparation of payroll and maintenance of personnel records

Present system

Under your present system, just two members of staff are entirely and equally responsible for the maintenance of personnel records and preparation of the payroll. Furthermore, the only independent check of any nature on the payroll is that the chief accountant confirms that the amount of the wages cheque presented to him for signature agrees with the total of the net wages column in the payroll. This latter check does not involve any consideration of the reasonableness of the amount of the total net wages cheque or the monies being shown as due to individual employees.

Implications

It is a serious weakness of your present system, that so much responsibility is vested in the hands of just two people. This situation is made worse by the fact that there is no clearly defined division of duties as between the two of them. In our opinion, it would be far too easy for fraud to take place in this area (eg by inserting the names of 'dummy workmen' into the personnel records and hence on to the payroll) and/or for clerical errors to go undetected.

Recommendations

(i)   Some person other than the two wages clerks be made responsible for maintaining the personnel records and for periodically (but on a surprise basis) checking them against the details on the payroll.

(ii)   The two wages clerks be allocated specific duties in relation to the preparation of the payroll, with each clerk independently reviewing the work of the other.

(iii)   When the payroll is presented in support of the cheque for signature to the chief accountant, that he should be responsible for assessing the reasonableness of the overall charge for wages that week.

Our comments have been discussed with your finance director and the chief accountant and these matters will be considered by us again during future audits. We look forward to receiving your comments on the points made. Should you require any further information or explanations do not hesitate to contact us.

This letter has been produced for the sole use of your company. It must not be disclosed to a third party, or quoted or referred to, without our written consent. No responsibility is assumed by us to any other person.

We should like to take this opportunity of thanking your staff for their co-operation and assistance during the course of our audit.

Yours faithfully

ABC & Co

Question

Reporting control weakness

List the most important reasons for the auditors to give a letter on internal controls to a client.

Answer

The principal purposes of a letter on internal controls are as follows.

(a)   To enable the auditors to highlight weaknesses in the accounting records, systems and controls which they have identified during the course of their audit, and which may lead to material errors.

(b)   To provide management with constructive advice on various aspects of the business which the auditors may have identified during the course of the audit.

(c)   To highlight matters that may have an effect on future audits.

(d)   To comply with specific requirements as laid down by, for example, government departments.

4 Communication of audit matters with those charged with governance

FAST FORWARD

The auditor should also remember to communicate with those charged with governance.

ISA (UK and Ireland) 260 *Communications of audit matters with those charged with governance* applies here. It says 'the auditor should communicate audit matters of governance interest arising from the audit of financial statements with those charged with governance of an entity'.

Key term

Governance is the term used to describe the role of persons entrusted with the supervision, control and direction of the entity. Those charged with governance ordinarily are accountable for ensuring that the entity achieves its objectives, financial reporting and reporting to interested parties. Those charged with governance include management only when it performs such functions.

The scope of the ISA is limited to matters that come to the auditors' attention as a result of the audit; the auditors are not required to design procedures to identify matters of governance interest. It says 'the auditor should determine the relevant persons who are charged with governance and with whom audit matters of governance interest are communicated'.

The auditors may communicate with the whole board, the supervisory board or the audit committee depending on the governance structure of the organisation. The auditor should ensure that those charged with governance are provided with a copy of the audit engagement letter on a timely basis. To avoid misunderstandings, the engagement letter should explain that auditors will only **communicate matters** that come to their attention as a **result** of the **performance** of the audit. It should state that the auditors are **not required** to **design procedures** for the purpose of identifying matters of governance interest.

The letter may also:

- **Describe** the **form** which any **communications** on governance matters will take
- **Identify** the **relevant persons** with whom such communications will be made
- **Identify** any **specific matters** of **governance** interest which it has agreed are to be communicated

4.1 Communicate what?

'The auditor should consider audit matters of governance interest that arise from the audit of the financial statements and communicate them with those charged with governance.' Matters would include:

- Relationships that may bear on the firm's independence and the integrity and objectivity of the audit engagement partner and audit staff
- The **general approach** or overall scope of the audit, including limitations or additional requirements
- Selection of, or changes in, **significant accounting policies**
- The potential effect on the financial statements of any **significant risks** and **exposures**, for example pending litigation, that are required to be disclosed in the accounts
- Significant **audit adjustments**
- **Material uncertainties** affecting the organisation's ability to continue as a going concern
- **Significant disagreements** with management
- **Expected modifications** to the audit report
- Other **significant matters** such as material weaknesses in internal control, questions regarding management integrity, and fraud involving management
- Other **matters** mentioned in **terms** of **engagement**

In addition, relevant matters include matters of independence and objectivity and planning matters.

Where the audited company is a listed company, auditors should:

(a)   Disclose in writing to the audit committee, and discuss as appropriate:

- All relationships between the audit firm and its related entities and the client entity and its related entities that may reasonable be thought to bear on the firm's independence and the objectivity of the audit engagement partner and the audit staff and
- The related safeguards that are in place and

(b)   Where this is the case, confirm in writing to the audit committee that, in their professional judgement, the firm is independent within the meaning of the regulatory and professional requirements and the objectivity of the audit engagement partner and audit staff is not impaired.

The ISA also requires auditors to outline the scope of the audit work and reports. Such matters might include materiality, material misstatements, approach to internal controls, extent to which external auditors intend to rely on internal auditors and any work to be undertaken by other auditors.

'The auditors should inform those charged with governance of those uncorrected misstatements aggregated by the auditor during the audit that we determined by management to be immaterial, both individually and in the aggregate, to the financial statements taken as a whole.'

Matters may be communicated orally or in writing, but they should be recorded in the audit working papers, however discussed. Auditors should make clear that the audit is not designed to identify all relevant matters connected with governance. Reporting should take place on a timely basis.

Auditors should have regard to local laws and regulations, and local guidance on confidentiality when communicating with management.

Exam focus point

You may be asked to draft paragraphs for a communication to management in the exam. You should follow the format we have used. The pilot paper contained 6 marks on items to be included in such a report.

Chapter Roundup

- Assurance on review assignments is given in the form of negative assurance.

- The internal auditors' report may take any form as there are no formal reporting requirements for internal review reports.

- Reports to management can be sent by external auditors after both the interim and final audits.

- The primary purpose of the report to management is to inform management of weaknesses in the system of internal controls but the letter can also be used for other purposes.

- The auditor should also remember to communicate with those charged with governance.

Quick Quiz

1   Complete the definition.

.... is moderate assurance given by auditors when no matters have come to their attention to indicate .... do not give a .... and .... view.

2   List the main contents of an internal review report.

1   ....

2   ....

3   ....

3   There are formal reporting requirements for internal review reports.

True   ☐

False   ☐

4   List six matters the auditors might wish to raise with management at the end of the audit.

1   ....
2   ....
3   ....
4   ....
5   ....
6   ....

Answers to Quick Quiz

1   Negative assurance, financial statements, true, fair

2   • Executive summary (background, major outcomes, key risks, key action points, summary of work to do)

     • Main body (full details of work carried out and still required, also responsibilities, time scale and cost)

     • Appendices

3   False

4   • Any **practical difficulties** encountered in performing the audit

     • Any **disagreements** with management relating to the financial statements

     • **Significant audit adjustments**, whether or not reflected in the financial statements

     • **Significant concerns** or problems relating to accounting policies and the disclosure of items in the financial statements that might lead to a modification of the audit report

     • Any **irregularities** or suspected non-compliance with laws and regulations which came to the attention of the auditors

     • **Significant risks** or exposures faced by the entity such as matters that have the potential to jeopardise the ability of the entity to continue as a going concern

     • **Recommendations** that the auditors wish to make as a result of the audit

Now try the question below from the Exam Question Bank

Number	Level	Marks	Time
Q20	Examination	20	36 mins

BPP
PROFESSIONAL EDUCATION

Part F

Not for profit
organisations

Not for profit organisations

Topic list	Syllabus reference
1 Objectives	4
2 Planning	4
3 Evidence	6
4 Reporting	7
5 Public sector	6

Introduction

This chapter looks at the audit of not for profit organisations. Remember, that such entities may or may not be required to have a **statutory audit** under legislation. They may choose to have a **non statutory audit** under the terms of a charitable deed, or as part of good practice.

Once thing an auditor should do when conducting a non statutory audit is confirm that a statutory opinion is not required.

The points made in this chapter about the issues inherent in these entities are **relevant for any kind of assurance work in not for profit organisations**, that is, internal auditors and external auditors undertaking audits or reviews. These entities will have inherent features, the most obvious being the difference in **objective** of the entity, which will **affect the way the work is carried out**.

Study guide

28 – Not for profit organisations

- Apply audit and review techniques to small not for profit organisations
- Explain how the audit review of small not for profit organisations differs from the audit and review of for-profit organisations

Exam guide

The study guide refers to questions being about **small** not for profit organisations, so it seems reasonable to expect one.

1 Objectives

FAST FORWARD

> There are various types of organisations which do not exist for the purpose of maximising shareholder wealth, which may require an audit.

In Chapter 1, we looked at some of the objectives of directors of companies, the key of which was to manage well the shareholders' investments. In a large majority of cases, 'manage the shareholders' investment' means 'create a profit', as this will create returns to the shareholders in the terms of dividends or growth in the capital value of the share.

Also in Chapter 1, we made reference to the fact that some companies and other entities who do not operate for the purpose of making profit will require an audit, either statutory or otherwise.

1.1 Not for profit organisations

Before considering what a not for profit organisation's audit will entail, it will be helpful to consider what sort of entities might exist with objectives other than to make a profit and what their objectives are, as these will impact on the way that they report and the audit that is carried out.

Question	Not for profit organisations

List as many types of not for profit organisations as you can.

The following diagram shows a number of organisations you might have come up with in your answer to the question.

You may be thinking that some of the associations above might aim to operate at a profit, and you are correct, not for profit organisations may (conversely it may seem) operate at a profit, however, this may not be their key aim.

1.2 Example

A hospital could operate at a profit by not spending all the money it receives in its budget. However, the key objective of a hospital is to provide health services to the public, not to make a profit. As its income is wholly fixed, it is more likely to focus on **cost-saving** so that it can operate within its budget.

Question	Objectives

Identify the key objectives and focus of the types of association listed above.

Answer	

Charities and friendly societies	To meet the 'raison d'etre' of the charity, that is, to carry out the charitable purpose. May involve fund-raising, receiving donations, managing invested funds, controlling costs.
Schools	To provide education. Likely to involve managing a tight budget (either from fees or government funds).
Clubs, associations, societies, unions	To further the aims of the club, provide a service to members. May include managing subscriptions paid and keeping costs of running the club down.
Housing association	Managing the related houses and providing facilities for residents. May involve rent collection and maintenance costs or even building costs of future developments.
Local councils, public services	To provide local services to a budget based on public money. Likely to be focused on value for money as they are in the public eye.

1.3 Reporting

We noted in Chapter 1 that many of these organisations are legislated for and the Acts which relate to them may specify how they are to report their results.

Many of the organisations mentioned above may be companies (often companies limited by guarantee) and so are required to prepare financial statements and have them audited under companies legislation.

Some of the entities will have statements of recommended accounting practice. In the UK, there is a charities SORP outlining what a charity's accounts should comprise. It suggests:

(a) A **statement of financial activities** (SOFA) that shows all resources made available to the charity and all expenditure incurred and reconciles all changes in its funds

(b) Where the charity is required to prepare accounts in accordance with the 1985 Companies Act, or similar legislation, or where the governing instrument so requires, a **summary income and expenditure account** (in addition to the SOFA) in certain circumstances

(c) A **balance sheet** that shows the assets, liabilities and funds of the charity. The balance sheet (or its notes, see (e) below) should also explain, in general terms, how the funds may or, because of restrictions imposed by donors, must be utilised

(d)   A **cash flow statement**, where required by accounting standards

(e)   **Notes**

1.4 Audit

Where a statutory audit is required, the auditors will be required to produce the statutory audit opinion concerning the truth and fairness of financial statements.

Where a statutory audit is not required, it is possible that the organisation might have one anyway for the benefit of interested stakeholders, such as the public or people who give to a charity.

It is also possible that such entities will have special, additional requirements of an audit. These may be required by a Regulator, or by the constitution of the organisation. For example, a charity's constitution may require an audit of whether the charity is operating in accordance with its charitable purpose.

1.5 Conclusion

An audit of a not for profit organisation may vary from a 'for profit audit' due to:

- Its objectives and the impact on operations and reporting
- The purpose an audit is required

When carrying out an audit of a not for profit organisation, it is vital that the auditor establishes:

- Whether a statutory audit is required
- If not, what the objectives of the engagement are
- What the engagement is to report on, and
- To whom the report should be addressed, and
- What form the report should take

As we have seen, there are many types of not for profit organisation and their audits could all be different depending on the purpose the audit is required and correspondingly, the objectives of the organisation. The study guide specifically focuses on small not for profit organisations, so for the rest of this chapter we shall focus on the following scenarios.

Exam focus point

> You should think around the issues raised for the audit in relation to all the following entities, and be able to apply similar facts and reasoning to any not for profit organisation which comes up in the exam. Remember, the issues relating to small companies that we have discussed throughout this Study Text may also apply to small not for profit organisations as well.

Small charity scenario

Headington Hospice Co is a small, local charity which operates a small children's hospice and two charity shops which raise money for the ongoing work of the hospice. The hospice receives grants from the health authority, sponsorship from some local businesses, receives income from the charity shop which is entirely voluntarily operated and receives donations from individuals. It employs three nurses, a part-time hospice manager and an accountant donates his time to keep the books and produce the annual accounts. As the company's turnover falls below the exemption limit, it is not required to have an audit by law, but the terms of its constitution require that an audit of the accounts is required for the benefit of the trustees that gives an opinion as to whether the financial statements give a true and fair view and to whether the charity is meeting its objects, as set out in the constitutional document.

Small association scenario

The Midvale League is a small association. It runs several local football leagues for various ages and stages. It employs a general administrator and some casual bar staff. Any player who appears in more than 30% of a team's games for the season is required to pay a subscription to the association. The subs pay for the administrator's wages, the referee's fees, team coaches' expenses and a lease on a sport's club comprising a clubhouse and changing facilities and three football pitches. The administrator also acts as groundsman. There is a bar in the clubhouse which is run for the benefit of members at a profit which covers bar staff wages and contributes to other expenses of the club. The association pays a local firm of accountants to prepare management accounts every quarter and to produce annual financial statements which it then audits for the benefit of members of the club.

2 Planning   12/03

FAST FORWARD ▶

The audit risks associated with not for profit organisations may well be different from other entities.

2.1 Small charity

When planning the audit of a charity, the auditors should particularly consider the following:

- The **scope** of the audit
- Recent **recommendations** of the **Charity Commissioners** or the other regulatory bodies
- The **acceptability of accounting policies** adopted
- **Changes in circumstances** in the sector in which the charity operates
- **Past experience** of the effectiveness of the charity's accounting system
- **Key audit areas**
- The **amount of detail included** in the financial statements on which the auditors are required to report

In the case of Headington Hospice, the scope of the audit is two-fold. The auditors are to report on the truth and fairness of the financial statement for the benefit of the trustees and also on whether the charity is meeting its objectives. The auditors should therefore establish what the objectives are, and consider how they are to identify whether the objectives are being met.

The auditors should consider whether any recommendations of the Charity Commissioners apply to Headington Hospice. It is unlikely that there have been any substantial changes in the sector in which it works.

In order to identify the key audit areas, the auditors will have to consider audit risk.

2.1.1 Audit risk

FAST FORWARD ▶

Cash may be significant in small not for profit organisations and controls are likely to be limited. Income may well be a risk area, particularly where money is donated or raised informally.

There are certain risks applicable to charities that might not necessarily be applicable to other small companies. The auditors should consider the following:

Problem	Key factors
Inherent risk	• The complexity and extent of regulation
	• The significance of donations and cash receipts
	• Difficulties of the charity in establishing ownership and timing of voluntary income where funds are raised by non-controlled bodies
	• Lack of predictable income or precisely identifiable relationship between expenditure and income
	• Uncertainty of future income
	• Restrictions imposed by the objectives and powers given by charities' governing documents
	• The importance of restricted funds
	• The extent and nature of trading activities must be compatible with the entity's charitable status
	• The complexity of tax rules (whether Income, Capital, Value Added or local rates) relating to charities
	• The sensitivity of certain key statistics, such as the proportion of resources used in administration
	• The need to maintain adequate resources for future expenditure while avoiding the build up of reserves which could appear excessive
Control risk	• The amount of time committed by trustees to the charity's affairs
	• The skills and qualifications of individual trustees
	• The frequency and regularity of trustee meetings
	• The form and content of trustee meetings
	• The independence of trustees from each other
	• The division of duties between trustees
	• The degree of involvement in, or supervision of, the charity's transactions on the part of individual trustees
Control environment	• A recognised plan of the charity's structure showing clearly the areas of responsibility and lines of authority and reporting
	• Segregation of duties
	• Supervision by trustees of activities of staff where segregation of duties is not practical
	• Competence, training and qualification of paid staff and any volunteers appropriate to the tasks they have to perform
	• Involvement of the trustees in the recruitment, appointment and supervision of senior executives
	• Access of trustees to independent professional advice where necessary
	• Budgetary controls in the form of estimates of income and expenditure for each financial year and comparison of actual results with the estimates on a regular basis
	• Communication of results of such reviews to the trustees on a regular basis

In the case of Headington Hospice, the auditor will need to devote attention to cash receipts and income, as the Hospice receives donations from the public and also receives cash income from the charity shop.

It will also be necessary to consider non current assets, to determine whether the premises the hospice and the charity shop should be included on the balance sheet of the charity. The auditor will also need to assess the nature of the grants received from the health authority to determine how they should be accounted for. These things should all be considered as part of the accounting policy review. The auditor should also be aware of issues such as depreciation during this review, as the hospice may own specialised medical equipment which makes such issues complex.

Another matter which the auditor must consider is the issue of going concern. This will include an assessment of the sponsorship deals which the charity has in place and any consideration of future sponsorship. The grant position must also be considered, as must the likelihood of future donations. The auditors should also consider matters such as personnel, for example, whether any existing arrangements with doctors' practices will continue in existence.

2.1.2 Internal controls

Small charities will generally suffer from internal control weaknesses common to small enterprises, such as **lack of segregation of duties** and use of **unqualified staff**. Shortcomings may arise from the staff's lack of training and also, if they are volunteers, from their attitude, in that they may resent formal procedures.

The auditors will have to consider particularly carefully whether they will be able to obtain adequate assurance that the accounting records do reflect all the transactions of the enterprise and bear in mind whether there are any related statutory reporting requirements.

The following sorts of internal control might be typical of a number of charities.

Cash donations	
Source	**Examples of controls**
Collecting boxes and tins	Numerical control over boxes and tins
	Satisfactory sealing of boxes and tins so that any opening prior to recording cash is apparent
	Regular collection and recording of proceeds from collecting boxes
	Dual control over counting and recording of proceeds
Postal receipts	Unopened mail kept securely
	Dual control over the opening of mail
	Immediate recording of donations on opening of mail or receipt
	Agreement of bank paying-in slips to record of receipts by an independent person

Other donations	
Source	**Examples of controls**
Deeds of covenant	Regular checks and follow-up procedures to ensure due amounts are received
	Regular checks to ensure all tax repayments have been obtained
Legacies	Comprehensive correspondence files maintained in respect of each legacy,
	Regular reports and follow-up procedures undertaken in respect of outstanding legacies
Donations in kind	In case of charity shops, separation of recording, storage and sale of stock

Other income	
Source	**Examples of controls**
Fund-raising activities	Records maintained for each fund-raising event
	Other appropriate controls maintained over receipts
	Controls maintained over expenses as for administrative expenses
Central and local government grants and loans	Regular checks that all sources of income or funds are fully utilised and appropriate claims made
	Ensuring income or funds are correctly applied

Use of resources	
Resource	**Examples of controls**
Restricted funds	Separate records maintained of relevant revenue, expenditure and assets
	Terms controlling application of fund
	Oversight of application of fund money's by independent personnel or trustees
Grants to beneficiaries	Records maintained, as appropriate, of requests for material grants received and their treatment
	Appropriate checks made on applications and applicants for grants, and that amounts paid are intra vires
	Records maintained of all grant decisions, checking that proper authority exists, that adequate documentation is presented to decision-making meetings, and that any conflicts of interest are recorded
	Control to ensure grants made are properly spent by the recipient for the specified purpose, for example requirements for returns with supporting documentation or auditors' reports concerning expenditure, or monitoring visits

For Headington Hospice, the issues relating to cash donations and grants will be particularly relevant.

2.2 Small association

The Midvale League (ML) requires an audit for the benefit of its members. This makes the audit of ML similar to any small company audit such as those which we have considered throughout this Study Text.

However, the nature of the association may give rise to some particular audit risks and control issues.

Question   **Audit risks**

Identify any audit risks arising from The Midvale League.

Answer

Inherent risks

The classification of the sport's club **lease** may be problematic. It is certainly likely to be their biggest financial commitment. The auditor will need to determine whether the terms of the lease mean that it should be included on the balance sheet as an asset, showing the corresponding liability or whether it does not so qualify. If the terms of the lease agreement imply that the lease is merely an operating lease, the auditors should consider whether this has implications for the **going concern** of the association, as if it obtains no long-term benefit from the lease, it might be faced with the situation where it has nowhere to operate in the foreseeable future, in which case, the purpose of the association is gone.

The auditors will also have to consider the role of the general administrator, who fulfils a number of roles. He is clearly a **key man** to the association, and it might find that it had difficulties if he was incapacitated, not least perhaps in affording a replacement and any sickness benefit they were required to pay by law.

It is unclear what degree of financial record keeping the administrator takes on. The audit firm are hired to produce quarterly management **accounts**. They will gain some assurance from the fact that they prepare the accounts themselves, but there is also a risk that day to day transactions are not **properly recorded**, as there appears to be no one with financial expertise 'at the coal face'. Given that the administrator will record or maintain the relevant records to be passed on to the accountancy firm, there is also an issue of **segregation of duties** here.

The auditors should also be aware of any legal issues relating to the bearing of a license for the bar, particularly perhaps the danger that the license might be jeopardised by the sale of liquor to underage drinkers. The loss of the license to serve alcohol could severely diminish the income of the club to the point where it could no longer function.

The auditors will also need to pay attention to the membership of the association from the point of view of completeness of income.

3 Evidence

Obtaining audit evidence may be problem, particularly where associations have informal arrangements and there might be limitations on the scope of the audit.

3.1 Small charity

When designing substantive procedures for charities the auditors should give special attention to the possibility of:

- **Understatement or incompleteness** of the **recording of all income** including gifts in kind, cash donations, and legacies
- **Overstatement of cash grants or expenses**
- **Misanalysis** or misuse in the application of funds
- **Misstatement** or omission of **assets** including donated properties and investments
- The existence of **restricted or uncontrollable funds** in foreign or independent branches

Completeness of income can be a particularly problematic area. Areas auditors may check:

- Loss of income through fraud
- Recognition of income from professional fund raisers
- Recognition of income from branches, associates or subsidiaries
- Income from informal fundraising groups
- Income from grants

Particular matters which might be an issue at Headington Hospice are:

- Completeness of cash income from various sources
- Accounting for the grants from the local authority

3.1.1 Overall review of financial statements

It will be necessary to ensure accounting policies used are appropriate.

The auditors must consider carefully whether the **accounting policies** adopted are **appropriate** to the activities, constitution and objectives of the charity, and are consistently applied, and whether the financial statements adequately disclose these policies and fairly present the state of affairs and the results for the accounting period.

In particular the auditors should consider the basis of disclosing income from fund-raising activities (for example net or gross), accounting for income and expenses (accruals or cash), the capitalising of expenditure on non current assets, apportioning administrative expenditure, and recognising income from donations and legacies.

Charities without significant endowments or accumulated funds will often be dependent upon future income from voluntary sources. In these circumstances auditors may question whether a going concern basis of accounting is appropriate.

3.2 Small association

In the case of the Midvale League, establishing the **number of members** might prove to be difficult. Once the number of members has been established, there should be good analytical evidence available about the income from subscriptions. It would also be sensible for the auditor to encourage the association to foster subscription by bank transfer, as this would reduce the problems associated with any subscriptions which are made by cash and would provide a record of subscriptions being made (the bank records).

The problem of the **maintenance** and **retention of relevant accounting records** for the association has already been mentioned. It is possible that the auditors might find that their audit suffers a **limitation in scope** if sufficient records have not been kept.

In the absence of the association employing qualified accountancy staff, the audit firm will also need to consider whether the association has accounted correctly for **income tax** on wages, as it is possible that significant **tax liabilities** could ensue if they have not.

3.2.1 Accounting policies

As has already been mentioned in connection with risk, the lease is likely to pose the biggest issue for the auditor in terms of accounting policies.

4 Reporting

The nature of the report will depend on statutory and entity requirements, but it should conform to ISA 700 criteria.

On not for profit audits where a statutory audit report is required, the auditors should issue the same report as we have considered in Chapter 19. They should also consider whether any additional statutory requirements fall on the audit report.

Where an association or charity is having an audit for the benefit of its members or trustees, the standard audit report may not be required or appropriate. The auditor should bear in mind the objectives of the audit and make suitable references in the audit report. However, the ISA 700 format will still be relevant. The auditor should ensure that he makes the following matters clear:

- The addressees of the report
- What the report relates to
- The scope of the engagement

- The respective responsibilities of auditors and management/trustees/directors
- The work done
- The opinion drawn

Exam focus point

The points made above are general points, the remember that not all clubs and charities will be the same. If you have a question in the exam relating to a charity, apply this general knowledge to the specifics given in the question and be **logical** when formulating your answer.

Question
Charity audit

You have recently been appointed audit of Links Famine Relief, a small registered charity which receives donations from individuals to provide food in famine areas in the world.

The charity is run by a voluntary management committee, which has monthly meetings, and it employs the following full-time staff:

(a) A director, Mr Roberts, who suggests fund raising activities and payments for relief of famine, and implements the policies adopted by the management committee; and

(b) A secretary (and bookkeeper), Mrs Beech, who deals with correspondence and keeps the accounting records.

You are planning the audit of income of the charity for the year ended 5 April 20X7 and are considering the controls which should be exercised over income.

The previous year's accounts, to 5 April 20X6 (which have been audited by another firm) show the following income.

	£	£
Gifts under non-taxing arrangements		14,745
Tax reclaimed on gifts under non-taxing arrangements		4,915
		19,660
Donations through the post		63,452
Autumn Fair		2,671
Other income		
Legacies	7,538	
Bank deposit account interest	2,774	
		10,312
		96,095

Notes

(a) Income from gifts under non-taxing arrangements is stated net. Each person who pays by deed of covenant has filled in a special tax form, which is kept by the secretary, Mrs Beech.

(b) All gifts under non-taxing arrangements are paid by banker's order – they are credited directly to the charity's bank account from the donor's bank. Donors make their payments by deed of covenant either monthly or annually.

(c) The tax reclaimed on these gifts is 1/3 of the net value of the gifts, and relates to income received during the year – as the tax is received after the year-end, an appropriate amount recoverable is included in the balance sheet. The treasurer, who is a voluntary (unpaid) member of the management committee, completes the form for reclaiming the income tax, using the special tax forms (in (a) above) and checks to the full-time secretary's records that each donor has made the full payment in the year required by the arrangement.

(d) Donations received through the post are dealt with by Mrs Beech, the full-time secretary. These donations are either cheques or cash (bank notes and coins). Mrs Beech prepares a daily list of donations received, which lists the cheques received and total cash (divided between the different denominations of bank note and coin). The total on this form is recorded in the cash book. She then prepares a paying-in slip and banks these donations daily. When there is a special fund-raising campaign, Mrs Beech receives help in dealing with these donations from voluntary members of the management committee.

(e)   The Autumn Fair takes place every year on a Saturday in October – members of the management committee and other supporters of the charity give items to sell (for example food, garden plants, clothing) – a charge is made for entrance to the fair and coffee and biscuits are available at a small charge. At the end of the fair, Mrs Beech collects the takings from each of the stalls, and she banks them the following Monday.

(f)   Legacies are received irregularly, and are usually sent direct to the director of the charity, who gives them to Mrs Beech for banking – they are stated separately on the daily bankings form (in (d) above).

(g)   Bank deposit account interest is paid gross of income tax by the bank, as the Links Famine Relief is a charity.

Required

List and briefly describe the work you would carry out on the audit of income of the charity, the controls you would expect to see in operation and the problems you may experience for the following sources of income, as detailed in the income statement above.

(a)   Gifts under non-taxing arrangements
(b)   Tax reclaimed on gifts made under non-taxing arrangements
(c)   Donations received through the post
(d)   Autumn Fair

Answer

The audit consideration in relation to the various sources of income of the Links Famine Relief charity would be as follows.

(a)   *Gifts made under non-taxing arrangements*

This type of income should not present any particular audit problem as the donations are made by banker's order direct to the charity's bank account and so it would be difficult for such income to be 'intercepted' and misappropriated.

Specific tests required would be as follows.

(i)   Check a sample of receipts from the bank statements to the cash book to ensure that the income has been properly recorded.

(ii)   Check a sample of the receipts to the special tax forms to ensure that the full amount due has been received.

Any discrepancies revealed by either of the above tests should be followed up with Mrs Beech.

(b)   *Tax reclaimed on gifts made under non-taxing arrangements*

Once again this income should not pose any particular audit problems. The auditors should check the claim form submitted to the tax authorities and ensure that the amount of the claim represents $1/3$ of the net value of the covenants recorded as having been received.

(c)   *Donations received through the post*

There is a serious problem here as the nature of this income is not predictable and also because of the lack of internal check with Mrs Beech being almost entirely responsible for the receipt of these monies, the recording of the income and the banking of the cash and cheques received. The auditors may ultimately have to express a qualified opinion relating to the uncertainty surrounding the completeness of income of this type.

Notwithstanding the above reservations, specific audit tests required would be as follows.

(i) Check the details on the daily listings of donations received to the cash book, bank statements and paying-in slips, ensuring that the details agree in all respects and that there is no evidence of any delay in the banking of this income.

(ii) Check the donations received by reference to any correspondence which may have been received with the cheques or cash.

(iii) Consider whether the level of income appears reasonable in comparison with previous years and in the light of any special appeals that the charity is known to have made during the course of the year.

(iv) Carry out, with permission of the management committee, surprise checks to vouch the completeness and accuracy of the procedures relating to this source of income.

(d) *Autumn Fair*

Once again there is a potential problem here because of the level of responsibility vested in one person, namely Mrs Beech.

Specific work required would be as follows.

(i) Attend the event to observe the proper application of laid down procedures and count the cash at the end of the day.

(ii) Check any records maintained by individual stallholders to the summary prepared by Mrs Beech.

(iii) Check the vouchers supporting any expenditure deducted from the proceeds in order to arrive at the net bankings.

(iv) Agree the summary prepared by Mrs Beech to the entry in the cash book and on the bank statement.

5 Public sector

FAST FORWARD

The public sector comprises a large number of different not for profit organisations.

The public sector in most countries comprises a great variety of organisations. They all must have their accounts audited by an independent external auditor, in order to provide external accountability to the community at large.

In the public sector there is a tendency for an external audit to cover a much wider scope than in the private sector. The scope of public sector audit includes not only auditing of financial records and auditing to check compliance with regulations but also auditing the achievement of economy, efficiency and effectiveness.

The audit is an important part of public accountability and it provides an independent check on how public funds have been raised and spent. More specifically audit is needed to ensure that:

(a) **Public funds** have been **spent on proper, authorised purposes** and **legally within statutory powers.**

(b) **Organisations install and operate controls** to limit the possibility of corrupt practice, fraud and poor administration.

(c) Arrangements are in place to secure **economy, efficiency and effectiveness** in the use of resources.

5.1 The regulatory framework

The public sector is often subject to a high degree of regulation. For most public sector audits, the scope and objectives of the audit are affected by the interests and requirements of certain third party organisations such as audit supervisory bodies and government sponsoring departments which have specific regulatory responsibilities.

The manner in which the auditors conduct their work is affected by auditing standards and other regulatory influences including:

- **Specific statutory requirements**
- Requirements of an **audit supervisory body** or sponsoring department
- **Contractual requirements** contained in terms of engagement

The nature of regulation affecting public sector bodies ranges from statutory to detailed administrative requirements.

The auditors of a public body are expected to take reasonable steps to consider compliance by the audited body with regulations relevant to its activities and operations, and to ensure that expenditure made is not *ultra vires*.

Chapter Roundup

- There are various types of organisations which do not exist for the purpose of maximising shareholder wealth, which may require an audit.

- The audit risks associated with not for profit organisations may well be different from other entities.

- Cash may be significant in small not for profit organisations and controls are likely to be limited. Income may well be a risk area, particularly where money is donated or raised informally.

- Obtaining audit evidence may be problem, particularly where associations have informal arrangements and there might be limitations on the scope of the audit.

- It will be necessary to ensure accounting policies used are appropriate.

- The nature of the report will depend on statutory and entity requirements, but it should conform to ISA 700 criteria.

- The public sector comprises a large number of different not for profit organisations.

Quick Quiz

1   Explain why income can be a problem when auditing charities.

2   Complete the table, giving two examples of controls in each area.

Cash donations	Other donations	Other income

3   All limited companies must have a statutory audit.

     True   ☐

     False   ☐

Answers to Quick Quiz

1   •   Loss of income through fraud
       •   Recognition of income from professional fund raisers
       •   Recognition of income from branches, associates or subsidiaries
       •   Income from informal fundraising groups
       •   Income from grants

2

Cash donations	Other donations	Other income
Numerical control over boxes and tins	Regular checks and follow up procedures to ensure due amounts are received	Records maintained for each fund raising event
Satisfactory sealing of boxes and tins so that any opening prior to recording cash is apparent	Regular checks to ensure all tax repayments have been obtained	Other appropriate controls maintained over receipts
Regular collection and recording of proceeds from collecting boxes	Comprehensive correspondence files maintained in respect of each legacy	Controls maintained over expenses as for administrative expenses
Dual control over counting and recording of proceeds	Regular reports and follow-up procedures undertaken in respect of outstanding legacies	Regular checks that all sources of income or funds are fully utilised and appropriate claims made
Unopened mail kept securely	In case of charity shops, separation of recording, storage and sale of stock	Ensuring income or funds are correctly applied
Dual control over the opening of mail		
Immediate recording of donations on opening of mail or receipt		
Agreement of bank paying-in slips to record of receipts by an independent person		

3   False

Now try the question below from the Exam Question Bank

Number	Level	Marks	Time
Q21	Examination	20	36 mins

The scenario and requirement of this question have been analysed in some detail in the Exam Question Bank because as well as being a question on a not for profit organisation, it is an example of a question where you are asked to identify **audit risks**, which is a key skill for the exam.

Exam question
and answer bank

Examination standard questions are indicated by mark and time allocations.

1 Princetown and Yale   15 mins

Princetown and Yale are in partnership. Previously accounts have been prepared by their bookkeeper but as their business is growing they are considering asking your firm to act as auditors to the partnership.

Required

(a)   State how a non-statutory audit could assist the partnership.

(b)   Identify the major difficulty you could potentially face in a non-statutory audit, and state how you would try to overcome it.

2 Corporate governance   36 mins

The objective of a system of corporate governance is to secure the effective, sound and efficient operation of companies. This objective transcends any legislation or voluntary code. Good corporate governance embraces not only making the company prosper but also doing business in a legal and ethical manner. A key element of corporate governance is the audit committee. The audit committee is a committee of the board of directors and is of a voluntary nature regulated by voluntary codes.

Required

(a)   Explain how an audit committee could improve the effectiveness of the external auditor's work.

(10 marks)

(b)   Discuss the problems of ensuring the 'independence' of the members of the audit committee.

(5 marks)

(c)   Discuss the view that the role of the audit committee should not be left to voluntary codes of practice but should be regulated by statute.   **(5 marks)**

(Total = 20 marks)

3 Standards   30 mins

You are required to discuss the advantages and disadvantages of accounting and auditing standards to auditors and the consequences of such standards being enforceable by statute.

4 Role of internal audit   36 mins

(a)   You are a member of the internal audit team at Golden Holdings plc, a listed company. The board of directors wants to raise the profile of the internal audit department in the company. They have asked the internal audit department to give a series of seminars on the corporate governance and the role of internal audit in achieving corporate objectives to other members of staff.

The head of internal audit has asked you to prepare some notes on this subject.

Required

Prepare the notes which the head of internal audit wants.   **(12 marks)**

You should cover the following matters:

(i)   The Board of Directors
(ii)   Accountability
(iii)   The meaning of risk management

(b) After the seminars, the various departments of Golden Holdings have been asked to carry out risk management brainstorming sessions to identify risks in each of their departments and to design internal control systems to reduce those risks. The sales director, Wayne, has asked you if you will attend the brainstorming session in the sales department and whether you will assist them in the risk identification and management process.

Required

Draft a memorandum to the Sales Director, answering his questions. **(8 marks)**

You should cover the following matters

(i) Whether you will attend the meeting, and in what capacity.

(ii) Whether you attend the meeting or not, what involvement you, as a member of the internal audit team, will have in the risk management exercise.

(Total = 20 marks)

5 Objectivity
36 mins

(a) Explain the concept of objectivity, with reference to

(i) External auditors
(ii) Internal auditors, who are members of ACCA,

outlining any general threats to objectivity that exist. **(8 marks)**

(b) *Scenario 1*

Bakers Ltd is an audit client of Hinkley Innes, a firm of Chartered Certified Accountants. The firm has had the audit of Bakers for 17 years and the fee represents 7% of firm income. Bakers is considering a major new project and has asked the firm if it would be happy to undertake some one off consultancy work for the firm. It is possible that the fee income for this contract would represent 10% of that year's income for Hinkley Innes. The new business services partner, who heads up a new division of the firm, is keen to take on the work, as this would represent his best contract yet.

Scenario 2

Peter works in the purchasing department of Murphy Manufacturing plc. He has been instrumental in setting up control systems in the purchasing department as part of a recent risk management exercise. He has a poor relationship with his immediate supervisor, the Purchasing Director. Murphy Manufacturing has just advertised the post of trainee internal auditor. Peter is interested in the work that internal audit do, having liased substantially with the department during the recent controls exercise. No formal accountancy qualifications are required for the post, because the successful candidate will be put through accountancy training. Peter has had a chat with the head of internal audit concerning the post and is seriously considering making an application.

Required

Discuss the threats and the safeguards to objectivity that could be implemented in the two situations given above. **(12 marks)**

(Total = 20 marks)

6 Audit evidence
36 mins

(a) For each of the following substantive tests you are required to state, together with any limitations, whether they provide strong or weak evidence of the completeness, existence, accuracy and valuation and (where applicable) ownership of the asset or liability at the financial year end.

(i) Inspecting inventories and testing perpetual records by making test counts and noting damaged, obsolete and slow moving items **(6 marks)**

(ii) Vouching fixed assets additions to supporting documentation **(3 marks)**

(iii) Verification of bank balances by bank confirmation request **(4 marks)**

(b) Explain why it is important that audit evidence is fully documented and list the details relating to the audit tests which should be recorded in the working papers. **(7 marks)**

(Total = 20 marks)

7 Glo   36 mins

Glo-Warm Ltd is a company which manufactures various heating products which it sells to both High Street and catalogue retailers.

The balance sheets for the years ended 2005 and 2006 are set out below. Last year, materiality was set at £10,000.

	2006		2005	
	£'000	£'000	£'000	£'000
Fixed Assets				
Tangible Fixed Assets		20		21
Investments		2		2
Current Assets				
Stock	52		179	
Debtors	78		136	
Cash at bank	12		34	
Cash in hand	1		1	
	143		350	
Creditors: amounts falling due within one year				
Trade creditor	121		133	
Bank loan	5		5	
	126		138	
Net current assets		17		212
Creditors: amounts falling due after more than one year				
Bank loan		(20)		(25)
Provision*		(20)		-
Total (liabilities)/assets		(1)		210
Capital and reserves				
Share capital		2		2
Profit and loss account		(3)		208
		(1)		210

*The provision of £20,000 consists entirely of a warranty provision.

Required

(a) Without carrying out any calculations, discuss whether the materiality level used in 2005 will be appropriate for this year's audit, giving reasons for your answer. **(3 marks)**

(b) Explain audit risk. **(3 marks)**

(c) Review the balance sheet given above and set out the areas on which audit work should be concentrated, giving reasons in each case. **(14 marks)**

(Total = 20 marks)

8 Using the work of an expert

36 mins

You are carrying out the audit of Ravenshead Construction plc. The company's business includes large civil engineering contracts (the construction of buildings and roads). It also owns investment properties which are let to third parties and these comprise offices and industrial buildings.

During the year ended 31 October 20X6 the company received a substantial claim for damages from Netherfield Manufacturing plc for faults in a building it had constructed. This claim includes the cost of repairs and damages, as the customer alleges that the building cannot be used because of the faults, so alternative accommodation has had to be found. The company has obtained advice on the likely outcome of this claim from a local solicitor.

In the year end accounts the investment properties had been revalued by an independent valuer and the long-term contract work in progress has been valued by an employee of the company who is a qualified valuer.

Required

Describe the matters you would consider and the other evidence you would obtain to enable you to assess the reliability of the work of experts in the following cases:

(a)   Legal advice obtained from the local solicitor on the outcome of the claim by Netherfield Manufacturing   **(7 marks)**

(b)   Valuation of the investment properties by the independent valuer   **(7 marks)**

(c)   Valuation of the long-term contract work in progress by the internal valuer   **(6 marks)**

(Total = 20 marks)

9 Internal controls

36 mins

(a)   State four objectives of an internal control system.   **(4 marks)**

(b)   Internal and external auditors may review internal control systems. Explain the reason for their reviews, distinguishing between them.   **(6 marks)**

(c)   Suggest the work an internal auditor could carry out to check procedures in a purchase system to minimise the risk of fraud and error.   **(5 marks)**

(d)   If the risk of fraud and error is assessed as higher than normal, how would that affect the work of an external auditor and an internal auditor?   **(5 marks)**

(Total = 20 marks)

10 Fenton Distributors

36 mins

Fenton Distributors Ltd is a small company which maintains its sales, purchase and nominal ledgers on a small PC, using a standard computerised accounting package. The company buys products from large manufacturers and sells them to shops which either sell or hire them to the general public. The products include drain clearing machines, portable generators, garden cultivators and wallpaper strippers.

You have been asked to carry out an audit of the nominal ledger system to verify that items are accurately recorded in the year. At the end of the year, the nominal ledger produces a trial balance, which is used to prepare the annual accounts.

The company employs a bookkeeper, who is responsible for posting the sales and purchase ledgers, and maintaining the nominal ledger. Data is posted to the nominal ledger as follows.

(a) At the start of the financial year, all the balances on the nominal ledger accounts are set to zero (using the standard year-end procedure of the computer package).

(b) The following procedures relate to purchase transactions.

    (i) When invoices are posted to the purchase ledger, the purchase analysis code (for the nominal ledger), the purchases value and the VAT value are entered. The total invoice value is posted to the purchase ledger.

    (ii) At the end of the month, the computer posts the following items to the nominal ledger.

        (1) The total of each category of invoice expense and VAT for purchase invoices and credit notes posted in the month (at the same time the computer prints details of the individual invoices making up the total of each invoice expense and VAT for the month).

        (2) The total of purchase ledger cash payments, discount received and adjustments posted to the purchase ledger in the month (the computer prints details of the individual items comprising the total cash discount and adjustments for the month).

        (3) Where there is no account in the nominal ledger relating to the items being posted, the computer posts the items to a creditors suspense account. Also, all adjustments are posted to the suspense account.

(c) Sales ledger data is posted to the nominal ledger in a similar way to purchase ledger data.

(d) Journals are posted manually to the nominal ledger for:

    (i) The opening balances at the start of the year
    (ii) Other cash book items (other than sales and purchase ledger cash)
    (iii) Petty cash payments
    (iv) Wages analysis (details are obtained from the computerised payroll system)
    (v) Adjustments, which include:

        (1) Correction of errors

        (2) Dealing with items in the sale and purchase ledger suspense accounts (adjustments posted to the ledger, and items where there is no account in the nominal ledger)

All these journals are written manually in an accounts journal book, and they must be authorised by the managing director before posting. The opening balances are posted to the nominal ledger when the previous year's accounts have been approved by the auditors. Although the employee wages are calculated using another computer package, the total wages expense is posted to the nominal ledger manually. The wages expense is calculated from the payroll's monthly summary, using a spreadsheet package, and the wages expense is analysed into directors, sales, warehouse and office wages (or salaries).

Your are required to list and describe the audit work you would perform on the computerised nominal ledger system, and in particular:

(a) The checks you would perform to verify the accuracy of purchases transactions which are posted to the nominal ledger. **(5 marks)**

(b) The checks you would perform to verify the validity and accuracy of journals posted to the nominal ledger. Also, you should briefly describe any other checks you would perform to verify the accuracy of the year end balances on the nominal ledger. **(15 marks)**

Note. You should assume that sales transactions are accurately recorded and correctly posted to the nominal ledger.

(Total = 20 marks)

11 Cheque payments and petty cash

36 mins

Mr A Black has recently acquired the controlling interest in Quicksand Ltd, who are importers of sportswear. In his review of the organisational structure of the company Mr Black became aware of weaknesses in the procedures for the signing of cheques and the operation of the petty cash system. Mr Black engages you as the company's auditor and requests that you review the controls over cheque payments and petty cash. He does not wish to be a cheque signatory himself because he feels that such a procedure is an inefficient use of his time. In addition to Mr Black, who is the managing director, the company employs 20 personnel including four other directors, and approximately three hundred cheques are drawn each month. The petty cash account normally has a working balance of about £300, and £600 is expended from the fund each month. Mr Black has again indicated that he is unwilling to participate in any internal control procedures which would ensure the efficient operation of the petty cash fund.

Required

(a) Prepare a letter to Mr Black containing your recommendations for good internal control procedures for:

    (i)   Cheque payments   **(9 marks)**

    (ii)   Petty cash   **(7 marks)**

    (Marks will be awarded for the style and layout of the answer.)

(b) Discuss the audit implications, if any, of the unwillingness of Mr Black to participate in the cheque signing procedures and petty cash function.   **(4 marks)**

    (Total = 20 marks)

12 Analytical review

30 mins

(a) Explain the purpose of analytical review and at what stages of the audit it should be carried out.

(b) Explain the importance of analytical review in a review assignment.

13 Boston Manufacturing

36 mins

You are the audit assistant assigned to the audit of Boston Manufacturing. The audit senior has asked you to plan the audit of fixed assets. He has provisionally assessed materiality at £72,000.

Boston Manufacturing maintains a register of fixed assets. The management accountant reconciles a sample of entries to physical assets and vice versa on a three-monthly basis. Authorisation is required for all capital purchases. Items valued less than £10,000 can be authorised by the production manager, items costing more than £10,000 must be authorised by the Managing Director. The purchasing department will not place an order for capital goods unless it has been duly signed.

The company has invested in a large amount of new plant this year in connection with an 8 year project for a government department.

The management accountant has provided you with the following schedule of fixed assets:

	Land and buildings £	Plant and equipment £	Computers £	Motor vehicles £	Total £
Cost	*				
At 31 March 2003	500,000	75,034	30,207	54,723	659,964
Additions		250,729	1,154		251,883
At 31 March 2004	500,000	325,763	31,361	54,723	911,847
Accumulated depreciation					
At 31 March 2003	128,000	45,354	21,893	25,937	221,184
Charge for the year	8,000	28,340	2,367	13,081	51,788
At 31 March 2004	136,000	73,694	24,260	39,018	272,972
Net realisable value					
At 31 March 2004	364,000	252,069	7,101	15,705	638,875
At 31 March 2003	372,000	29,680	8,314	28,786	438,780

*Of which, £100,000 relates to land.

Required

(a) Without undertaking any calculations, assess the risk of the tangible fixed assets audit, drawing reasoned conclusions. **(6 marks)**

(b) Outline the audit procedures you would undertake on fixed assets in respect of the following assertions:

    (i) Existence **(3 marks)**
    (ii) Valuation (excluding depreciation) **(4 marks)**
    (iii) Completeness **(3 marks)**

(c) Describe how you would assess the appropriateness of the depreciation rates. **(4 marks)**

(Total = 20 marks)

14 Sitting Pretty   36 mins

Sitting Pretty Ltd is a small, family run company that makes plastic chairs in a variety of shapes and colours for children and 'fun at heart' adults. It buys in sheets of plastic which can be cut and bent into the correct shape and a plastic leg that is custom made by another company to Sitting Pretty's requirements. All off-cut plastic is sent back to the supplier who melts it down and re-uses it, for which Sitting Pretty receive a 10% discount off their purchase price.

For the stocktake, the factory manager ensures that no work in progress is outstanding and closes down production for the day. The factory workers come in early on the day of the stocktake to count the stock, and they are entitled to go home as soon as stock is counted. Good controls have always been maintained over the stocktake in previous years. There are no perpetual stock records. Raw materials are all kept in the stores and are only taken out when they are required for production. Finished goods are kept in the end of the factory, near the delivery exit.

You are the audit assistant assigned to attend the stocktake. You have just rung the factory manager and he has mentioned that on the day of the stocktake a large consignment of plastic is going to be delivered. It is the only day that his supplier can make the delivery, and he needs the material to continue with production on the day after the stocktake.

The audit engagement partner has told you that he is aware that Sitting Pretty changed the specification of their customised leg recently, after a series of complaints over the stability of their chairs. Last year's stock was valued at £200,000 in the balance sheet, of which £30,000 related to raw material stocks.

Finished goods are all carried at the same valuation as each other as there is very little difference between the stock ranges. Planning materiality for this year has been set at £5,000 on the grounds, at this stage, that the figures are expected to be similar to last year.

Required

(a) Explain the importance of the stocktake in this situation.   **(3 marks)**

(b) Prepare notes for your audit supervisor detailing the procedures you propose to undertake in relation to your stocktake attendance.   **(7 marks)**

(c) Outline the procedures which should be taken in relation to cut off at the final audit.   **(5 marks)**

(d) List the audit procedures you would carry out on the valuation of stock at the final audit. **(5 marks)**

(Total = 20 marks)

15 Bright Sparks   36 mins

Bright Sparks Ltd distributes domestic electrical equipment from one warehouse. Customers are mainly installers of such equipment, but there is a 'cash and carry' counter in the warehouse for retail customers. The warehousemen are responsible for raising invoices and credit notes relating to credit sales as well as handling cash sales.

You have carried out your interim audit in respect of the year ending 31 December 20X0 which included a circularisation of 80 debtors as at 30 September 20X0 selected from a total credit customer list of 1,000. Replies were received from all debtors circularised. The interim audit work disclosed the following.

(a) Of the 80 customers accounts circularised, 8 disagreed but could be reconciled by bringing into account payments stated by the customers concerned to have been made before 30 September 20X0 but which in each case were recorded in Bright Sparks Ltd's books between 14 and 18 days after the dates stated by the customers as the date of payment.

(b) Your tests suggested that some 25% of credit customers were allowed settlement discounts of 2½% although payments were consistently received after the latest date eligible for discount.

(c) A large number of credit notes were raised representing approximately 12% of the total number of invoices raised. A review of the copy credit notes indicated that they usually arose from arithmetical and pricing errors on invoices raised.

You are required to set out the conclusions you would draw as a result of the interim audit and the work you would plan to carry out at the final audit on debtors at 31 December 20X0 based upon those conclusions.

(20 marks)

16 Newpiece   36 mins

Your firm is the auditor of Newpiece Textiles Limited and you are auditing the financial statements for the year ended 31 October 19X7. The company has a turnover of £2.5 million and a profit before tax of £150,000.

(a) The company has supplied you with the following bank reconciliation at the year end. You have entered the 'date cleared' on the bank reconciliation, which is the date the cheques and deposits appeared on the November's bank statement.

BPP
PROFESSIONAL EDUCATION

				£	£
Balance per bank statement at 31 October 19X7					(9,865)
Add: deposits not credited					

CB date		Type	Date cleared		
31 Oct		SL	3 Nov	11,364	
24 Oct		CS	3 Nov	653	
27 Oct		CS	4 Nov	235	
28 Oct		CS	5 Nov	315	
29 Oct		CS	6 Nov	426	
30 Oct		CS	7 Nov	714	
31 Oct		CS	10 Nov	362	
					14,069

Less: uncleared cheques

CB date	Cheque no	Type	Date cleared		
30 Oct	2163	CP	3 Nov	1,216	
31 Oct	2164	PL	18 Nov	10,312	
31 Oct	2165	PL	19 Nov	11,264	
31 Oct	2166	PL	18 Nov	9,732	
31 Oct	2167	PL	20 Nov	15,311	
31 Oct	2168	PL	21 Nov	8,671	
31 Oct	2169	PL	19 Nov	12,869	
31 Oct	2170	PL	21 Nov	9,342	
31 Oct	2171	CP	3 Nov	964	
					(79,681)
Balance per cash book at 31 October 19X7					(75,477)

Notes

1   'CB date' is the date the transaction was entered in the cash book

2   Type of transaction

    SL   sales ledger receipt
    CS   receipt from cash sales
    PL   purchase ledger payment
    CP   cheque payment (for other expenses)

3   All cheques for purchase ledger payments are written out at the end of the month.

Required

(i)   Describe the matters which cause you concern from your scrutiny of the bank reconciliation.

(ii) Describe the investigations you will carry out on the items in the bank reconciliation which cause you concern.

(iii) Describe the adjustments you will probably require to be made to the financial statements if your investigations confirm the problems you have highlighted in (i) above. **(10 marks)**

(b)   The manager in charge of the audit has asked you to consider the petty cash system and recommend what audit work may be necessary. You have found that petty cash is recorded in a hand written analysed petty cash book and it is not kept on an imprest system. From the petty cash book you have recorded the petty cash expenditure for each month.

19X6	£
November	855
December	6,243
19X7	
January	972
February	796
March	893
April	751
May	986
June	695
July	749
August	8,634
September	948
October	849
Total	23,371

Required

(i)   Advise the audit manager as to the desirability of performing further substantive procedures on petty cash. You should consider materiality and audit risk in relation to the petty cash system. **(4 marks)**

(ii)   Assuming the audit manager decides that further audit work is necessary, describe the detailed substantive tests of transactions and balances you should carry out on the petty cash system. **(6 marks)**

(Total = 20 marks)

17 Truro Electronics   36 mins

You are the audit senior in charge of the audit of Truro Electronics plc.

Required

State the audit procedures you would carry out to verify the following items appearing in the balance sheet at 31 March 20X8.

(a)	Trade creditors	£3,200,000	**(4 marks)**
(b)	Bank overdraft	£2,100,000	**(4 marks)**
(c)	Corporation tax creditor	£5,200,000	**(4 marks)**
(d)	Accruals	£2,300,000	**(4 marks)**
(e)	Value Added Tax creditor	£1,700,000	**(4 marks)**

(Total = 20 marks)

18 Going concern   36 mins

Carrington Joinery Ltd is a private company, owned by its directors, which manufactures wooden window frames, doors and staircases for domestic houses. It has prepared draft accounts for the year ended 30 September 20X6 and you are concerned that they indicate serious going concern problems. The profit and loss accounts and balance sheets for the last five years (each ended 30 September) are given below.

PROFIT AND LOSS ACCOUNTS

	20X2 £'000	20X3 £'000	20X4 £'000	20X5 £'000	20X6 £'000
Sales	625	787	1,121	1,661	1,881
Cost of sales	(478)	(701)	(962)	(1,326)	(1,510)
Gross profit	147	86	159	335	371
Other expenses	(88)	(86)	(161)	(240)	(288)
Interest	(6)	(9)	(58)	(90)	(117)
Net profit/(loss)	53	(9)	(60)	5	(34)

BALANCE SHEETS

	20X2 £'000	20X3 £'000	20X4 £'000	20X5 £'000	20X6 £'000
Fixed assets	89	161	544	600	587
Current assets					
Stock	67	133	181	307	449
Debtors	91	240	303	313	364
	158	373	484	620	813
Current liabilities					
Creditors	90	317	355	490	641
Bank overdraft	10	65	211	269	365
Hire purchase creditor	14	28	98	92	59
	114	410	664	851	1,065
Net assets	133	124	364	369	335
Capital and reserves					
Share capital	17	17	17	17	17
Reserves	116	107	47	52	18
	133	124	64	69	35
Long term loan	-	-	300	300	300
	133	124	364	369	335

The company has been in business for about fifteen years. In January 20X3 it decided to build a new factory on a site leased from the local authority which would allow a major increase in sales. This new factory with new machinery was completed a year later. The factory was financed by a long-term loan of £300,000 from a merchant bank and an increase in the bank overdraft.

The loan from the merchant bank is secured by a fixed charge on the leasehold factory and the bank overdraft is secured by a second charge on the leasehold factory, a fixed charge on the other fixed assets and a floating charge on the current assets.

The company purchases its main raw material, wood, from timber wholesalers. It sells about 75% of its production to about twelve local and national builders of new domestic houses. The remaining sales are mainly to smaller builders with a very few sales to local builders merchants.

Required

(a)   In relation to the accounts above, list and briefly describe the factors which indicate that the company may not be a going concern. You should also highlight certain figures and calculate relevant ratios in the accounts.   **(13 marks)**

  Note. You will only be given credit for going concern problems which can be determined from the accounts above.

(b)   Describe the investigations and checks you would carry out, in addition to those described in part (a) above, to determine whether the company is a going concern.   **(7 marks)**

(Total = 20 marks)

413

19 The standard external audit report
36 mins

(a) What are the main elements of the audit report prescribed by ISA 700? **(4 marks)**

(b) You are an audit partner and are reviewing the audit files of four clients, on each of which there is a significant matter arising.

    (i) The audit team were not informed about the year-end stock take until after it had taken place. Stock is material in the financial statements. **(4 marks)**

    (ii) No provision has been made against a material amount owed by a debtor who is now in liquidation. **(4 marks)**

    (iii) The accounts of a plc client do not contain a cash flow statement. **(4 marks)**

    (iv) A substantial claim has been lodged against the company by a major customer. The matter is fully explained in the notes to the accounts, but no provision has been made for legal costs or compensation payable as it is not possible to determine with reasonable accuracy the amounts, if any, which may become payable. The directors have received legal advice which appears to be reliable that the claim can be successfully defended. **(4 marks)**

Required

Explain what impact each of these matters would have on the audit report.

(Total = 20 marks)

20 Internal audit reporting
36 mins

You have been appointed manager of internal audit in a large organisation and asked to set up an appropriate department.

Required

You are required to produce a formal memorandum for the Board of Directors, briefing them on the following matters.

(a) Brief comparison of the role of external audit with internal audit. **(5 marks)**

(b) Explain the role of the internal audit function at the design stage of a new accounting system. **(7 marks)**

(c) Explain the format and nature of reporting that the internal audit department will carry out. **(8 marks)**

(Total = 20 marks)

21 'Tap!'   **36 mins**

You are an audit assistant in the firm Rogers and Smith. You have been asked to plan the audit of 'Tap!' for the year ended 30 June 20X4. It is the first time your audit firm has audited the charity, which has not been audited previously. The trustees have expressed interest in receiving a 'value added' audit and are particularly interested in business advice, especially in the area of systems controls.

'Tap!' is a registered charity that raises money for projects building wells in Africa through musical entertainment in the UK. The group consists of volunteers who travel around the country, putting on variety shows of music and dance, the proceeds of which are put towards building the wells. The main show is an tap dance production, acting out the difficulties many people face when they are not near a clean water supply.

The administrative offices of 'Tap!' are located in Leicester. It owns a house, donated by legacy in the past, where the administration is carried out and where the volunteers stay during off periods.

A large proportion of 'Tap!''s income comes from box office receipts which are taken by the theatre at which they are performing. The theatres usually waive their standard terms for use of the premises and merely take a 10% commission on ticket receipts to cover light and heat and other such expenses. Income usually comes in after every booking in the form of a lump sum cheque from the theatre, together with a break down of takings and commission.

Tap also receives donations towards the work. These come from a variety of sources:

- Cash donations from buckets passed around at the interval of each performance
- Cash donations on the (rare) occasion that the team do street performances
- Cash donations made over the phone or by post by interested donors

The troupe consists largely of volunteers so they are only paid expenses for their work. The cost of housing the group while they are on the road is borne by the charity. The charity employs an administrator who organises bookings, handles publicity and co-ordinates all the finances.

Required

(a)   Discuss the risks arising for the audit of the year ending 30 June 20X4.   **(8 marks)**

(b)   Outline the audit procedures you would undertake in respect of cash income in the financial
       statements.   **(6 marks)**

(c)   Outline some controls over cash which the charity should implement.   **(6 marks)**

                                                                          (Total = 20 marks)

Approaching the answer

You should read through the requirement before working through and annotating the question as we have so that you are aware what things you are looking for.

> First time audit for firm so little CAKE knowledge and experience.

> Impact on opening balances and compa-atives.

You are an audit assistant in the firm Rogers and Smith. You have been asked to plan the audit of 'Tap!'

for the year ended 30 June 20X4. It is the first time your audit firm has audited the charity, which has not

been audited previously. The trustees have expressed interest in receiving a 'value added' audit and are

particularly interested in business advice, especially in the area of systems controls.

> Not just a simple audit. This may make the engagement too risky – given the potential bad publicity that could result if there were problems with the audit.

 415

High degree of regulation. Do we have any experience in this field?

'Tap!' is a registered charity that raises money for projects building wells in Africa through musical entertainment in the UK. The group consists of volunteers who travel around the country, putting on variety shows of music and dance, the proceeds of which are put towards building the wells. The main show is an tap dance production, acting out the difficulties many people face when they are not near a clean water supply.

Where is the audit evidence? Also, is expenditure in line with the Trust Deed.

Is this common? Are there restrictions on expenditure? Also ensure accounts are correct for disclosures.

The administrative offices of 'Tap!' are located in Leicester. It owns a house, donated by legacy in the past, where the administration is carried out and where the volunteers stay during off periods.

Trust?

How accounted?

A large proportion of 'Tap!''s income comes from box office receipts which are taken by the theatre at which they are performing. The theatres usually waive their standard terms for use of the premises and merely take a 10% commission on ticket receipts to cover light and heat and other such expenses. Income usually comes in after every booking in the form of a lump sum cheque from the theatre, together with a break down of takings and commission.

Trust for completeness?

Cash income – risky

Again cash. Also, poor in future years for analytical evidence. Lack of good evidence available.

Tap also receive donations towards the work. These come from a variety of sources:

Again cash. Also, what are the controls here? Completeness has to be a problem.

- Cash donations from buckets passed around at the interval of each performance

- Cash donations on the (rare) occasion that the team do street performances

- Cash donations made over the phone or by post by interested donors

No salaries

Expenditure issues again.

The troupe consists largely of volunteers so they are only paid expenses for their work. The cost of housing the group while they are on the road is borne by the charity. The charity employs an administrator who organises bookings, handles publicity and co-ordinates all the finances.

Not a specialist? But drafting complex accounts.

You should have been noticing and annotating risks as you have worked through the scenario. Try and categorise them in your mind (inherent control, detection)

Required

Note you are looking specifically for **audit** risks.

(a) Discuss the risks arising for the audit of the year ending 30 June 20X4. **(8 marks)**

(b) Outline the audit procedures you would undertake in respect of cash income in the financial

statements.

Only cash income!!

(6 marks)

(c) Outline some controls over cash which the charity should implement. **(6 marks)**

A standard requirement, but you must **tailor** your answer to the scenario.

Think of control objectives and then design reasonable controls that meet the objective. There are more control problems in the scenario than you need to identify/solve for the marks.

Answer plan

Then organise the things you have noticed and your points arising into a coherent answer plan. Not all the points you have noticed will have to go into your answer – you should spend a few minutes thinking them through and prioritising them.

(a) Audit risks

Overall risk of being auditor to a charity in terms of potential bad publicity in the event of problems arising on the audit.

Inherent risk	Control risk	Detection risk
Cash – susceptible to loss or theft.	Appears to be very little control over cash.	First year audit – lack of detailed knowledge of the business on the part of the auditor.
Charity – high degree of regulation		First ever audit of the charity – need to take extra care over audit of opening balances, implications for comparatives, audit report.
Lack of an accounting specialist drafting the accounts		Whereabouts of audit evidence – some may be posted to Leicester – is it all retained there?
Completeness of income appears to be a problem		
Disclosure of income – net or gross of commission		
Expenditure – substantiating, in accordance with Trust Deed?		

(b) **Audit procedures**

Income from box office takings

Verified to bank records/statement from the theatre. Possible to circularise the theatres to get them to verify numbers of seats sold so as to gain a little more assurance about the completeness of income?

Income from buckets

Are there any original records of cash counts? Verify from them to the banking documentation if so.

Income from other donations

Original documents such as letters/forms or original records of cash received should be traced to banking documentation and bank records.

(c) **Controls over cash**

Box office

The theatre should try and get more assurance re completeness of income. Is it possible to get a schedule of seats sold from the theatres – this should be available on their system.

Buckets

Two people should collect and count to avoid loss, misappropriation and/or error.

The money should be made more secure both during collection and between banking: use collecting tins, have a transportable safe and bank frequently.

An initial record of the cash count should be kept, signed by both the counters.

Other income

Other income should be recorded on pre-numbered forms to help ensure completeness.

The Trustees should carry out a periodic review of the work of the administrator to protect both the charity and the administrator.

1 Princetown and Yale

> **Tutorial note**. This is not an exam standard question but it includes the simple benefits of an audit which you must understand and be able to outline. However remember that in a small company, these same benefits could also be provided by an alternative assurance service, perhaps a review. You need to be able to evaluate the difference between the levels of assurance given.

(a)   A non-statutory audit could assist the partnership of Princetown and Yale in the following ways.

    (i)   It would highlight any weaknesses in the partnership's systems, and should provide constructive suggestions for improvements.

    (ii)   It would help to substantiate the partnership accounts in case of any disagreement between the partners or any query arising as to the results shown in the accounts.

    (iii)   Audited accounts carry more weight with interested third parties such as the Inland Revenue, Customs and Excise and bankers or other potential sources of loan finance or credit.

(b)   There is a risk that, in the absence of statutory guidance, auditors and clients have different expectations of the non-statutory audit. For instance, as discussed in (b) above, the client may expect the audit to be aimed at detecting fraud. A letter of engagement should be sent by the client to the auditors, having been discussed and agreed by both parties, setting out the areas to be covered by the audit. This should help to ensure that the client understands what degree of comfort the audit will give, and that the auditors are aware of the client's requirements.

2 Corporate governance

(a)   **Improving the effectiveness of audit**

- Increasing assurance from stronger corporate governance and internal controls

- Providing an opportunity to discuss the terms and scope of external audit in an impartial way.

- Strengthening the ability of the external auditor to request changes in control systems

- Ensuring that there is minimal duplication of work where internal auditors are involved, by discussing the audit plan with the external auditors via the audit committee.

- Ensuring that directors' statements on internal control as required by Cadbury are reviewed by the audit committee

- Reviewing going concern issues and ensuring that appropriate disclosures are made

- Acting as a forum for resolving problems between the directors and the external auditors

- Resolving difficulties over the availability of information and key client personnel

- Reviewing draft financial statements before presentation to the auditors and the executive board

(b)   **Independence of audit committees**

- The members should be **independent** and declare any interests in the company.

- Non-executive directors often sit on several boards, so **conflicts of interest** can easily arise.

- Salaries are paid by the company so **financial independence** can be compromised.

- Members of the audit committee tend to have **other roles** at the client, eg personnel. They act in several capacities and **independence may be reduced**.

- Members may have had **previous involvement** in executive positions and could have share options or pension schemes, again **compromising independence.**

(c) **Statutory regulation**

Statutory regulation could impose additional costs and regulatory burdens, which might not justify the end in all cases and could sometimes be detrimental to shareholders.

However, an argument in favour of statutory regulation is that **voluntary codes of practice** may not be applied consistently by companies. Another is that the non-executive audit committee may not feel able to criticise management unless they have **statutory backing**.

Shareholders do not readily understand the role of the audit committee. If it was statutorily appointed and governed this role might be better understood, but this is not necessarily the case. There is no evidence that shareholders understand legal regulations any better than voluntary ones in many cases. It is difficult to arrive at a **'model' audit committee** suitable for all entities, as would be required if statutory regulation were introduced. Companies are unique, and have unique requirements.

A **statutory monitoring report** upon the audit committee would be required. This would further increase costs for the company. It would be very difficult to set **standards for non-executive directors** on audit committees.

3 Standards

> **Tutorial note**. Although not exam style, this is a useful discussion about important issues which could be examined. The examiner has stated that an understanding of the overall regulatory environment is essential. Auditing standards were specifically examined in December 2001.

The major *advantages* of accounting standards and auditing standards can be summarised as follows.

(a) *Accounting standards*

   (i)   They reduce the areas of uncertainty and subjectivity in accounts.

   (ii)   They narrow the areas where different accounting policies can be adopted.

   (iii) They increase the comparability of financial statements.

   (iv) They codify what is considered in most circumstances to be best accounting practice.

   (v)   They give an indication of the interpretation of the concept 'true and fair' in many circumstances.

(b) *Auditing standards*

   (i)   They give a framework for all audits around which a particular audit can be developed.

   (ii)   They help to standardise the approach of all auditors to the common objective of producing an opinion.

   (iii) They assist the court in interpretation of the concept of 'due professional care' and may assist auditors when defending their work.

   (iv) They increase public awareness of what an audit comprises and the work behind the production of an audit report.

(v)   They provide support for auditors in a dispute with clients regarding the audit work necessary.

The possible *disadvantages* include the following.

(a)   *Accounting standards*

(i)   They are considered to be too rigid in some areas and too general in others, making their application difficult in some circumstances.

(ii)   They can be onerous for small companies to adopt.

(iii)   Their proliferation could be said to increase proportionately the number of qualified audit reports thereby reducing the impact of such qualifications.

(iv)   They can create divisions within the profession of those who agree and those who disagree with a particular standard.

(v)   They would be difficult to change once they become statutory as alterations to company law can take years rather than months to enact.

(b)   *Auditing standards*

(i)   It may appear that they impinge on, rather than assist, professional judgement.

(ii)   They are considered by some to stifle initiative and developments of new auditing methods.

(iii)   They may create additional and unnecessary work and thus raise fees, particularly on the audit of small companies.

If either type of standard were to be enforceable by statute it would mean that there would be government intervention in areas currently controlled solely by the profession itself. This might ultimately lead to a diminished role in self-regulation. To be enforceable by statute the standards would have to be applicable to all circumstances and thus need to be very general and broad in their instructions. This might reduce their usefulness to the auditors. Auditors might spend unnecessary time ensuring that they have complied with the law rather than considering the quality of their service to their clients.

Finally, it should be considered whether full statutory backing for standards would force auditors into narrow views and approaches which might gradually impair the quality of accounting and auditing practices.

Note. A legal opinion on truth and fairness, accounting standards and the law in the *Foreword to Accounting Standards* strengthens the legal backing for accounting standards and UITF pronouncements.

4 Role of internal audit

Tutorial note. The examiner has recently written an article on the role of internal audit in risk management, and has stated that it is an important area both in practice and in this syllabus. It is important that you get to grips with the all the issues relating to internal audit and risk management.

Part (a) of this question requires you to state what you know about the background corporate governance issues and any requirements which companies must meet. Note that Golden Holdings is a listed company, so things such as the Combined Code are mandatory.

Part (b) requires you to apply the role of internal audit in a practical situation. It demands that you draw some conclusions about what your role will be. You should provide reasoning for the conclusions you draw, so that the marker can credit you both for your conclusions and your thought-processes. As internal auditor you have been asked to educate the senior management about the role of internal audit, so in practice it would be appropriate for you to appraise the director of your reasoning.

(a)   **Notes on the role of internal audit**

    (i)   *Requirements in relation to the Board of Directors*

As a listed company, Golden Holdings is bound by the requirements of the Combined Code. This contains the following requirements:

- Board must meet regularly
- There should be a clearly accepted division of responsibilities
- Positions of Chief Executive and Chairman should be distinct
- A formal schedule of matters for referral to the Board should exist
- There should be a balance of executive and non-executive directors on the board

Companies should also set up remuneration committees comprised of non-executive directors to determine executive remuneration. Committee should report annually to the shareholders setting out the company's policy to remuneration and making disclosures about director's remuneration packages.

These recommendations specifically relate to listed companies, and if listed companies do not comply with the recommendations, they must explain themselves. However, they also represent good practice for other companies.

    (ii)   *Requirements in relation to accountability*

The Combined Code contains the following matters in relation to accountability:

- Directors must explain their responsibility for preparing accounts
- Directors must report on the going concern status of the company
- The Board should establish an audit committee

In addition, the financial statements must be audited by an independent auditor who qualifies for the position under legislation. The company is required as part of the annual report to include a narrative statement of how it has applied the principles of the combined code.

    (iii)   *Risk management*

The Combined Code requires that the directors review the effectiveness of internal control systems at least annually.

Internal control systems are maintained to enable the business to operate efficiently, to ensure that assets are safeguarded and that reliable records are maintained. An internal control system reduces risk to a company.

As such, an internal control system is part of a company's risk management. Directors are required to review the system as part of their risk management exercise, to ensure that the system is still reducing risks, and that all risks have been considered.

The directors are also required to appraise the need for an internal audit department annually. Internal audit have a role in monitoring the risk management of an entity.

(b)   **Sales department brainstorming session**

MEMORANDUM

To: Sales director

    (i)   I should be able to come along to your brainstorming session in July. However, it is probably best that I attend in an **advisory and interested capacity** only.

As we shall be involved in monitoring the systems which the sales department put into place to mitigate risks in the business, it is **inappropriate** for me to get **too involved** in the initial systems **design stage**, as this will **impair my future objectivity** when **monitoring** how the system is operating and achieving its objectives.

(ii)   In terms of **assessing risks**, I am not best qualified to undertake this role. You guys work in the department everyday, **you are the specialists** and should be able to identify the major risks arising in the department.

Just to give you a better idea of what my role can be, I can say that internal audit are able to provide three things:

- **Objective assurance** on the operation of systems once you have them up and running

- Assistance in setting up a process to help you identify risks

- Assistance in strengthening the control process once you have identified risks.

In other words, if you are struggling to identify risks at the meeting, I can give you some pointers on how to go about it, but after that my job will be looking at the systems you come up with, and helping you improve them continually.

See you at the meeting, if not before,

Internal auditor

5 Objectivity

Tutorial note. It is important to be able to discuss ethical issues from the point of view of both external and internal auditors. This question focuses on your ability to do that.

Part (b) of this question breaks down into four parts: the two situations, and the two requirements (threats and safeguards). Do not spend so much time on the first scenario that you lose the chance to obtain any of the marks available for the second one.

As you read through both the scenarios, highlight or underline key words and scribble notes in the margin (we have bracketed notes which you could have scribbled in the margins). The following approach may have been helpful:

'Bakers Ltd is an audit client of Hinkley Innes, a firm of Chartered Certified Accountants. The firm has had the audit of Bakers for **17 years** [LONG ASSOCIATION]and the fee represents **7% of firm income**[WITHIN ACCA FEE RULES]. Bakers is considering a major new project at the present time and has asked the firm if it would be happy to undertake some once off **consultancy** [OTHER SERVICE] work for the firm. It is possible that the fee income for this contract would represent **10%** of that year's income [NOT RECURRING FEES] for Hinkley Innes. The **new business services partner**, who heads up a **new division** [NEW DEPARTMENT – SEGREGATED] of the firm, is keen to take on the work, as this would represent his best contract yet.'

'Peter works in the purchasing department of Murphy Manufacturing plc. He has been **instrumental in setting up control systems** [RISK OF REVIEWING HIS OWN WORK] in the purchasing department as part of a recent risk management exercise. He has a **poor relationship** [IA NEED OBJECTIVITY IN RELATIONSHIPS] with his immediate supervisor, the Purchasing Director. Murphy Manufacturing has just advertised the post of trainee internal auditor. Peter is interested in the work that internal audit do, having liased substantially with the department during the recent controls exercise. No formal accountancy qualifications are required for the post, because the successful candidate will be put through accountancy training. Peter has had a **chat with the head of internal audit** [NEED OBJECTIVITY IN RECRUITMENT PROCESS] concerning the post and is seriously considering making an application.'

> There are fewer pointers in scenario 2, so you are required to notice the relevant issues contained amongst the other information and apply this to the other issues you know exist for internal auditors. Any internal auditor could not review systems he has designed, so this will be an issue for Peter. Given the importance of objectivity to internal auditors, how will the recruitment process be handled, now that Peter and the head of internal audit have had an informal chat about the post? Use details in the scenario to remind you of the key issues in such a situation.

(a)   **Objectivity**

Objectivity is defined by the ACCA as being 'a state of mind which has regard to all considerations relevant to the task in hand but no other. It pre-supposes intellectual honesty.'

(i)   **External auditors**. Objectivity is usually hallmarked by '**independence**' in the case of external auditors. The auditor must be, and be seen to be, independent. ACCA provides a number of guidelines as to how an auditor should maintain his independence.

(ii) **Internal auditors**. Internal auditors are usually employees of the people they report to, so independence is a more difficult issue to understand here. However, it is vital that they maintain objectivity towards their tasks within a company, so they must **avoid conflicts of interest** and maintain **integrity in their relationships** with other staff members.

In particular, as an ACCA member, an internal auditor is bound by the ACCA's Fundamental Principles and Rules of Professional Conduct. Objectivity is a fundamental principle.

Threats to objectivity

The following are all threats to objectivity:

*   **Personal interest** (for example, fear of losing fees or a good relationship with a client/fellow staff member)

*   **Review of own work** (for example, if an auditor audits financial statements he has compiled, or an internal auditor monitors systems he has designed)

*   **Disputes** (for example, with a client, or where an audit firm advocates for its client, or where an internal auditor has a personal issue with a staff member)

*   **Long association or undue sympathy** (for example, through close personal relationships)

*   **Intimidation** (this is linked to self-interest. For example, fear of losing a client or an internal auditor losing his job)

(b)   **Two situations**

Scenario 1

(i)   **Threats**

The situation raises three potential threats to objectivity.

The first is the issue that the firm has had a **long association** with the audit client. It is unclear whether the same engagement staff have been associated with the entity in that time.

The second is that the firm has been offered the opportunity to carry out work other than audit for the firm. ACCA guidance states that **provision of other services** can affect objectivity.

Connected to the previous point is the fact that a **self-interest threat** arises through the **substantial fee income** that this client may generate in the current year. ACCA's guideline in respect to recurring income is that 15% of office income from one client is likely to adversely affect objectivity (for a Ltd company). The income in this year is likely to be 17%, but much of that is not recurring. However, the firm should consider that the result of the consultancy might be that the business expands and the audit fee might rise in the future. They should lay down contingency plans.

(ii) **Safeguards**

In relation to the other services, the key inherent safeguard is that it is a **one off project**, as stated above. It appears that it will also be carried out by a **department other than the audit department**, which will help to maintain objectivity.

In terms of the audit, as the client has been associated with the audit firm for a number of years, the firm should consider laying out procedures for **rotation of the engagement partner** in relation to the client, so that the relationship cannot become too close over time.

If this is considered inappropriate, it might consider instituting a **second partner review** as another measure to maintain objectivity.

Scenario 2

(i) **Threats**

If Peter was to get the job in the internal audit department, there would be considerable threat of **self-review**, as he would have to monitor the systems which he has set up in the purchasing department.

As Peter is a current employee of the company, there is also a risk that his objectivity towards an internal audit role would be affected by his **relationships with fellow employees**.

This is particularly the case with regard to his relationship with his current boss, the **Purchasing Director**, as he has a **poor relationship** with him. As a member of the internal audit department, Peter would in all likelihood have to report directly on matters relating to this director.

(ii) **Safeguards**

If Peter gets the job, an important safeguard would be that he **did not work on matters relating to the purchasing department for a period of time**, or perhaps until the systems have been reviewed again and/or the Purchasing Director moves on.

It would also be important to address the issue of objectivity as part of the recruitment process. The issue of **relationships with staff** would have to be **discussed** and **understood**.

Lastly, it would is important to have **objectivity in the recruitment process**. As Peter has had an informal discussion with the head of Internal Audit, the head of Internal Audit should ensure that other staff members are included in the recruitment process.

6 Audit evidence

Tutorial note. Each of the numbered sections in this question could form part of a question on auditing a specific balance sheet area. In such a question, you could be asked to set out the audit procedures you would undertake (what evidence would you seek) and ask for an assessment of the quality and quantity of that evidence, (that is, how much evidence do you need and why).

(a)   (i)   Inspecting inventories and testing perpetual records by making test counts provides:

         (1)   Strong evidence of completeness with the limitation that items not physically in stock or on the perpetual records will not be identified. This may apply to goods in the receiving area at the time of the stocktake

         (2)   Strong evidence of existence

         (3)   Strong evidence of accuracy

         (4)   Weak evidence of valuation, and

         (5)   Weak evidence of ownership as stock items may be on consignment or help under Romalpa conditions.

   (ii)   Vouching fixed asset additions to supporting documentation provides:

         (1)   Weak evidence of completeness as such a test will not highlight omissions only overstatement

         (2)   Weak evidence of existence as, although the additions were purchased by the company, there is no evidence that they are physically held by the company at the year end

         (3)   Strong evidence of accuracy

         (4)   Strong evidence of valuation in respect of cost but not for any subsequent fall in value, and

         (5)   Strong evidence of ownership as the purchases will be invoiced in the company name. However, this assumes no subsequent sales or transfers.

   (iii)   Verification of bank balances by bank confirmation request provides strong evidence for existence, accuracy, valuation and ownership for balances at the particular bank circularised. However, only weak evidence is given of completeness, because undetectable balances may be held at other banks. The same applies to liens.

(b)   Audit evidence should be fully documented so that the auditor has a written record of the work and conclusions thereon on which he has based his audit opinion.

Documentation also acts as a means of quality control on the work done providing evidence for the reviewer. It is particularly important in litigation situations.

The details relating to the audit tests which should be regarded are as follows.

   (i)   Detailed audit tests carried out, the reasons for the timing and level of the tests and the objectives of the tests

   (ii)   Notes of errors or exceptions found and action taken

   (iii)   Conclusions drawn by staff who performed the tests

7 Glo

Tutorial note. In part (a) you must discuss the issues raised by the question. It is not appropriate to answer a 3 mark question by saying 'no, it will not be appropriate.' The question asks you to discuss, so you must explain your reasoning and come to a conclusion.

Part (b) should represent easy marks. However, remember to explain what you know swiftly to bank those marks and then move on to section (c) where a large number of marks are available for identifying risk areas in practice.

BPP
PROFESSIONAL EDUCATION

In part (c) you need to identify what looks odd in the balance sheet because this will indicate that it is potentially a risk area requiring a higher level of audit work. However, you should not just read through the balance sheet and compile an answer which lists the balance sheet areas in balance sheet order, explaining they are risky because 'stock has fallen' etc.

You should explain **why things may be risky** for the audit, in other words, **explain what the balance sheet movement may indicate**. Stock may have fallen because a large amount of stock held at a third parties wasn't included in the stocktake, or because of a tremendous recent marketing push. The first explanation shows the risk that the financial statements are materially misstated in terms of stock completeness.

You should **structure your answer** in terms of what you feel is the **greatest risk**. This may involve **making links between the various lines of the balance sheet** and pulling together an **overview of the situation**. In our answer below, we highlight the issue of going concern. There is no point in auditing the balance sheet in its current form if the going concern basis is inappropriate, therefore going concern is a key risk in this audit. There are various indicators that the going concern assumption may be inappropriate: fall in value in the whole balance sheet, retained loss, fall in cash position, suggestion of fall in activity.

(a) **Materiality**

It is **never appropriate** to apply the prior year's materiality figure to the current year figures. Materiality should be assessed in each year.

If the financial position has not changed much, and the results are very comparable with the prior year, it is possible that the materiality assessed year on year is very similar, but this does not mean that the auditors should not assess it for each audit. When assessing materiality, the auditor must consider **all known factors at the current date**. In this case, the position has changed considerably, increasing the risk of the audit, which may lower materiality in itself.

As the **balance sheet position** has **changed considerably**, so when materiality is assessed, it is unlikely that it will be similar to the prior year. Using the information available, **materiality is likely to be assessed extremely low** in monetary terms, due to the overall decrease in assets and the loss that appears to have been made in the year. It is also possible that given the current balance sheet position, the balance sheet figures will not be used to assess materiality in this year.

(b) **Audit risk**

Audit risk is the risk that the auditor will give an inappropriate opinion on financial statements. It is made up of three different elements of risk:

- **Inherent risk**: the risks arising naturally in the business and specific accounts/transactions
- **Control risk**: the risk that the accounting system will fail to detect and prevent errors
- **Detection risk**: the risk that the auditors will not detect material misstatements

Detection risk is comprised of **sampling risk** (the risk that the auditors' conclusion drawn from a sample is different to what it would have been, had the whole population been tested) and **non-sampling risk** (the risk that auditors may use the inappropriate procedures or misinterpret evidence).

Inherent and control risk are assessed by the auditors. Detection risk is then set at a level which makes overall audit risk acceptable to them.

(c) **Specific audit areas of risk**

A review of this balance sheet suggests that audit work should be directed in the following areas:

Going concern

The **balance sheet has reduced considerably in value** since the previous year. Net current assets has fallen from £212,000 to £17,000, and the total position in 2002 is **net liabilities**, albeit this is only marginal. Although the profit and loss account has not been reviewed, the balance sheet shows a **retained loss** for the year of £211,000.

Net assets shows a **reduction in both stock and debtors**, which **suggest a decrease in activity**, although trade creditors does not seem to have fallen so considerably. However, this could be accounted for by Glo-Warm not paying its suppliers in a similar fashion to the previous year. It will be **necessary to review** the **profit and loss account** to substantiate whether activity has reduced.

The **cash position has also worsened**, with cash falling by £22,000. The cash flow statement should reveal more detail about this fall. However, the company has paid of £5,000 of its bank loan, reducing over all net debt.

In summary, audit work should be directed at going concern as **several indicators of going concern problems** exist in the balance sheet. This will be further amplified when the profit and loss account is available.

Stock

Stock has been mentioned above in the context of going concern. Audit work should be directed at stock specifically as this **balance has fallen significantly** from the previous year, which seems **odd in a manufacturing company**. There is no suggestion on the balance sheet for why this should be so (for example, debtors are not correspondingly high, suggesting high pre-year end sales, and creditors are not correspondingly low, suggested low pre-year end purchases). It may be that the stocktake did not include every item of stock. Alternatively it could simply point to a fall in activity (discussed above).

Warranty provision

A provision of £20,000 has been included in 2005 for warranties. The reasons for this must be investigated and the auditors must check that it has been accounted for correctly in accordance with FRS 12.

It seems **odd that a warranty provision should suddenly appear in a balance sheet**. It suggests a change in the terms of contracts given to customers, or a change in the customers themselves (with different terms then applying). Alternatively it suggests that **FRS 12** has been **wrongly applied in the current year, or should have been applied in the previous year**, and was not.

Other material items

As stated above, given the indications of loss and the reduction in total asset value, it is likely that materiality will be assessed low in monetary terms. In this case, most balances on the balance sheet are likely to be material (excluding investments and cash in hand which appear to be very low risk).

However, as the bank loan is likely to have good audit evidence available, the most risky of the other balances are **trade debtors** and **trade creditors**, for reasons discussed above in going concern. More detail is required to make a judgement about the risk of tangible fixed assets.

8 Using the work of an expert

Tutorial note. Note that as well as considering the independence and qualifications of experts, auditors should consider the scope of the expert's work and carry out *some* confirmation work on the expert's opinion. You do not need (and would not be expected to have) a detailed knowledge of valuation of long-term contracts to be able to answer Part (c)

(a)   In assessing the reliability of the legal advice obtained from a local solicitor on the outcome of the claim by Netherfield Manufacturing plc, the auditors should consider the following.

(i)   The materiality of the claim is important as the significance to the company of the amount involved would clearly affect the extent of the audit work required.

(ii)   The qualification, experience, reputation and standing of the local solicitor would be relevant. Presumably the solicitor would be qualified, but it would also be necessary to consider his suitability to advise on this type of claim. The experience of the solicitor and his firm and their reputation in this field of litigation would be an important factor in determining the extent of reliance to be placed on the solicitor's advice. In particular, consideration should be given as to whether the solicitor had advised the company in respect of similar litigation in the past and how reliable his advice had proved to be on those earlier occasions.

(iii)   The independence of the solicitor must be checked as any suggestion that the solicitor or his firm had any direct connection with the company or its management would tend to reduce somewhat the reliability of the evidence provided.

(iv)   The nature and extent of the evidence provided by the company to the solicitor, and on which he has based his opinion, should be carefully reviewed to ensure that the solicitor's decision appears to have been based upon all relevant facts available to the company.

(v)   The solicitor's opinion should be examined and its reasonableness assessed, in the light of the auditor's knowledge and experience of similar cases against both Ravenshead and other clients engaged in similar activities.

(vi)   If the auditors consider the amount of the claim to be material, and there is uncertainty in relation to the outcome of the claim and/or the solicitor's evidence, the auditors should consider recommending to the client that a second opinion from an independent specialist in the field be obtained. If the client was not agreeable to this action or if the auditors still considered there to be material uncertainty, then a qualification of the audit report would probably be required.

(b)   The factors to be considered by the auditors in assessing the reliability of the valuation of investment properties by an independent valuer would be as follows.

(i)   The independence of the valuer should be considered in a similar way to that of the local solicitor, and for the same reasons.

(ii)   The qualification, reputation and experience of the valuer should be considered. The valuer should be a qualified member of a professional valuation body with experience of valuing similar properties within the same geographical area as the properties owned by Ravenshead. If the valuer does not have experience of the type of properties held by the company or of the areas in which they are located, then the value of his evidence is likely to be considerably reduced. The reputation of the valuer or his firm would also affect the reliability of his evidence so far as the auditors are concerned, with the likelihood that more reliance could be placed on a valuation made by a large firm with a good reputation, than one obtained from a little-known small firm.

(iii)   The actual valuation of the properties by the valuer should be carefully examined. The auditors would need to satisfy themselves that a reasonable basis for the valuation had been adopted. Typically, an open market value based upon existing usage would be expected. The valuation of leasehold properties should be assessed in the light of the remaining length of the leases and the value of freehold properties would be affected by whether or not they are leased and, if they are, the remaining period of the leases, the amount of the rental income and the frequency of rent reviews.

(iv)   Any change in the valuation of the properties since the time of the previous valuation should be assessed. The validity of any significant changes in the valuation of the properties should be considered in the light of any statistical or other evidence available for similar properties.

(v)   The reasonableness of the valuations should be considered against any profits or losses made on any properties disposed of in recent times, as this could be a good indication of any tendency to over or under value the properties to a material extent, either over or under valuation being likely to distort the truth and fairness of the financial statements.

(vi)   The reasonableness of the valuations could also be considered by the auditors comparing the valuations with those used by other clients holding similar properties in the same locations.

(c)   The matters to be considered when assessing the valuation of the long-term contract work in progress by an internal valuer would be as follows.

(i)   How material is this asset in the financial statements: as it is likely to be highly material, it needs to be valued accurately.

(ii)   The basis of the valuation should be carefully checked to consider the extent to which it appears to comply with the requirements of SSAP 9.

(iii) Recognition of the fact that, as the valuer is an employee of Ravenshead, this will reduce the reliability of the evidence provided. However this may be countered to a certain extent by the fact that the valuer should have a more detailed knowledge of the work in progress than it would perhaps ever be possible for an independent valuer to obtain.

(iv)   Confirmation should be sought that the valuer had actually visited all of the contract sites, or otherwise obtained satisfactory evidence as to the stage of completion of the contracts in order to provide himself with a reliable basis for their valuation.

(v)   The valuer's basis of determining costs to date should be ascertained and the auditor would need to be satisfied as to the reliability of the company's records in this respect and, in particular, that a consistently applied satisfactory basis of overhead recognition had been employed.

(vi)   The valuer's estimates of the further costs to completion of the contracts should be carefully reviewed and confirmation obtained that reasonable allowance had been made for increases in the costs of material and labour having regard to the current and projected rates of inflation.

9 Internal controls

Tutorial note. Parts (a) and (b) to this question should be reasonably straightforward. Part (c) requires you to set out the work that the internal audit department would routinely do to reduce the risk of fraud and error. Remember that one of the risks facing the purchases department is that fraud may be perpetrated: internal controls have been put in place to ensure that this risk is reduced. Therefore, on a routine basis, this would fall within the role of the internal audit department checking that controls are operating effectively. In your answer to part (c) then, you should identify what controls would exist to mitigate against fraud and set out the procedures that internal audit would carry out to test their effectiveness.

In part (d), you are asked how a risk assessment would affect the work of both internal and external auditors. You are not asked specifically for procedures that would be carried out. You should therefore note that as a higher than normal risk has been identified, more work would be carried out than usual. For the external auditor this would mean a higher number of the same procedures, for the internal auditor, it might mean a special investigation. However, you could also note that internal audit might disguise their special operations as normal operations so as not to alert the suspected party that they are investigating him. If fraud was expected to have a material impact on the financial statements, the external auditors would carry out some procedures that they might not have otherwise carried out (for example, a creditors' circularisation). You should note these in your answer.

(a)   **Four objectives of an internal control system**

- To enable management to carry on the business of the company in an orderly and efficient manner

- To satisfy management that their policies are being adhered to

- To ensure that the assets of the company are safeguarded

- To ensure, as far as possible, that the enterprise maintains complete and accurate records

(b)   **Review of internal control systems**

External auditor

As part of his audit, the external auditor is required to **ascertain the system and controls**. Once the system has been ascertained, the external auditor will walkthrough the systems to ensure that they operate as he has been led to believe that they do.

The auditor will then determine his **audit approach**. If he is planning to rely on the controls in the system, he has to evaluate the controls in the accounting system to assess whether they are **reliable enough to produce financial records which are free of material misstatement**. In other words, he is assessing whether the systems achieve the fourth objective given above.

He will conduct tests of controls to ensure that the controls have operated properly in the year. If these tests produce good results, the auditor can rely on the systems and undertake reduced substantive testing on the financial statements.

The auditor will decide not to undertake tests of controls if the controls do not appear effective, or it is more cost effective to undertake high substantive procedures.

Internal auditor

Internal audit is an appraisal or monitoring activity established by the directors. It functions, amongst other things, by **examining and evaluating the adequacy and effectiveness of components of the accounting and internal control systems**.

Internal audit therefore review and test internal control systems to assess whether the systems are **achieving the four objectives** stated above.

Conclusion

The external auditor is interested in the internal control systems which help to produce the financial statements which he is auditing. Internal auditors are interested more generally in internal controls to ensure that they meet their objectives of helping the business to operate effectively and reduce risks.

(c)   **Internal auditor work**

The sort of frauds which could be carried out in a purchases system are: processing non-businesses expenses as business expenses or paying fictional suppliers inflated prices.

The work an internal auditor could carry out to check procedures in the purchase system and to lessen the risk of fraud and error is as follows:

(i)   Check individual purchases to the invoice, agreeing the details to the purchase order and delivery note. If these items are not available this should be noted.

(ii)   Review individual purchases to ensure that they are related to **business expenses**. If an item appears questionable, it should be investigated further.

(iii) Review the **prices paid** for purchases and ensure that alternative supply options have been considered (either on an individual basis, or on a yearly basis)

(iv)   Test **cheque payments** to ensure that they **related to approved invoices**

(v)   Perform **reconciliations to supplier statements** to ensure that payments have been made to the **correct suppliers for genuine invoices**

(vi)   Check reconciliations made between the purchase ledger and the purchase control account to ensure that **all differences have been investigated and reconciled**.

(vii)   Review the purchase ledger on a regular basis to ensure that there are **no unusual or unexplained balances or debits**.

(d)   **Risk of fraud and error**

The auditors should consider the reasons that the risk of fraud and error has been assessed as high, as this will affect the work that they do. The factors that cause each set of auditors to assess risk as high may be different.

External auditors' work

Auditors should plan and perform their audit procedures and evaluate and report the results thereof, recognising that fraud or error may materially affect the financial statements. When planning the audit the auditors should assess the risk that fraud or error may cause the financial statements to contain material misstatements.

In this case, the risk has been assessed and it appears to be higher than normal. This means that the external auditor will have to perform **additional procedures** to **reduce the risk that the financial statements are materially misstated** as a result of fraud. The additional risk would mean that materiality was assessed lower. This would result in a greater proportion of transactions and balances being subject to evidence gathering.

If a purchase ledger fraud was suspected, the external auditors would **circularise creditors**, to obtain third party evidence as to the value of creditors at the year end. If a sales ledger fraud was suspected, they would conduct a debtors' circularisation, or extend the sample from previous years.

They would scrutinise the ledgers for indications of suppliers or customers who may be connected to management.

The external auditors might also carry out detailed transactions tests such as have been outlined above in part (c) to be carried out by internal audit.

Internal auditors' work

Internal auditors might assess the risk of fraud or error as high if they had **specific suspicions** about a particular member of staff. This would direct their additional work.

Investigating fraud would be a special project for the internal audit department, outside of the scope of their normal work. However, it is possible that they would want the operation to be covert, so as to ensure that the person suspected would not be alerted to their suspicions. The special project would involve scrutinising past records, looking for **evidence of controls having been bypassed**, particularly evidence of authorisation not being sought. This would be done by scrutinising documents for evidence of controls being kept, for example, authorising initials, or 'paid' stamps. They would interview staff to assess whether if controls are maintained as they should be. They would also observe the system operating at the current time.

They might also run company searches on all the suppliers on their central suppliers' register to ensure that they did not appear to be connected to members of staff.

If the suspicions of fraud were strong, the company might hire specialist forensic practitioners to assist the internal audit department's investigations.

10 Fenton Distributors

> **Tutorial note**. In (b) significant emphasis is placed on testing unusual or suspicious items (particularly the adjustment journals). Note also the importance of accounting controls at the year-end. Correct categorisation of expenses is important from the viewpoint of the statutory accounts (directors' emoluments), and in ensuring the quality of management information, which the auditors may use for analytical procedures.

(a) To verify the accuracy of the purchases transactions posted to the nominal ledger I would perform the following checks.

    (i) I would check that the bookkeeper was up to date with the monthly posting of all purchases transactions to the nominal ledger.

    (ii) Specific checks on purchase transactions will include the following.

        (1) Purchase transactions will be traced from the invoice to the nominal ledger and the analysis and analysis code will be checked.

        (2) The total invoice value will be traced to the nominal ledger.

        (3) The category of invoice expense and the expense amount will be checked to confirm that it appears correctly on the detailed computer list for the month concerned.

        (4) The total of the items on the detailed list will be checked to the nominal ledger.

        (5) Transactions will also be traced backwards from the entries in the nominal ledger making up the monthly total posted to the purchase ledger back to both the detailed analysis and the individual invoice.

        (6) The amount of the invoice expense will be agreed with the amount posted to the nominal ledger.

    The tests above check accounting entries forwards and backwards within the system and any errors would be fully investigated as to their type, cause, materiality and pattern.

    (iii) The test checks on the detailed list and total postings of cash payments, discounts received and adjustments will follow the same procedure as for invoices and credit notes. The monthly cash book total will be checked to the total posted from the purchase ledger to the nominal ledger.

    (iv) A check on the analysis and coding of purchase invoices will be carried out to establish the level of accuracy achieved. Particular care will be taken to see that the expense category 'purchases' is correctly identified and coded from invoices and is not confused with other categories, for example stationery, rates, gas and telephone. Incorrect analysis and/or coding may be indicated where the expense category is high or low in comparison with its budget to date.

    Large variations between actual and budget on expense categories should be test checked to verify that they are not due to errors in analysis, coding or posting.

(b) To verify the validity and accuracy of the journals posted to the nominal ledger I would carry out the following checks.

    (i) Firstly, I would check the opening balances at the start of the financial year. To do this I would check the value of each trial balance item on the opening trial balance back to the closing entries on the previous year's accounts. After this, each item would be checked to the nominal ledger ensuring that both the value and analysis are correct. These opening postings should be the first entries in the new year as all nominal ledger balances should have been set to zero, and this should be confirmed.

(ii) Other cash book items would be test checked to the nominal ledger to confirm that postings are correct as to value and expense category. Large items would require a larger sample size and large, unusual or suspicious items should all be checked and evidenced by supporting documentation or Board approval.

(iii) The year-end balances of cash and bank on the nominal ledger should be agreed with the year-end balances in the cash book. This would require the last month to be checked as the closing balances at all previous month-ends will have been checked already.

(iv) The checks on petty cash payments transactions would include the following.

(1) Check that transactions are supported by vouchers and correctly posted to the right nominal ledger account. This would include checking that transactions are valid and coded to the correct expense category.

(2) Check that petty cash transactions are within any limits, regarding the type of expenditure or maximum value, established by management.

(3) Check that the petty cash balance in the nominal ledger at the end of each month and at the financial year-end agrees with the balance in the petty cash book.

(v) The wages expense is posted manually to the nominal ledger from the monthly payroll summaries by means of a journal. To verify that the journals are correctly posted I would select several journals and check the following matters.

(1) The totals of the analysis columns on the monthly summary shown on the spreadsheet should be posted to the journal, and forward to the nominal ledger.

(2) The breakdown of wages expense into directors and the several departmental categories will be checked. The correct identification of directors' pay is important as this requires statutory disclosure. I would obtain the current list of directors. I would add up the totals in the analysis columns to confirm the summary total, and consider its reasonableness.

(3) Amounts owing at the year-end for PAYE, NI, accrued pay, superannuation and other deductions will be verified and any reconciliation drawn up by the bookkeeper agreed.

(4) Any additions to, or amendments of, weekly wages records posted to the nominal ledger through the adjustments journal will be fully investigated and their validity established.

(5) The analysis of wages expense for the year will be compared with the budget and an explanation will be sought for any significant variances.

(vi) Adjustment journals are potentially a high-risk area and any checks would include the following.

(1) Check that all the manually written adjustment journals were authorised by the managing director and supported by documentation and proper narratives.

(2) Check journals are posted in numerical order and there should be no missing numbers gaps in the postings.

(3) Examine all large adjustments and the reasons given for the errors. These will be traced to the nominal ledger to ensure that postings do correct the errors.

(4) Investigate closely recurring errors to establish their cause and whether these can be avoided in future by management action.

(5)   Examine the purchase ledger suspense account (creditors suspense) and trace all postings in and out.

(6)   Where there was no account in the nominal ledger, check back to the purchase invoice, establish the account number and verify that the item has been posted from the suspense account to the correct account.

(7)   Where the adjustment is due to the wrong account number being used, check that the journal correctly transfers the item to the right account.

(8)   Where the bookkeeper has created contra entries between the purchase ledger and the sales ledger, check that the creditor/debtor company concerned is posted with a purchase ledger and sales ledger contra of the same value.

(9)   All other adjustments will be checked for validity and supporting documentation.

Reasons will be established for postings that increase or reduce purchase ledger balances.

(vii)   Year-end balances on the nominal ledger would be further checked as follows.

(1)   Any balances remaining on the purchase ledger and sales ledger suspense accounts should be itemised on a supporting schedule and the existence of each item justified.

(2)   Nominal ledger balances for the cash book, petty cash book, sales ledger and purchase ledger should agree to, or be reconciled to, the cash book, petty cash book, total sales ledger and total purchase ledger balances at the year end. I will check that any difference is reconciled and explained. It may be that further adjustments are required to reduce or eliminate a difference.

(3)   All fixed asset movements should be checked, including purchases, sales, revaluations and depreciation.

(4)   All outstanding liabilities should be verified and their size reviewed for reasonableness.

(5)   The bank reconciliation should establish the correctness of balances on all types of bank account, ie loan, current, deposit, special transactions and so on.

(6)   A review of the financial statements would be carried out to ensure that material changes in assets, expenses, revenues, liabilities and share capital are justified and explained. Justification would be sought in both relative and absolute terms.

11 Cheque payments and petty cash

Tutorial note. This question asks you to asses the controls over a particular area of a business. As such, it could have been posed to either an internal or an external auditor – remember that either would be possible in the exam. Notice that the answer refers to the objectives of the suggested controls as well as the controls themselves. Thinking through the control objectives in any given area will help you to suggest relevant controls. In another situation, it might help you to explain why current controls are weak.

(a)   A Black Esq   MNO & Co
Managing Director   3 Green Street
Quicksand Limited   Anytown
12 Kelvin Street
Anytown

Date

Dear Mr Black

You recently requested that we should advise you on good internal controls over cheque payments and petty cash. We should like to make the following recommendations.

The main objectives of control over payments are to ensure that payments are made only in respect of valid transactions and that they are suitably authorised.

The following control procedures will contribute toward attaining these objectives.

Cheque payments

(i)   Cheques should be raised only on the basis of authorisation, for example a purchase invoice which has been suitably authorised.

(ii)   Cheques should be signed by people other than those who approve invoices.

(iii)   There should be two independent signatories for each cheque, for instance, two directors might act as signatories. Signatories should inspect the documents supporting the cheque to ensure that the details agree. They should also mark the document so that it cannot be reused.

(iv)   Cheques should be restrictively crossed.

(v)   Unused cheques should be kept in a secure place. Cheques should never be signed in blank.

(vi)   Cheques should be under sequential control and all numbers should be accounted for. Spoilt cheques should therefore be retained.

(vii)   When cheques have been signed, they should be despatched immediately.

Petty cash

(i)   Petty cash payments should be made only on the basis of suitably authorised vouchers, which should be under sequential control. Vouchers should be retained for subsequent references. Where independent evidence is also available, for example invoices and receipts, this should be retained.

(ii)   An imprest system should be used to control petty cash. This means that the petty cash float is maintained at a specific amount and is reimbursed at regular intervals on the basis of vouchers showing the payments which have been made. It is suggested that the float should be kept at a level of £300 and be reimbursed on a weekly basis.

(iii)   The petty cash float should be subject to a periodic surprise counts by a responsible person not involved with the petty cash system. The balance on hand should be reconciled to the imprest account by reference to the vouchers not yet reimbursed.

(iv)   The size of individual payments out of petty cash should be subject to a maximum to be agreed by the directors.

(v)   Staff should not be allowed to cash personal cheques or borrow from petty cash.

I hope that the above information is useful to you in designing your systems of internal control. If you require any more information, please let me know.

Yours sincerely,

A Smith

(b)   Mr Black presumably feels that involvement in cash and cheque controls will be time-consuming, and that he is too busy to be involved in it. He may feel that he does not want to play a direct part in the petty cash function. Because of the small amounts involved, he may wish to delegate this function to another director. He should appreciate, however, that involvement at least in the authorisation of cheque payments would help to ensure that he is aware of major transactions in his business. He might consider the possibility of authorising cheques in excess of a given amount; this would minimise the demands on his time, while exercising control and keeping him informed of significant outgoings from the business.

Auditors may wish to consider whether Mr Black's lack of involvement may be symptomatic of insufficient attention being given to financial matters by the board.

12 Analytical review

> **Tutorial note**. This is not an exam standard question, but it is a useful look at what analytical procedures are and when they should be used. It is easy to fall into a trap of thinking that analytical procedures are only relevant at the start and end of the audit. This is not the case. They are valid procedures to use in the audit of every balance sheet area, and so might fall into an answer setting out procedures for the audit of any area. Analytical procedures are very important as part of a review.

(a)   Analytical review involves studying **significant ratios**, **trends** and other **statistics** and investigating any unusual or expected variations. The precise nature of these procedures and the manner in which they are documented will depend on the circumstances of each audit.

What determines comparisons made

The comparisons which can be made will depend on the nature, accessibility and relevance of the data available. Once the auditors have decided on the comparisons which they intend to make in performing analytical procedures, they should determine what variations they expect to be disclosed by them.

Investigation and evaluation of results

Unusual or unexpected variations, and expected variations which fail to occur, should be investigated. Explanations obtained should be verified and evaluated by the auditor to determine whether they are consistent with his understanding of the business and his general knowledge. Explanations may indicate a change in the business of which the auditors were previously unaware in which case they should reconsider the adequacy of their audit approach. Alternatively, they may indicate the possibility of misstatements in the financial statements; in these circumstances the auditors will need to extend their testing to determine whether the financial statements do contain material misstatements.

Analytical review at different stages of the audit

Auditors use analytical review in audit planning to help them understand the client's business and to identify areas of particular audit risk. Analytical procedures help auditors decide on the nature, timing and extent of audit procedures. Auditors can use various sources of information at the planning stage, including budgets, management accounts and bank and cash records.

Auditors may use analytical procedures as substantive tests. Various factors determine how much they will do so. These include the level of detail available, the predictability of the data being studied, and the objectives of the audit tests.

At the final stage of the audit auditors will use analytical procedures (such as ratio analysis and comparisons with previous years) to help them draw a conclusion about the accounts. Auditors will carefully review the results of the procedures undertaken to see whether they are consistent with the results of other audit procedures and the auditors' knowledge of the business.

(b)   Analytical procedures are likely to be used heavily as part of a review exercise. A review exercise will consist largely of observation and enquiry. Analytical procedures will be the key substantive procedure used.

13 Boston Manufacturing

Tutorial note. In part (a), where you are required to assess the risk of the tangible fixed assets section of the audit, you should assess each of the components of audit risk in relation to the information given to you and then draw a conclusion about overall audit risk. However, this does not mean you should give detailed definitions of each component of audit risk. That will not gain you any marks in this question. The requirement clearly asks you to assess audit risk in this situation. You need to understand what each component is in order to be able to assess the risk here, but this question requires application of your understanding, not explanation.

Part (b) is a very typical auditing question at this level. You should expect a question requiring you to set out appropriate procedures relating to any of the balance sheet areas you have studied. You should have a good knowledge of the sort of tests you are likely to carry out in respect of each balance sheet assertions, however, remember also to use information given to you in the question to direct you in the specific case.

For example, in this situation, there has been a heavy investment in plant in the year. A high proportion of the total fixed assets figure relates to this new plant. Information given to you about these assets should affect your answer to part (c) when you consider how the depreciation rate should be set and assessed. However, it is also clearly relevant to part (b). Knowing that depreciation on the new plant should in the region of £25K should point you towards the fact that there may be plant which is fully written down in the financial statements. This may in fact be plant which has been replaced by the new plant. If the plant is not in use, it should not be included in the balance sheet.

(a)   **Risk in the tangible fixed asset audit**

Control risk

The controls over fixed assets at Boston Manufacturing appear to be strong. The company maintains and reconciles a fixed asset register and there are authorisation procedures in operation. These controls should be tested, and if they prove effective, control risk could be assessed low.

Inherent risk

The tangible fixed assets are material on the basis of the proposed materiality level. There has been a substantial movement on the plant and equipment account this year, but this appears to be supported by the information given by the management accountant. There appear to be no disposals in the year, which may indicate that they have been omitted, or that obsolete items are included in the register. It is also unclear whether land is being depreciated. It would be inappropriate if it was being depreciated. Overall, the inherent risk seems to be medium.

Detection risk

Given that inherent risk has been assessed as moderate and control risk has been assessed as low, detection risk will be assessed as higher. However, there is usually good evidence in relation to existence and valuation of fixed assets and these are the key assertions which the auditors are interested in. There will also be scope to carry out good analytical procedures, such as proof in total of depreciation.

BPP
PROFESSIONAL EDUCATION

Conclusion

The audit of fixed assets appears to be medium to low risk.

(b) **Audit procedures**

   (i)   **Existence**

In many cases it is self-evident that land and buildings exist. However, it is important for the auditors to verify all components of land and buildings contained within the balance sheet, if they are on a site different to the one which the auditors are primarily attending, for example. Land and buildings should also be verified to **title deeds** to ensure that they **not only exist**, but that **they are owned** by the client.

The other classes of asset should be **inspected**. A sample of assets from the **register should be agreed to the physical asset**. There may be scope to rely on the work that the management accountant has undertaken here. The auditor should check a reconciliation which the accountant has undertaken. The auditors should make use of any identification marks on assets recorded in the register, for example, security tags or bar codes which are kept on assets to distinguish them. The auditor should inspect the **condition** of the assets and ensure that they are **in use**.

The motor vehicles should be **reconciled in terms of number of vehicles existing at the opening and closing positions**. Again, to ensure that they not only exist, but are owned by the company, the auditors should check the **registration documents** to ensure that the company is the registered owner.

For all the above assets, the external auditor should also review the insurance provision for the assets. This gives **third party evidence** of the existence of assets as the insurer would not insure a non-existing asset.

   (ii)   **Valuation (excluding depreciation)**

Land and buildings appear to be stated at historic **cost** as the schedule does not contain the words 'or valuation'. The auditors should **confirm** that this is the case with the management accountant. The cost can then be **agreed to brought forward figures** as there have been no additions in the year. These figures will have been audited in the previous year. If the assets are held at valuation, the auditors must ensure that the requirements of FRS 15 in relation to revaluations are being complied with.

Similarly, as there have been no movements in the year, **motor vehicles** can be agreed to the **opening position**.

To audit the valuation of **plant and computers**, the auditors should **agree the opening position**. They should then **obtain a schedule of additions** to fixed assets, which can be **agreed to purchase invoices** to verify valuation.

Lastly, the auditors should investigate whether the cost figures include any **fully-written down assets**. This is implied by the fact that the depreciation charge on plant excluding additions is low. If so, the auditor should find out whether these assets **are still in use**, and if not, consider whether they **should be excluded** from the cost and accumulated depreciation figures contained within the notes to the accounts. Excluding them would have a net effect on the reported figure of £0.

   (iii)   **Completeness**

The schedule of fixed assets prepared should be reconciled to:

- The **opening position** (that is, the previous balance sheet)
- The **closing position** (what is disclosed in the financial statements)
- The **underlying records** (the nominal ledger)

If the fixed asset register contains details of the cost and accumulated depreciation of each asset, the **register should also be reconciled to the schedule**. Explanations should be sought for any differences.

The additions of the schedule should also be checked to ensure that the opening and closing positions reconcile within the schedule.

The auditors should also carry out a test on some of the **individual additions**, tracing the transaction through the system, from purchase orders to delivery notes and invoices and through the ledgers to the financial statements to ensure that additions have been included completely.

(c) **Depreciation**

(i) **Appropriateness**

The appropriateness of the rates should be considered and discussed with management. **Relevant factors** to consider are matters such as;

- The **replacement policy** for the asset
- The pattern of **usage** in the business
- The **purpose of the asset** being owned

In this instance, the auditors should establish the rationale behind the depreciation rates applied, particularly in the case of plant. In the case of the plant purchased this year, the depreciation rate applied is 10%. However, the assets have been purchased in relation to an 8 year project, so 12.5% might be a more appropriate rate.

(ii) **Audit procedures**

Depreciation on **buildings** can be verified by agreeing the purchase date of the buildings to last year's file or historic invoices/purchase documents and the valuation applied to the building portion.

For the other classes of asset, depreciation should be agreed for individual assets, as it is not possible to agree them in total. The auditors should obtain a **breakdown of the charges** for the year. They should be able to **recalculate the depreciation** from details in the fixed asset register and compare the results.

14 Sitting Pretty

Tutorial note. This question covers all the important aspects of stock; existence, valuation and cut off. Part (b), which is for the most marks, requires you to plan the stocktake attendance. As you are planning, you should look for risk areas given to you in the question, just as you would in a more standard planning question.

In part (a) don't just give a standard answer about the importance of a stocktake (although this should form part of your answer). The question asks you to be specific about this situation.

The Study Text gives three useful steps in planning a stocktake attendance (on page 250) so you should bear these in mind, although not all the matters it mentions there are important in this case. You must practice being able to use standard lists of matters to consider but to *apply* them to a given scenario.

Similarly in parts (c) and (d), do not just write down everything you know about auditing cut off and valuation of stock. You must tailor your answer to the facts given in the question. In part (d), therefore, you will have to make a comment about the 10% discount, for example.

(a) **Importance of the stocktake**

The stocktake provides important **audit evidence** as to the **existence** and **completeness** of stock included in the financial statements.

In this case, the stocktake is particularly important because the **company does not maintain perpetual stock records**. As no perpetual records are maintained, the only basis for the stock entries in the financial statements is the results of this stocktake.

Stocks are **generally material** to the balance sheet of a manufacturing company and they are also one of the **higher risk areas** on the balance sheet. The stocktake provides important audit evidence reducing the risk of a material misstatement in relation to stock.

(b) **Planning for attendance**

Gain knowledge: I must review the notes of last year's stocktake and I must contact the factory manager to obtain details of this year's. I must review this year's details to ensure that the stocktake appears to be planned efficiently and effectively.

> **Tutorial note**. It is possible you assumed that this part of planning was already completed as the question tells you that you have just rung the factory manager. If so, you should have stated that assumption, or to cover yourself as we have, noted that this is a requirement. However, you should not have spent long on this aspect of the question.

Assess key factors: There are various key factors given in the scenario:

(i) **Nature and volume of the stocks**. There should be no WIP, so I will count raw materials (approximately 10% of the stock) and finished goods. However, raw material plastic should be low because a delivery is required to continue with production.

(ii) **Possible obsolescence**. I must make a note of the number of old chair legs maintained in raw materials as these are now obsolete, a new specification having been agreed.

(iii) **Cut off issues**. I need to ensure that the delivery on the day is isolated and that I obtain details of the delivery made during the stocktake. I need to determine whether this should be included as deliveries for the year, but most of all ensure that it does not get counted twice (as it arrives, and if it is put into stores). I should also obtain copies of the relevant documents, for example, the last invoices in the year and the last goods received and despatched notes.

(iv) **Off-cuts**. I need to consider whether any off cuts are maintained on site and whether these are being included in the stocktake. As the company receives a discount relating to them, they are unlikely to legally be considered Sitting Pretty's and so should not be included.

(v) **Staff issues**. It appears that the stocktake is undertaken by the people who work in the factory and handle the stock on a daily basis. This is not best practice, although in practical terms it is difficult to avoid. However, I should discuss this with the factory manager to assess whether staff can be allocated to counting stock they have not produced. Also, as the staff are allowed to go home as soon as the stocktake is completed, there is a risk that the stocktake will be rushed and mistakes will be made. The manager should ensure that it is made clear that the stocktake should be thorough and that no one will leave before checks on the thoroughness of the counts have been made.

Plan procedures: I need to determine my sample sizes and whether there is a need for expert assistance at this stocktake.

(i) **Procedures**. I will carry out test counts, checking from a sample of items to the count sheets and a sample of items from the count sheets to the physical items.

(ii)   **Samples**. There are no higher value items that I should concentrate particularly on. Materiality for the year has been set at £5,000 currently. Dividing last year's figures for stock by this materiality level would give a sample size of 6 items for raw materials and 34 items for finished goods. I need to determine the batches in which stock is valued to ensure that I count the correct items. I need to assess the levels of stock when I arrive to ascertain whether this remains appropriate.

(c)   **Cut off at final audit**

General procedures

The audit team should take a **sample of delivery notes** for sales and purchases on either side of the year end and **trace** these to **invoices** and **ledgers** and **stock** records to ensure that **sales and purchases have been included in the correct period** and that **stock is accounted for where appropriate**. (That is, sales have not be counted twice and purchases have been included in stock.) As the factory has been shut down, there is a lower risk that sale cut off is inappropriate than purchase cut off.

Stocktake delivery

Once it is determined whether this delivery should count as this year's stock (which it should if the stocktake was the year end date), the delivery information should be traced to purchase invoices and ledgers to ensure that the purchase is recorded in the year and that the creditor is accounted for in the year. The stock should then be included also.

Other matters

If **stock returns** are material, the stock returns after the year end should be reviewed to ensure that items are not included as sales in the year and that the stock is added to the stock figure unless it is now obsolete, whereupon it should be written off.

(d)   **Valuation of stock**

The auditors should obtain the client's working papers relating to the valuation of stock. Items which the auditor sampled at the stocktale should already have been verified to the stocktake records as part of the verification of existence.

Cost

The auditors should then **trace a sample of items to purchase invoices** to ensure that **cost has been correctly applied**. Cost of purchase (per SSAP 9) excludes trade discounts and rebates, so the auditors should ensure that the valuation **cost excludes the 10% discount** received for returning the off-cuts of plastic.

The auditors should then ensure that for a sample of finished goods items, **costs of conversion** (comprising costs of labour and overheads) have been included. This should be on a comparable basis to the previous year and therefore can be audited by analytical review.

Net realisable value

The auditors should ensure that **cost is lower than net realisable value** by tracing their sample to **after date sales**. If no invoices are yet available, the auditors can make confirmations by reviewing sales orders and price lists.

Obsolete

Lastly, the auditors should ensure by review and by discussion with management that stock which has been identified as **obsolete** at the stocktake has **not been attributed value** and has been **scrapped**.

Analytical procedures

The auditors will undertake general analytical procedures to ensure that the stock figure stacks up. This could include calculating ratios such as stock turnover and ensuring that they stack up with the facts that have been presented them in the course of the stock audit.

15 Bright Sparks

> **Tutorial note**. This question looks at the issue of control problems arising from an interim audit and then it asks you to draw conclusions for the final audit. The second part of this question is in effect a planning exercise. It requires you to look at specific procedures as a result of what has been done at the interim stage, however, you also need to include some more general procedures in your answer. This question is slightly unusual in that an interim audit has already been done. In an exam you are more likely to have to set out procedures from scratch. However, this question is also good practice in evaluating the results of procedures performed. This could also be examined, perhaps in the context of drawing conclusions for the audit report.

(a)   *Conclusions to be drawn as a result of the interim audit*

       The following weaknesses exist in the company's systems.

       (i)   In any system of internal control, one person should not be able to process a whole transaction:

            (1)   Authorisation
            (2)   Execution
            (3)   Recording

           The most serious deficiency in the company's system is that warehousemen can:

            (1)   Sell goods
            (2)   Receive cash from cash sales
            (3)   Raise sales invoices for credit sales
            (4)   Raise credit notes

           Moreover, there appears to be no procedure for checking any of their work. Since the accounting records are written up on the evidence of these invoices and credit notes, any errors made by the warehousemen will be carried into the records. It may also be the case that the issue of credit notes is not authorised by a senior member of staff.

           Possible consequences

            (1)   Errors on invoices may not be detected except by customers

            (2)   Risk of unauthorised or fraudulent invoices or credit notes being raised without detection

            (3)   Risk of goods leaving the premises without being invoiced, whether through error or fraud (this is particularly dangerous in a business such as this, with a variety of high-value items)

            (4)   Time wasted by needless disagreements with customers about amounts owing

       (ii)   There appears to be a weakness in the recording of cash received by the company. The dates recorded in the books are presumably the dates when the entries were written up. If so, there is clearly an excessive delay in recording cash received, and possibly also in banking it. There may also be no record of cash received made when incoming mail is opened.

Possible consequences

(1)   Errors and defalcations can arise where a cash received system is weak.

(2)   The longer the gap between receipt and recording, the more likely it is that discrepancies can occur.

(3)   Specific possibilities:

- Falsification of records leading to misappropriation of cash (teeming and lading)

- Mislaying of cheques if not banked promptly

- Errors in the records, especially concerning dates

(iii)   Stricter control is needed over the granting of cash discounts (assuming that it is the actual receipt of cash which is later than the due date, not merely the late recording of same).

Possible consequence

Discounts given to a standard list of customers who may be friends of staff or regular customers, not necessarily prompt payers.

(b)   *Audit work on debtors at the final audit*

(i)   *Second circularisation*

(1)   Consider circularising all debtors, or at least a larger sample than before of debtors not circularised at 30 September.

(2)   Circularise, and investigate disagreeing replies. Discover if reasons are similar to those given at 30 September circularisation.

(ii)   To gain further evidence about the rights and obligations and existence of debtors

(1)   Check the sales invoices which make up the balances with backing documentation, for example purchase orders and despatch notes (if the latter exist).

(2)   Ascertain extent of cash received from debtors after the year-end; reconcile the individual invoices to ensure that no discrepancies exist.

(3)   Obtain explanations for invoices remaining unpaid after subsequent invoices have been paid.

To gain evidence about the valuation of debtors, I would review the cash received after date and would also carry out the following tests.

(1)   Check calculation of outstanding invoices.

(2)   Carry out further tests on settlement discounts and ascertain whether the position has improved or deteriorated since the time of the interim audit.

(3)   Confirm necessity/adequacy of provision against write-off of specific debts by review of correspondence, solicitors' debt collection, agencies' letters, liquidation statements.

(4)   Consider whether amounts owed may be not recovered where there have been round sum payments on account or invoices unpaid after subsequent invoices paid.

(5)   Review customer files/correspondence from solicitors and debtors' circularisation results for evidence of potential bad debts.

(6)   Confirm any general provisions for bad debts, considering how well previous year's provision considering predicted actual bad debts and whether the formula used is reasonable and consistent with previous years.

I would check the completeness of debtors by carrying out cut-off tests at 31 December to ensure that all goods leaving the premises by that date (and only those) have been included in sales. I would also check that all returns of goods after the year-end relating to 20X0 sales have been correctly recorded.

Other general tests include:

(1)   Agree the opening balance on the sales ledger control account with the previous year's working papers to ensure all the necessary adjustments were put through last year.

(2)   Scrutinise sales ledger control for unusual entries.

(3)   Check list of debtor balances to and from sales ledger, and reconcile with sales ledger control account.

(4)   Carry out analytical procedures, particularly reviewing changes in the debtor turnover period, and changes in the age profile of debtors.

(5)   Check that trade debtors have been separately disclosed in the notes to the accounts.

16 Newpiece

Tutorial note. The bank reconciliation is extremely important when auditing bank. It links the good, third party evidence of a bank letter to the client's actual position after timing differences. If a question on auditing bank comes up, it is likely to involve procedures relating to auditing a bank reconciliation, so this is good practice. Part (b) looks at some audit considerations in relation to petty cash.

Always remember to consider (and write down that you have) materiality with regard to petty cash. It is often immaterial, and this should affect the audit approach you take.

(a)   (i)   The matters that are of concern in the bank reconciliation are as follows

(1)   **Delay in banking cash sales**. Cash received does not appear to have been banked until a week after the cash was received. A **teeming** and **lading fraud** could have occurred, where an embezzlement of receipts is covered up by an apparent delay in banking subsequent receipts.

(2)   **Delay in presentation of cheques by suppliers.** Most suppliers would bank cheques within seven to ten days. However payments to the majority of suppliers entered on October 31 have not been cleared for over two weeks. Cheques, although entered prior to the year-end, may not therefore have been sent to suppliers until some time after the year-end. The reason for doing this would be to **improve** the appearance of the company's **liquidity** in its accounts, by decreasing cash and creditors, and hence improving the company's current and acid test ratios.

(ii)   **Cash sales**

The following tests should be carried out.

(1)   **Compare** the **date** on the **bank statement** with the **date** stamped on the **paying-in slip**. If the dates are the same or a day apart, then that is strong evidence of when the cheques were actually banked.

(2)   **Compare amounts banked** with **cash records** for the day (invoices or the till roll).

(3)   **Compare sales ledger cash received** per **cash book** with **daily listing** of cash received.

(4) Carry out **further investigations** if there does appear to be a **significant delay** between **collecting** and **banking cash**. Investigations should cover other periods of the year and the situation at the date of the audit.

(5) If there is **unbanked cash** at the date of the **audit, inspect** this **cash**. Failure to produce this cash would be strong evidence of fraud.

Uncleared payments

The following tests should be carried out.

(1) **Ask cashiers** and others involved in sending cheques out **when** the **cheques** were **actually sent.**

(2) **Obtain suppliers' statements** after the year-end, and **check** the **date** the **cash** is **shown as received.** If this date is similar to the date shown on the bank statement, the cheques would probably have been sent out after the year-end.

(iii) (1) If the **cash receipts** represent monies that have been **embezzled,** these **receipts** should be **excluded** from the **cash balances** at the year-end (£2,705). If the **money** is **irrecoverable,** it should be charged as an **expense** in the profit and loss account; if it appears to be **recoverable,** it should be charged as an **amount owing.**

(2) **Cash** and **creditors** should be **increased** as it appears that the true date of the cheques, the date that the cheques were sent to suppliers, was after the year-end. Thus the bank balance and creditors due within one year should be increased by £77,501, the total of cheques 2164 to 2170.

Thus the true cash book balance will be £681 overdrawn.

(b) (i) **Materiality**

Two commonly used measures of materiality are **1% of turnover** and **5% of profit** before tax. For Newpiece these two measures would suggest materiality levels of £25,000 and £7,500 respectively. Total petty cash expenditure is well over the profit measure and slightly under the turnover measure, and this indicates that on balance it should be audited. However about £15,000 of total expenditure occurred in two months. This suggests that testing should be concentrated on these months, with a briefer review taking place of other months, since material fraud and error is unlikely to occur during those months.

Audit risk

Petty cash is a high risk audit area for the following reasons.

(1) Cash is the **most liquid asset**, and hence there is a high risk of defalcation.

(2) **Supporting documentation** for payments may be **limited.**

(3) The failure to keep petty cash on an imprest system means that it may **not** be **subject** to **regular management review.**

(4) Risk would be increased by a **large petty cash balance** (say over £1,000), as this would offer greater opportunity for fraud.

(ii) The audit tests that will be carried out are as follows.

Initial procedures

(1) **Agree opening balances** to working papers for last year.

(2) **Check additions** in **petty cash book.**

(3) **Check** that **petty cash book totals** have been **posted** to the **general ledger.**

(4) **Check** that **payments** in the **main cash book** shown as payments to **petty cash** have been shown as receipts in the **petty cash book**.

Review of unusual items and analytical review

(1) Review cash payments in the general ledger and investigate unusual transactions.

(2) Carry out analytical procedures on balances by comparing amounts with cash flow forecasts.

Transactions (to test existence, completeness and rights and obligations)

(1) **Verify individual payments** in petty cash book (concentrating on the larger items) to **supporting documentation** and check that employee has acknowledged receipt of cash.

(2) **Check cash cut-off** procedures have been performed by **reviewing reconciliation** at the year-end, and checking that all reconciling items can be satisfactorily **explained** and have **subsequently been cleared**.

Cash counts (to verify existence, completeness, rights and obligations and valuation)

(1) **Count all balances simultaneously** and **agree** to **petty cash book** or other record.

(2) **All counting** should be **done** in the **presence** of the **individuals responsible**. They should sign at the end of the count to acknowledge funds returned are complete.

(3) **Enquire** into any **IOUs** or **cashed cheques** outstanding for unreasonable periods of time.

(4) **Obtain certificates** of **cash in hand** from responsible officials.

(5) **Confirm** that bank and cash **balances** as reconciled above are **correctly stated** in the **accounts**.

Follow-up procedures should include the following tests.

(1) **Obtain certificates** of **cash-in-hand** as appropriate.

(2) **Check unbanked cheques/cash receipts** have subsequently been **paid in** and **agree** to the **bank reconciliation**.

(3) **Check IOUs** and **cheques cashed** for **employees** have been **reimbursed.**

(4) **Check IOUs** or **cashed cheques outstanding** for **unreasonable periods** of time have been **provided for**.

(5) **Check** the **balances** as **counted** are **reflected** in the **accounts** (subject to any agreed amendments because of shortages and so on).

Presentation and disclosure

Check presentation of cash balances in the accounts is **correct**.

17 Truro Electronics

Tutorial note. Again we have focused our answer round the financial statement assertions. This answer is longer than you would be expected to produce in an exam. The question is not really exam style – in the exam you might be asked a similar requirement, but probably in the context of a fuller audit scenario.

The substantive procedures that might be performed to verify the specified balance sheet items are as follows.

(a) *Trade creditors: £3,200,000*

We should carry out the following general tests on trade creditors

(i) Agree the opening balance on the purchase ledger control account with the previous year's working papers to ensure all the necessary adjustments were put through last year.

(ii) Obtain a list of purchase ledger balances in respect of the year-end and:

(1) Test check to and from purchase ledger accounts to list of balances.

(2) Check total of list with control account balance at year-end (obtain explanations if any reconciliation necessary).

(3) Cast list of balances and control account.

(iii) Carry out analytical review of statistics such as ratio of trade creditors to purchases and gross profit ratio; compare to previous periods and obtain explanations for major variances.

(iv) Scrutinise ledger balances for unusual entries especially items that are large and occur around the year-end.

Reconciliation of suppliers' statements with purchase ledger balances will be a key test of rights and obligations, valuation and existence. A creditors' circularisation should be carried out if suppliers' statements for significant creditors are not available.

The following tests should be carried out to check creditors are completely recorded.

(i) Check purchases cut-off.

(1) Check from goods received notes with serial numbers before the year-end to ensure that invoices are either:

– Posted to purchase ledger prior to the year-end; or
– Included on the schedule of accruals.

(2) Review the schedule of accruals to ensure that goods received after the year-end are not accrued.

(3) Check from goods returned notes prior to year-end to ensure that credit notes have been posted to the purchase ledger prior to the year-end or accrued.

(4) Review large invoices and credit notes included after the year-end to ensure that they refer to the following year.

(5) Reconcile daily batch invoice totals around the year-end to purchase ledger control account ensuring batches are posted in the correct year.

(6) Review purchase ledger control account around the year-end for any unusual items.

(ii) Compare current listing of creditors with that of the previous year and note any significant changes, for example changes in major suppliers, proportion of debit balances.

We should also check that trade creditors are disclosed separately in the notes to the accounts, and other necessary disclosures (for example amounts payable by instalments) made.

(b) *Bank overdraft: £2,100,000*

The bank letter will provide vital evidence concerning the financial statement assertions that relate to the bank overdraft We should carry out the following tests that relate to the bank letter and the year-end bank reconciliation.

(i)   Check arithmetic of bank reconciliation.

(ii)   Trace cheques shown as outstanding from the bank reconciliation to the cash book prior to the year-end and to the after date bank statements and obtain explanations for any large or unusual items not cleared at the time of the audit.

(iii)   Verify by checking pay-in slips that uncleared bankings are paid in prior to the year end, and check uncleared bankings are cleared quickly after the year-end.

(iv)   Verify balances per cash book according to the reconciliation with cash book and general ledger.

(v)   Verify the bank balances with reply to standard bank letter and with the bank statements.

(vi)   Scrutinise the cash book and bank statements before and after the balance sheet date for exceptional entries or transfers which have a material effect on the balance shown to be in hand.

(vii) Obtain explanations for all items in the cash book for which there are no corresponding entries in the bank statement and vice versa.

The following tests relate specifically to rights and obligations.

(i)   Ensure that bank overdraft is within company's agreed limit with the bank.

(ii)   Consider balance in terms of:

    (1)   Right of set-off with other balances

    (2)   Any security granted for the borrowing (if there is a charge over the assets it should be registered)

    (3)   The company's borrowing limits per its articles and authorisation in the directors' minutes

We should consider the classification of the overdraft in the accounts as current or longer term, and check that it has been disclosed separately in the notes to the accounts.

(c)   *Corporation tax creditor: £5,200,000*

The main emphasis will be checking the calculation and reasonableness of the provision. The auditors will carry out the following tests:

(i)   Obtain and recompute corporation tax computation for the current year, check that current year's provision has been computed at the correct rate, and reconcile the tax charge in the profit and loss account with tax at current rate applied to the profit before tax.

(ii)   Check position regarding computations for previous years; note agreed computations and verify that provisions for computations not yet agreed appear reasonable. (*Note.* The provision of £5,200,000 may be in respect of more than one accounting period.).

(iii)   Confirm tax paid to receipts from Inland Revenue.

The following tests should be carried out to check the completeness of the provision and also rights and obligations:

(i)   Ensure that all disallowable items have been identified and added back by reviewing the financial and management accounts in conjunction with our own detailed working papers.

(ii)   Review correspondence with the Inland Revenue for unusual items.

We should also check that the taxation provision is separately disclosed in the accounts, ensuring that the balance is properly identified as tax currently payable (within one year).

(d) *Accruals: £2,300,000*

We should obtain the list of accruals and check the list to the accounting records to confirm its accuracy.

We should check the valuation of accruals by carrying out the following tests:

(i) Verify the amounts of accruals by reference to subsequent payments and supporting documentation (this also provides evidence of rights and obligations).

(ii) Consider basis for any round sum accruals and ensure it is consistent with prior years.

(iii) Carry out analytical review of accruals.

The main emphasis on testing accruals will be on testing that accruals have been completely provided. We shall carry out the following tests.

(i) Scrutinise payments made and invoices received after year-end to ascertain whether any further accruals are necessary.

(ii) Compare with prior year's list of accruals. Investigate any items brought forward and items normally paid in arrears not included on current year's list.

(iii) Ascertain why any payments on account are being made and ensure full liability has been provided.

(iv) Consider whether there are any items which might not be invoiced until a long time after the year-end.

We should also check that accruals are disclosed separately in the notes to the accounts.

(e) *VAT creditor: £1,700,000*

The following tests should be carried out on the valuation of the creditor:

(i) Check that VAT accrual is correct amount outstanding by checking to returns/accounting records.

(ii) Ensure that no non-deductible tax is reclaimed.

(iii) Vouch payments or refunds of VAT to cash book from VAT returns.

We should perform the following tests to confirm the completeness of the creditor, also to confirm rights and obligations:

(i) Obtain VAT returns for the period, and check returns have been properly prepared and filed promptly (attention should be paid to the default surcharge provisions for late submission of returns or late payment of VAT due).

(ii) Test VAT totals from prime records to monthly/quarterly summaries and test cast summaries and scrutinise for unusual items.

(iii) Review correspondence with HM Customs & Excise and results of any recent control visits.

18 Going concern

Tutorial note. Part (a) demonstrates what can be deduced from the calculations for example short-term funds used to purchase fixed assets and delayed payments to creditors. It is vital when you approach questions like this that you do not spend so long calculating ratios that you fail to make comments and draw conclusions from your work. Equally, having been asked in the question to undertake some calculations, it would be wrong not to do so. You must apply judgement in the balance between calculations and analysis in your answer, remembering that you will score better marks for analysis. Of course, to get those marks, you must have something to analyse ...

Workings

The following significant accounting ratios are based on the accounts provided in the question.

	20X2	*20X3*	*20X4*	*20X5*	*20X6*
Gross profit (%)	23.50	10.90	14.20	20.20	19.70
Other expenses: sales (%)	14.10	10.90	14.40	14.40	15.30
Interest: sales (%)	0.90	1.10	5.20	5.50	6.20
Net profit (%)	8.50	(1.10)	(5.40)	0.30	(1.80)
Current ratio	1.39	0.91	0.73	0.73	0.76
Liquidity ratio	0.80	0.59	0.46	0.37	0.34
Gearing	0.18	0.75	9.52	9.58	20.69
Stock (months)	1.68	2.28	2.26	2.77	3.57
Debtors (months)	1.75	3.66	3.24	2.26	2.32
Creditors (months)	1.73	4.83	3.80	3.54	4.09

Notes

$$\text{Stock age} = \frac{\text{Year end stock}}{\text{Cost of sales}} \times 12$$

$$\text{Debtors age} = \frac{\text{Year end debtor}}{\text{Sales}} \times 12$$

$$\text{Creditors age} = \frac{\text{Year end creditor}}{\text{Sales}} \times 12$$

$$\text{Gearing} = \frac{\text{Long-term loans} + \text{Bank overdraft} + \text{Hire purchase}}{\text{Shareholders' funds}}$$

(a) The various factors in the accounts which may be indicative of going concern problems are as follows.

(i) Only losses or low profits are being made; the company is not generating sufficient funds to finance the expansion required.

(ii) There has been a dramatic increase in the level of overdraft over the last year, there seems little prospect of the borrowing being reduced and the security is threatened.

(iii) There are signs of overtrading as the expansion has been financed by borrowings and the increase in current assets is being financed by creditors.

(iv) The gearing is high and increasing, with very little security being available for the loans.

(v) There is a low current ratio; short term funds are being used to finance long term assets.

(vi) The liquidity ratio is low and decreasing and the company's ability to meet its liabilities on demand must be very questionable.

(vii)   Stock levels are increasing, suggesting that one or more of the following problems may exist: deteriorating sales, poor stock control, obsolete or slow moving stocks.

(viii)   The value and age of creditors is increasing: some creditors must be having to wait a considerable time before being paid and it can only be a matter of time before pressure is put on the company by one or more of its creditors.

(ix)   High and increasing interest charges make the company very vulnerable, especially in a period of recession and high interest rates.

(x)   The fluctuating gross profit would suggest that the company's profit margins are under pressure. The present level of gross profit does not seem sufficient given the company's high level of expenses.

(b)   The other important steps to be taken by the auditors in determining whether or not the company may be properly regarded as a going concern at the year end would include:

(i)   Review carefully the cash and profit forecasts for the next year to see if they suggested any improvement in the company's position; consider the basis of preparation of these forecasts and whether they appear comprehensive.

(ii)   Seek some evidence that the company's bank is prepared to continue supporting the company.

(iii)   Review the level of post balance sheet trading to see if this supports the forecasts and show any signs of improvement in the company's position.

(iv)   Examine correspondence files for any evidence that creditors might be putting pressure on the company for repayment of monies owing.

(v)   Consider how the company's position compares with similar companies in the same business.

(vi)   Discuss generally the situation with management and review any recovery plans which they may have in mind.

19 The standard external audit report

Tutorial note. The study guide states that you are required to be able to describe the unqualified audit report. Part (a) is a simple test of your knowledge in this area. Part (b) looks at some situations which have arisen in audits and asks you to assess the impact that each will have on the audit report. This is a higher skill. Think 'what impact will this have on my audit work?' – if it causes a limitation and there is no good alternative evidence available, the audit report will be affected by that. Think 'what is the best accounting practice?' – if it is not being followed and there is no good reason for non-compliance, the audit report will be affected by that.

(a)   **Elements of the audit report**

(i)   A title identifying the addressee of the report
(ii)   An introductory paragraph identifying the financial statements audited
(iii)   A scope paragraph
(iv)   An opinion paragraph
(v)   The signature of the auditors and their address
(vi)   The date of the auditors' report

(b)   **Situations**

(i)   *Stock take*

It is good practice for auditors to attend the stock take where stocks are material in the company's financial statements and the auditor is placing reliance on management's stock take in order to provide evidence of existence of stock.

There therefore appears to have been a material limitation on the scope of this audit.

The implications of this for the audit report would be that:

The basis of opinion section of the report should state

(1)   The evidence available to us was limited because we could not attend the stock take

(2)   We were unable to carry out alternative procedures necessary to give sufficient assurance as to the existence of stock (presumed)

(3)   The amount of the stock involved

The opinion section of the report should be headed up as 'Qualified opinion due to limitation of scope'. The section should state that the accounts give a true and fair view except for any adjustments that may have been necessary had the auditors been able to gain sufficient evidence about stock. It should also state that in respect of the limitation relating to stock, we did not obtain all the information and explanations that we considered necessary for the purpose of our audit and we were unable to determine whether proper accounting records had been kept.

(ii)   *Debt*

It appears in this instance that there is no prospect of the debt being recovered. Best accounting practice would be to provide against that doubtful debt.

The audit opinion should therefore be qualified on the grounds of disagreement. The opinion section should be headed 'Qualified opinion arising from disagreement about provision for debtor'. It should state that the accounts give a true and fair view except for the disagreement about the debtor provision.

In a paragraph above the opinion paragraph, the auditors should give details of the disagreement.

(iii)   *Cash flow statement*

As the client is a plc, its accounts should include a cash flow statement.

The audit opinion should therefore be qualified on the grounds of disagreement. This disagreement is not pervasive to the accounts, it is limited to the cash flow statement, so this would be an except for qualification.

The opinion section should be headed 'Qualified opinion arising from disagreement over the omission of the cash flow statement'. It should state that the accounts give a true and fair view and have been properly prepared in accordance with the Companies Act except for the omission of a cash flow statement.

The omission should be detailed in a paragraph above the opinion section, where the auditors should give details of the net cash flows and state that in our opinion, information about the cash flows is necessary for a proper understanding of the company's affairs.

(iv)   *Legal claim*

The auditors need to determine whether the legal claim is a material matter and even whether it is pervasive to the accounts as a whole. For example, if the customer involved is a major customer, it could be that an adverse outcome could affect the going concern basis of the company.

It appears that the disclosure in the financial statements is adequate and there appears to be no basis on which to make a provision in the financial statements. Therefore there is no question that there is a disagreement in the audit.

However, the audit report will be affected by the fact that there is an uncertainty affecting the business. The auditors will have to decide whether the inherent uncertainty is material or fundamental. If material, it does not need to be mentioned in the audit report. However, if we decide that it is fundamental, the report should contain a paragraph giving the appropriate details. It should also state that the opinion is not qualified in relation to this matter.

Thereafter, no reference should be made to the legal claim in the opinion section of the report.

20 Internal audit reporting

Tutorial note. This is a useful question to work through as it covers issues relating to the objectives of internal audit as well as how internal audit will report on matters arising within the company. While there is no formal requirements for how internal audit reporting will be presented, it is important that the Board are familiar with the customs that will be set up so that they are best placed to interact with the internal audit department and to facilitate the department's suggestions.

MEMORANDUM

To: Board of Directors
From: Head of Internal Audit
Date: June 2006
Subject: Internal audit objectives and reporting

(a) **Objectives of internal and external audit**

The main functions of internal and external audit are very different, although some of the means of fulfilling their objectives are the same.

The external auditors are appointed by the shareholders to report on the stewardship of the directors. The role of the external auditors is defined by statute and the report produced by the auditors states whether the financial statements give a true and fair view and have been properly prepared.

In contrast, internal auditors are employed directly by the managers of the company. They are not independent of the management of the company, but work for it. Their work is likely to be more varied and wide-ranging than the external auditors, and they report to the Board or to the Audit Committee on the results of that work.

The internal auditors will be concerned with monitoring the effectiveness of all controls within a business and with the risk management policies of the business. The objectives of the internal audit team are controlled by management.

(b) **Design of a new accounting system**

The internal auditors should be involved in some degree at all stages of the design of a new accounting system.

There are three main stages of development:

- Feasibility studies
- System development
- System specification and construction

At each of these stages, the internal auditor is in an ideal position to ensure:

- All the proper controls that are required have been built in to the system design
- The system meets company standard along with the design process itself

In effect, the internal auditors will be putting their customary skill of internal control evaluation into practice even before the system is devised and is running. The internal auditors will look for key attributes in the planned system:

- Is the benefit worth the cost of the system?
- Is the planned system complete?
- Are the outputs (reports) relevant and will they be produced in a timely manner?
- Will the system be secure from internal and external tampering?
- Is staff training on the new system necessary and has it been planned?

During the feasibility stage, the auditors should ensure that all user departments have been consulted and had input as to the key risks which the system is trying to answer. The internal auditors should assess any assumptions which have been made as part of the planning, for example, estimates of future trading growth.

As the development stage commences, the internal auditors should ensure that the system development is properly documented. Once the system has been developed, the internal auditors will be required to test the new system. The tests should also be properly recorded.

(c) **Reporting**

As has been mentioned above, the internal audit department report to the Board of Directors and/or the Audit Committee. It is up to the directors to determine whether they would prefer that the internal audit department report routinely to the Audit Committee, with any pressing matters being passed on to the full Board. In either case, there may be occasions and some matters where it appropriate for issues to be reported directly to the audit committee, only. An example of such instances could include the suspicion of a senior management/director fraud.

In contrast to the external auditors, internal auditors are not required by law or other regulation to produce a particular format of report. Therefore, how the internal audit department report is also dependent to a degree on the requirements of the Board.

However, there are some basic elements of internal audit reporting that are likely to be included in most reports.

Internal audit will largely produce two types of report:

- Risk-based reports
- Performance enhancement reports

In the scenario looked at in (b) above, where the auditors were reporting on the design and operation of a new system, this would be a risk-based report. However, the new system might have been investigated because internal audit produced a performance enhancement report suggesting future action.

Both types of report will probably conform to the accepted business report which consists of an executive summary, followed by a detailed report and appendices. They are likely to include recommendations and action points, together with details of how such plans would be implemented, when, by whom, and at what cost.

Internal audit reports will usually come with a distribution list to enable each reader of the report to know who is also reading it. They will also come with a date and a reference number. The report should also state whether it is final or draft. Internal audit reports may be produced so that they may be modified when feedback is obtained. Modified reports should state clearly that they have been modified and indicate the feedback that led to the modification.

21 'Tap!'

Tutorial note. In part (a) you are asked to discuss the audit risks in the scenario. Remember that there will be some inherent risk in the audit from the fact that this client is a charity (such as additional regulatory requirements and unusual income) but there these are not exclusively the inherent risks. Don't put an imaginary 'charity hat' on to the exclusion of everything else. Breaking your answer down into the components of audit risk helps to structure your answer. If you are thinking in terms of the components of risk as you read through the scenario, it might help you see the various risks that are contained in the scenario. Don't be afraid to mark your question paper as well – scribble things down as they strike you.

Part (b) should be fairly straightforward. Remember, when suggesting audit procedures, be explicit about what you are going to do. Don't just 'check invoices'. Explain which invoices and why.

In part (c) you should be able to think of many more than 5 marks worth of controls which the charity could implement over cash, as you have not been told of any that they have. Remember to think in terms of control objectives – why is a control needed and what is it trying to achieve? Then you will be suggesting relevant controls. Try and be realistic as well. The Trustees want genuine business advice, not crazy schemes.

(a)   **Audit risks**

There is a higher audit risk associated with a charity as in the event of problems arising and litigation taking place, the audit firm could experience a significant amount of bad publicity.

Inherent risks

This 'overall' risk comes before all the others

(i)   **Cash**. The charity operates with a high number of cash and cheque transactions. A substantial part of their **income** comes from cash donations. Put another way, it is likely that very little of their income comes from direct bank transfers. Also, it is likely that many of the **expenses** which 'Tap!' incurs are also cash expenses. Cash is **risky for audit purposes** because it is **susceptible to loss, miscounting or misappropriation**.

(ii)   **Charity**. The theatre company is a charity, and is therefore subject to a high degree of **regulation**. This raises the risk for our audit.

(iii)   **Accounting specialist**. The charity employs an administrator, but there is no mention of an accountant. It is **unclear who is going to draft the charity accounts** (which must comply with specialist requirements) but it does not appear that a specialist exists to undertake this job. This increases the risk of errors existing in the accounts.

(iv)   **Completeness of income**. As the charity appears to have **no control** over the primary collection of income from box office receipts, there is a significant **risk that income is understated** and that the theatres have not accounted properly to the theatre.

(v)   **Disclosure of income**. The disclosure of income must be considered. It is unlikely to be appropriate to show the 'net income from theatres' figure. Rather, the gross income less commission should probably be disclosed.

(vi)   **Expenditure**. The charity expenses may be well-recorded, or they may be **difficult to substantiate** – this is not clear. It may also be difficult to substantiate payments made to build wells in Africa. We currently have no knowledge about how that aspect of the charity operates. It will be important to check that expenditure is made in accordance with the trust deed. Some necessary administrative expense will not necessarily be conducive to the aims of the charity. We must ensure that it is all analysed correctly.

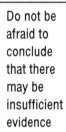

Structuring your answer by components of risk makes it logical/easy to read

Control

There currently appear to be **no controls over cash** in the charity.

Detection

This is a **first year audit**, so there is little knowledge of the business at present. It is also the **first ever audit** of the charity, so the comparatives are unaudited. We must make this clear in our report, and we will need to undertake more detailed work on the **opening balances**. As the charity is to a large degree **peripatetic**, we may find audit evidence difficult to obtain, if it has not be properly returned to the administrative offices.

Conclusion

This appears to be a high risk first year audit. It is likely to result in a qualified audit opinion.

(b) **Audit procedures**

Income from box office takings

Income from box office can be **verified to the statement from the theatre** and the **bank statements** to ensure that it is complete. The **commission** can be agreed by **recalculation**.

It might be necessary to **circularise** a number of the theatres and request **confirmation of the seats sold** for each performance to ensure that income is completely stated on the return from the theatre. [However, if theatres have been defrauding the charity, they are unlikely to confirm this to the auditors. This may have to be an area which is aided by stronger controls over income.]

Income from buckets (theatres and streets)

We must discover whether the charity fill out 'counting sheets' when the buckets of money are originally counted. If so, the **money in buckets can be verified from the original sheet to the banking documentation**.

Do not be afraid to conclude that there may be insufficient evidence

However, in the **absence of strong controls** over the counting, it will be **impossible to conclude that this income is complete**.

Income from other donations

Donations made over the phone should have been noted on documents then retained at the administrative offices. Donations made by post should have **original documents**. A sample of these should be **traced to banking documentation** and bank statements.

Again, in the **absence of originating documentation**, it will be **difficult to conclude that income is fairly stated**.

(c) **Controls over cash**

> **Tutorial note**. Three good suggestions should be sufficient to gain you 6 marks. We have included others as there are a large number of suggestions that can be made.

Income from box office takings

It would be a good control over completeness of income to request a **schedule of seats sold** from the theatres for every night a performance is given. This is likely to be information that theatres can print off their systems with no trouble. This will lead to the theatre company having more assurance as to the completeness of income.

Income from buckets

As this income is highly susceptible to loss or misappropriation, strong controls should be put in place:

(i)   **Number of people**. If possible, the charity should assign **two people** to each bucket during the collection phase and two people should count the money in the bucket at the end of the day. These people will act as a **check on each other** to ensure that cash is kept more secure.

(ii)   **Security**. The security arrangements for buckets should be strong. The charity could invest in a **transportable safe** in which to store the money between collection and banking. It might also be wise to use **collecting tins** rather than buckets, as this simple measure would ensure that the cash was less open to the public. The cash should also be **banked frequently**. It should not be kept not banked for 24 hours after collection.

(iii)   **Recording**. A record should be made of cash counts and it should be signed by both the people that undertook the count. These can provide an initial record of the cash takings.

Other income

The controls over other income will be restricted by the number of staff at the Leicester office. It appears that only the administrator may work there regularly. If this is the case, it is going to be difficult to introduce supervision into the cash operations.

All phone donations should be **recorded on pre-numbered documentation** so as to give evidence of completeness.

As the administrator largely works alone, it would be a good idea for the Board of Trustees to carry out a cyclical review of the work of the administrator. This would provide a useful protection from problems for both the charity and the administrator.

Make sure your suggestions are relevant and possible

Index

Note: **Key Terms** and their page references are given in **bold.**

Review Form & Free Prize Draw – Paper 2.6 Audit and Internal Review (6/06)

All original review forms from the entire BPP range, completed with genuine comments, will be entered into one of two draws on 31 January 2007 and 31 July 2007. The names on the first four forms picked out on each occasion will be sent a cheque for £50.

Name: _____ Address: _____

_____

_____

How have you used this Text?
(Tick one box only)

☐ Home study (book only)

☐ On a course: college _____

☐ With 'correspondence' package

☐ Other _____

Why did you decide to purchase this Text? *(Tick one box only)*

☐ Have used BPP Texts in the past

☐ Recommendation by friend/colleague

☐ Recommendation by a lecturer at college

☐ Saw advertising

☐ Saw information on BPP website

☐ Other _____

During the past six months do you recall seeing/receiving any of the following?
(Tick as many boxes as are relevant)

☐ Our advertisement in *ACCA Student Accountant*

☐ Our advertisement in *Pass*

☐ Our advertisement in *PQ*

☐ Our brochure with a letter through the post

☐ Our website www.bpp.com

Which (if any) aspects of our advertising do you find useful?
(Tick as many boxes as are relevant)

☐ Prices and publication dates of new editions

☐ Information on Text content

☐ Facility to order books off-the-page

☐ None of the above

Which BPP products have you used?

Text	☑	Success CD	☐	Learn Online	☐
Kit	☐	i-Learn	☐	Home Study Package	☐
Passcard	☐	i-Pass	☐	Home Study PLUS	☐

Your ratings, comments and suggestions would be appreciated on the following areas.

	Very useful	Useful	Not useful
Introductory section (Key study steps, personal study)	☐	☐	☐
Chapter introductions	☐	☐	☐
Key terms	☐	☐	☐
Quality of explanations	☐	☐	☐
Case studies and other examples	☐	☐	☐
Exam focus points	☐	☐	☐
Questions and answers in each chapter	☐	☐	☐
Fast forwards and chapter roundups	☐	☐	☐
Quick quizzes	☐	☐	☐
Question Bank	☐	☐	☐
Answer Bank	☐	☐	☐
Index	☐	☐	☐

Overall opinion of this Study Text   Excellent ☐   Good ☐   Adequate ☐   Poor ☐

Do you intend to continue using BPP products?   Yes ☐   No ☐

On the reverse of this page are noted particular areas of the text about which we would welcome your feedback. The BPP author of this edition can be e-mailed at: catherinewatton@bpp.com

Please return this form to: Nick Weller, ACCA Publishing Manager, BPP Professional Education, FREEPOST, London, W12 8BR

Review Form & Free Prize Draw (continued)

TELL US WHAT YOU THINK

Please note any further comments and suggestions/errors below

Free Prize Draw Rules

1   Closing date for 31 January 2007 draw is 31 December 2006. Closing date for 31 July 2007 draw is 30 June 2007.

2   Restricted to entries with UK and Eire addresses only. BPP employees, their families and business associates are excluded.

3   No purchase necessary. Entry forms are available upon request from BPP Professional Education. No more than one entry per title, per person. Draw restricted to persons aged 16 and over.

4   Winners will be notified by post and receive their cheques not later than 6 weeks after the relevant draw date.

5   The decision of the promoter in all matters is final and binding. No correspondence will be entered into.